PRIMER ON INDIVIDUAL EMPLOYEE RIGHTS

Second Edition

PRIMER ON INDIVIDUAL EMPLOYEE RIGHTS

Second Edition

Alfred G. Feliu

The Bureau of National Affairs, Washington, D.C.

Copyright © 1996
The Bureau of National Affairs, Inc.

Library of Congress Cataloging-in-Publication Data

Feliu, Alfred G.
    Primer on individual employee rights / Alfred G. Feliu. -- 2nd ed.
        p.   cm.
    Includes index.
    ISBN 0-57018-026-1 (softcover)
    1. Employee rights--United States. 2. Labor laws and legislation-
-United States. I. Title.
KF3319.F45   1996
344.73'01--dc20
[347.3041]
                                                         96-10893
                                                              CIP

Authorization to photocopy items for internal or personal use, or the
internal or personal use of specific clients, is granted by BNA Books
for libraries and other users registered with the Copyright Clearance
Center (CCC) Transactional Reporting Service, provided that $1.00
per page is paid directly to CCC, 222 Rosewood Dr., Danvers, MA
01923. 0-57018-026-1/96/$0 + $1.00.

Published by BNA Books
1250 23rd St. NW, Washington, DC 20037
International Standard Book Number: 0-57018-026-1
Printed in the United States of America

"to the treasured memory of my
father, Mario"

Foreword

Few legal topics are more relevant and important to most Americans than the topic of this book, the rights of individual employees. Most of us are employees, or rely on someone else who is. Our jobs are very important to us for income, security, dignity, and even pleasure. Thus, the topic of this book affects tens of millions of employees in fundamental and pervasive ways. And, of course, it affects millions of employers—large and small—in important ways, too.

This book does exactly what a primer should do; it provides a lucid, informative overview of the topic. It is an exceptionally valuable resource for anyone wanting to know more about the topic—whether an employee with little knowledge, an experienced human resources professional, or an attorney who handles employment matters. Even as an employment law expert, I learned a lot from this book.

Three aspects of this book are especially notable.

First, it is extremely well organized, presented, and written. Legal subjects can be dry and complicated; and as the Preface and the Afterword point out, the law on individual employee rights is often complicated, confusing, and contradictory. Nonetheless, the author sets forth the law in a way that is practical, clear, and understandable. For example, he raises typical employment issues (*e.g.*, job references) and then sets forth not only the relevant legal considerations, but also the practical considerations for employees and employers. On each issue, the legal rules in various jurisdictions are carefully compared and contrasted, often with descriptions or briefs of illustrative cases. Moreover, the writing itself is a model of clarity and elegant simplicity.

Second, this book is uncommonly interesting and informative. Rather than merely outlining legal rules, the author puts the legal issues into context and explains how and why the law got to be the way it is. Thus, Chapter 1, "A Survey of U.S. Employment Law," provides the historical background and context for the law of individual employee rights, while the Afterword suggests where the law may be going. Chapter 2, "Application of Traditional Contract Principles to the Employment Setting," contains an excellent mini-course on contract law, which provides a valuable foundation for Chapter 3, "Modern Expansion of Traditional Contract Law." The discussions on employee testing in Chapter 6 include interesting background information on the types of tests used, on the practical problems with such tests, and on the real interests of employees, employers, and the public that such tests affect.

Third, the author presents the law of employee rights in a scrupulously fair and accurate manner. The legal and economic interests of employees and employers are often in sharp conflict. As an attorney who specializes in representing individual employees, I am acutely aware of the possibilities for tilting a presentation of the law toward one side or the other on many issues. I can vouch that this primer can be relied on for a balanced presentation of the issues.

Many dozens of books on employment law have been published in recent years. Virtually all of them are addressed to specific audiences: employees, personnel administrators, employees' attorneys, employers' attorneys, law students, etc. This primer—addressing the subject of employee rights in a comprehensive, interesting, and balanced fashion—deserves a place on the bookshelf of each of those people. More important, it should be read thoroughly before going on the shelf and consulted regularly while there.

Wayne N. Outten
Partner, Lankenau, Kovner & Kurtz
President, National Employment Lawyers
    Association/New York
New York, New York

Preface

Individual employee rights were hardly known to the law prior to the 1970s. Employee rights, to the extent that they existed, were principally the collective rights of unionized employees, the rights conferred on a protected class of individuals under antidiscrimination laws, or the rights gained by contract by that rare employee with significant bargaining power. Then in the 1970s and 1980s, individual employees, with the help of their attorneys, successfully expanded existing case law and prompted legislation of new rights. This trend has continued into the 1990s. These developments are the focus of this book.

The term "individual employee rights" is an umbrella under which such unrelated subjects as contract rights, privacy issues, defamation, and negligence principles are covered in this book. The term, while hardly precise, is functional and provides a framework for analyzing important recent developments in employment law.

Some book subjects organize themselves. For example, a review of a major statute such as the Employee Retirement Income Security Act can rely on the structure of the statute itself for organization. The topic of individual employee rights, principally based as it is on inconsistent and constantly evolving federal, state, and local legal developments, resists easy organization and permits a variety of options, none fully satisfying.

Two basic methods of organizing this text suggest themselves: the first, based on the law, relies on causes of action and statutory grounds for structure; and the second, based on personnel function, relies on such management concerns as hiring, disciplining, and discharge. I chose neither, and both.

This book is not a legal treatise but rather an introduction to a topic of great importance to lawyers, managers, personnel specialists, academics, and employees at all levels. To present this subject in terms of tort and contract law and statutory rights would be satisfactory to the lawyers alone. Nonetheless, the law does drive this text as it focuses on individual *legal* rights of employees. On the other hand, to organize the book along personnel function lines would render the text repetitive and unwieldy because the same legal developments would have to be reviewed and revisited in several different areas.

Instead, I chose as a method of organization the use of overarching legal areas such as contract law, negligence, and privacy, which are subdivided, for the most part, functionally. After several false starts, this approach seemed most suited to this book's anticipated audience of managers, personnel specialists, lawyers new to the topic, academics with an interest in individual and employee rights and common law developments, and employees.

Unfortunately, because the law in this area is still emerging, a simple, definitive exposition of the state of the law on most topics is not possible. This is further complicated by the fact that the law related to individual employee rights is principally rooted in state law. Each state serves as its own laboratory— unburdened by the precedent of other states—from which will eventually emerge that state's body of law. The trends between and among states are often contradictory and on most issues a consensus has yet to be reached and may likely never emerge. The reasons for this diversity of opinion and approach are many. Suffice it to say that this area of law may rightly be viewed as a litmus test of each state's perception of the role of the law in establishing and protecting individual rights.

This book has been divided into nine chapters. Many of the chapters are obviously related; others stand alone. Great effort was made to minimize the overlap between and among chapters.

Chapter 1 briefly surveys the development of employment law in the United States from the nineteenth century to the present. In particular, the text traces the birth and expansion of the fundamental rule of employment law in the United States, the "employment-at-will doctrine."

Chapter 2 reviews the traditional principles of contract law applicable to the employment setting.

Chapter 3 analyzes the modern expansion of basic contract principles in the employment context and the application of those principles to the hiring process, and employer writings, statements, policies, and practices.

Chapter 4 reviews an employee's right to know information affecting the employee's health or employment in the possession of his or her employer, and the employee's right of access to such information. This chapter also addresses plant closings and related issues.

The obtaining of information related to employees or prospective employees and the disclosure by employers of that information is the focus of Chapter 5. Such topics as the obtaining and disclosure of credit and medical information, employee searches and surveillance, and defamation are addressed in this chapter.

Chapter 6 deals with the controversial issues associated with employer testing, including drug and alcohol, honesty, AIDS-related, and genetic testing.

The limitations on employers' right of discipline and discharge based on public policy, the exercise of an employee's civic duties, and whistleblowing are the subjects of Chapter 7.

Chapter 8 reviews such lifestyle and personal privacy issues as romance in the workplace, appearance and grooming standards, sexual harassment, sexual orientation and sexual freedom, marital status discrimination, and personal habits and addictions.

Chapter 9 explores the expansion of traditional negligence principles into the employment relationship, including the emerging actions of negligent hiring and retention.

The Appendices, taken from The Bureau of National Affairs' Individual Employment Rights Manual and Labor Relations Expediter, include the text of the Employment At Will State Rulings Chart as well as the text of Michigan's Access to Employee Records Law, the Worker Adjustment and Retraining Notification Act, Fair Credit Reporting Act, Omnibus Drug Testing Law, Employee Polygraph Protection Act, New Jersey's Conscientious Employee Law (Whistleblower Law), Uniformed Services Act, and New York's Lawful Activities Law.

In each area covered by this book, the law is responding to changing societal perceptions of the workplace and of the relationship between employer and employee. The emerging law presents a fascinating and current case study of the adaptability of the common law, the case law borrowed from Britain and adapted to meet the needs of our society, and, to a lesser extent, the responsiveness of Congress and state legislatures to new societal norms.

In sum, this book, as its title denotes, is a primer, that is, an *introduction* to a rapidly evolving topic. Its purpose is to introduce its readers to the topic and assist them in spotting issues. It is not a "how to" guide to responding to such issues. As with all legal rights, an employer or an individual with a particular legal problem touched on in this book should seek legal counsel and *not* rely on the general comments or the specific holdings of cases briefly noted in this book. This is particularly so because the law is changing quickly and is based on the inconsistent positions taken by many jurisdictions.

It is a rare pleasure for an author to introduce an audience to a subject as intrinsically interesting and indisputably relevant to all our lives as is the topic of individual employee rights in the 1990s.

Alfred G. Feliu

Acknowledgments

As might be expected, many hands, hearts, and minds played roles in the researching, writing, and production of this book. They have each in their own way earned my deepest appreciation.

The research for and writing of this text was, in many ways, a collaborative effort. My law firm, Paul, Hastings, Janofsky & Walker, fully supported this project both in spirit and with the generous provision of its resources.

In particular, my colleague Mark A. Gloade was the principal reviewer, researcher, and rewriter for the Second Edition. For his tireless efforts, I offer my most sincere appreciation. I also want to thank my partner Vicki Cundiff in our New York office for her excellent rewrite of the "Agreement Limiting Competition" section of Chapter 3 and my colleague Mary Dollarhide in our Stamford office for her review and thoughtful revisions to the drug testing discussion in Chapter 6. I would also like to recognize the able assistance of my colleagues Elizabeth A. Fealy and David Levin and our former legal assistant, Myra A. McGinley, and the valuable contributions of our Firm's 1995 summer associates, including Michael Feinsod, Michael A. Berlin, Richard Salisbury and, most especially, Susan Schick.

I also gratefully acknowledge the contribution of my mentor in this area of the law, as in so many others, the esteemed Dr. Alan F. Westin of Columbia University. Dr. Westin not only tutored me on the topics addressed by this book but helped define and establish the many developments covered by this book as a body of law. For his many insights and encouragement through the years I am most appreciative.

As can be imagined, the production work associated with preparing this text was substantial. The rewrites were frequent, the table of cases massive, and the updates seemingly endless. I gratefully acknowledge the substantial efforts of the Paul, Hastings' New York staff, with a special thanks to my very dedicated and opinionated (the two can live in harmony) secretary, Anne Sheridan, and the many members of our Document Processing Department for their professionalism and willing and capable assistance in bringing this project to fruition.

Like a patient with a medical problem, I sought second opinions in the form of readers to help assure that the text was accurate, informative, and literate. I made a particular effort to ensure that the text was readable to non-lawyers, in other words, the real world. To this end, I express my sincere thanks to Wayne N. Outten and Louise Sobin who served as readers of the First Edition and whose many suggestions were almost uniformly adopted. My warmest thanks go to my brother Joe, a businessman, manager, friend, and most important, a non-lawyer. His guidance, support, biting commentary, intolerance of legal jargon, and numerous insights have greatly influenced this text as well as its author.

Finally, I give my love and thanks to my wife, Susan L. Hobart, and my children, Julie, Danny, and Gregory. I can only hope that my frequent absences while working on this text made me only a less visible, and not a lesser, husband and father.

CONTENTS

1

A SURVEY OF U.S. EMPLOYMENT LAW

The notion of individual employee rights is relatively new to U.S. law. Until recent years, the employer–employee relationship was viewed in basic contractual terms with little adjustment made for the disparity in the respective bargaining powers of the parties.

The foundation upon which U.S. employment law is built is the "employment-at-will" doctrine. Introduced into U.S. law in the 1880s, the employment-at-will doctrine simply states a legal presumption that all employment relationships that do not provide for a duration of employment or a standard for dismissal are terminable by either party at will without penalty. Legal presumptions can be rebutted by the particular facts of a case. Over time, however, the employment-at-will presumption was transformed into a *rule* not subject to rebuttal except in extraordinary circumstances. The at-will rule effectively barred all employee claims of wrongful discharge and remained virtually unchanged until the 1970s.

A brief review of nineteenth-century U.S. employment law and the introduction of the employment-at-will doctrine provide the necessary context for understanding current developments in employment law.

I. EVOLUTION OF EMPLOYMENT-AT-WILL DOCTRINE

For both judges and litigants in the latter half of the nineteenth century, the law governing the emerging relationship between employers and employees was a curiosity. A stepchild of domestic relations law, it did not yet command a distinct identity. Employers were not "employers," but rather, in the borrowed parlance of the common law, "masters"; employees were "servants." Master–servant law is most noteworthy for its quaint paternal leanings and its status-based view of the employment relationship.

In England, the birthplace of the common law, the practice had developed that the hiring of domestic servants for an unspecified period of time was presumed to be a hiring for one year. This was most appropriate in the agricultural setting in which this presumption developed. According to the legal scholar Sir William Blackstone, "natural equity" required that a master–servant relationship be maintained "throughout all the revolutions of the respective seasons." In that way, masters were assured of labor during the planting and harvesting seasons, while servants were secure in the knowledge that they would be cared for during the harsh winter months. This presumption, born to accommodate agricultural and domestic labor, eventually came to be universally applied.

As the nineteenth century progressed, it became apparent that master–servant law was ill-equipped to handle relations in the new industrial workplace. Masters were no longer estate holders, caring for devoted domestics, but rather absentee industrialists concerned with maximizing productivity and profits. Servants were more likely to be day laborers or factory workers than farmhands or domestics. The "revolution of the seasons" was little felt on a dimly lighted, frantic factory floor.

Judges, while acknowledging the British practice of presuming a general hiring to be for a year, and on occasion professing adherence to it, nonetheless went about fixing the duration of employment where none was specified in notoriously different ways. Varying approaches were employed and contradictory conclusions reached in often identical settings. Employment relations law in the United States, reflecting the socioeconomic upheaval brought on by industrialization, was in turmoil.

Finally, in 1877, Horace Gay Wood, a respected attorney from Albany, New York, published a treatise entitled *Master and Servant*, which authoritatively announced that in the United States "the rule is inflexible, that a general or indefinite hiring is *prima facie* a hiring at will, and if the servant seeks to make it out a yearly hiring, the burden is upon him to establish it by proof." Although Wood's analysis has subsequently been fully discredited, the rule he announced was uniformly followed by U.S. courts. By the turn of the twentieth century the employment-at-will doctrine was generally applied.

Wood's "rule" in fact was merely a legal presumption that could be rebutted by evidence to the contrary. Courts almost immediately turned Wood's presumption into Wood's rule. In turn, Wood's rule brought certain defeat to employees challenging their discharges and thus discouraged potential suits. The employment-at-will doctrine provided American industry with a steady and flexible workforce that helped propel the economic growth of a rapidly industrializing nation for nearly a century, but not without injury to the notion of fairness and equity in the workplace. The resulting inequities, however, helped fuel the nascent labor movement that would dramatically change the dynamics of labor–management relations in the twentieth century.

II. THE LABOR MOVEMENT AND COLLECTIVE RIGHTS

Early in the twentieth century, Congress and the state legislatures enacted laws designed to protect the growing labor movement. Just as often, courts struck down this legislation on constitutional or other grounds.

Employee rights as a distinct body of law was born, however, during this period with the enactment of such major federal labor legislation as the Railway Labor Act of 1926 and the National Labor Relations Act of 1935 (also known as the Wagner

Act). Through this legislation, Congress recognized workers' rights to unionize and engage in other collective activity. As a result, a significant portion of the labor force was provided with job rights and security gained through the collective-bargaining process, removing these employees from the vagaries of the at-will doctrine.

The Supreme Court upheld this legislation in the face of substantive due process challenges that had prevailed earlier in the twentieth century. The Depression-era Court found that "the right of employees to self-organization and to have representatives of their own choosing for the purpose of collective bargaining is often an essential condition of industrial peace." The Court saw the need for unions emerging from "the necessities of the situation," that is, that single employees relying on their jobs to maintain their families were powerless to resist unfair or arbitrary treatment. Unions, in contrast, offered employees the opportunity to deal on an equal basis with their employers. (*NLRB v. Jones & Laughlin Steel Corp.*)

As anticipated by Congress, enactment of labor legislation led to vibrant unions and enhanced job security for covered workers. These employee rights, however, were basically *collective* rights inuring solely to members of unions. Unorganized employees were just that—unorganized—and remained subject to termination at will. The only relief available to the individual employees was the very limited protection of traditional contract law until the 1960s.

III. CIVIL RIGHTS MOVEMENT

The civil rights movement of the 1960s produced legislation that changed employment law dramatically. For the first time, individual employees were empowered by civil rights legislation, enacted to protect designated classes of employees, to enforce their rights *individually* against discriminatory employment decisions. The significance of this development cannot be overstated. The civil rights movement and the legislation it generated helped establish a mandate of fairness in the workplace that essentially ended employers' unrestricted authority over personnel decisions in the nonunion setting. Equally significant, attorneys specializing in civil rights litigation demonstrated a willingness and ability to challenge and expand the law of the workplace on behalf of individual employees and, in doing so, permanently altered the dynamics of the American workplace.

By the end of the 1980s, courts increasingly began to view the employment-at-will doctrine, strictly applied, as an anachronism. Employees, with the help of counsel, began to challenge their employer's actions through the lens of "fairness" in ever expanding ways. Management came to view at-will employment as increasingly less terminable at its will. The law of contracts was rethought and employee rights were increasingly recognized and applied. Tort law, the law related to civil rather than contractual wrongs, was expanded to recognize new bases for employee suits. Congress and state legislatures enacted more legislation in the 1970s and 1980s addressing employee rights than had been enacted in all of U.S. history to that point. By the end of the 1980s, the previously preeminent employment-at-will doctrine was notably less preeminent and at its expense the rights of individual employees greatly expanded.

2

APPLICATION OF TRADITIONAL CONTRACT PRINCIPLES TO THE EMPLOYMENT SETTING

Individual employee rights until the 1970s were principally rooted in the traditional law of contracts. Job security and benefits were negotiated directly with employers and were purely a function of bargaining position and strength. Few employees, however, possessed sufficient leverage with prospective or current employers to be in a position to "negotiate" significant terms of the employment relationship. Individual employee rights based on contract were more a function of employer benevolence than negotiating strength.

Exceptions, of course, existed. Key corporate executives, athletes, and performing artists often offered unique services for which the law of contracts proved to be an ally. Babe Ruth earned more than the President of the United States not merely because he had a better year than the President, as he said at the time, but because he had the bargaining leverage to exact such a salary. Few employees, however, could compare their bargaining position to that of the "Babe."

In short, the law of contracts, favoring as it does the party with the stronger bargaining position, significantly benefited employers. To a lesser degree, it continues to do so today. Unless such disproportionate bargaining strength produced unconscionable results, the employment contract was ruled enforceable. Few courts found strict application of the employment-at-will doctrine to be troublesome, let alone unconscionable. Consequently, employees were almost invariably on the losing side of the application of traditional contract law principles until the 1970s.

This chapter will review the basic principles of contract law and their traditional application to the employment setting. Chapter 3 will review how these traditional notions became an increasingly significant force in the expansion of individual employee rights. By the 1990s, contract law became more closely linked to employee rights' claims than at any previous time in U.S. legal history.

I. THE BASICS OF EMPLOYMENT CONTRACTS

All employment relationships are contractual. The contract need not be in writing and the term "contract" need not be used. It is enough that (1) one agrees to perform services for an individual or entity or actually performs those services, (2) these services are performed in exchange for some benefit, and (3) the parties share an understanding about the basic terms and conditions of the relationship.

A contract can be unilateral, that is, a promise in exchange for performance, or bilateral, the exchange of promises. A unilateral contract is a contract "in which the employer promises to pay an employee wages in return for the employee's work. In essence, the employer's promise constitutes the terms of the employment agreement; the employee's action or forbearance in reliance upon the employer's promise constitutes sufficient consideration to make the promise legally binding." (*Bankey v. Storer Broadcasting Co.*) With a bilateral contract, the employee's acceptance is in the form of a promise to perform (or not to perform) rather than in actual performance or in an agreement not to perform an act.

Certain key terms help define the employment relationship, including compensation, benefits, job duties, hours of work, duration of employment, vacation, holiday and sick day policies, promotion rights, standards for termination, seniority rights, and other terms specific to each employer and job. These terms may be in writing, stated orally, or fairly implied from the employer's actions. An employer's deeds can be as binding as its words.

The duration of employment is perhaps the term with the most legal significance in any employment relationship. Employment can be for a set term—one year, for example—or for an indeterminate period, otherwise known as an employment-at-will or at-will relationship. Most employment relationships in the United States are at-will; that is, either party may freely terminate the relationship without penalty.

This distinction between set-term and at-will employment relationships is both basic and crucial. At-will contracts may be severed at any time; set-term contracts are for designated periods. Under set-term employment contracts, the employment relationship ends on a specified date. As with any other contract, however, a failure to perform adequately during the term of the contract, whether it is to manufacture nails on schedule or to perform one's job duties competently, may constitute a breach of the agreement.

The parties to a set-term employment agreement will often expressly provide that employment may be terminated for good or just cause that may or may not be defined in the agreement. In any event, most courts will imply a just-cause provision in set-term contracts if none is present. (*Alpern v. Hurwitz*) This assures that the employer retains the benefit of the bargain if the employee should not perform as required during the term of the agreement. In contrast, in at-will relationships, courts will imply a just-cause requirement for termination only where warranted by the particular facts of that case. (*Weiner v. McGraw-Hill, Inc.*)

II. REQUIREMENTS FOR AN ENFORCEABLE CONTRACT

An enforceable contract requires an offer, the acceptance of the offer, and "consideration" for the contract.

A. Offer

The formation of an employment contract begins with an offer of employment. Job offers may be made directly to the applicant by the potential employer either orally (*Hartung v. Billmeier*) or in writing (*Sartin v. Mazur*). A job offer also may be tendered by a third party with the authority to do so, such as an employment agency. (*Travelers Ins. Co. v. Workmen's Comp. Appeals Bd.*)

An offer can be conditional (for example, based on the receipt of good references) or unconditional. The applicant's failure to comply with the offer as stated, such as by not accepting by the time or in the manner required, constitutes a rejection of the offer. In one case, an applicant for a position as district sales manager with Coca Cola Bottling Company filled out an employment application expressly providing that as a condition of employment he agreed to submit to and pass a physical examination including a preemployment drug test. His conditional offer of employment was revoked following receipt of his drug test results that indicated the presence of marijuana. The court concluded that no contract had been established as the applicant had never fulfilled a condition of the offer, namely, passing a drug test. (*Jevic v. Coca Cola Bottling Co.*) Once the requirements of a conditional offer are satisfied, however, the offer becomes binding and sets forth the terms of the employment relationship.

To be enforceable, an offer of employment must be sufficiently clear and definite to be acted on. Merely providing applicants with company materials, such as the employer's bylaws, does not constitute a job offer. (*Terrebone v. Louisiana Ass'n of Educators*) Similarly, a statement that an employee "will always have a job" was found to be not sufficiently definite to constitute an offer. (*O'Brien v. A.B.P. Midwest, Inc.*) An employer's statement that the employee would remain in her position as long as adequate federal funding was awarded was similarly ruled to be too indefinite to constitute an offer. Such a statement is nothing more than a hedge against a contingency beyond the control of both the employer and the employee, which, rather than vesting the plaintiff with a fixed term of employment, bespeaks indefiniteness. (*Miller v. Sevamp, Inc.*) Further, a promise from a company's vice-president that the company's president would make an offer of employment with terms and conditions comparable to those under which the employee had been previously employed with another company was held merely to be an agreement to agree and did not rise to the level of an offer. (*Bower v. Atlis Sys.*) Similarly, an offer merely to permit an individual to apply for employment is not enforceable as an offer of employment. (*Wright v. Ford Motor Co.*) Moreover, the terms of employment stated in a newspaper job advertisement do not constitute a job offer on which a reader may rely. (*Eng v. Longs Drugs*)

An offer of at-will employment is generally terminable at any time. For example, an applicant for a registered nurse position at a state correctional facility received a letter informing her that she had been "selected" for the position and directed her to report to work on a certain day. The applicant resigned her current position and appeared for work and was subsequently told that the offer was withdrawn because she had failed to complete fully her employment application. The court held that since the offer was for at-will employment "it would be illogical to hold" that the offer, like the employment, was not also terminable at will. "It would be absurd to require an employer, which had changed itc mind after an offer had been made, to actually employ the applicant for one hour or one day so that the employee could then be discharged." (*Sartin v. Mazur*) However, an applicant who has relied to his or her detriment on an offer of employment that is revoked may have a basis for suit under the doctrine of promissory estoppel, as discussed below.

In contrast, an offer of at-will employment has been held not terminable when the applicant was required to comply with certain conditions, and did so, only to have the offer then withdrawn. In one case, an applicant was promised employment by a certain date if he passed a physical examination, resigned from his current job, and moved to a designated city. The applicant performed each condition. Nonetheless, the employer withdrew the offer before the applicant's start date. The court emphasized that the employer expressly required that the applicant, among other things, resign his current employment, and on this basis found that the applicant had stated a breach-of-contract claim. (*Comeaux v. Brown & Williamson Tobacco Co.*) Similarly, termination of a set-term contract by an employer prior to the employee's start date constitutes an anticipatory breach of the agreement for which the employee can recover damages. (*Songer v. Mack Trucks, Inc.*)

B. Acceptance

An offer, to be enforceable, must be accepted in the manner required and on the terms as offered. (*Tow v. Miners Memorial Hosp. Ass'n*) Consequently, a contingent offer can be accepted only through satisfaction of the contingency. (*Scheck v. Francis*) For example, an offer of employment expressly conditioned upon the approval of the board of directors was deemed not accepted where only informal approval of two directors was received. (*Santandrea v. Siltec Corp.*) An applicant who places conditions on the acceptance of an offer has not accepted the offer; rather, he or she has made a counteroffer that the employer must accept before an employment relationship is established. The same holds true if the employer responds to an applicant's offer of his services with terms different than those offered by the applicant. (*Ferrero v. Amigo, Inc.*) The acceptance of an offer of employment conditioned on a change in the start date from July 10 to July 15 was ruled by the court to be a counteroffer rather than acceptance of the offer. (*Foster v. Ohio State Univ.*)

The acceptance of an offer of employment is most obvious when a job applicant simply agrees to the employer's offer orally or in writing on the terms as offered. An offer can also be deemed accepted by commencing employment on the terms as offered by the employer or by continuing employment after the terms of the original agreement have been modified. (*Dallenbach v. MAPCO Gas Prods.*)

C. Consideration

Not every promise made by an employer is binding. For a promise or a contract to be enforceable, it must be supported by "consideration." Consideration is the exchange of a promise for the other party's:

- Promise to perform or not perform an act;
- Actual performance of an act or failure to do so; or
- Agreement to create, modify, or terminate a legal relationship.

In the typical employment setting, the employer provides consideration by agreeing to employ and compensate an individual and the employee provides consideration by promising to work for the employer (in a bilateral contract) or by actually beginning to work (in a unilateral contract). Continued employment by the employee typically satisfies the employee's requirement for consideration. For example, an employee concerned about her job security in the face of the potential sale of the company who obtained a written agreement for a severance package of six months' pay provided consideration for this agreement through her continued employment. (*Mohr v. Arachnid, Inc.*)

The issue of consideration in the employment setting often arises when an employee seeks to enforce a particular promise made by the employer in addition to the promise to employ. Common examples of such promises include a promise to promote the employee within a designated period of time or to terminate the relationship only where just cause exists. Some courts have ruled that continued employment constitutes the necessary consideration for such promises. Others have found such promises to be enforceable only if the employee provides "additional consideration," that is, some benefit to the employer or detriment to the employee beyond continued employment. (*Merritt v. Edson Express, Inc.*)

In those states applying the additional consideration doctrine, an applicant's promise to perform or the actual performance constitutes the consideration for the employment agreement; his or her relocation at the request of the employer, for example, constitutes the additional consideration for the limitation of the employer's ability to terminate at will. In one case, an employer promised to treat its employee handbook as a binding contract in exchange for the employees' promise to vote against union representation. The Hawaii Supreme Court concluded that the employees' rejection of the union constituted consideration for this agreement and, consequently, the employer's promise, found in its employee handbook, to terminate only for just cause was ruled enforceable. (*Kinoshita v. Canadian Pac. Airlines*) Similarly, an applicant who accepted an employer's offer and relocated from one city to another at the employer's urging was found to have provided additional consideration for the employer's promise to transfer the employee if the position did not work out. (*Rodie v. Max Factor & Co.*)

In contrast, additional consideration claims have been rejected in the following circumstances:

- Employees who decided to transfer to a new five-year project were terminated when the project was canceled unexpectedly. The court characterized the transfer decisions as "simply reasoned choices of new career goals and did not constitute additional consideration for continued employment"; (*Schleig v. Communications Satellite Corp.*)
- Employee's relocation following acceptance of a job offer that required the employee to live within 30 minutes of the work site did not constitute independent consideration that converted the employee's at-will status to that of an employee terminable only for cause; (*Lavery v. Southlake Ctr. for Mental Health*)
- Relinquishment of a union job with job security for a supervisory position without job security did not constitute consideration for an alleged promise of job security made at the time the supervisory position was offered; (*Koch v. Illinois Power Co.*) and
- Assignment of inventions or patents to the employer did not constitute additional consideration for a just-cause claim. (*Thompson v. St. Regis Paper Co.*)

Courts rejecting the additional consideration doctrine, such as the California Supreme Court, have reasoned that it is contrary to the general principle of contract law that courts should not inquire into the adequacy of consideration. "There is no analytical reason why an employee's promise to render services, or his actual rendition of services over time, may not support an employer's promise both to pay a particular wage (for example) and to refrain from arbitrary dismissal." (*Foley v. Interactive Data Corp.*)

Support for the doctrine of additional consideration is decreasing and, consequently, courts are more likely to hear and address employee breach-of-contract claims than in the past without the requirement that additional consideration be present.

III. BEYOND CONTRACT LAW

Traditional contract principles do not always provide the means for recovery in cases where recovery seems otherwise warranted. In response, the law has developed alternative routes for recovery where contract law fails.

The first addressed here, promissory estoppel, attempts to cover the circumstance in which the employer has induced reliance on a promise to the detriment of an applicant or employee. This doctrine is typically invoked when a promise of employment is wrongfully withdrawn after the prospective employee acts on that promise, for example, by resigning from prior employment.

The doctrine of quasi-contract or *quantum meruit* provides a remedy to avoid unjust enrichment to a party. Under this doctrine, an employee who has provided services with the unrealized expectation of compensation may sue to recover the value of those services even though no employment contract can be shown to have existed. In contrast to promissory estoppel (where the employer's promise is required), an individual seeking recovery in quasi-contract is relying not on an employer's promise but on the unfairness of permitting the employer to benefit from the provision of services without compensation.

An employee whose employment agreement has been breached as the result of actions of a third party may seek a remedy in the realm of civil wrongs known as tortious interference with contract.

A. Promissory Estoppel

Even in the absence of an employment contract, employers may be legally bound to carry out a promise to an applicant or individual performing services for it. The legal doctrine of promissory estoppel may be invoked in the absence of a contract to prevent injustice to an individual who in good faith relied upon employer actions or representations, ultimately to the individual's detriment.

Generally, for the doctrine of promissory estoppel to apply (1) the promise must be clear and definite, (2) reliance should have reasonably been expected by the employer, (3) reliance on the promise in fact occurs to the employee's or applicant's detriment, and (4) the actions taken were reasonably induced by the promise.

Courts have found the following promises to be "clear and definite" enough to satisfy the requirements of the doctrine of promissory estoppel:

- An offer to hire a pharmacist with knowledge that the pharmacist, in response, would resign from his current job; (*Grouse v. Group Health Plan, Inc.*) and
- An offer to reinstate an employee with back pay if criminal charges were resolved in his favor. (*Mers v. Dispatch Printing Co.*)

In contrast, oral representations from a company's owner and vice president that "good employees are taken care of" to an employee negotiating a transfer were found not to be "clear and definite" enough to support a promissory estoppel claim. (*Ruud v. Great Plains Supply*)

Even if a promise is "clear and definite," detrimental reliance is required to establish a promissory estoppel claim. An employee or applicant who passes up other employment opportunities, who relocates based on the employer's promise, or who incurs reasonable expenses in reliance on the employer's promise generally will be found to have satisfied the detrimental reliance requirement. (*Scholtes v. Signal Delivery Serv.*) However, detrimental reliance has been found lacking where:

- The employee does not turn down other employment, but instead simply continues to work for the employer based on the employer's promise of job security; (*Dumas v. Kessler & Maguire Funeral Home*)

- The employee simply accepts management's promise of a commission rate of seven percent for an indefinite period; (*Dumas v. Auto Club Ins. Ass'n.*)
- The employee's rejection of a job offer from another company was based on grounds different than those on which he based his promissory estoppel claim; (*Rynar v. Ciba-Geigy Corp.*)
- The employee failed to advise the employer of another job offer, which she purportedly rejected in favor of the defendant-employer's promise of long-term employment; (*Moore v. Merrill Lynch*)
- The employee was a sophisticated businessman who had earned an MBA from Harvard; (*Krisak v. Gourmet Coffees of Am.*) and
- The employee transfers from one at-will job to another with the same employer, and the employee does not need to relocate. (*Chrisman v. Philips Indus.*)

The doctrine of promissory estoppel may be applied even if the employment is at-will and may be terminated for any or no reason without repercussion. For example, in one case, 23 telephone repair persons were told that they were going to be laid off, but were promised clerical positions as soon as a company warehouse was converted into office space. Based on this promise, the employees turned down other job offers and delayed searching for other employment. Ultimately, the employer reneged on the promise and refused to hire any of the laid-off employees. The court awarded damages to the employees based on their detrimental reliance, even though the employer could have hired and immediately fired the employees. (*Bower v. AT&T Technologies*)

Damages under the doctrine of promissory estoppel are restricted. Generally, a court may award damages based on the employee's reasonable reliance on a promise not otherwise enforceable by law. (*Bower v. AT&T Technologies*) Courts will not typically order the employer to actually hire or rehire the aggrieved employee or applicant. An employer may be required, however, to reimburse an employee for expenses incurred, such as relocation costs, and damages resulting from the failure to live up to the promise upon which the employee relied. In one case, for example, a salesman quit his job and incurred expenses for moving his family to make himself available to start a new job offered by the prospective employer; the court held that he was entitled to recover his "reliance damages" when the employer wrongfully withdrew its offer. (*Comeaux v. Brown & Williamson Tobacco Co.*)

B. Quasi-Contract

Under certain circumstances, an individual may render services in expectation of receiving compensation without express agreement by the employer or under circumstances in which an agreement is not enforceable for other reasons such as the lack of consideration. Contract law will provide no remedy because of the lack of the basic requirement of an agreement. To compensate the provider of services and avoid the unjust enrichment of the employer in such circumstances, a legal remedy known as quasi-contract or *quantum meruit* was born. (*Reprosystem, B.V. v. SCM Corp.*)

Quasi-contract claims are not contractual in the traditional sense and, consequently, the normal requirements for the formation of a contract need not be satisfied. With a contract, it is the agreement of the parties that defines their respective duties. With quasi-contract, the promise of the employer is implied based on the actions of the employee to avoid the employer's unjust enrichment.

The requirements for a quasi-contract claim in the employment setting are that (1) an individual render services beneficial to the employer with the expectation of compensation, and (2) the benefit conferred on the employer is unjust. Failure to demonstrate that a benefit has been conferred on the employer will result in the dismissal of the employee's quasi-contract claim. (*Nelson v. Stanley Blacker, Inc.*)

For example, the president of a company continued to work beyond the expiration of his contract while a new agreement was being negotiated. No new agreement was signed and the now former president sued to recover for his services rendered after expiration of his contract. The court found recovery for that period warranted on a quasi-contract basis at the rate offered by the employer during negotiations for the new contract. (*Ellis v. Photo Am. Corp.*)

If, however, the party claiming damages cannot show that his services conferred any benefit on the company, he cannot recover on a quasi-contract theory. For example, a New York appellate court held that a potential investor who worked for a company to assess the business was not entitled to payment on a *quantum meruit* theory where one of the clients he allegedly recruited went bankrupt without paying the company and where he could not identify the revenues generated by a second client. (*Reisner v. Recco Temporary Servs.*)

Recovery under quasi-contract is limited to the reasonable value of the services actually rendered. (*Holman v. CPT Corp.*)

C. Tortious Interference With Contract

A "tort" is a civil wrong, that is, a violation of a duty imposed by law for which damages may be recovered. In the employment setting, tort claims have proliferated in recent years in a variety of forms. One such tort that has been increasingly invoked is the claim of tortious interference with contract. Tortious interference claims encompass both existing and prospective business relationships. (*Toney v. Casey's Gen. Stores*) This legal action is typically asserted when a third party, not part of the employment relationship, intentionally injures that relationship or prospective relationship to the detriment of one or both parties. (*Hannigan v. Sears, Roebuck & Co.*)

While the *existing* business relationship tort requires a contract, the *prospective* business relationship tort requires only a reasonable expectancy of forming a contract. (*Torbett v. Wheeling Dollar Sav. & Trust*) In the employment setting, most legal challenges have involved existing business relationships. Such claims have generally been sustained even where the relationship is terminable at will, since it is assumed that parties to an at-will employment relationship may intend to continue employment indefinitely, and therefore third-party interference should be actionable. (*Lewis v. Oregon Beauty Supply Co.*) In any event, both branches of tortious interference claims share similar legal standards.

The basic requirement for a tortious interference with contract claim is the existence of, or prospect of, a contract. Generally, the offending party must be aware of the existence of the contract or prospective contract between two other parties and must intentionally and improperly interfere with the performance of the contract or prospective contract, although direct, overt action is not required. (*Hannigan v. Sears, Roebuck & Co.*) Liability will result if the third party induces or otherwise causes a party to the contract not to perform or enter into the contract.

The following factors may be considered in determining whether interference is improper: the nature of the offending actor's conduct; the actor's motive; the interests of the other with which the actor's conduct interferes; the interests the actor seeks to advance; the social interests in protecting the actor's freedom of action and the contractual interests of the other; the proximity or remoteness of the actor's conduct to the interference; and the relations between the parties. Unlawful interference has been found to exist where:

- The former employer secures a former employee's termination from a new position by actively soliciting his termination; (*Pratt v. Prodata, Inc.*)
- The former employer submits reports concerning the employee's job performance, which it knew were inaccurate, to a potential employer and fails to respond timely to another potential employer's inquiries concerning the former employee; (*Purgess v. Sharrock*)
- The employee's access to equipment and information necessary to perform her job is maliciously restricted; (*Sorrells v. Garfinckel's*)
- The employee is retaliated against for complying with state fire laws which required that patients who desired to cook their meals be supervised; (*Hobson v. McLean Hosp. Corp.*) and

- A current employer, by deceit, induces an employee to revoke his acceptance of an offer from another company while, at the same time, the employer is seeking to replace him. (*Shebar v. Sanyo Business Sys.*)

A tortious interference claim typically cannot be asserted against one of the parties to the contract that is at issue inasmuch as one cannot tortiously interfere with one's own contract. For example, supervisors or corporate officers are generally considered parties to the employment relationship between an employer and its employees, as long as they are acting within their official capacities. (*Wells v. Thomas*) As such they are generally sheltered from liability for tortious interference with contract. If this were not so, every termination or disciplining of a subordinate would arguably subject a supervisor to suit. Consequently, tortious interference claims will be rejected where the officer or supervisor acts within his or her official capacity, without malice or not for personal interests. (*Medina v. Spotnail, Inc.*)

In contrast, liability may result if the supervisor or officer is shown to have acted based on personal interests. For example, a female employee began dating her supervisor. When she later refused to date him, the supervisor swore at her, threw things at her, and generally harassed her for six months until she quit. A tortious interference claim against the supervisor was permitted. (*Lewis v. Oregon Beauty Supply Co.*)

In another case, an employee was discharged after he questioned his supervisor's choice of supplier. The supervisor was found to have a surreptitious relationship with the supplier and therefore was acting for his own ulterior motive, not for the benefit of the company. A tort claim was permitted based on the supervisor's actions toward the employee. (*Haupt v. International Harvester Co.*)

Liability also has been found where employers ill-advisedly attempt to enforce the terms of a restrictive covenant. For example, the Utah Supreme Court held that a former employer interfered with a former employee's economic relations when it secured the employee's termination from a new job based on a restrictive covenant that had expired and which did not, in any event, cover the work the employee performed for his second employer.

(*Pratt v. Prodata, Inc.*) Liability also may be predicated upon an attempt to enforce a restrictive covenant where the employer seeking to enforce the covenant has no protectable interest at stake. In one case, a former employer threatened to sue a former employee's subsequent employer based on the employee's execution of a restrictive covenant. Faced with the prospect of defending a lawsuit, the new employer terminated the employee. The West Virginia Supreme Court affirmed the jury's verdict in favor of the employee and held that inasmuch as the prior employer did not have a legitimate business interest warranting the protection of the covenant, its attempt to enforce it was reckless and showed a willful disregard for the employee's rights. (*Voorhees v. Guyan Mach. Co.*)

Liability may include an award of damages (generally lost salary and benefits) reflecting the lost fruits of the employment contract, compensatory damages for such injuries as emotional distress, and punitive damages. For example, the West Virginia Supreme Court of Appeals upheld an award of $157,005, which included compensatory and punitive damages as well as prejudgment interest, in a tortious interference claim. (*Voorhees v. Guyan Mach. Co.*) In another case, a federal appeals court applying New York law upheld a $700,000 award for a tortious interference with contract claim. (*Purgess v. Sharrock*)

IV. LIMITATIONS ON CONTRACT

The scope of contract law applicable to the employment setting may be limited by the application of traditional contract principles and devices such as disclaimers, the requirement of a writing under state statutes of fraud, the parol evidence rule, and statutes of limitations. Each of these limitations on contract law will be addressed in turn.

A. Disclaimers

Employee rights are both granted and limited by the terms of the same agreement. A common term of an employment agreement that serves to limit employee rights conferred by contract is a disclaimer, that is, a reservation of rights by an employer generally retaining employer prerogatives such as the ability to discharge without cause. Disclaimers are generally written, although oral disclaimers are also permissible. Disclaimers are used by employers most typically to preserve the employment-at-will status of their employees.

Generally, to determine the validity of a disclaimer, courts will consider the context in which it appears with reference to the norms and expectations of the parties. (*Zaccardi v. Zale Corp.*) Factors considered in determining the enforceability of a disclaimer include the prominence of the disclaimer; its specificity; the surrounding circumstances, including the extent to which employees were apprised of the disclaimer; whether the disclaimer was signed; its effect on the terms of the employment relationship; and, to a lesser extent, the intent of the drafters.

An enforceable disclaimer in the setting of a personnel manual, for example, would state in a prominent place in the document that the terms of the manual are meant to be only advisory and are not legally enforceable; that the employer remains free to change the terms set forth in the manual and all other working conditions without having to consult anyone and without anyone's agreement; and that the employer retains the authority to fire anyone with or without good cause. (*Woolley v. Hoffman-La Roche, Inc.*)

In contrast, the Alaska Supreme Court found that a "one-sentence disclaimer, followed by 85 pages of detailed text covering policies, rules, regulations, and definitions, does not unambiguously and conspicuously inform the employee that the manual is not part of the employee's contract of employment." In that case, a registered nurse was discharged after the hospital issued a revised personnel policy manual providing that the new manual was not contractual; this had not been stated in the previous manual. The court explained that the personnel manual contained many provisions relating to employee rights and consequently a one-sentence disclaimer is not automatically sufficient to preserve the employment-at-will status of employees. (*Jones v. Central Peninsula Gen. Hosp.*) A disclaimer was found to be enforceable under Wyoming law, however, where the disclaimer was printed in capital letters and was the only text appearing on a separate page, which the employee signed, and was unambiguous in putting any reasonable signatory on notice that employment was at will. (*Hatfield v. Converse County*)

The disclaimer used by Sears, Roebuck and Company in its employment application has been the subject of extensive litigation. The disclaimer, which is typical of disclaimers used in the employment setting, reads as follows:

> In consideration of my employment, I agree to conform to the rules and regulations of Sears, Roebuck and Co., and my employment and compensation can be terminated, with or without cause, and with or without notice, at any time, at the option of either the company or myself. I understand that no store manager or representative of Sears, Roebuck and Co., other than the president or vice-president of the Company, has any authority to enter into any agreement for employment for any specified period of time, or to make any agreement contrary to the foregoing.

(*Reid v. Sears, Roebuck & Co.*) The enforceability of this disclaimer has been repeatedly upheld.

For example, a Sears employee was discharged for avoiding a security guard's questioning relating to a box the employee was carrying out of a store. The employee claimed that Sears was not permitted to discharge him without just cause. The court refused to uphold the employee's claim since the disclaimer specifically preserved the employment-at-will status of employees. The court explained that "there is no way that the [employee] could reasonably have had a legitimate expectation of a right to a just cause determination prior to termination." (*Novosel v. Sears, Roebuck & Co.*)

Disclaimers such as the Sears disclaimer may also serve to bar employees' reliance on supervisors' promises which contradict the terms of the disclaimer. If a disclaimer specifically limits the circumstances under which it may be modified, then it may be modified only in the manner provided. For example, a court found that the language of the Sears disclaimer precluded an action based on subsequent representations by management. "The contract expressly precludes reliance upon subsequent representations which are contrary to the written employment contract." (*Summers v. Sears, Roebuck & Co.*)

Some courts have ruled that without such an express limitation, however, a disclaimer may be overridden by the subsequent representations of management. (*Reid v. Sears, Roebuck & Co.*) Put another way, the absence of a disclaimer providing that the terms of a handbook may not be modified except in writing leaves open the possibility that later oral modifications will supersede the handbook provisions. (*Kern v. Levolor Lorentzen, Inc.*) Moreover, inconsistent disclaimers or representations may negate the enforceability of an otherwise enforceable disclaimer. In one case, the applicability of a disclaimer contained in an employee's benefit manual to policies contained in an employer's Memorandum of Working Conditions was found to raise a question of fact, which required a trial. (*Swanson v. Liquid Air Corp.*)

Courts differ as to the enforceability of a disclaimer contained in a later document that modifies otherwise enforceable terms of an employment relationship. The Michigan Supreme Court has ruled that a disclaimer in a new employee handbook providing that the employment relationship is at will is enforceable and defeats an employee's breach-of-contract claim based on past promises of job security. (*Scholz v. Montgomery Ward & Co.*) A disclaimer contained in a modified handbook was found, however, not to bar a discharged employee's breach-of-contract claim where the transmittal memorandum misled employees by suggesting that the differences between the original and amended handbooks were merely a matter of form rather than substance. (*Elliott v. Montgomery County Community College*)

In a case involving an Atlantic City casino, a handbook issued in 1980 guaranteed employees, among other things, "maximum job security." The policy of maximum job security was reinforced in a policies and procedures manual. The casino added a disclaimer in a subsequently issued handbook, which stated that the terms of the handbook were not intended to be contractual. The court found the disclaimer to be inadequate because it failed to explain the relationship between the disclaimer and the promise of maximum job security. The court pointed out that the first handbook was issued during an orientation meeting and that the second handbook was merely distributed along with a request that it be read and that the detachable acknowledgement form be signed and returned. The court found that the casino's failure to reorient the employees and to state clearly the impact of the disclaimer rendered the disclaimer unenforceable. (*Preston v. Claridge Hotel Casino*)

Disclaimers are a notably effective means for management to clarify the terms and conditions of employment and have served as the death knell for many claims by employees. Disclaimers are most likely to survive a legal challenge if they are clearly stated and conspicuously placed in an appropriate document, and where receipt is acknowledged by employees. The enforceability of a disclaimer is strengthened where the disclaimer itself provides that it may be modified only in writing. Employers that include disclaimers in their policies should carefully review the terms and conditions of employment, including disclaimers, with new employees and should review periodically company policies, including the limitations on the enforceability of those policies, with employees.

B. Requirement of a Writing (Statute of Frauds)

One significant defense to claims of oral contracts by employees is the long-standing doctrine of the statute of frauds. Under the statute of frauds, a contract that cannot be performed within a year must be in writing to be enforceable. This legal doctrine typically is invoked when an oral agreement of employment for a set term is at issue.

The law has long favored written, as opposed to oral, agreements to minimize later disputes between the parties. This principle was codified in seventeeth-century England by the Statute of Frauds. Almost every state has adopted its own statute of frauds.

The statute of frauds requires *written* documentation for any agreement that, by its terms, cannot be performed within one year. In the absence of such documentation, the agreement is invalid and a legal action may not be based on it. In the employment setting, depending on the state, employee handbooks or related documents generally have been ruled insufficient to satisfy the requirement of a writing. (*Bowser v. McDonald's Corp.*)

Although the standards vary, a valid writing generally must list the agreement's material terms such as salary, job description, and duration. (*Tallini v. Business Air, Inc.*) Failure to fill in the salary and bonus terms in a proposed contract was held to be fatal to enforcement of the contract under the statute of frauds. (*Ferrera v. Carpionato Corp.*)

Courts apply the requirement of a writing only to those agreements whose performance could not possibly be completed within one year. In other words, a writing is not required as long as there is *any* possibility the agreement can be performed within a year. (*Ohanian v. Avis Rent A Car*) What *actually* occurs is irrelevant. For example, an employee alleged that his discharge violated an oral promise that he would be discharged only for cause. The court ruled that the statute of frauds did not bar the claim because under the agreement the employer could discharge the employee within one year if cause was shown. (*Wanamaker v. Columbian Rope Co.*)

Moreover, many courts have ruled that a promise of employment for life, or until retirement, does not require written documentation because the employee may quit, die, or retire within a year. In one case, an assistant counsel for a bank, Hodge, sought new employment and interviewed with a financial services firm. In his second interview, Hodge stated, "I want to be here until I retire." The interviewer for the financial services firm orally agreed. Hodge accepted a job offer and was fired within a year. The court ruled that, while the oral agreement of employment until retirement was binding, a writing was not required and the statute of frauds was inapplicable. The court reasoned that Hodge may have retired or died within a year and, consequently, the contract did not require a writing. (*Hodge v. Evans Fin. Corp.*) In this area of contract law, however, directly contrary results are not uncommon. For example, a Texas court held that, under that state's statute of frauds, an offer of permanent employment had to be in writing to be enforceable. (*Cortez v. Humana Hosp. Corp., Inc.*) The court reasoned that a contract promising employment until retirement had to be in writing because it would not be performed within one year, because the employee was 47 years old and normal retirement is at age 65.

An employer may be prevented or equitably estopped from asserting a statute of frauds defense when to do so would inflict an unconscionable injury (*Whitco Indus., Inc. v. Kopani*) or where the party seeking shelter from the statute of frauds defense is guilty of material misrepresentation. (*Evans v. Certified Eng'g & Testing Co., Inc.*) For example, an employer was equitably estopped from asserting a statute of frauds defense when its employee, relying on the employer's oral (and unfulfilled) promise that he would receive part ownership in the business after ten years' employment, left his prior job where he received more money and worked ten years for the company. (*Jarrett v. Epperly*)

C. Parol Evidence

Parol evidence is oral evidence such as promises communicated to employers by employees orally. The parol evidence rule provides that evidence inconsistent with the terms of a written agreement will not be admitted into evidence. This long-standing rule of contract construction is intended to enhance the predictability and stability of contractual relations by eliminating collateral challenges to written contracts.

Parol evidence is admissible, however, as proof of the intent of the parties where (1) the terms of a written agreement are ambiguous (*Stancil v. Mergenthaler Linotype Co.*) or (2) the oral statement addresses a matter not covered in the written agreement and is not inconsistent with that agreement. (*Hall v. Hotel L'Europe, Inc.*) Parol evidence may also be admitted when the written agreement is not "fully integrated," that is, it does not constitute a complete expression of the parties' agreement. (*Litman v. Massachusetts Mut. Life Ins. Co.*) For example, statements on a pre-printed employment application were found not to constitute an integrated agreement thereby allowing the admission of evidence of contemporaneous oral agreements. (*Harden v. Maybelline Sales Corp.*) Similarly, a contract was held not to be integrated because it was silent as to the grounds for termination and was the only one of its kind where the practice was to enter into oral agreements. (*Esbensen v. Userware Int'l.*) In addition, parol evidence may be considered when the written agreement was procured by fraud. (*Hall v. Integon Life Ins. Co.*)

Under each of these circumstances, parol evidence may be admitted to demonstrate additional terms of the agreement.

D. Statute of Limitations (Limitations Period)

A legal claim has a life span known as the period of limitations within which it must be asserted to be viable. After the limitations period lapses, a claim, whether or not it has merit, is not enforceable. The period of time within which a claim may be asserted varies depending on the jurisdiction and the nature of the claim.

The limitations period for contract actions is generally six years. (*Minto v. County of Suffolk*) A number of states have enacted statutes with shorter limitations periods. For example, California has a four-year limitations period for written contracts and a two-year period for oral contracts. (*McMahon v. Pennsylvania Life Ins. Co.*)

Statutes of limitations serve a variety of functions. As time passes, there is an increased likelihood of lost evidence and faded memories. Moreover, individuals are discouraged from postponing action; closure to an action promotes the security and stability of involved parties by limiting the threat of litigation.

Generally, limitations periods begin to run the moment one has a right to commence an action. In the employment setting, this is often when the employee is aware, or should be aware, of an alleged wrongful action whether or not it has yet occurred. (*Prouty v. National R.R. Passenger Corp.*) For instance, in cases involving termination of employment, the period of limitations will generally begin to run the moment the termination decision is communicated to the employee, *not* when the employee is actually discharged. (*Delaware State College v. Ricks*) A negative performance evaluation was held, however, not to trigger the statute of limitations where the implications of the evaluation were unclear and the employee had no reason to believe that the evaluation would lead to his termination. (*Colgan v. Fisher Scientific Co.*)

Notice of termination need not be "official" for the statute of limitations to begin running. In one case, a community college employee was discharged and more than three years later claimed the discharge was based on his political activities in violation of his constitutional rights. The court determined that the limitations period started to run with receipt of an earlier letter received *more* than three years before the filing of the claim, rather than a later, more official letter notifying the employee of the termination received *less* than three years prior. Therefore, the employee's claim under the applicable three-year statute of limitations was barred. (*Bates v. Board of Regents*)

E. Remedies

The general aim of a court in remedying a breach of contract is to place the injured party in the position that the party would have enjoyed if a breach had not occurred. In the employment setting, remedies for an employee could include compensation for lost pay and benefits. The employee could also recover liquidated damages (that is, an amount, if any, set forth in the contract to be paid in the event of a breach). Equitable relief, including reinstatement to the former or a substantially equivalent position, is warranted only in extraordinary cases such as where the injured party will suffer irreparable harm. (*Ezekiel v. Winkley*) Similarly, punitive or compensatory damages are generally not available under a breach of contract claim (*Patton v. University of Chicago Hosps.*), but have been awarded in some states where the contract breach was willful, wanton, or fraudulent in nature. (*Ainsworth v. Franklin County Cheese Corp.*) Damage awards that would put the employee in a better position than the employee would have been in had the contract been performed have been reduced or rejected. (*Paul v. Lankenau Hosp.*)

Recovery for lost compensation is fairly easy to calculate. A wrongfully discharged employee is entitled to the compensation lost from the time of the breach to the date of the court's decision, with interest. Deductions from that amount may include any earnings received by the employee (*e.g.*, other employment) during that period. (*Hendler v. Manageable Info. Sys., Inc.*) The general rule is that unemployment compensation may not be deducted from back pay awarded. Some courts have allowed such deductions, reasoning that the employee should not be doubly compensated. (*Mers v. Dispatch Printing Co.*) If the employment agreement provides for termination upon notice, for example 60 or 90 days, recovery generally will be limited to the notice period.

Future damages, that is, damages for a period of time after the court's finding of a contract breach, while generally not rewardable have been awarded under limited circumstances. (*Ritchie v. Michigan Consol. Gas Co.*) For example, future damages may be awarded if an employment contract which has been breached lacks a fixed term. A diminution in future earning power is not included in this recovery. (*Lindsey v. University of Ariz.*) Courts awarding future damages look to the facts of the particular case to determine the period of time the employee could reasonably be assumed to have remained employed under the breached employment agreement. (*Osterkamp v. Alkota Mfg. Inc.*) A "front pay" period of 26.5 years was awarded in one extreme case in which the court calculated damages by taking the difference between the salary received from the breaching employer and the lower salary received currently and multiplying that figure by the number of years until retirement, which in that case was 26.5 years. (*Diggs v. Pepsi-Cola*) Other courts have refused to award future damages in breach-of-contract cases. (*Lesmeister v. Dilly*)

Lost profits, while generally not awarded in breach-of-contract cases (*Broersma v. Sinor*), may be awarded if the employee's compensation is based in whole or in part on company profits. (*Brawthen v. H&R Block, Inc.*)

Recovery for lost fringe benefits also may be awarded in contract actions. (*Neiman-Marcus Group v. Dworkin*) Such fringe benefits may include vacation pay (*Jackson v. Minidoka Irrig. Dist.*), unused sick time (*Logue v. City of Carthage*), health benefits (*Acree v. Minolta Corp.*), and life insurance (*Panhandle E. Pipe Line Co. v. Smith*). Lost bonuses, benefits under stock purchase plans, severance pay, or commissions may also be awarded depending, in part, on each employer's requirements for the earning of each.

Liquidated damages—a fixed amount of damages set at the time the agreement is reached—are almost always recoverable where the stated damages are reasonably related to the damages anticipated to be incurred from breach of the agreement. (*Robbins v. Finlay*) Anticipating the damages to be suffered as the result of a prospective breach is often difficult, particularly where the relationship is not for a set term. Courts in those circumstances will look to the reasonableness of the terms and the good faith of the parties in determining the enforceability of a liquidated-damages clause. Courts will not enforce such clauses where they constitute a penalty rather than a reflection of anticipated actual damages. (*Acree v. Minolta Corp.*)

In extraordinary circumstances, a court also may award equitable relief such as an injunction (which requires a party to do or not do an act) or an order of reinstatement. (*Dania Jai Alai Int'l, Inc. v. Mura*) To obtain injunctive relief, the employee must be able to show irreparable injury and likelihood of success on the merits of the claim. An injunction may not be obtained where calculable monetary damages are at issue.

Reinstatement may be awarded as well. (*Stafford v. Electronic Data Sys. Corp.*) One court illustrated the extraordinary nature of this remedy when it reversed a lower court's order permitting an employee to amend his complaint to seek reinstatement. In rejecting the reinstatement claim, the court concluded that full redress for the employee's breach-of-contract claim was available by an award of damages and, in any event, reinstatement was found to be inappropriate in light of hostilities between the employer and employee (*Zahler v. New York State Ass'n for Retarded Children, Inc.*)

An employee seeking recovery for a breach of contract may not avoid finding new employment while waiting for a court award, but rather has a duty to mitigate his or her damages by seeking new employment. An award of contract damages will be reduced not only by the employee's interim earnings but also by what the employee could have earned with the exercise of reasonable diligence. (*Beggs v. Dougherty Overseas, Inc.*)

In determining whether an employee has satisfied the duty to mitigate, the court will look to the employee's experience, skills, and education and will measure those factors against the efforts expended in marketing those attributes in seeking gainful employment. The duty to mitigate would not require a physician terminated by a hospital to accept work as a janitor, but could require that the physician explore opportunities for physicians in nonhospital settings. Whether the duty to mitigate has been satisfied depends on the facts of each case, taking into account the reasonableness of the employee's efforts to find new work in the particular setting and at the particular time, and with the employee's skills, experience, and education in mind.

Mitigation is not required, however, where the employee is wrongfully discharged out of malice (that is, where the employer "willfully and deliberately violated the employee's rights under circumstances [the employer] knew or with reasonable diligence should have known of the employee's rights"). In that case, the employee is entitled to a flat back pay award without regard to the employee's interim earnings. (*Mace v. CAMC*) Furthermore, mitigation is waived where the employee is not capable of reasonable efforts to mitigate damages. For example, where an employee was 70 years of age at the time of trial and was left 80% permanently disabled due to an on-the-job injury, the court held that no other employment could have been obtained by using reasonable diligence. (*Lee-Wright, Inc. v. Hall*)

3

MODERN EXPANSION OF TRADITIONAL CONTRACT LAW

Contract law as applied to the employment relationship evolved in the 1970s and 1980s as courts expanded traditional contract law principles to meet the rising expectations of employees and the societal norms they reflected. This trend has continued full force in the 1990s.

An employer's authority to terminate the employment relationship at will with no repercussions—known as the employment-at-will doctrine—had for many years been used by employers to defeat employee legal challenges. Increasingly, this doctrine has been treated not as a hard-and-fast rule but as a legal presumption that can be overcome by the facts of any individual case. As stated by one California appeals court, the at-will presumption is "subject, like any presumption, to contrary evidence. This may take the form of an agreement, express or implied, that ... the employment relationship will continue indefinitely, pending the occurrence of some event such as the employer's dissatisfaction with the employee's services or the existence of some 'cause' for termination." (*Pugh v. See's Candies*)

Courts generally look to an employer's documents, statements, and practices to determine the enforceable terms of the employment relationship. An employer's documents and statements may serve to establish company policy or may evidence an adopted practice. Courts, in reviewing company documents and statements, focus on the employer's words, whether written or oral, which may represent an enforceable term of the employment contract. When addressing employer practices, courts look to the employer's actions and seek to determine whether, based on the employer's acts or pattern of behavior, a particular contractual term exists and is enforceable. Appendix A lists those states permitting employees to sue based on their employers' documents (such as handbooks), policies, and practices.

The basic terms of the employment relationship are set at the time of hiring and may be modified or expanded during the period of employment. This chapter reviews some of the current legal issues based on the law of contracts that may arise at the time of hire or during the employment relationship and that may expand or limit individual employee rights.

I. THE HIRING PROCESS

The hiring process is the gateway to the employment relationship. The terms as well as the tone of the relationship are established at this time.

Individual employee rights are both established and limited during the hiring process. For example, statements found in the employment application, promises made during job interviews, and the express terms stated in a written contract may all serve to establish employee rights.

A. Job Application

Job applications tend to be innocuous. Just as consumers rarely read the fine print on credit sales slips, few job applicants dwell on the fine print of an application form when seeking employment. As with the consumer sales agreement, however, job applications may provide or waive significant legal rights.

An employer may require as a condition of employment that an application form be completed. (*Armstrong v. Ryder Truck Rental, Inc.*) Misrepresentations made on an application form may constitute grounds for termination if the applicant is hired. (*Adams v. Texas & Pac. Motor Transp. Co.*)

The enforceability of the terms of employment applications are increasingly the subject of litigation. Employers in particular have been successful in invoking employment applications in defense of employee contract claims. A properly drafted application, including clear statements of the employer's policies, can help guard against unintentional contractual promises. Most employers have added to the text of employment applications, for example, disclaimers stating that the employment relationship is terminable at will. As discussed in Chapter 2, such disclaimers are generally enforceable. (*Butzer v. Camelot Hall*) For example, the Sears employment application provides that the applicant understands that the employment is at will. Three employees who were terminated allegedly without good cause sued, claiming that Sears, through its documents and representations, had promised job security to the employees. The court rejected this claim and concluded that the disclaimer in the employment application was enforceable and established an employment-at-will relationship. (*Reid v. Sears, Roebuck & Co.*) Similarly, an offer letter, which stated that the employer believed "it could provide [the applicant] with the opportunity for both professional and career advancement" was held to be insufficient to establish a promise of job security in the face of a clear disclaimer in the employment application establishing at-will employment. (*Fournier v. U.S. Fidelity & Guar. Co.*)

A disclaimer on an employment application also has been ruled sufficient to defeat a claim of job security based on a subsequently provided employee handbook (*Suter v. Harsco Corp.*) or, in the alternative, as strong evidence of the parties' agreement to waive such claims (*Harden v. Maybelline Sales Corp.*).

B. Job Interviews

The job interview is obviously crucial in establishing the tone and terms of most employment relationships. Job interviews are best used from the employer's perspective for screening purposes and from the applicant's perspective to determine the nature of the job and the opportunities it presents. Many statements may be made in the interview as the employer attempts to sell the position to a qualified applicant and determine his or her qualifications and as the applicant tries to market his or her qualifications. Both sides may be guilty of puffery, or worse.

Statements or promises made by an employer's representative in an interview may constitute enforceable terms of the employment relationship, whether or not the employer so intended. The significant risk that an interviewer may knowingly or unwittingly overstate or misstate the terms of employment argue for the careful training of interviewers and for the exercise of great care and discretion by interviewers.

Whether a promise made in an interview is enforceable as part of the employment "contract" depends on a number of factors, most notably, the applicable state law. As evidenced below, quite similar statements may be treated differently under different states' laws. As a general rule, a promise is more likely to be enforceable when it is specific and made under circumstances in which the employer or its representative evidenced an intent to be bound. Courts have found the following to be enforceable promises:

- The job would last until the applicant reached retirement; (*Eales v. Tanana Valley Medical-Surgical Group*)
- Someday the applicant (the son of the president) would become president of the company; (*Larson v. Kreiser's, Inc.*)
- The applicant would be discharged only for a "substantial mistake" that would cause the company a sizeable loss, or for wrongdoing; (*Sivel v. Readers Digest, Inc.*)
- The individual would have "a position for life if you can do the job"; (*Yaris v. Arnot-Ogden Memorial Hosp.*) and
- The employer responded to the applicant's statement that he wanted a year to bring the business up with the statement, "I can understand that, if you are not doing the job in a year, you are not going to be here anyway." The court held this created a factual question for the jury as to

whether a one-year contract of employment had been established. (*Schneider v. Equibank*)

In contrast, the following statements made in job interviews have been ruled by courts *not* to be enforceable as the result of a lack of specificity or due to the conditional nature of the promise:

- The job is "here for as long as you want it"; (*Merritt v. Edson Express*)
- The applicant would retire from the company if he could successfully centralize and computerize his department; (*Gross v. Goldome*)
- The manager wanted the new hire to remain with the company fifteen years or longer; (*Pratt v. Brown Mach. Co.*)
- The applicant would not get rich working for the company but would have "job security"; (*Corum v. Farm Credit Servs.*)
- The applicant would not be discharged as long as she met her sales quota and was honest; (*Rowe v. Montgomery Ward & Co.*)
- The individual had a "promising future with the company"; (*Hartman v. R.P. McCoy Apparel, Ltd.*), and
- The applicant could have the job for as long as he wanted and it would take two years to get a grasp of the job. (*Allen v. Dayco Prods.*)

The different results in often comparable factual situations are evidence of the lack of uniformity under various state laws on the question of the requirements for an enforceable promise in an at-will setting.

C. Job Offers

Job offers typically include the terms of the proposed employment relationship, which, if the offer is accepted, form the general outline of the relationship.

Failure by the employer to abide by the terms of the job offer may be found by a court to constitute a breach of an agreement.

For example, the failure to grant severance pay upon termination may constitute breach of the agreement. (*Mohr v. Arachnid, Inc.*) A promise of lifetime employment as long as the applicant for a sales position did not steal, coupled with the potential for high commissions, was ruled to be an enforceable term of the employment contract by the Michigan Supreme Court. This oral contract could be enforceable, the court determined, even in the face of contradictory written policies. (*Bullock v. Automobile Club of Mich.*) Similarly, an employer's hire letter, which outlined in detail a sales director's territory, the production requirements for three years, and his salary, coupled with the party's subsequent behavior, constituted an enforceable contract. (*Integon Life Ins.Co. v. Vandegrift*) In contrast, a court found language in an offer letter simply referring to a "guaranteed salary" does not create a one-year contract at the guaranteed amount. The court pointed out that in this context "guaranteed" was used to distinguish the salary offered from potential bonus. (*Cassel v. Ancilla Devel. Group.*) Similarly, the statement by the personnel director for the Chicago Cubs to a ball girl that she could have the job for "as long as [she] wanted" was found to be unenforceable for, among other reasons, "indefiniteness." (*Schoeneck v. Chicago Nat'l League Ball Club, Inc.*)

Documents provided at the time of hiring may be made part of the job offer. The most notable example is the personnel handbook or policies manual. The terms in the handbook or manual, if sufficiently definite, are enforceable under the laws of many states. (*Lewis v. Equitable Life Assurance Soc'y*)

On occasion, employment offers are withdrawn or rescinded and applicants who acted on those offers, for example, by resigning their employment, are injured. Offers of at-will employment generally have been held to be terminable at any time without repercussion "[b]ecause the actual employment was terminable at will, [and] it would be illogical to hold . . . that somehow the offer of such employment was not terminable at will." (*Sartin v. Mazur*) Nonetheless, applicants injured as the result of a withdrawn offer of at-will employment may recover, as discussed in Chapter 2, on such alternate grounds as promissory estoppel or tortious interference with contract.

Under certain circumstances, an otherwise enforceable promise made in a job interview may be modified or rescinded after the employee starts work. For example, an applicant for a parts and service representative position was promised during the job interview that he could relocate from Minneapolis to northern Minnesota. When the employer rescinded the offer to relocate after the employee began work, the employee relocated anyway three months later and was terminated for gross insubordination. A jury denied the employee's breach-of-contract claim and found that a new or modified agreement was reached when the employer denied the employee's relocation request and the employee nonetheless remained on the job. (*Pershern v. Fiatallis N.A., Inc.*)

D. Written Employment Agreements

Written employment agreements eliminate much of the uncertainty about the terms of an employment relationship. Written employment agreements can be detailed documents drafted by lawyers or terms scribbled on a napkin. As long as the requirements for the formation of a contract are met as described in Chapter 2, the agreement is enforceable. Written agreements also supersede prior oral agreements on the same points and, if they so provide, may prohibit subsequent oral modification of the agreement. (*Eyerman v. Mary Kay Cosmetics, Inc.*)

Employees may sue to enforce an employment agreement as they would any other contract. The court's job is to implement the intent of the parties and the ends they sought to achieve.

A court will not enforce any provision of the agreement that is contrary to law, even if it is agreed to by the parties and satisfies the requirements of a contract. For example, an action brought by a physician to enforce an employment agreement against a hospital, which hired him knowing he was not licensed, was rejected as against public policy. (*Tovar v. Paxton Community Memorial Hosp.*) Similarly, an employment agreement that required the forfeiture of all commissions earned, but not yet paid, should the employee resign was held unenforceable as contrary to that state's wage payment law. (*Weinzirl v. Wells Group, Inc.*)

Employee rights most often litigated under written employment agreements are those related to wages, benefits, and termination of the employment relationship. Other common and generally enforceable terms of a written employment agreement beyond those specifically related to the employment relationship are:

- An arbitration clause, that is, a choice to submit disputes to private resolution by means of an agreed-upon panel of neutrals or rules of arbitration;
- A choice-of-law provision, that is, the selection of a body of law by which the agreement will be governed;
- A "no oral modification" clause, which requires amendments to the agreement to be in writing; and
- An "integration" clause, which states that the agreement constitutes the entire agreement between the parties.

Terms may also be *implied* in a written contract where appropriate. For example, it is implied in an employment agreement that the employer is a lawful employer authorized to hire employees for the purpose stated. A contract to pitch for the New York Yankees entered into with someone who neither owns nor is authorized to act on behalf of the Yankees is unenforceable.

Implied terms can go to the very heart of the employment relationship. For example, a just-cause requirement is generally implied in every written employment agreement for a set term (in contrast to an at-will agreement) so the employee will not be denied the benefits of his or her bargain as the result of an arbitrary dismissal. (*Alpern v. Hurwitz*)

In contrast, no agreement to provide a smoke-free workplace was found where an employee's resume indicated that she was allergic to smoke, that she was initially provided with a private office, and that she kept a no-smoking sign on her desk. The court in that case noted that the employer's knowledge of her preference was not equal to a promise to accommodate it. (*Bernard v. Cameron & Colby Co.*) Similarly, New York's highest court rejected a breach-of-contract claim alleging that the employee was entitled to a higher bonus than he received. The court held that the written employment contract unambiguously left management with full discretion to determine bonuses and, consequently, attempts to introduce evidence of promises to the contrary were rejected. (*Namad v. Salomon, Inc.*)

II. DURING THE EMPLOYMENT RELATIONSHIP

Once the employment relationship begins, a court will look to an employer's documents, statements, and practices to determine which terms of the employment relationship are enforceable.

A. Employer Documents

Employers provide or show countless documents to employees during the course of employment. These documents may be in the form of postings, memoranda, personnel handbooks, letters, policy statements, schedules, performance evaluations, benefits reports, or numerous variations on these themes. To be effective, communications between management and employees should be precise, informative, and detailed.

The documents also may be less formal. For example, they may take the form of a note from a supervisor, or written comments on a report submitted by the employee or on the employee's performance evaluation.

In each instance, the document may be sufficient to establish a term of employment enforceable against the employer. It is the very effectiveness of the written word as a means of communication that makes it a likely and reliable source for the terms of the employment relationship and the focus of most employment litigation.

1. Personnel Handbook or Manual

Undoubtedly the document most frequently invoked in litigation by employees seeking to establish a particular term of the employment relationship is the personnel handbook or manual.

Almost invariably, the personnel handbook is cited to establish a "just cause" standard for termination or to require an employer to follow certain mandatory steps before disciplining or discharging an employee.

Handbooks for many years had been treated by both employers and the courts simply as guidelines for management and staff and not as enforceable contracts. The logic was simple: Handbooks were unilaterally issued by employers for their own convenience and as a tool of communication, and employees did not assent to the terms of the handbook or participate in their establishment. Certainly, it was argued, if management intended to set forth terms of an enforceable contract with its employees, it would do so with the care it would invest in negotiations with a union over a new labor agreement, not by means of issuing an employee handbook.

Beginning in the late 1970s, courts took a new and more critical look at employee handbooks. Courts for the first time began to enforce promises made in clear language in personnel manuals and handbooks distributed to employees in the normal course of employment. Among the factors arguing for the enforceability of handbooks or manuals are the context of their issuance, namely, as a compilation of management policies; the care with which they are prepared; and the documents' titles, for example, the company's policies or practices manual. "As every employee knows, when superiors tell you 'it's company policy,' they mean business." (*Woolley v. Hoffman-La Roche, Inc.*)

Whether a particular term in a personnel manual is enforceable is a question of fact for a judge or jury to decide. (*Hepp v. Lockheed-California Co.*) Relevant to this inquiry is, among other things, the language used in the manual along with the employer's course of conduct and representations regarding the relationship. In one case, the California Supreme Court cited three factors that supported a jury verdict in favor of two employees who had been demoted for poor performance in contravention of the company's policy: (1) the company's policy manual stated that the disciplinary process outlined in the manual was intended to be uniformly applied to all employees; (2) the company's personnel managers testified that the company expected employees to rely on the company's disciplinary policies; and (3) the company failed to produce any evidence that its disciplinary policies were guidelines to be followed at its management's discretion. (*Scott v. Pacific Gas & Elec.*)

While the trend among the courts is to enforce the provisions of employee handbooks, this view is not universal. For example, the Missouri Supreme Court has held that the issuance of a handbook does not constitute a contractual offer; rather, the handbook is better viewed as an informational statement of self-imposed policies. (*Johnson v. McDonnell-Douglas Corp.*) Still other courts have taken the position that unilaterally issued handbooks stating general policies are not enforceable. This will generally be the case when the employer reserves the right to modify the terms of the handbook (*Johnson v. McDonnell-Douglas Corp.*) or where the handbook contains an express disclaimer (*Pratt v. Brown Mach. Co.*). The applicable state law must be reviewed to determine the enforceability of the terms of the manual in a particular case.

The terms of a personnel manual may serve as a shield for employers as effectively as it can be a sword for employees. Management, in the collective-bargaining setting, often cites the terms of a collective-bargaining agreement in support of its personnel actions. Similarly, employers often refer to the terms of the personnel manual in support of disciplinary actions or personnel decisions such as refusals to promote. Courts have rejected employee claims where they are contrary to the terms of an enforceable personnel handbook, for example, by failing to exhaust contractual grievance procedures as set forth in the handbook. (*Fregara v. Jet Aviation Business Jets*) The New Mexico Supreme Court denied a breach-of-contract claim based on a layoff because the handbook provided that layoff decisions were in the purview of management solely. (*Shull v. New Mexico Potash Corp.*) Similarly, an employee's attempt to be reinstated after a four-month leave of absence was defeated where the employer's handbook specifically provided that reinstatement was not guaranteed following a leave of absence but, rather, depended on the employer's staffing requirements at the time. (*Nguyen v. CNA Corp.*)

Personnel handbooks are generally applicable at minimum to all nonsupervisory employees and in most instances to all employees including supervisory personnel. Supervisory manuals, in contrast, are often prepared to assist in the application of company policies and procedures. The question has arisen whether employees may seek to enforce the policies and procedures set forth in supervisory manuals that have not been distributed to employees. Supervisory manuals are, of course, evidence of company policy. (*Kelly v. Georgia-Pac. Corp.*) Courts have generally concluded, however, that supervisory manuals are not, by themselves, enforceable against the employer, particularly when they were not distributed or available generally to all employees. (*Owens v. American Nat'l Red Cross*) For example, a single copy of corporate guidelines found in a personnel office, even if shown to the manager, has been ruled not to constitute an employment contract. (*Anderson v. Hewlett-Packard*) Similarly, a former director of human resources' memorandum standardizing disciplinary procedure that was distributed only to managers was found not to constitute an implied contract. (*Leong v. Hilton Hotels Corp.*) In contrast, a personnel manual distributed only to supervisors was found to be enforceable as representing the official expression of company policy. (*Taylor v. National Life Ins. Co.*) In that case, the employee alleged that he had been discharged without good cause in violation of the provisions of the company's manual. The court found that the manual's express statement that it was the official source of company policy (where contradictions existed between the manual and a widely distributed employee handbook) and that it was "binding" created an issue concerning whether the employee could be discharged only for just cause.

Courts have generally permitted employers to revise the terms of a handbook after its issuance, even if the revision is detrimental to employees. This is so even if the right to modify an employment policy has not been expressly reserved. "[A] 'policy' is commonly understood to be a flexible framework for operational guidance, not a perpetually binding contractual obligation. In the modern economic climate, the operating policies of a business enterprise must be adaptable and responsive to change." (*Bankey v. Storer Broadcasting Co.*) For example, an employer was allowed to modify its handbook from a termination-for-cause standard to a termination-at-will standard on the ground that the employee accepted this modification by continuing to work for the employer. (*Chambers v. Valley Nat'l Bank*)

Nonetheless, some courts have ruled that an employee must assent to any significant modification of a unilateral agreement such as a handbook. (*Toth v. Square D Co.*) Moreover, the Michigan Supreme Court, while recognizing an employer's right to change its written policies, nonetheless required that employees be given reasonable notice of the change. (*Bankey v. Storer Broadcasting Co.*) Similarly, a federal court rejected a disclaimer added to a handbook where the employer made no mention of the change in a cover letter transmitting six pages of changes in the handbook. Instead, the disclaimer "was buried in a glossary definition, and there was no effort to highlight the fact or the effect of the disclaimer." (*Durtsche v. American Colloid Co.*)

2. Other Writings

Personnel manuals, while perhaps most conspicuous, are not the only forms issued by employers. Courts have adopted the same analysis in determining the enforceability of other writings as has been adopted for personnel manuals. For example, a benefits package summary and a supervisor's manual that merely stated general corporate goals were found *not* to be contractual. (*Gmora v. State Farm Mut. Auto. Ins.*) One court has even determined that the Girl Scout Promise, while laudable, does not establish contractual rights on behalf of employees of the Girl Scouts. (*Slattery v. Girl Scouts of Am.*) Where an employer document is binding, however, the mere failure to receive or review it does not necessarily prevent its enforceability. (*Grow v. General Prods.*)

Written statements of policy or employment terms found to be enforceable by courts include:

- A list of standard operating procedures; (*Jimenez v. Colorado Interstate Gas Co.*)
- A college faculty manual; (*Rose v. Elmhurst College*)
- An internal memorandum recounting a promise of reassignment if the employee was unable to perform a new

position effectively; (*Robertson v. Atlantic Richfield Petro-leum Prods.*) and

- A letter from the employer informing the employee of a bonus. (*McGraw v. Bill Hodges Truck Co.*)

In contrast, courts have ruled that written policy statements or employment terms were insufficient to support breach-of-contract claims in the following cases:

- A statement provided that, "when possible," the company would "normally" place 10-year employees in jobs similar in content to a past position; (*Schuler v. Polaroid Corp.*)
- A memorandum listing examples of misconduct was found to be not sufficiently specific to rise to the level of a contract. The employee contended that discipline on grounds other than what was listed was precluded. The court rejected this claim; (*Doe v. First Nat'l Bank*)
- Policy directives related to affirmative action, equal employment opportunity, job posting, minimum job qualifications, and job offers were found not to constitute an implied contract regarding promotions and hiring; (*MacGill v. Blue Cross of Md.*)
- A performance appraisal system that provided no assurance of job security whenever a positive evaluation was received; (*Palmer v. Richard L. Schlott Realtors*) and
- The company's sexual harassment policy did not establish a contract by which a supervisor who alleges that he was wrongfully accused of sexually harassing employees could sue his employer for failing to rebut workplace rumors. (*Martin v. Baer*)

In sum, the more authoritative the employer document upon which an employee relies and the more precisely it states company policy, the more likely it is that a court will find that the employer is bound by its terms.

B. Oral Statements and Promises

Not all terms and conditions of employment are—or can be—communicated to employees in writing. By necessity, an employer, through its managers and supervisors, also communicates with its employees orally. For example, the employee handbook may caution employees against tardiness, but in an era of flexible scheduling it is likely that such matters as the hours of employment for each employee will be communicated orally to employees during the hiring process or on the first day of the job.

Oral statements made by a manager or supervisor at the time of hire or in the course of employment may rise to the level of contract and may serve to bind an employer in the same way as a written promise. For example, a promise made at the time of hiring that the applicant would be paid a certain sum if an offer of employment were accepted or that the applicant would be terminated only for good cause may be as enforceable as written promises, if they are proved.

Certain key factors in determining the enforceability of an orally communicated contract term include the terms in question, the authority of the one making the promise, the circumstances surrounding the making of the promise, and the specificity of the particular terms.

Any term of the employment relationship can be established orally. For example, the South Dakota Supreme Court found that a father's promise to make his son president of the family business, if proven, could be found enforceable by a jury. In that case, the son alleged that he accepted employment with and toiled for the family business for 20 years based on his father's oral promise that he would soon take over the business. When his father fired him in the twentieth year of his employment, the son sued and the court concluded that he was entitled to prove that an oral contract existed promising him the presidency of the family business. (*Larson v. Kreiser's, Inc.*)

To be enforceable, the terms must be reasonably certain. For example, statements that the employee has a promising future with the company (*Hartman v. R.P. McCoy Apparel, Ltd.*); that the company wanted the employee to work 15 years and that he had become a "permanent" employee following completion of probation (*Pratt v. Brown Mach. Co.*); and that a boss would take care of a secretary's financial needs for the rest of her life in exchange for her services (*Saunder v. Baryshnikov*) have been ruled not sufficiently definite to constitute enforceable terms of the employment agreement. In the *Baryshnikov* case, the dancer's private secretary alleged that in exchange for her "substantial services" including translating, making travel arrangements, serving as appointments secretary, and organizing dinners, Mr. Baryshnikov agreed orally to "take care of her and her financial needs for the rest of her life." The court, pointing out that the private secretary could provide none of the relevant details of this arrangement, concluded that it could not enforce a contract whose terms could not be established.

An important factor in determining the enforceability of any oral promise is the position and authority of the employee making the promise. A co-worker's promise of a pay raise to another employee cannot bind the employer because a co-worker has no authority to determine pay raises. In contrast, a promise by a supervisor or high-level official who traditionally sets pay raises may bind the employer.

The circumstances under which a promise was made must also be taken into account. A comment made in a job interview or in the boss's office will more likely rise to the level of contract than one made on the softball field at the company outing.

The more specific the promise, the more likely it is to be enforced. Vague promises and optimistic hopes are typically held not to be specific enough to be construed as a contract. For example, an employer prepared a videotape reviewing its personnel policies to be shown to new hires. Company representatives on the tape stated that the company would "honor its responsibilities," "conduct fair performance evaluations," and would make "every effort to provide stability of employment." A court rejected a breach-of-contract claim based on these statements, finding them to be too indefinite to limit the employer's prerogatives. (*Allen v. MCI*) A statement made 23 years prior to a termination to the effect that the company never discharged people for economic reasons was found not to be enforceable, particularly when the policy was eliminated following acquisition by another company. (*Nixon v. Celotex Corp.*)

The following statements or promises have been found by courts *not* to be contractual:

- The employee's "position was not in jeopardy"; (*Fleming v. AT&T Info. Servs., Inc.*)
- The corporate president would remain employed as long as the company remained profitable; (*Geib v. Alan Wood Steel Co.*)
- The company hoped that the new hire would be with the company 15 years or longer; (*Pratt v. Brown Mach. Co.*) and
- A vice president's statement to a salesman that "so long as you do your job you can be here until you're a hundred." (*Mursch v. Van Dorn Co.*)

In contrast, the employer statements or promises in the following cases were ruled enforceable:

- The promise of employment until retirement age; (*Eales v. Tanana Valley Medical-Surgical Group*)
- "[A]s long as your performance is satisfactory, you won't have to worry about [termination]"; (*Diggs v. Pepsi-Cola*) and
- A promise to employ an attorney as general counsel until he qualifies for 100 percent vesting in each of the benefit plans. (*Slifkin v. Condec Corp.*)

The differing results in comparable settings reflect the varying approaches of the states in enforcing oral promises against employers.

Oral promises that directly contradict the written terms of the employment contract are generally not enforceable. As discussed in Chapter 2, to the extent that these promises are made prior to or contemporaneously with the signing of the written agreement, they are unenforceable under the parol evidence rule. (*Eyerman v. Mary Kay Cosmetics, Inc.*) Such promises will also be barred subsequent to the signing of the written agreement where the written agreement provides, as is often the case, that no oral modification of the agreement is permitted. (*Jackson v. Action for Boston Community Dev.*) Breach-of-contract claims based on oral statements that contradict an enforceable disclaimer similarly have been rejected. (*French v. Foods, Inc.*)

In one case, the employee alleged that the employer established a just-cause contract when the plant manager told him
that he would not lose his job if he performed well, and he received a memorandum stating that he could return to his prior
position if he failed in the position to which he was promoted.
The court, in rejecting this claim, pointed out that a previously
issued handbook provided that employment was at will, that this
policy could be modified only by the company's chief executive
officer, and that such a modification had not occurred. (*Vollrath v.
Georgia-Pac. Corp.*)

Further, failure to object to a change in the terms of an at-
will employment relationship coupled with continued employment may constitute an agreement to a modification of the employment contract. (*Facelli v. Southeast Mktg. Co.*) Courts are less
likely to rule so, however, where the modification serves to deny
the employee a vested benefit. (*Drans v. Providence College*) For
example, a court concluded that a salesman who refused to accept a reduced commission rate and who resigned two weeks
later was entitled to commissions at the prior rate for the two-
week period while he was still employed after the commission
rate had been changed. (*Ebling v. Gove's Cove, Inc.*)

Oral promises present a ripe field for potential litigation, as
the circumstances in which enforceable statements may have been
made by managerial or supervisory personnel are endless and
ultimately beyond an employer's ability to control fully.

C. Implied Contract and Employer Practices

An express contract is based on agreed terms, whether written or oral. An implied contract, in contrast, is based on the
employer's practices, course of conduct, documents, and statements. Implied contracts (sometimes referred to as implied-in-
fact contracts) are enforceable in the same manner as express contracts. In the employment context, implied contract arguments
are most often raised by at-will employees asserting claims of
job security following termination.

As with claims of oral contracts, a court may consider a number of factors in determining whether an implied contract in the

employment setting exists, such as "the personnel policies or practices of the employer, the employee's longevity of service, actions, or communications by the employer reflecting assurances of continued employment, and the practices of the industry in which the employee is engaged." (*Pugh v. See's Candies*)

An employee asserting an implied contract claim of job security has to overcome the strong presumption in favor of at-will employment present in most states. For example, a court denied an implied contract claim of permanent employment, despite the employee's allegation of having received "many" corporate documents providing that longevity of employment is a corporate goal, many promises of fair and consistent treatment, and a supervisor's assurance that his "position was not in jeopardy" and "as long as I have a branch, you have a job." The court found the employee's evidence to be "manifestly insufficient to rebut the at-will presumption." (*Fleming v. AT&T Info. Servs., Inc.*)

Similarly, a court rejected an implied contract claim where the employer "continuously encouraged, fostered, placed great importance upon and rewarded long, faithful, even lifetime service to the company." (*Sprott v. Avon Products*) In another case, an employer issued documents just prior to the vote in a union election guaranteeing that the company would not terminate employees as long as they performed well and there was sufficient work. The court ruled that under Mississippi law such promises were not enforceable unless the employee conferred some additional benefit or consideration on the employer beyond continued employment. (*Windfield v. Groen Div., Dover Corp.*)

Such claims, however, are not necessarily doomed to fail. States differ in their willingness to recognize implied contract claims. Courts have recognized implied contract rights to job security based on:

- Repeated oral assurances of job security; promotions, salary increases, bonuses consistent with these assurances; a violation of the company's own written termination procedures; and execution of a noncompetition agreement; (*Foley v. Interactive Data Corp.*)
- A general manager's investment in the company, loan to the company, and divesting himself of partnership in-

terest in another company (*Malarkey Asphalt Co. v. Wyborney*)

- A long employment history; numerous promotions and commendations; the company's general policy favoring more senior employees; oral representations that reductions in force would not occur; and the foregoing of other employment opportunities; (*Krause v. Dresser Indus.*) and
- A course of conduct over 28 years of employment. (*Shipkowski v. United States Steel Corp.*)

Mere length of service, however, does not assure job security. Two pharmacy employees were terminated when they refused to confess to embezzling money from the owner. One employee had worked for the owner 40 years. He sued, alleging an enforceable promise of job security. The employee's claim of job security, based on the employment history and performance of certain tasks without compensation, was rejected by the court. (*Benishek v. Cody*)

Implied contract claims are not limited to job security. For example, employees have raised implied contract claims related to the following personnel policies:

- Demotion; (*Bullock v. Automobile Club of Mich.*)
- Compensation; (*Dumas v. Auto Club Ins. Ass'n*)
- Health insurance benefits; (*Omer v. Tagg*)
- Annual performance evaluations; (*Buttell v. American Podiatric Medical Ass'n*) and
- Procedures required for termination. (*Hillsman v. Sutter Community Hosps.*)

Implied contract claims based on the following grounds have been rejected:

- An obligation to select the most qualified candidate for remaining available positions following layoff; (*Dabrowski v. Warner-Lambert Co.*)
- Promise of a smoke-free environment based on notice to employer of allergic reaction to tobacco; (*Bernard v. Cameron & Colby Co.*)

- Subjective belief that company policy was to lay off employees based on seniority; (*Boynton v. TRW*)
- An uncirculated management manual's provision that seniority would be taken into consideration when determining which employees would be terminated; (*Kreiney v. Hercules, Inc.*)
- Unwritten just-cause policy; (*Muscarella v. Milton Shoe Mfg. Co.*) and
- Failure to perform annual performance appraisals in accordance with internal management policy resulting in loss of salary increase. (*Lieber v. Union Carbide Corp.*)

Ironically, the success of an implied contract claim depends on, to a great degree, the employee's ability to distance his or her claim from its implied nature and instead associate it with the express or conscious policies of agreed-upon terms with the employer.

III. IMPLIED GOOD-FAITH REQUIREMENT

The law implies in every contract a good-faith term, known as the implied covenant of good faith and fair dealing, by which each party must not do anything that would deny to the other party the benefit of their agreement. The good-faith covenant is designed to achieve the reasonable expectations of the parties; however, in doing so, it may not be used to achieve a result contrary to the express terms of a valid contract.

Until recently, suits based on the good-faith covenant in the employment-at-will setting were rarely if ever seen. Today, their occurrence is much more frequent and the courts' application of the covenant has been, in the words of the North Dakota Supreme Court, "somewhat erratic." (*Hillesland v. Federal Land Bank Ass'n*) If broadly applied, the covenant would inject a good-faith requirement for all terms of an employment agreement, including termination. At-will employment would be less at will and would be to a greater degree subject to a third party's assessment of the appropriateness of the decision to terminate that relationship.

Some states have applied the covenant to employment agreements broadly, others more narrowly, and most others not at all. Those courts endorsing the application of the covenant point out that no exemption exists for the application of the covenant, which is implied in all contracts, in the employment area. Those courts rejecting application reason that for courts to imply a good-faith standard in every employment contract is an inappropriate exercise of judicial authority and would transform courts into bargaining agents for all employees. For example, the Utah Supreme Court has rejected application of the covenant of good faith and fair dealing in the employment setting because to do so would be to imply new independent rights not agreed to by the parties. (*Brehany v. Nordstrom, Inc.*)

Among the states applying the covenant to employment agreements are Alaska, California, Nevada, and Wyoming. A full list of those states recognizing employment suits based on the good-faith covenant is contained in Appendix A. The covenant has been held to apply where:

- An applicant who accepted a job out of state, quit his job, began to relocate, and was terminated before he commenced employment; (*Sheppard v. Morgan Keegan & Co.*)
- An employee who participated in the company's investigation of a discrimination claim by providing information supporting the allegations was subsequently transferred and denied other job opportunities; (*Price v. Federal Express Corp.*)
- An employee was not provided with work and work surroundings commensurate with his status, which, in turn, undermined his ability to perform his obligations under an employment contract that previously had been renewed three times; (*Hoffman v. Hill & Knowlton, Inc.*) and
- An employee was terminated for refusing to submit a urine sample as part of a drug test. (*Luck v. Southern Pac. Transp. Co.*)

Even in those states recognizing the covenant, limitations exist. For example, the Arizona Supreme Court has limited the application of the good-faith covenant to an employer's failure to pay earned benefits. (*Wagenseller v. Scottsdale Memorial Hosp.*) Similarly, the Massachusetts Supreme Court has limited claims under the good-faith covenant to those cases where employers gain a readily definable financial windfall as the result of the employee's termination, such as the forfeiture of earned commissions (*McCone v. New England Tel. & Tel. Co.*), and the Wyoming Supreme Court has limited claims to tortious conduct in an employment agreement involving a special relationship of trust and reliance. (*Wilder v. Cody County Chamber of Commerce*)

Most courts have rejected application of the covenant as an undue intrusion on management prerogative, particularly as it relates to job security. (*Thompson v. St. Regis Paper Co.*) "[I]n the absence of express terms limiting the right of an employer to discharge for any or no reason and in the absence of provisions establishing procedures by which a discharge should be effectuated, it would be inconsistent to hold that an employer, on the basis of the implied covenant of good faith, is bound to a substantive limitation on the employer's right to discharge." (*Brehany v. Nordstrom, Inc.*) Since such a broad application of the covenant to the employment setting would, in effect, undermine the employment-at-will relationship, it has been observed that such a decision is best left to the state legislatures rather than the courts. (*Murphy v. American Home Prods. Corp.*)

The damages recoverable for a violation of the covenant of good faith and fair dealing in those states that recognize the action vary depending on the state. The determining factor is whether the action is viewed as being contractual under the state's law, in which case damages are limited, or in the nature of a civil wrong or tort, in which case damages are broader and can include punitive damages. Nevada allows broader remedies including compensatory and punitive damages. (*K-Mart Corp. v. Ponsock*) California, in contrast, applying the prevailing view, limits recovery to contract damages with the aim of putting the employee in the position he or she would have been in but for the violation of law. (*Foley v. Interactive Data Corp.*)

IV. PARTICULAR CONTRACT TERMS

While any term of the employment agreement may be subject to legal challenge, certain terms have been challenged with particular frequency. A review of some of the more litigated terms follows.

A. Just Cause

Perhaps the most frequently litigated term of the employment relationship is a claimed limitation on at-will employment based on a just-cause requirement for termination. In the absence of a set term of employment, a just-cause requirement is the most notable limitation on the presumption of at-will employment. In short, job security in an otherwise at-will employment relationship invariably translates into a just-cause standard for termination.

In reviewing a just-cause claim, a court is confronted with two basic questions. First, is just cause required for disciplining or termination? Second, was there just cause for the action taken by the employer in the particular case under review? The importance of the first question is to remove the employment relationship from the realm of at-will employment. The second question requires that a court determine what constitutes just cause and apply that standard to the facts underlying the employee's claim.

1. Existence of Just-Cause Requirement

On occasion, an employer may agree to a just-cause standard for termination, or the parties may negotiate its requirement. In those instances, just cause may be defined in writing or a representative list of actions that would constitute just cause may be provided, for example, in a handbook or a written employment contract. The just-cause requirement may apply across the board as, for example, where the promise of just-cause employment is a standard term in agreements with all employees, or is contained in a personnel handbook, or can be based on the terms of an individual agreement. In the latter case, a review of the particular promises made to an individual employee is required.

Whether a court will imply a just-cause standard into the employment relationship depends as much on the state law to be applied as on the strength of the employee's case. The differing results "can also be explained by a difference in attitude, some courts continuing to be concerned with the adverse impact on employers of long-term employment contracts, while others are concerned with the adverse impact on employees when apparent commitments are not honored." (*Woolley v. Hoffman-La Roche, Inc.*)

More often, an employee asks the court to imply the just-cause requirement from the actions, practices, or words of the employer. Under these circumstances, it is for the judge or jury to determine, based on the facts as established on the record, whether just cause is required to terminate the employment relationship.

The New Jersey Supreme Court has ruled that a personnel manual promising just-cause termination may be applicable to all employees in the work force. The court reasoned:

> Whatever else the manual may deal with . . ., one of its major provisions deals with the single most important objective of the work force: job security. The reasons for giving such provisions binding force are particularly persuasive. Wages, promotions, conditions of work, hours of work, all of those take second place to job security, for without that all other benefits are vulnerable. (*Woolley v. Hoffman-La Roche, Inc.*)

Most states recognize an exception to at-will employment based on representations of job security in personnel handbooks, though not all as broadly as New Jersey.

Individual claims of just-cause contracts come in infinite variety. Employees' claims typically center on promises of fair treatment as evidenced in assertions of job security, establishment of progressive disciplinary policies and procedures, or past practices limiting an employer's authority to discipline or discharge its employees.

2. What Constitutes Just Cause?

Parties to an employment contract can, of course, define the terms of that relationship, including establishing just cause as a standard and defining what is required to establish just cause. In general, an employee bargaining from a position of strength will seek to limit the scope of a permissible just cause termination, for example, to gross misconduct or unlawful activity. In contrast, the employer will seek to broaden its discretion by using an expansive definition of just cause. In either case, the question of whether just cause exists, if challenged in court, is a question of fact to be determined based on the evidence presented in the case. (*Diggs v. Pepsi-Cola*) For example, a jury rejected an employer's claim that the discharge of a manager of a meat-packing plant was for just cause after the manager demonstrated that, in fact, he was fired because of his efforts to compel the company to comply with Department of Agriculture regulations. (*Stiles v. Skylark Meats, Inc.*)

Various attempts have been made to define just cause when it is not expressly defined by the parties. For example, the Washington Supreme Court offered the following definition: "'Just cause' is a fair and honest reason, regulated by good faith on the part of the party exercising the power . . . [A] discharge for 'just cause' is one which is not for any arbitrary, capricious, or illegal reason and which is one based on facts (1) supported by substantial evidence and (2) reasonably believed by the employer to be true." (*Baldwin v. Sisters of Providence, Inc.*)

Typically, more than the employer's good faith is required to demonstrate just cause; the employer's action must also be objectively reasonable. (*Stiles v. Skylark Meats, Inc.*) The following have been held to constitute "just cause" for termination:

- A business decision to reorganize operations; (*Clutterham v. Coachmen Indust.*)
- A reduction in force; (*Caldwell v. Ford, Bacon & Davis Utah, Inc.*)
- Falsification of expense records; (*Rush v. United Technologies*)
- Cost-cutting in anticipation of a drop in business; (*Cecil v. Cardinal Drilling Co.*)
- Keeping employer's critical, time-sensitive mail in a locked desk drawer for more than two months, by which time

some of the deadlines stated in mail had lapsed; (*Enis v. Continental Ill. Nat'l Bank & Trust Co.*)

- Sleeping on the job in violation of no-sleeping policy; (*Bolen v. E.I. DuPont de Nemours & Co.*)
- Alleged, although yet unproven, violation of federal banking laws by a bank vice president, which at minimum constituted the appearance of impropriety; (*Desuasido v. Sanwa Bank of Cal.*) and
- Overstaffing. (*Wilde v. Houlton Regional Hosp.*)

Employers failed to demonstrate just cause sufficient for discipline or discharge in the following cases:

- Reliance by an attorney on his professional code of ethics in refusing to implement management's policies; (*Mourad v. Automobile Club Ins. Ass'n*)
- The filing of a defamation claim against the employer; (*Tacket v. Delco Remy*)
- A reduction in force shown to be pretextual; (*Harlan v. Sohio Petroleum Co.*) and
- Use of alcohol on the job without a showing that it interfered with performance. (*Walker v. Goodson Farms, Inc.*)

The burden of proving a breach of the employment agreement, that is, that just cause did *not* exist, is generally on the employee. (*Baldwin v. Sisters of Providence, Inc.*) At least one court, however, has applied to the employer the burden of proving just cause for the dismissal if the employee provides evidence of the necessary components of a claim, namely, a just-cause contract, performance under that contract, and damages resulting from its alleged breach. (*Diggs v. Pepsi-Cola*)

B. Disciplinary Procedures

An employer's disciplinary procedures, if not followed, may be the source for a breach-of-employment contract claim. Typically, the claim is made by a discharged employee alleging that proper procedures were not followed in reaching the termination decision. For example, the procedures could be progressive, that is, they could require that a certain number of formal warnings be given to the employee prior to termination, or the procedures could require that a certain level of supervision approve the termination decision. Conversely, an employee who fails to submit an employment-related dispute for resolution under a grievance procedure established by his or her employer runs the risk of forfeiting the claim.

Employee claims that the employer failed to follow its own disciplinary procedures have yielded mixed results in the courts. The decisions typically turn on the purpose of the procedures as communicated by the employer. If the procedures are mandatory and specific, then a court is more likely to determine that failure to follow these procedures constitutes a breach of the employment contract. (*Brown v. Ford, Bacon & Davis Utah, Inc.*) If the procedures merely serve as guidelines or are discretionary, they are less likely to be enforceable. (*Shankle v. DRG Fin. Corp.*)

In one case, a hospital employee handbook provided that employees who survived probation "are never dismissed without prior written admonitions and/or investigation that has been properly documented" and that except for extremely serious offenses "three warning notices within a twelve-month period are required before an employee is dismissed." The handbook did not contain a disclaimer. A nurse was terminated for unsatisfactory performance without the prior warnings required by the handbook. The Illinois Supreme Court found that the nurse had sufficiently alleged a breach-of-contract claim. The court found that the handbook language "is such that an employee would reasonably believe that after the expiration of the initial probationary period the progressive disciplinary procedure would be part of the employer's offer." The court also noted that the handbook contained no disclaimers and, indeed, the handbook emphasized that it was clarifying both the employees' rights and duties. (*Duldulao v. St. Mary of Nazareth Hosp.*) Similarly, the Nebraska Supreme Court ruled that a nurse terminated for dishonesty could sue for breach of contract when the hospital failed to follow its three-step grievance procedure. (*Jeffers v. Bishop Clarkson Memorial Hosp.*)

In contrast, the Massachusetts Supreme Judicial Court denied an employee's breach-of-contract claim based on his employer's alleged failure to follow proper disciplinary procedures. In that case, the employer expressly reserved its right to modify the terms of the handbook and by its own terms merely provided "guidance" as to the employer's policies. (*Jackson v. Action for Boston Community Dev.*) Similarly, the South Dakota Supreme Court held that Citibank's employee handbook did not state a "for cause only" requirement for employee terminations and, consequently, the bank was free to bypass its corrective action procedures detailed in its handbook. (*Butterfield v. Citibank*)

In one informative decision, the court, while recognizing an employer's contractual obligation to abide by its grievance procedures, nonetheless rejected the employee's breach-of-contract claim because, in the court's words, the employee "got all the procedure she was due under the employment contract." The employee, a chemical dependency counselor, was accused of and later fired for having a sexual relationship with a former patient in violation of the institution's rules. The counselor complained that the members of the investigatory committee were not properly trained; the investigation was not begun quickly enough; a member of the committee had a conflict of interest; and the fact that the former patient had reached a settlement with the institution had not been disclosed to the committee. The court rejected each one of these claims, finding that, while the counselor understandably wanted more extensive procedures, her private expectation of due process was not required to be met and that the institution had provided her with what its policies mandated. (*Meleen v. Hazelden Found.*)

If the employer intends to reserve its rights, it is best to do so with specificity. In one case, a college established procedures to be followed except in "extenuating circumstances" in the event of unsatisfactory performance. The court held that by not reserving to itself the right to determine what constituted "extenuating circumstances," the college would be required to prove that such circumstances existed, excusing its failure to follow the proper procedures. (*Goldhor v. Hampshire College*) In contrast, a policy stating that a disciplinary procedure would not be adhered to in cases involving "serious misconduct" was sufficient to uphold the summary discharge of an employee who violated the company's sexual harassment policy. (*Jewell v. Palmer Broadcasting Ltd. Partnership*)

Grievance procedures found only in supervisors' manuals have been ruled not to apply to nonsupervisory employees. (*Adler v. Ryder Truck Rental*) Conversely, grievance procedures established for employees do not necessarily apply to supervisors. In one case, a foreman sued after being terminated for sexually harassing subordinates, alleging that his employer did not follow disciplinary procedures set forth in the employee handbook. The court, in denying the supervisor's claims, noted that higher standards of behavior are required of supervisory personnel and different levels of punishment are applicable to them. (*Williams v. Maremont Corp.*)

The contractual nature of grievance procedures has not been limited to employee terminations. A Colorado court held that an employee could challenge his demotion, which allegedly failed to follow the requirements of the employer's policy and procedures manual, based on breach-of-contract grounds. (*Salimi v. Farmers Ins. Group*)

Contract rights created by employer documents also can be limited in the same document. For example, Michigan courts have decided that failure to exhaust grievance procedures contained in a handbook before going to court bars the subsequent contract action in court. (*Dahlman v. Oakland Univ.*) But an employee will not be bound by the decision rendered under employer grievance procedures which are unfair and deny basic procedural due process to the employee. (*Renny v. Port Huron Hosp.*)

Employers may also establish an alternative to litigation for the resolution of employment-related claims—for example, by means of outside arbitration—as part of the employment relationship. Such terms are enforceable and an employee seeking the benefits afforded by an employment agreement is also bound by its obligations, in this case, the submission of a claim to arbitration. (*Zeniuk v. R.K.A., Inc.*) Further, the Supreme Court has ruled that standardized agreements to arbitrate claims in the securities industry are enforceable and require the arbitration of federal age discrimination claims. (*Gilmer v. Interstate/Johnson Lane Corp.*) A vast majority of courts have expanded this ruling beyond the securities industry and include race, sex, disability and other discrimination claims under both federal and state laws. (*Mayo v. Shearson Lehman Hutton Inc.* and *Fletcher v. Kidder, Peabody & Co.*)

C. Layoffs or Reductions in Force

Courts increasingly have been asked in the context of breach-of-contract suits to review the legality of layoffs or reductions in force. The contract claims fall basically into two categories: that the employer failed to follow proper procedures or to enforce certain standards applicable to layoffs; or that the layoffs failed to constitute just cause for dismissal where just cause is required by contract.

Courts in some states have determined that employers must abide by established policies and procedures in conducting economically based layoffs or reductions in force. For example, policies requiring that layoffs be conducted based on strict seniority may be enforceable. (*Boynton v. TRW*) In contrast, a claim that the employer's policy was to retain only the "most qualified candidates" for the limited positions available prior to a layoff was held not to support a breach-of-contract claim. (*Dabrowski v. Warner-Lambert Co.*) Of course, an employer whose policies expressly provide that management reserves the right to terminate employees based on a reduction in force may apply such policies. Such an express reservation of rights generally will be upheld upon review. (*Pytlik v. Professional Resources*) As with disclaimers, however, such a reservation must be sufficient to negate any seemingly contradictory provision. In a recent case, the employer's handbook set forth a procedure for work force reductions that detailed severance pay amounts and bumping rights. The handbook also contained a reservation-of-rights clause, which provided that "in the final analysis, specific judgment and discretion will govern." This provision, it was held, was insufficient to negate the handbook's more specific work force reduction procedure. (*Mycak v. Honeywell, Inc.*)

Moreover, in situations where just cause is required for termination of employment, courts have consistently concluded that layoffs resulting from adverse economic conditions constitute just cause. (*Boynton v. TRW*) This is so even if the employer did not expressly define just cause to include economic difficulties. (*Taylor v. National Life Ins. Co.*) Once an employer determines that adverse economic conditions require a reduction in the work force, a court generally will refrain from substituting its judgment for that of the employer as to the manner in which that decision is effectuated. (*Nixon v. Celotex Corp.*) For example, an employer's decision to select a "lousy manager" for layoff on that basis was ruled not subject to challenge. (*DeMinico v. Monarch Wine Co.*) Similarly, the Michigan Supreme Court refused to submit to a jury a breach-of-contract claim when an advertising executive failed to present evidence that his discharge as part of a reduction in force was for a reason other than "economic necessity." (*McCart v. J. Walter Thompson, Inc.*) The Montana Supreme Court went one step further when it concluded that an employer is not obligated to exercise reasonable care in its decision-making and on that basis rejected a claim that an employee's layoff for economic reasons was negligently decided by his employer. (*Heltborg v. Modern Mach.*)

The mere recitation by an employer that a layoff was for economic reasons is generally not sufficient to constitute just cause. For example, the Connecticut Supreme Court has stated, "An employer may not use a reduction in force as a pretext to terminate other employees in violation of contractual obligations, public policy grounds or statutory rights." (*Coelho v. Posi-Seal Int'l*) In that case, the court found that the employee had presented sufficient evidence for a jury to find that the layoff was not for economic reasons but due to a conflict between two competing departments.

D. Agreements Limiting Competition

Employers have an undisputed interest in protecting their trade secrets and proprietary information from unauthorized disclosure. Similarly, they have an interest in avoiding the "raiding" of employees and the "pirating" of clients. Employees, in contrast, have an interest, shared by society in general, in free, unrestricted access to employment opportunities and in using their full knowledge and skills in each new employment opportunity. These interests can clash, and certainly must be balanced, when an employer requests that an employee enter into an agreement that seeks to protect employer information and interests by limiting the employee's ability to use such information or to interfere with such interests as a competitor of the employer.

Such "restrictive covenants" come in various forms. The most common are noncompetition agreements (what courts generally refer to as "restrictive covenants"), customer and employee nonsolicitation agreements, and the least restrictive, confidentiality agreements and patent and invention assignment agreements.

While state laws in this area vary, certain general principles can be discerned. With few exceptions, the law in this area is governed by state case law, although some states' unfair competition laws or laws specific to restrictive covenants may apply. Courts tend to take a strict view of restrictive covenants under the assumption that they are anticompetitive. Society has a strong interest, it is maintained, in removing barriers to free employability of individuals and in increasing competition. Restricting an individual from being employed in his or her occupation or profession is generally not favored.

In ruling on the enforceability of any restrictive covenant, a court will inquire whether:

- The employer has a legitimate interest it is seeking to protect;
- The restriction is reasonably necessary to protect that legitimate interest;
- The restriction is reasonable; for example, in the case of noncompetition agreements, in scope of activity proscribed, time, or geography; and

- Enforcement of the restrictive covenant is not offensive to the public interest.

The burden is typically on the employer to demonstrate the enforceability of the restriction. A discussion of specific requirements attendant to each category of restrictive covenants follows.

1. Noncompetition Agreements

Noncompetition agreements are not enforceable if the employer does not have a legally protectible interest, such as genuine trade secrets, longstanding customer relationships, a substantial investment in training programs, a truly "unique" employee, or the acquisition of a business and its attendant good will. Some employers make the mistake of concentrating on the formalities of drafting the covenants—is the geographic limitation properly specified, for example—before assessing this threshold issue. It is important to keep in mind that noncompetition agreements are not enforceable as a matter of right. Most courts are extremely solicitous of the employee's interest in mobility and gaining the greatest compensation for his or her services and will enforce restrictive covenants only if thoroughly satisfied that they are necessary to protect legitimate interests of the employer.

An agreement not to compete with an employer upon termination of the employment relationship will generally be found unenforceable if the restraint imposed is broader than necessary to protect the employer's legitimate interest. For example, a noncompetition agreement that prohibited a former employer from working "in any capacity" in the business of marketing structured settlement agreements—that is, even in some capacity that would not place the employer's legitimate interest at risk—was ruled to be overbroad. (*National Settlement Assoc. v. Creel*) Not all employment by a competitor places an employer's legitimate interests at risk. More narrowly tailored restrictions, such as a temporary prohibition on marketing particular kinds of agreements directly to particular categories of customers, however, would more likely be enforceable.

By contrast, focusing on the protectibility of the goodwill a company had helped its employee to develop, the Georgia

Supreme Court found a television station had a legitimate, protectible interest in the image it projects and enforced a limited noncompetition agreement against television broadcast activities by a television weatherman. The station had promoted extensively its "on air" team including the weatherman. After the weatherman joined a competitor, the television station sued and succeeded in barring the weatherman from appearing on television for six months within a radius of 35 miles of the station. The court concluded, "For a limited time and in a narrowly restricted area, [the television station] is entitled to prevent [the weatherman] from using the popularity and recognition he gained as a result of [the station's] investment in the creation of his image so that [the station] may protect its interest in its image . . . ." The court noted that the agreement prohibited the weatherman only from being "on air" and not from working in the industry altogether. (*Beckman v. Cox Broadcasting Corp.*)

Once the fundamental issue of whether the employer has a narrowly defined legally protectible interest is resolved, attention to formalities and controlling case law, usually of the state where the employment occurs, is critical. Some states insist that precise formations be followed or the agreement will not be enforced.

A restrictive covenant may place a substantial burden on the employee. It must, therefore, be supported by consideration, that is, a benefit to the employee supporting the agreement. When the agreement is reached at the time the employment relationship is formed, most states will find the employment relationship itself constitutes sufficient consideration, although a few states, like Texas, require further consideration even at the outset of the employment if the employment relationship is to be at will. Courts often, but not always, require meaningful additional consideration when the agreement is entered into after employment has commenced. Additional compensation, such as a promotion or bonus, or other employment benefits beyond what the employee had been receiving would generally constitute adequate compensation for a noncompetition clause. In one case, additional compensation was found to be present where the former employee was compensated for each month during the one-year noncompetition period in an amount equal to at least 1/24 of his base salary. (*Hekimian Lab., Inc. v. Domain Sys., Inc.*)

A noncompetition agreement must be reasonably limited in geography and time. A reasonable geographic limitation, for example, may be the geographic area in which the employee worked or had responsibility (*AMF Tuboscope v. McBryde* and *Paramount Termite Control Co. v. Rector*), although a few states, including Georgia and Texas, might view such a prohibition as unduly vague if it did not contain an explicit recital of the affected counties. The following geographic limitations were ruled to be overbroad under the specific circumstances presented:

- Within 100 miles of any company office where the effect would have been a statewide ban; (*Lamp v. American Prosthetics, Inc.*)
- A 400-mile circular area and another geographic area in which the employee rendered services; (*North Am. Paper Co. v. Unterberger*)
- Nine counties in which neither the employer nor the employee performed services; (*Brewer v. Tracy*)
- Nationwide; (*Medline Indus. v. Grubb*) and
- Within 50 miles of any city where the employer operated. (*Diversified Human Resources Group v. Levinson-Polakoff*)

Under other facts and circumstances, however, such geographic limitations may have been reasonable.

Some industries conduct business nation- or even worldwide and are as much injured by unfair competition across the country as by such activities within the same county. In those limited circumstances, an agreement barring competition anywhere in the country or world may be appropriate, particularly where the agreement recites the nation- or worldwide character of the business. (*Hulsenbach v. Davidson Rubber Co.* and *Herkimian Lab., Inc. v. Domain Sys., Inc.*) Not every court will accept this approach, however. As with all other aspects of noncompetition agreements, therefore, the employer should carefully consider the formalities imposed by the laws of the affected states.

The definition of a reasonable time period for a valid noncompetition agreement also will vary with the facts of each case. As a general rule, a restriction that lasts longer than is necessary to protect an employer's legitimate interests will be found to be unenforceable. For example, an agreement not to compete for five years after execution of the agreement or three years after termination, whichever was longer, has been ruled unenforceable (*Lawter Int'l v. Carroll*). In contrast, a prohibition against competing for eighteen months in the propane business in one county has been ruled lawful. (*B. Cantrell Oil Co. v. Hino Gas Sales*). In each case, the court's determination may have been different under different circumstances and in light of the information and relationships to be protected.

Many states will seek to enforce the lawful portions of a restrictive covenant and "blue pencil" out of the agreement those provisions that are unenforceable or otherwise modify the agreement to make it lawful. For example, an agreement that is lawful in all respects except its three-year term may be modified in a "blue pencil" state by reducing its term to one year. (*Dean Van Horn Consulting v. Wold*) Some states, however, such as Arkansas, Georgia, North Carolina, and Wisconsin, decline to modify judicially or "blue pencil" restrictive covenants that, without modification, would not be enforceable. Even states that are prepared to "blue pencil" may simply strike offending clauses altogether rather than take the further step of modifying the remaining provisions. Further, some states view an employer's request for extensive modification of a restrictive covenant at trial as troubling evidence that the employer was improperly trying to use the original formulation to frighten employees away from legitimate activities, a circumstance that could result in an award of attorneys' fees against the employer.

Courts differ on the question of whether noncompetition agreements without express time and geographic limitations are enforceable. In those states that will modify or "blue pencil" agreements to render them enforceable, agreements lacking time or geographic limitations will likely be so modified. (*Ellis v. James V. Hurson Assoc.*) In contrast, an Indiana court declined to modify, on the basis of the customer list, a noncompetition agreement with no geographic limitation. (*Commercial Bankers Life Ins. Co. v. Smith*)

Finally, courts are more likely to enforce restrictive covenants when the employee resigned his or her employment than when they find that the employee was improperly terminated. (*Ma & Pa, Inc. v. Kelly*) Even if the employee was properly terminated, courts may nonetheless decline to enforce the restrictive covenant. For example, a Pennsylvania court held that a covenant was not enforceable where the employee was terminated for unsatisfactory performance (*Insulation Corp. of Am. v. Brobston*). The court found that a salesman who is discharged for poor sales performance does not pose the same competitive threat to his employer's business interests as the satisfactory salesman who resigns voluntarily to join a direct competitor. Under such circumstances, the courts are likely to find the employer's legitimate practicable interest to be diminished and the employee's interest in freely gaining new employment paramount.

2. Solicitation of Clients

Limitations on the solicitation of customers following employment, sometimes known as antipiracy agreements, may be enforced under the laws of most states to the extent necessary to protect an employer's legitimate interests, such as its trade secrets or confidential information. The same requirement of geographical and durational reasonableness applied to noncompetition clauses applies to nonsolicitation clauses. The key to the enforceability of such a provision is whether the customer information and relationship are in fact legally protectible.

For example, a former employee of a defense contractor who violated an agreement not to solicit the business of former clients, resulting in his former employer losing a major contract, was required to pay approximately $91,000 in damages. The employee used highly confidential pricing and related information to assist his new employer in drafting a proposal to perform the last phase of a project that his former employer had completed to that point. (*Support Sys. Assoc. v. Tavolacci*) Similarly, an accounting firm's antipiracy clause that for two years prohibited former employees from contacting or performing services for the firm's clients or, in the alternative, required employees to pay any fees earned to the employer, was ruled enforceable. (*Rehmann, Robson & Co. v. McMahan*)

Over-reaching, however, will result in an unenforceable agreement. If the customers are readily identifiable, a nonsolicitation provision is unenforceable. (*Scott v. Snelling & Snelling, Inc.*) A ban on soliciting *any* customers of the former employer, including those about whom the employee did not learn confidential information or with whom the employee did not establish relations, is also unlikely to be enforceable, because it is broader than necessary to protect confidential information. An employer also may generally not seek to bar a former employee from contacting customers if those customers were known to the employee before commencing work for the employer. (*Fidelity Fund, Inc. v. DiSanto*) Further, a former employee's recollections of a former employer's clients and their needs, unaided by stolen documents, are generally not confidential and therefore not subject to a nonsolicitation restriction. (*Best Metro. Towel & Linen Supply v. A & P Coat*)

3. Customer Lists

To be protected, customer lists must either rise to the level of a trade secret or, in states differentiating between "trade secrets" and "confidential information," qualify as confidential information and fall within the express provisions of a confidentiality agreement.

A list of customers generally known within the relevant industry will not be protectible as a trade secret. For example, a claim of trade secret protection was rejected when the employer's customers were known to be listed as advertisers in the apparel industry's *Redbook* magazine. (*Primo Enter. v. Bachner*) Similarly, if a competitor can easily duplicate the list, trade secret status will be denied. If the list must be painstakingly assembled over substantial time, however, even from publicly available information, it may be protectible. (*Velo-Bind, Inc. v. Scheck*)

A customer list is most likely to be considered a trade secret where some or all of the following are present:

- The list includes such details as the customer's location, individual characteristics or preferences, credit rating, and the names of principal contacts;
- The number of potential customers is large;
- Customers tend to do business only with a small percentage of potential suppliers;
- Extensive time, effort, and expense was incurred in compiling the list;
- The list is regularly updated;
- Only a select number of employees are permitted access to the list or employees are permitted access only to those parts of the list relevant to their work; and
- The list is treated as a confidential document within the company.

A customer list put together following a termination or compiled through legitimate means, that is, by using publicly available information or independent recollection, may properly be used by a former employee. (*Aetna Bldg. Maintenance Co. v. West*) However, physically taking and copying employer customer lists or files from which customer lists can be derived is generally not protected, although if the list did not contain confidential information and the employee did not remove all copies, it is unlikely that the court would find that the employee had caused any legal harm.

4. *Solicitation of Employees*

A common target of restrictive covenants is the solicitation of current employees by a former employee. When one employee leaves, the employer risks losing not merely the departing employee, but also one or more other members of the team. An employee nonsolicitation agreement generally will be enforced to the extent it is necessary and reasonable to protect the employer's legitimate interests. For example, two executive bank officers signed, among other restrictive covenants, nonsolicitation-of-employees clauses when exercising stock options equaling $1.8 million and $800,000 respectively. The court held these provisions enforceable, noting that the executives were "more than adequately compensated" for their troubles. (*Central Bancshares v. Puckett*)

In certain instances, salary information may be viewed as confidential information that may not be used to benefit a new employer. This has led to a trade secrets-based rationale for enforcing an employee nonsolicitation agreement. (*Bancroft-Whitney Co. v. Glen*)

Employees who solicit other employees of their former employers and succeed in enticing them to end their employment may be subject to suit on interference-with-contract grounds as discussed in Chapter 2. To succeed on such a claim, the employer must demonstrate the existence of a contract, the former employee's knowledge of the contract, and intentional interference with the contract inducing the breach and damages. (*First Wyoming Bank v. Mudge*) Interference-with-contract claims in this setting are more likely to succeed if the employment agreement breached was for a set term rather than at will. (*National Recruiters, Inc. v. Cashman*) An exception to this rule is where the motivation for the interference with the at-will relationship is malicious or where the former employees used confidential information in effectuating their plan. (*Frederick Chusid & Co. v. Marshall Leeman & Co.*)

5. Trade Secrets

The vast majority of states have adopted the Uniform Trade Secrets Act (UTSA), although a few key industrial states, including New York and Texas, have not. Those states that have not adopted the UTSA nonetheless provide for comparable trade secret protection. The UTSA prohibits the misappropriation of protectible trade secrets. To constitute a trade secret, the information must have independent economic value, it must not be known or readily accessible to the general public, and it must be treated confidentially by the employer. While an employee's general knowledge and skill do not constitute a protectible trade secret, specific knowledge or confidential information gained solely through employment may. For example, a Massachusetts court prohibited a former employee from marketing chocolate chip cookies based on a recipe improperly obtained from his former employer. The court noted that the former employer had used reasonable efforts to keep the recipe secret (it was stored in a safe) and that the former employee had gained access through a ruse. (*Peggy Lawton Kitchens, Inc. v. Hogan*) Protection for a protectible trade secret may be lost by inadvertent disclosure or by failure to keep the information confidential within the organization.

Information that is easily obtained by means other than misappropriation does not constitute a trade secret. For example, client lists put together through review of public documents or information gained about a competitor's product through reverse engineering, that is, the disassembling of a competitor's product to learn the product's component parts, are not protected.

While an "idea" by itself may not constitute a trade secret, a procedure based on or application of that idea may be so protected. (*Gonzales v. Zamora*) For example, a computer program, which is an application of an idea at its core, may be a protectible trade secret. (*Aries Info. Sys. v. Pacific Management Sys.*) Further, a new idea that incorporates readily available information may be a trade secret if the combination itself is not generally known. (*Integrated Cash Management Svcs., Inc. v. Digital Transactions, Inc.*) A particularly useful new guide to the specific facts that may make a critical difference in evaluating a trade secrets claim is the *Restatement of the Law: Unfair Competition*, recently released by the American Law Institute.

6. Confidentiality

Employers have a legitimate interest in protecting confidential business information. Such protection, however, does not extend to situations where the true purpose is unlawfully to prevent or inhibit competition. Thus, an agreement to hold secret information that is already widely known is not enforceable. (*Arthur Murray Dance Studios, Inc. v. Witter*)

For the same reason, if the employer imposes a very general obligation to keep "all confidential information" confidential, a court may find that the employee was not given adequate guidance about what specific information was not to be disclosed. In these cases, the courts may not enforce the agreement as it relates to particular categories of information that were not obviously confidential. (*R.R. Donnelley & Sons Co. v. Fagan*)

Because confidential information may have a long life if not disclosed, courts typically do not insist on a time or geographic limitation on nondisclosure, as long as the agreement makes clear that the confidentiality obligation ends once the information becomes generally known. This approach is preferable to imposing a specific time limitation on the nondisclosure duty, since that limitation may prove to be either too short or too long. The UTSA does not include a requirement for confidentiality agreements to include specific time or geographic constraints. (*Pepsico, Inc. v. Redmond*)

Unauthorized use of confidential employer information for competitive purposes may be enjoined by a court, even in the absence of a confidentiality agreement, on the grounds of unfair competition. Such was the finding when former employees took their employer's master list of customers, which included the customers' sales activities and credit ratings, as well as customer cards containing information related to the customers and the operation of their businesses. (*Advanced Magnification v. Minuteman Optical Corp.*) Conversely, even a confidentiality agreement does not bar former employees from competing for customers where the former employees do not use confidential information to do so.

7. Patents and Inventions

The law generally provides that an invention is the property of the inventor who conceived, developed, and perfected it. That right, however, may be contracted away.

As a general rule, an employee hired to design a specific invention or solve a specific problem has a duty to assign or surrender the resulting information or ideas or patent to his or her employer. Further, an employee's invention conceived during working hours or through use of the employer's equipment or resources may be used by the employer on a nonexclusive basis under the so-called "shop right" rule. Under this rule, an employee is treated as having authorized or licensed the employer to use the resulting invention. (*Solomons v. United States*)

Many employers require their employees to assign by express contracts all rights to their inventions, ideas, and patents to their employers. Where used, such agreements should not be limited to requiring transfer of patents, since trade secrets the employee develops may also have great value to the employer. A few states, such as California, Minnesota, Illinois, North Carolina, and Washington, have by statute limited the enforceability of such agreements. Consequently, employers in these states cannot require employees to assign away rights beyond what the law currently allows and generally must provide the employee with a copy of the pertinent statutory language as part of any assignment agreement.

In determining the enforceability of such an assignment agreement, courts apply a test of reasonableness. An invention or patent assignment agreement generally will be found to be unreasonable and therefore not enforceable if it:

- Extends beyond what is necessary to protect the employer's legitimate interest;
- Prevents the employee from seeking other employment; or
- Otherwise injures the public interest.

A particularly controversial variation of the assignment of inventions and patents is what is known as "holdover" agreements, that is, agreements that extend beyond the term of employment and purport to apply to postemployment inventions. Such agreements are designed to protect an employer's "legitimate interests in preventing employees from using the thoughts and ideas generated by the employee and fellow workers while being paid by and using the resources of the [former] employer to invent a product that directly competes with the [former] employer's product." (*Ingersoll-Rand Co. v. Ciavatta*) Employers generally will not be able to enforce such agreements where the former employee shows that he or she has developed, subsequent to his or her employment, a new idea or concept independent of the knowledge gained while employed by the employer.

The Copyright Act gives the employer ownership of all copyrightable works (including computer programs, films, drawings, and music) made in the scope of the employee's employment by operation of law. A written assignment may be necessary, however, to make such transfers enforceable abroad.

4

EMPLOYEES' RIGHT TO INFORMATION

Employers are the repositories of a wide variety of information about their employees. The information can come from a number of sources, including the employees themselves, the government, credit agencies, medical personnel, former employers, supervisors, clients or customers, and unions. Payroll information, disciplinary records, medical information, health and safety data, and insurance information are all likely to be found in the records maintained by employers. An employee's right of access to this information, the focus of the first part of this chapter, depends on applicable federal and state laws, company policy, and the information being sought.

Employers, in addition to maintaining information specific to individual employees, also possess information affecting groups of or all employees, such as information regarding health hazards or decisions related to the scope or nature of operations. Employees may be entitled to this information as well. For example, under federal law employees have a legal right to know of the potential chemical hazards they face in the workplace. The scope of "right to know" legislation is addressed in this chapter as well.

Finally, Congress and a number of state legislatures have enacted plant and business closing legislation that requires prior notification to employees of such closings or mass layoffs. An overview of these statutes concludes this chapter. Issues related to the disclosure by employers of information concerning its employees are addressed in Chapter 5.

I. ACCESS TO PERSONNEL FILES

Most, although not all, information directly related to an employee maintained by an employer is typically contained in the employee's personnel file or employer data base. Some employers maintain elaborate personnel files while others keep such information on a strictly ad hoc, informal basis. In either case, an employee clearly has an interest in the information maintained by an employer, the use of that information, and the circumstances under which that information may be disclosed.

Employees' access to their own personnel files is authorized under a number of states' laws, including Alaska, California, Connecticut, Delaware, Illinois, Iowa, Maine, Massachusetts, Michigan, Minnesota, Nevada, New Hampshire, Oregon, Pennsylvania, Rhode Island, Washington, and Wisconsin. These laws vary in scope and application. Most provide that an employee may review and copy, on a periodic basis and at a reasonable time and place, his or her own personnel records. Certain documents, such as those related to an internal investigation, management planning documents, letters of reference, and documents containing confidential information are often excluded from this right of access. Some state laws provide employees with the opportunity to seek correction of erroneous information contained in their personnel records.

Penalties for employers who violate these state laws may include damages, awards of attorneys' fees, and, occasionally, criminal penalties. Statutes in states such as Wisconsin, which provide only for civil penalties, do not permit private actions brought by employees who then must look to the government to pursue their rights. (*Graves v. Katahdin Found., Inc.*)

In those states not authorizing access, employees are entitled to review their personnel records only if their employer's policy so provides or if legal process, such as a subpoena, is issued. Of course, an employer can always agree to provide access whether or not a company policy on the subject exists. If an employer chooses to permit access to personnel files, it is well-advised to put the policy in writing, communicate it simply and clearly to employees, and take steps to ensure that it is consistently applied.

II. ACCESS TO MEDICAL FILES

The federal Americans With Disabilities Act (ADA) requires that employers maintain employee medical records in a file separate from an employee's personnel file. The ADA does not, however, require that employees be given access to this separate medical records file. Most states do not authorize employee access to employer-maintained medical records. A few states, such as Connecticut, Delaware, Massachusetts, Michigan, Ohio, Rhode Island, and Wisconsin, provide such access by defining personnel records to include medical information either in laws authorizing access to personnel records or in separate statutes expressly authorizing access to medical records.

Those states authorizing disclosure of medical information have adopted different approaches. For example, Connecticut requires disclosure to a physician designated by the employee. Wisconsin permits employers to disclose medical information to the employee's physician where direct disclosure to the employee may be detrimental to the employee. North Carolina permits an employer to exempt from disclosure information that "a prudent physician would not divulge to a patient." A number of states, including Arkansas, Massachusetts, and Wyoming, require that results be turned over to employees only if the employer requires an employment-related physical examination. Iowa requires disclosure where a health hazard is present in the workplace.

The federal Occupational Safety and Health Administration (OSHA) has issued a number of "standards" that mandate medical examinations for employees working with such materials as asbestos, vinyl chloride, benzene, and lead. The results of these examinations may be disclosed only to OSHA, the National Institute of Occupational Safety and Health, the employee, and, with the employee's specific written consent, to the employee's representative (a physician, attorney, family member, fellow employee, or union representative).

Federal occupational and safety law also mandates access to employee medical records pertaining to employees' exposure to toxic substances or harmful physical agents. "Exposure records" are defined as any record that monitors the amount of a toxic substance or harmful physical agent to which the employee has been exposed. "Employee medical records" are defined as any record concerning the health status of an employee made or prepared by health care personnel.

The right to review employee exposure and medical records is, by statute as augmented by regulation, provided to both employees and their designated representatives such as their union representatives or health professionals. OSHA also may have access to exposure records but may have access to employee medical records only where a written access order has been issued by the Assistant Secretary upon the recommendation of the OSHA Medical Records Secretary. Employers are obligated to maintain such records for the duration of employment plus 30 years. Employers must provide such access, if requested, at a reasonable time and place and in a reasonable manner within 15 days of the request. The employer must provide a copy of exposure and medical files if requested or otherwise permit copying of the file.

Public employees generally have greater rights of access to their personnel and medical records than do employees in the private sector.

Federal employees are provided extensive rights of access under the Privacy Act of 1974. The Privacy Act governs the maintenance and disclosure of "records," including personnel records, maintained by a federal agency. Federal government employees are entitled to access to their personnel records maintained by agencies, which must promulgate rules establishing the procedures to be followed in permitting employee access. A federal employee has the right to photocopy his or her record and may request that an error in the record be corrected. If that request is denied, the federal employee may prepare a statement of disagreement that must be disclosed by the agency whenever the personnel record containing the disputed information is disclosed.

A number of states permit employees access to their government personnel records comparable to that authorized by the Privacy Act. These states include Arkansas, California, Kansas, Maine, North Carolina, South Dakota, Tennessee, Utah, and Vermont.

III. RIGHT TO KNOW: ACCESS TO CHEMICAL HAZARDS INFORMATION

Employees have a right to know the chemical hazards and hazardous substances to which they may be exposed in the workplace. This right is established in federal law as the Toxic and Hazardous Substances Hazard Communication Standard (Hazard Communication Standard or the Standard) and, in certain instances, supplemented by state and local law. The government agency principally responsible for administering this legislative mandate is OSHA. The full penalties available under the Occupational Safety and Health Act of 1970 apply to violations of the Hazard Communication Standard. Significantly, the most common citation issued by OSHA inspectors is for a violation of the Standard. A 1991 General Accounting Office study revealed that more than 50 percent of randomly selected employers were not in compliance with the key requirements of the Standard.

The goal of "right to know" legislation is clear. Chemicals, chemical products, and chemical processes are present in and essential to many workplaces. Employees, and sometimes employers, are often unaware or not fully aware of the hazards of these chemicals. Exposure can be catastrophic. This lack of full knowledge about the hazards to which employees may be exposed in the workplace denies employees the opportunity to choose for themselves whether they are willing to risk a particular hazard for the sake of a job.

For these reasons, OSHA formulated the Hazard Communication Standard, which, among other things, grants to employees the right to know the chemical hazards they may confront in the workplace. OSHA concluded in implementing the Standard that the program would reduce the incidence of chemical-related occupational illnesses and injuries in the workplace and would assist employers in devising appropriate protective measures and employees in taking necessary steps to protect themselves.

The Standard imposes obligations on chemical manufacturers, that is, employers in whose workplaces chemicals are produced for use or distribution, and employers in whose workplaces chemicals are used. The Standard applies to any hazardous chemical present in the workplace to which employees may be exposed under normal conditions or under a foreseeable emergency. For purposes of the Hazard Communication Standard, hazardous chemicals are defined as chemicals that present either a physical hazard or a health hazard.

Employees' "right to know" extends to the existence of chemical hazards they may confront in the workplace. No such affirmative right, however, extends to information concerning the presence of hazardous waste on an employer's premises. To the extent that employees may be exposed to or come in contact with hazardous wastes, or are actually required to handle such wastes as part of their employment, employers are obligated to train employees in proper handling of such wastes and in proper safety procedures.

A. Obligations of Manufacturers and Importers

Manufacturers and importers of chemicals must determine whether chemicals produced in their workplaces or imported by them are hazardous. Manufacturers and importers must ensure that a "material safety data sheet" (MSDS) accompanies each hazardous chemical that they produce or import. The MSDS must, among other things, identify the chemical, its ingredients, its common names, its physical and chemical characteristics, the physical and health hazards associated with it, the recognized OSHA exposure limits, generally applicable precautions or control measures known to the manufacturer or importer, any applicable emergency or first aid procedures, the date the MSDS was prepared, and the address of the manufacturer. Manufacturers, importers, and distributors must ensure that all containers leaving a workplace are labeled to identify the hazardous chemical they contain, any applicable hazardous warnings, and the identity of the manufacturer or importer.

B. Obligations of Employers

Employers are required to develop and administer a written "hazard communication program" in their workplaces that describes the employer's approach to implementing the Standard. The written program must list hazardous chemicals used in the workplace known to the employer. An employer may rely on the hazard determination made by a chemical manufacturer or importer. An employer that chooses to do its own evaluations, however, is responsible for the accuracy of its hazard determination. The written program must be available upon request to employees, to their representatives, such as unions, and to the government.

Employers are required to ensure that containers of hazardous chemicals present in their workplaces are labeled to identify the hazardous chemicals. As an alternative, an employer may use signs, operating procedures, or other written materials that identify which warnings apply to which chemicals. The required written materials must be accessible to employees in their work areas, be in plain English, and be legible.

Employers are also obligated to train employees at the time they are assigned to work with hazardous chemicals. Additional training is required whenever a new hazard, not merely a new chemical, is introduced into the work area. An employee who has been previously trained by the employer, a past employer, a union, or other entity need not be completely retrained but, at minimum, must be instructed on the specifics of the employer's hazard communication program in effect at the time. Training need not address each specific chemical found in the workplace but may be conducted by categories of hazards.

Training typically includes proper responses to emergency situations and focuses on the use of the information included in the hazard communication program. Mere distribution of the program by itself will not satisfy the training requirement.

C. State Plans

OSHA encourages states to develop and operate their own workplace safety programs. A state program may be approved by OSHA if it is "at least as effective as" the federal program, in which case OSHA pays 50 percent of the state program's operating costs. State law on the subject of hazard communication that is not approved by OSHA may be preempted by federal law. Where state plans are approved, federal enforcement activity will cease to the extent that the state program is applicable. To maintain its approved status, a state program must adjust to changes in federal standards. States with approved state programs include Alaska, Arizona, California, Hawaii, Indiana, Kentucky, Maryland, Michigan, Minnesota, Nevada, New Mexico, North Carolina, Oregon, South Carolina, Tennessee, Utah, Vermont, Virginia, Washington, and Wyoming.

A number of states, including Delaware, Florida, Illinois, Maine, New Jersey, New York, Oklahoma, Pennsylvania, Texas, and Wisconsin, have enacted their own hazardous communication standard laws that expand upon OSHA's Hazardous Communication Standard. These laws often grant additional rights to employees and impose additional recordkeeping and employee notification requirements. For example, Florida's law permits employees to refuse to work with a chemical or hazardous substance where the employer has failed to provide the applicable MSDS within five days of a request to review it. Maine's law requires that employers make available to employees upon request any measurements taken as part of an exposure monitoring effort. Each state law should be consulted for its own applicable terms.

IV. PLANT CLOSINGS OR MASS LAYOFF NOTIFICATION REQUIREMENTS

Business closings and mass layoffs are becoming more frequent in an increasingly competitive marketplace. Until the passage of the Worker Adjustment and Retraining Notification Act (WARN), also known as the "Plant Closing Law," a copy of which is included as Appendix B, employers were generally not obligated by law to provide employees any prior notice of a plant closing or layoff. However, driven by a recognition of the potentially devastating effect of a sudden loss of employment for a significant number of employees—not merely on the employees and their families, but on the affected community as a whole—Congress enacted WARN in 1988. It provides that employees must be given 60 calendar days notice of a plant closing or mass layoff as those terms are defined in the statute.

As a result, any employer considering laying off significant numbers of employees or closing either a facility or an operation must determine whether the notice requirements of WARN apply to its situation. This determination may not be simple, as the statute is burdened by defined terms and complex tests. An employer failing to provide the necessary notice to its employees faces various penalties as described more fully below.

A. Who Is Covered by WARN?

WARN applies to any business enterprise, including nonprofit organizations, (1) employing 100 or more full-time employees or (2) employing 100 or more employees including part-time workers, if these employees in the aggregate work at least 4,000 hours per week not including overtime. The term "part-time employee" is defined as an employee who works on the average fewer than 20 hours a week or has been employed less than 6 of the prior 12 months. A part-time employee is still entitled to 60 days notice under WARN even though he or she may not be counted for purposes of determining whether the employer met the minimum threshold to be covered under the law. (*Carpenters v. Dillard Dep't Stores*)

The 100 employee minimum number applies to an employer's entire operation, not to each separate site. For example, a manufacturer with 60 employees at one plant and 60 employees at a second plant falls within the statute and, should that employer close one plant, would be required to provide notice to affected employees. Independent contractors and wholly or partially owned subsidiaries are treated as separate employers or as part of the parent company based on the degree of their independence from the parent company. (*Teamsters Local 952 v. American Delivery Serv. Co.*)

Non-profit organizations of the requisite size are subject to WARN. Federal, state, and local governments are generally not covered unless a separately organized public or quasi-public entity with independent authority engages in a business of a commercial nature.

B. Plant Closings and Mass Layoffs

WARN's 60-day notice period applies to both plant closings and mass layoffs.

A plant closing occurs when there is a permanent or temporary shutdown of either (1) a "single site of employment," that is, a plant or employer site or group of locations in close proximity, or (2) one or more facilities or operating units, such as a department or division within a plant. Facilities located "across town" from each other will rarely be considered a single site of employment unless employees are rotated between the two locations and both sites share staff and equipment. (*Williams v. Phillips Petroleum Co.*) The shutdown must result in an "employment loss" at that operation during any 30-day period for 50 or more full-time employees. As noted above, employees working less than six months are considered part-time for purposes of WARN. (*Solberg v. Inline Corp.*)

An "employment loss" is defined by WARN as an employee termination, a reduction in the hours of work of individual employees of more than 50 percent during *each* month of any six-month period, or a layoff exceeding six months. A discharge for cause, voluntary departure, or retirement does not constitute an "employment loss" for purposes of WARN. If a layoff was initially announced as being for less than six months, but is eventually extended beyond six months, it will be considered an employment loss unless the extension was unforeseeable when originally announced.

Employees who are laid off and recalled are not to be included in the number of laid-off employees when determining the minimum threshold for a WARN notice obligation. This is so even if the recalled employees are subsequently laid off again, as long as the temporary recall was not implemented for purposes of evading the law. (*Office & Professional Employees Int'l Union v. Sea-Land Serv.*)

A "temporary shutdown" triggers the notice requirement only if there are sufficient numbers of terminations, layoffs exceeding six months, or reductions in hours of work as specified under the definition of employment loss.

Employees terminated as the result of a "mass layoff" are entitled to 60 days' notice of their loss of employment. A mass layoff can occur in two ways. First, the employer can lay off at least 50 employees constituting at least 33 percent of its full-time work force. Second, the employer can lay off 500 or more employees, no matter what percentage of the work force is implicated. In either case, the layoff must occur at a single site of employment and must not constitute a plant closing under WARN.

The distinction between a plant closing and a mass layoff as defined in WARN is significant. In particular, a fewer number of employees as described above must be affected as the result of a plant closing than a mass layoff in order to trigger WARN's notice requirements. For example, if an employer has 200 employees, it must issue a WARN notice if it closes a plant that results in the permanent layoff of more than 50 employees. In contrast, if 50 employees are laid off as part of a mass layoff, WARN is not applicable because less than 33 percent of the work force was affected by the mass layoff.

C. Relevant Time Period

The relevant time period for determining the number of affected employees under WARN is 30 days. If the requisite number of employees are affected within a 30-day period, the notice requirements of the statute are triggered. The statute also allows for the aggregation of separate and distinct actions over a 90-day period that affect the requisite number of employees during that period. Consequently, an employer may not stagger a plant closing or mass layoff in order to defeat the purposes of the statute.

D. Notice Requirements

Notice under WARN must be specific, in writing, and provided at least 60 calendar days in advance of a plant closing or mass layoff based on the best information available to the employer at the time. Proper notice must also be given to any union representing affected employees, local elected officials, and state labor department officials. The written notice must:

- Provide the anticipated date of the closing or layoff;
- State whether the entire plant will be closed and whether the action is permanent or temporary;
- Note the existence of bumping rights (the right created by contract, usually a collective-bargaining agreement, of a more senior employee to displace a less senior employee), if any;
- Provide the name and phone number of a company official to contact for further information; and
- Provide any other information useful to the employees.

The particulars of the notice requirement should be followed meticulously. For example, one court concluded that notice of a mass layoff sent to the local union and not to the chief elected official of the national union would likely be found to be insufficient under the statute. (*United Elec. Workers v. Maxim, Inc.*)

E. Exceptions to Notice Requirements

There are certain narrow exceptions to WARN's notice requirements. It does not apply:

- To a closing of a temporary facility;
- To a closing or layoff as the result of the completion of a particular project or undertaking, if the affected employees were hired with the understanding that their employment was limited to the duration of the facility, project, or

undertaking; (*New Orleans Clerks & Checkers v. Ryan-Walsh Inc.*) or

● To a closing or layoff resulting from a strike or lockout.

Further, under certain limited circumstances, WARN provides for a reduction in the 60-day notice period. If an employer is seeking business or financing that would have made the notice unnecessary, and the employer reasonably believes that giving the notice would prevent it from getting the business or financing sought, the 60-day period may be shortened. This is known as the "faltering company" exception. It must be emphasized that this exception is narrowly drawn and unlikely to be applied often. An attempt to find a purchaser for a plant, rather than seek new capital or business, has been found not to be sufficient to come within this exception. (*Local 397 IUE v. Midwest Fasteners*)

The 60-day notice period also may be shortened if the plant closing or mass layoff is based on unforeseeable business circumstances such as a natural disaster; a principal client of the employer suddenly and unexpectedly terminating or repudiating a major contract; or some other sudden, unexpected dramatic change in business conditions. For example, a court ruled that the closing of an Atlantic City casino by a state enforcement agency constituted an unforeseen business circumstance. (*Finkler v. Elsinore Shore Assoc.*) Similarly, notice under WARN was not required where a bank was closed by federal authorities. (*Office and Professional Employees Int'l Union v. Federal Deposit Ins. Corp.*) Nonetheless, the employer must give as much notice as possible in such circumstances. (*Alarcon v. Keller Indus.*)

In one case, which involved a downturn in an entire industry, the court ruled that the employer could rely on the unforeseen business circumstances exception to avoid liability for its failure to provide WARN notice. (*Chestnut v. Stone Forest Indus., Inc.*) In that case, the employer asserted that its industry, yellow pine lumber sales, was particularly volatile and, accordingly, was difficult to forecast. Sales had been strong prior to August 1988 but dropped in the following months. Although there was a rebound from November 1988 to March 1989, sales fell again in April. Fearing crippling losses, the employer laid off 81 of its 175 employees. The court ruled that the employer did not violate WARN as it exercised its commercially reasonable business judgment.

The business circumstances exception was found to apply when J.C. Penney, the largest and most profitable client of one plant of a hosiery company, suddenly withdrew a vast majority of its business because of delays in delivery and poor quality of product. Within two months, the company lost $19 million of its $20 million worth of business from J.C. Penney, constituting 40 percent of the total business of the plant. One month later, after final efforts to regain the lost business failed, the decision to close the plant was made and scheduled to be implemented in phases over a two-month period, including the immediate and permanent layoff of 496 employees. The court found that the company had cause to believe that it would have additional time to improve its performance and that the loss of business was sudden and unexpected and outside the control of the company. Consequently, the business circumstances exception was found to apply. The court concluded, however, that the company's one-month delay in announcing and commencing implementation of the decision was not commercially reasonable and found a failure to give proper notice of a plant closing under WARN for that one-month period. (*Jones v. Kayser-Roth Hosiery*) Similarly, the arrest of a company's four top managers for customs violations was found not to be an unforeseen business circumstance where the company had notice of the investigation, which began eight months earlier. (*Parsley v. Kunja Knitting & Mills*)

F. Sale of Business, Relocation, or Consolidation

The Department of Labor's WARN regulations specifically provide that if there is a sale of the employer's business, the seller is responsible for providing notice for any plant closing or mass layoff up to and including the effective date of the sale. After this date, the purchaser is responsible for providing notice. Anyone who is an employee of the seller at the effective date of sale is considered an employee of the purchaser immediately after the effective date of the sale.

Even where the purchaser changes the employees' terms and conditions of employment after the sale, a WARN Act event has not occurred. One court concluded that since the only modification of a condition of employment of which Congress applied WARN's notice requirements was a 50 percent reduction in work hours in each month during any six-month period, the statute did not apply to any other modifications of employees' terms of employment. (*IATSE v. Compact Video Servs.*) In that case, the seller's employees were employed by the purchaser but at lower wages and with reduced benefits (after the sale employees were required to make health plan co-payments and many lost union pension plans). The court ruled that these modifications were not covered by WARN.

If a plant closing or mass layoff is the result of a relocation, reorganization, or consolidation, an employment loss technically does not occur. Therefore, the notice requirements do not apply if (1) the employer offers to transfer the employee to a different site of employment within a reasonable commuting distance with no more than a six-month break in employment or (2) the employer offers to transfer the employee to any other site of employment regardless of distance with no more than a six-month break in employment, and the employee accepts within 30 days of the offer or of the closing or layoff, whichever is later.

G. Penalties

Employees denied proper notice of a plant closing or mass layoff, or their designated representatives, may initiate a civil lawsuit seeking back pay for a maximum of 60 days. It is generally accepted that the amount of back pay is limited to the number of days the employee would have worked during the 60-day notice period rather than the calendar days during that period. (*Frymire v. Ampex Corp.*) One court held, however, that employees are entitled to back pay for 60 calendar days. (*United Steelworkers of Am. v. North Star Steel Co.*) Employees may also recover costs of any employee benefit programs to a maximum of 60 days, and their attorneys' fees if their suit is successful. Pre-judgment interest has also been awarded to employees entitled to damages under WARN. (*Carpenters v. Dillard Dep't Stores*) Vacation and severance pay are not owed to the employee under WARN. Indeed, where such payments are voluntarily and unconditionally made to the employee, WARN allows the employer to set off the payments against its WARN obligations. (*Carpenters v. Dillard Dep't Stores*) Punitive damages are not awardable under WARN. (*Finnan v. L.F. Rothschild & Co.*) Corporate officers or directors are not directly liable under WARN because they are not employers as that term is defined in the statute. (*Carpenters v. Dillard Dep't Stores*)

A local government that does not receive the 60-day notice may also bring a civil action for a penalty of not more than $500 for each day the employer violated WARN's notice requirements. The amount of the penalty can be reduced if the employer establishes that it had a good-faith, reasonable belief that its conduct did not violate WARN. (*Oil, Chem. and Atomic Workers v. American Home Prods. Corp.*)

An employer cannot be enjoined from completing its plant closing or mass layoff. A court may issue an injunction, however, to secure money that may subsequently be awarded as damages under WARN. (*Local 397 IUE v. Midwest Fasteners*)

H. State Plant Closing Laws

A number of states, including Connecticut, Hawaii, Maine, Massachusetts, and Wisconsin, have enacted plant closing laws. These laws do not extend WARN's 60-day notification requirement but may impose additional requirements on employers and confer additional benefits on employees. The details of these laws should be consulted in plant closing or mass layoff situations in those states.

5

GATHERING AND DISCLOSURE OF INFORMATION

More than ever, employers are carefully scrutinizing job applicants to determine job skills, education, background, and personality. Both business and legal reasons support diligent preemployment investigation of job applicants.

The decision to employ a job applicant is perhaps one of the most significant business decisions an employer can make. Employers often have been guilty of expending more effort in the selection of computer software, machinery, or office equipment that may be obsolete in a handful of years than in the hiring of an employee who may remain employed for several decades, an investment that could easily cost millions of dollars in salary, benefits, and training over the term of employment.

Recent developments in the law greatly encourage the selection of competent individuals on whom an employer can rely. An employer is potentially liable whenever a manager, and to a lesser extent, an employee, violates the law. The scope of liability has been greatly enhanced by the recent development of novel doctrines such as negligent hiring and retention (discussed more fully in Chapter 9), by which employers may be liable for failing to investigate or address properly the fitness of an employee who subsequently causes injury to another person.

A more competitive marketplace has also served to highlight the growing problem of resume fraud. This, in turn, has prompted the greater use of diligent background checks and has helped establish a preemployment information services industry.

This chapter will review the types of information typically collected or reviewed by employers in investigating employees, such as criminal records, credit history, medical history, and information related to an individual's general character and reputation. The relevant law in each area will be reviewed, as will the laws applicable to employee searches and surveillance and to investigating employees.

This chapter also will explore the thorny issues raised by the application of defamation law to the employment setting. Disparaging remarks made by managers or supervisors regarding subordinates' performance or character may subject the employer, as well as the manager or supervisor involved, to potential liability for defamation. Job references are, as a result, increasingly difficult to obtain reflecting the legitimate employer concern for potential lawsuits brought by former employees receiving less than favorable reviews. This chapter will conclude with a discussion of the application of defamation law specifically to the employee screening and evaluation settings, to disciplining and terminating employees, and to the giving of job references.

I. INVESTIGATING EMPLOYEES

Employers may choose to conduct a variety of preemployment investigations, security investigations, and general employee monitoring for a number of legitimate business reasons.

Job applications and interviews are the most common means of gathering information about job applicants. With the information provided, an employer may do its own investigation, for example, by directly contacting schools, former employers, or references. The employer may also hire specialized services to perform such functions as credit or criminal history checks. An employer also may retain a private investigator or investigation service to conduct a thorough background search.

The kind of investigation conducted will, of course, depend on the information sought to be gathered or verified. For many nonessential positions, a routine check may include simple resume verification. However, for a top security position or for one implicating public health and safety, a more thorough investigation can be expected. In addition, searches of employees' persons or property and the surveillance of employees on and off the job may be conducted to monitor and investigate employee practices.

Employer investigations into these areas and the use of these techniques, while permissible, must nonetheless be conducted within the bounds of the law. This section will focus on the permissible bounds of employer investigations of employees and the remedies available to employees whose rights have been violated.

A. Preemployment Inquiries

Most employers rely on job applications, resumes, and preemployment interviews as their principal sources of information about job applicants. The accuracy of the information, without an independent investigation, depends principally on the honesty of the applicant. Many employers decline to verify such information generally on the grounds that to do so is too time-consuming and costly. Further complicating the process are numerous laws limiting the use of such information as criminal and credit history, as discussed later in this chapter, and the reticence of former employers to respond to reference requests out of fear of liability for defamation.

Failure to conduct a proper and diligent inquiry into the qualifications of job applicants or candidates for promotion may subject employers to liability upon such grounds as negligence. For example, an employer is increasingly likely to be held liable for the negligent hiring of a candidate for a janitor position who is a former sex offender and who takes advantage of the access to tenants' residences to commit a further crime. Beyond screening out the dangerous employee, an employer also has a legitimate interest in confirming that an applicant possesses the education, skills, and experience which the candidate represented during the hiring process.

An applicant for employment or a candidate for a promotion who falsifies a preemployment application or resume may be denied the employment or the promotion on that ground. Courts have dismissed employee discrimination or wrongful discharge lawsuits, for example, where the employee misrepresented that he had a law degree for a lawyer's position of copyright examiner at the Library of Congress, even though his performance was adequate (*Williams v. Boorstin*), or where a postal service employee falsified a medical questionnaire by concealing that he had been diagnosed as paranoid schizophrenic. (*Russell v. Frank*)

Moreoever, resume fraud is often discovered not at the time of hiring but during the course of employment or, as is increasingly the case, after the now former employee has filed suit against the employer. The issue has arisen—does the belated discovery of resume fraud negate the former employees's claim? The Supreme Court has ruled, in the related setting of post-hire misconduct, that proof of employee wrongdoing first discovered in the midst of litigation, which has come to be known as "after-acquired evidence," does not require the dismissal of a discrimination suit but, rather, may limit the employee's recovery should the claim of discrimination be upheld. The Court went on to rule that the employee's recovery will be limited only if the employer demonstrates that it would have terminated the employee on the basis of the misconduct alone if the employer had known of it prior to or at the time of the termination. (*McKennon v. Nashville Banner Publishing Co.*) Where the misconduct was such that the employee would have been terminated, courts have generally ruled that the employee is not entitled to reinstatement or front pay even if he or she succeeds on the claim of discrimination; the employee can still recover, however, all other forms of damages provided by law. (*Miller v. Bircham, Inc.*)

In resume or job application fraud cases, the alleged misrepresentation must be material and not merely tangential. For example, a security guard's failure to disclose on her employment application her prior drug use, job terminations, and mental illnesses was found to be material (*Churchman v. Pinkerton's, Inc.*) while an employee's 40-year-old criminal conviction for contributing to the delinquency of a minor by having sex with a 17-year-old girl when he was 18 years old was found not to be material to his fitness to drive a truck. (*Schmidt v. Safeway, Inc.*)

The following case is instructive. Shattuck sued his employer for age discrimination. The employer learned just prior to trial that Shattuck misrepresented on his employment application that he was a college graduate when, in fact, he had completed less than one year of college. The employer alleged that it would not have hired Shattuck had it known that he was not a college graduate and would have fired him had it learned this fact during his employment. The federal appeals court ruled that the question was not whether Shattuck would have been hired, as an employer may still retain an employee who has performed well even if the employee lacked the necessary qualifications for the job. Rather, the question was whether the employee would have been fired upon discovery of the wrongdoing. The court noted that the "rationale underlying consideration of after-acquired evidence is that the employer should not be impeded in the exercise of legitimate prerogatives and the employee should not be placed in a better position than he would have occupied absent the discrimination. Cutting off relief at the time that a legitimate discharge would have occurred accomplishes these ends." In this case, the employer failed to demonstrate that it would have fired the employee once it discovered the truth, and the court, on this basis, rejected the employer's after-acquired evidence defense. (*Shattuck v. Kinetic Concepts, Inc.*)

B. Criminal History

Society has an interest in integrating those convicted of a crime back into its mainstream. Similarly, those arrested but not convicted of a crime have an interest in not being stigmatized by their arrest record, with the presumption of innocence in mind, in their future endeavors. Several states, responding to these concerns, have limited the extent to which an employer may inquire into a job applicant's or employee's prior arrests or, to a lesser extent, convictions.

State laws limiting the obtaining or use of arrest records come in two basic varieties: states such as Colorado, Ohio, and Virginia forbid inquiries into arrest records that have been expunged or sealed, or permit the individual to answer questions as if the arrest had not occurred; and states such as California, Illinois, Michigan, and New York forbid inquiries into arrest records outright if they did not result in a conviction. Connecticut requires that an employer keep arrest record information confidential and limit access to such information to the personnel department.

In one case, an employer was able to avoid the limitations on the use of arrest records by successfully arguing that the basis for the discharge was not the employee's arrest but rather injury to the employer's reputation if the employee were retained. In that case, the employee worked as a passenger agent for an international airline and was arrested for conspiracy to distribute cocaine. The court concluded that the airline's concern for the harm to its reputation under the facts of the case was warranted and justified the termination. (*Kinoshita v. Canadian Pac. Airlines*)

Employers generally have much greater discretion in the obtaining and use of conviction records. Indeed, some states require employers to inquire into sex-related criminal convictions when hiring for certain positions in the education and day-care fields. Arizona makes it a felony for a person convicted of a dangerous crime against children to fail to notify a prospective employer when applying for a position supervising children. Several states, including Pennsylvania and New York, limit use of conviction records unless the crime relates to the individual's suitability for the position sought. A number of states, such as Colorado, Florida, Maryland, and Massachusetts, take a more limited approach and forbid the obtaining or use of conviction records that have been sealed or expunged or permit the individual to respond to inquiries as if no conviction had occurred.

Employer use of arrest or conviction records may also be subject to challenge on discrimination grounds as the use of such information has been shown to have a disproportionate impact on minorities. (*Gregory v. Litton Sys., Inc.*) Policies that automatically disqualify applicants based on a conviction record generally have been rejected as discriminatory (*Green v. Missouri P. R. Co.*), whereas policies that consider such information as merely one component in its hiring process generally have been upheld. (*Hill v. U.S. Postal Serv.*) For example, a hotel rejected applicants convicted of serious crimes for safety-sensitive positions, such as bellstaff, that provided access to guests' luggage and rooms. The court found that the policy was narrowly tailored to fit its legitimate needs. (*Richardson v. Hotel Corp. of Am.*)

An employer's discriminatory application of its policy may also result in liability. In one case, a black employee was terminated for misrepresenting criminal record information on his employment application. The employee alleged that white employees who had made similar misrepresentations were not similarly terminated. The court ruled that the employee could pursue a claim of intentional infliction of emotional distress on this basis. (*Walker v. South Cent. Bell Tel. Co.*)

As discussed in greater detail in Chapter 9, employers who fail to conduct a diligent preemployment investigation, including a review of an applicant's criminal history, run the risk of liability for negligent hiring. The risk is greater for positions in which the prospective employee will have (1) significant contact with or will regularly serve the public, such as members of uniformed services, employees of common carriers, and restaurant or hotel workers, (2) special access to individuals or their homes, such as deliverymen, health care professionals, or janitorial staff, or (3) special access to a vulnerable class of individuals, such as children, the mentally ill, or the elderly.

In sum, criminal history is relevant and, indeed, constitutes important information for an employer to consider in assessing the suitability of an applicant for employment. Public policy and the laws of certain states, however, circumscribe the lawful gathering and use of such information. Employers as well as applicants with criminal records should determine, before requesting or disclosing such information, the legality of doing so in their jurisdictions.

C. Credit History

Information related to a job applicant's or employee's credit history and rating is available to employers from consumer reporting agencies such as TRW, Inc., Equifax, Inc., and Trans Union Credit Information Company. Credit checks have become a regular part of some employers' hiring and promotion procedures. Such employers argue that an individual's financial and credit history reflects his or her character and level of responsibility.

Employers are prohibited from terminating employees based on a garnishment of wages under the Consumer Credit Protection Act. Actions to enforce the statute can be brought only by the Secretary of Labor. (*Martin v. Hawkeye Int'l Trucks*) Otherwise, use by employers of credit and consumer information is generally lawful. However, significant reporting requirements exist. The federal Fair Credit Reporting Act (FCRA), which is included as Appendix C to this text, and various analogous state laws govern the collection and use of credit history information.

FCRA and comparable state laws regulate the use of consumer reports, that is, any information possessed by a consumer reporting agency that bears on an individual's creditworthiness or general character or reputation that is or may be used for employment purposes. Other than the usual report issued by TRW, Equifax, and Trans Union, the following documents have been found to be "consumer reports" within the meaning of the FCRA:

- Reports from check approval company; (*Estiverne v. Saks Fifth Avenue*)
- A drug-testing report prepared by a professional lab; (*Hodge v. Texaco, USA*) and
- Report issued by a landlord service to landlords concerning rent payment pattern of prospective tenant. (*Cotto v. Jenney*)

FCRA permits employers to request and use consumer reports in making employment decisions but requires employers to advise the applicant or employee of the name and address of the agency supplying the consumer report if an adverse employment action is taken based on the report. Further, the information that may be included in the report is greatly limited if the position at issue pays a salary of less than $20,000 a year. An employer will be liable under FCRA for obtaining a consumer report from a consumer reporting agency under false pretenses such as by posing as a bank employee processing a loan application. Courts have found that obtaining a consumer report on a political candidate to evaluate the candidate's fitness for employment as a public official was not for an employment purpose (*Hansen v. Morgan*) and that a consumer report concerning an employee was not for employment purposes where the report was not sought until the employee announced his resignation. (*Russell v. Shelter Fin. Servs.*)

An employer is liable for the actual damages, as well as costs and reasonable attorneys' fees, caused to an applicant or employee by the employer's negligent violation of FCRA. (*Jones v. Credit Bureau*) A willful violation will result in punitive damages. (*Russell v. Shelter Fin. Servs.*) The statute of limitations for an FCRA action is two years although it may be longer if the employer's actions are willful.

In a leading case, a salesman was interviewed and offered a position. Based on this offer, he resigned his employment, moved, and was ready to begin new employment. His start date was delayed and then the offer was withdrawn based on a consumer report indicating a poor credit history. The salesman was informed of this fact. After the salesman filed suit, the employer ordered an additional consumer report to assist in the defense of the suit. The employer was found to have violated FCRA by obtaining the second consumer report that was not for employment purposes; no violation was found for obtaining the initial preemployment report. (*Comeaux v. Brown & Williamson Tobacco Co.*)

As with the use of criminal records, employers using credit reports may be subject to discrimination claims where the practice has a discriminatory or disproportionate impact on minorities or women and where the practice is not justified by business necessity. (EEOC Decision No. 72-0427, August 31, 1971)

State law in this area may be more protective of the interests of applicants and employees than FCRA. For example, California law limits what may be contained in a consumer report for positions earning less than $30,000, rather than the $20,000 threshold under FCRA. Further, New York law requires that the employer obtain authorization from the consumer, including job applicants and employees, *prior* to obtaining the consumer report.

D. Medical Questionnaires and Examinations

The Americans With Disabilities Act (ADA) prohibits employers from requiring or giving medical examinations prior to making an offer of employment. Once a job offer has been made, an employer may condition actual employment upon the passing of a medical examination. To be lawful, the post-offer examination must be required of all entering employees in the same job category. An employer may not withdraw an offer of employment unless the reason is job-related and consistent with business necessity and no reasonable accommodation, as that term is defined by and applied under the ADA, can be made that will allow the applicant to perform the essential functions of the job. A job offer may be withdrawn if a medical examination shows that the applicant would pose a "direct threat" to the applicant's health and safety or the health and safety of others.

Employers' discretion in requiring that existing employees submit to medical examinations is also limited to situations in which the examination is necessary to determine fitness for duty or where there is evidence of a performance or safety problem. A fitness for duty test, such as lifting and carrying a heavy weight for a sanitation worker, measures the employee's ability to perform the essential functions of the position. Postemployment medical examinations are also permitted where the examination is performed to monitor compliance with federal, state, or local laws. Medical examinations may also be conducted as part of a voluntary employee health program as long as the information obtained is not used in violation of the ADA.

The ADA also prohibits employers from inquiring into the physical or mental condition of a job applicant whether by questionnaire, application, or interview. Employers also are prohibited from inquiring into an applicant's prior workers' compensation filings. An exception to this rule exists for federal government contractors who, under Section 503 of the Rehabilitation Act of 1973, may invite applicants to identify their disability and any accommodations required to perform the job. An employer may ask an applicant if he or she can perform the essential functions of the position.

Information obtained from a post-offer medical examination must be maintained in a separate medical file and must be treated as a confidential medical record. It is not appropriate under the ADA to include medical records and similar information in an employee's personnel file. An employer may, however, disclose to supervisors and managers information necessary to accommodate the needs of a disabled employee and to health and safety personnel the information necessary to permit them to respond to the needs of a disabled employee in the case of an emergency.

E. Employee Searches

Employers' security concerns vary widely. In employment settings in which trade secrets or proprietary information are present, an employer's concern may be with keeping that knowledge or information confidential. In a retail business, theft of goods or services will undoubtedly be a prevalent employer concern. In these and numerous other settings, searches of an employee's person, property, or work area are often conducted by employers as a means of protecting their property.

Government employers are subject to the restraints of the Constitution and any search by a government employer must be in accordance with the Fourth Amendment of the Constitution and, as such, reasonable under all the circumstances of the case. Private-sector employers, in contrast, are not bound by the Fourth Amendment unless they are acting under the auspices of the government. Nonetheless, such searches are subject to challenge on a wide variety of legal grounds if they are not conducted appropriately.

1. Searches by Government Employers

The Fourth Amendment states, in part, "The right of the people to be secure in their persons, houses, papers, and effects, against unreasonable searches and seizures, shall not be violated." This constitutional mandate applies to federal, state, and local governments. An employer search, in order to be unlawful, must infringe upon an expectation of privacy that society deems reasonable. (*United States v. Jacobsen*)

The key case in this area of government intrusion into employee privacy is the Supreme Court decision in *O'Connor v. Ortega*. The leading opinion for a divided Court distinguished between work-related areas and items on the one hand and personal belongings, such as a handbag or briefcase, on the other. It is more likely that an employee will have an expectation of privacy in his or her personal belongings than in work-related space or items. An employee's expectation of privacy, however, "may be reduced by virtue of actual office practices and procedures, or by legitimate regulation." The greater the access to the employee's workplace, the lesser is the reasonable expectation of privacy. Searches related to worker misconduct or for such a non-investigative reason as to retrieve a needed file or document will presumptively be lawful. For example, in one case, the court found that a search of an employee's desk while the employee was on medical leave was proper because the search was not associated with an attempt to discover employee misconduct but, rather, to locate documents. (*Williams v. Philadelphia Housing Auth.*) Search warrants are not required for work-related searches unless the search is related to a criminal investigation.

In *O'Connor v. Ortega*, a physician for a state hospital was put on an administrative leave of absence following allegations of impropriety on his part. In his absence, his office was searched and personal items such as a photograph, a Valentine's card, and a book of poetry by a former physician at the hospital were seized. The Court held that the physician had a reasonable expectation of privacy in his desk and file cabinets and sent the case back to the lower court to determine if the search was reasonable under all the circumstances of the case.

An employee's prior consent to a challenged search precludes a Fourth Amendment action. For example, postal workers who accepted lockers with the knowledge that the lockers would be subject to inspection at any time waived their constitutional claim to privacy. (*American Postal Workers Union v. United States Postal Serv.*) Mere acceptance of employment with the government, however, does not constitute consent to searches in violation of the Fourth Amendment. (*Bateman v. Florida*)

Searches are more likely to be upheld where the employee works in a safety-sensitive position or in a highly regulated industry. (*Kirkpatrick v. Los Angeles*) For example, a government hospital demanded that a licensed practical nurse whose roommate had AIDS disclose the results of an AIDS test he had taken. The nurse refused, in part, arguing that the forced disclosure of the test results would constitute an unlawful search under the Fourth Amendment. The court rejected this claim and, pointing to the hospital's position of requiring employees to disclose infectious diseases, concluded that the hospital's strong interest in a safe workplace and in limiting the spread of infection outweighed the limited intrusion on the nurse's privacy. (*Leckelt v. Board of Commr's.*)

In contrast, violations of the Fourth Amendment have been found where:

- Employees of a health services agency were required to submit to mandatory testing for the virus that causes AIDS and for hepatitis B where the risk of disease transmission from employees to the agency's clients was miniscule; (*Glover v. Eastern Neb. Community Office of Retardation*)
- Police officers were subjected to random urinalysis testing where there was nothing in the record to show that a drug problem existed or that there was a public perception of problems arising from the use of drugs; (*Guiney v. Police Comm'r of Boston*)
- All cars leaving the employee parking lot on a given day were searched and the employer did not proffer any reason for the search that would justify the invasion of pri-

vacy; (*McGann v. Northeast Ill. Regional Commuter R.R. Corp.*) and

- Correctional facility employees were subject to routine strip searches or body cavity searches where there was no legitimate penological objective for such searches. (*Security & Law Enforcement Employees, Dist. Council 82 v. Carey*)

Employees whose Fourth Amendment rights have been violated may recover for the emotional shock or physical harm of the unlawful search but may not recover for any resulting injury to their employment status or position. (*Bivens v. Six Unknown Agents of the Fed. Bureau of Narcotics*)

2. Searches in the Private Sector

Searches conducted by private employers may be subject to legal challenge on a number of grounds. Such challenges, however, are rare and even more rarely successful.

Private employers who are acting on behalf of the government are an exception to this general rule and are subject to the Fourth Amendment limitations against unreasonable searches or seizures. For example, an employer who participates in a joint investigation with police is viewed as an arm of the government and subject to the constitutional limits on searches and seizures. (*People v. Jones*)

Private security guards who are licensed by the state and empowered to serve as special police officers are generally considered agents of the government for constitutional purposes. (*Griffin v. Maryland*) Mere licensing of security guards by the state, however, is generally not sufficient to convert the guards into state actors for these purposes. (*United States v. Lima*)

A reasonably conducted search by a private employer of employees as part of a legitimate workplace investigation or as part of an announced policy is likely to be held lawful in the face of invasion of privacy suits or other legal challenges. Employees who are likely to succeed on these claims are those who can show that a reasonable expectation of privacy has been dashed by the employers' behavior. For example, an employer was found to have unreasonably intruded into an employee's privacy by removing his personal lock from his company locker. (*K-Mart Corp. v. Trotti*) Similarly, a strip search of a retail store checker in a public bathroom in the presence of a customer who had accused her of stealing $20 was found to be unlawful. (*Bodewig v. K-Mart, Inc.*)

Such cases are the minority as few challenges to employer searches have succeeded. For example, employees who refuse to submit to a search, even one that would otherwise be illegal, may not claim that their privacy was invaded for the alleged unlawful behavior never occurred. (*Gretencord v. Ford Motor Co.*) Further, the taking of photographs of an employee at work in common areas does not constitute a search (*State v. Dickerson*) or an invasion of the employee's privacy. (*Thomas v. General Elec.*) In addition, the use of metal detectors to detect weapons or stolen goods has been found to be lawful by an arbitrator. (*General Paint & Chem.*)

Searches by private employers are more likely to be found lawful where (1) a policy exists and has been promulgated to employees authorizing searches and stating under what circumstances and in what manner they will be conducted, (2) consent from the employee has been obtained, and (3) the search has been conducted in a responsible, non-discriminatory manner.

F. Surveillance

The term "employer surveillance" sounds ominous as it suggests espionage and clandestine activities. Employer surveillance can, in fact, be ominous; it can also be quite routine. Advances in technology have greatly enhanced the means and manner by which such surveillance can be conducted. This, in turn, furthers the threat to the legitimate privacy interests of employees. The legality of the surveillance will depend on its nature and purpose.

Employer surveillance comes in three basic forms: visual; voice; and electronic or computer-based. In each circumstance, the key factor in determining the legality of employer surveillance is the employee's reasonable expectation of privacy under the particular circumstances.

1. Visual Surveillance

Employer surveillance may be as simple as the observation of employee activities by a supervisor or security guard or by a video camera. For example, an employer may guard against potential theft of its inventory by hiring a security guard to monitor activities at a warehouse or distribution center or by means of a video camera. Clearly, both activities are lawful.

Surveillance of employees may be found to be unlawful where the employee is observed in a non-public area in which the employee had a reasonable expectation of privacy. For example, an Ohio court found that an employer intruded into an employee's seclusion where her supervisor spied on her by positioning himself in the ceiling of a bathroom for more than seven hours during an investigation of alleged wrongdoing by the employee. (*Speer v. Department of Rehabilitation and Correction*)

Some states have codified these privacy concerns. For example, Connecticut, Georgia, and Michigan statutes prohibit surveillance of employees in rest rooms, locker rooms, or lounges. Massachusetts law restricts the use of two-way mirrors for employee surveillance purposes. The law in other states is less clear. For example, no violation of privacy was found where the surveillance was of a dressing room that could be easily observed from the adjoining corridor (*In re Deborah C.*) or where notice of employer surveillance was posted. (*Lewis v. Dayton Hudson Corp.*) Similarly, an invasion of privacy claim was not established where the employer allegedly had a hidden camera in a room containing a jewelry storage safe, sink, counters for wrapping packages, and a phone, and which also doubled as a changing room for employees. (*Fazo v. Nordstrom*)

Surveillance of employees while off the job presents different issues and is more likely to run afoul of the law. An employee justifiably has a greater expectation of privacy while off the job than while at work. For example, the surveillance by a private investigator of a union official from the bottom of a stairwell outside the official's motel room while on a rendezvous with his girlfriend was found to constitute an invasion of privacy. A "detection device" was placed on the motel room door. In contrast, surveillance of that same union official outside his own residence, outside his girlfriend's residence, in a shopping center, and along public roads was ruled lawful as the union official had no reasonable expectation of privacy in those public areas. (*Pemberton v. Bethlehem Steel Corp.*)

Employer videotaping or photographing of employees on the worksite will be found lawful in most instances. For example, a court upheld an employer's practice of taking and using videotapes for the purposes of documenting the layout of equipment and machinery and the movement of employees while performing their jobs. The court noted that the videotapes were an efficient, effective, and economical means of studying and establishing safe and effective standards and procedures. (*Thomas v. General Elec.*) Similarly, observing and recording the performance of temporary employees during a study of computer equipment was found not to be an intrusion upon the employees' seclusion. (*Barksdale v. IBM*)

Employers sometimes use undercover operatives (sometimes called "shoppers") in the workplace to obtain and provide the company with information concerning employee morale, performance, misconduct, and the presence of illegal activities such as theft or drug use. The use of the information provided by the operative, however, may be limited by state law. Nevada, for example, prohibits the discipline or discharge of an employee based on the report of an operative unless the employee has a hearing in which the employee can confront the operative. (*Nunez v. Shara Nevada Corp.*) Similarly, California law requires employers who discipline or discharge employees based on a shopper's report to provide the employee with a copy of the report before taking action. (Cal. Labor Code § 2930)

2. Voice Monitoring

The federal Omnibus Crime Control and Safe Streets Act of 1968 makes it unlawful to intentionally intercept wire, oral, or electronic communications, that is, to bug or wiretap another's communication. One who violates the statute may be imprisoned and fined, and an individual whose communications are unlawfully intercepted may recover damages, including punitive damages and attorneys' fees. A minimum recovery for a violation is $100 a day for each day of the violation or $10,000, whichever is greater. One court has even permitted recovery for emotional distress for a violation of the Act. (*Gerrard v. Blackman*) Most states have enacted comparable legislation.

Federal and most state laws provide for a "telephone extension" exception important to the employment setting. Employers under this exception may monitor employee calls "in the ordinary course of business." For example, a court ruled that an employer who informed employees that telephone calls were being monitored to help improve service was protected under the telephone extension exception. (*James v. Newspaper Agency Corp.*) Similarly, an employer was entitled to record an employee's business calls to determine if the employee was violating previous warnings not to disclose confidential information to competitors. (*Briggs v. American Air Filter Co.*) In the course of monitoring business calls, employers may not purposefully listen in on personal phone calls once it is clear that the nature of the call is not business-related. (*Watkins v. L. M. Berry & Co.*) For example, a court found no legitimate business purpose was served by an employer's recording of personal calls, many involving conversations of a sexual nature, in an effort to discover whether an employee had participated in the theft of $16,000. (*Deal v. Spears*) The liquor store owners further violated the law when they disclosed this information to the spouses of the employee and her phone companion.

A second exception—the "provider" exception—permits providers of wire communication services, such as telephone companies, to monitor calls for mechanical or service checks.

Oral communications may not be intercepted under federal and state wiretapping laws absent a consent or warrant. The term "oral communications" is broadly defined to include those communications "uttered by a person exhibiting an expectation that such communication is not subject to interception." However, oral communications can be intercepted where one party has given prior consent to the interception.

Some state wiretapping laws, such as those in California, Delaware, Florida, Illinois, Louisiana, Maryland, Massachusetts,

Michigan, Montana, Oregon, and Pennsylvania, are stricter than the federal law by barring the interception of conversations without the approval and consent of all parties.

3. Electronic or Computer Surveillance

New technology has meant new and expanded means of surveillance. For example, computer technology permits employers to carefully monitor employee production and performance such as the times the employee's machine is on, the time it takes to perform certain functions, and the employee's error rate.

Congress enacted the Electronic Communications Privacy Act of 1986 (ECPA), which amended the Omnibus Crime Control Act of 1968, to respond to these developments. The term "wire communication" was expanded to include digital voice transmissions and voice transmissions by radio or fiber optic cable, and the term "electronic communications" was added to include electronic mail, digitized transmissions, and video teleconferences. Interestingly, at least one court has indicated that an unauthorized interception of e-mail messages can be found to violate the ECPA only where the e-mail message is "intercepted" (and not simply read after it has been delivered) by a non-intended recipient. (*Steve Jackson Games, Inc. v. U.S. Secret Serv.*)

Further, pen registers, devices that record the numbers dialed from a particular telephone, may not be used under the ECPA without first obtaining a court order. Providers of electronic or wire communication services, however, are given broad discretion to employ pen registers to protect the users of the service; for example, by helping to trace crank or harassing phone calls.

G. General Character and Reputation

Employers may, under certain circumstances, obtain information about an individual's character, general reputation, personal characteristics, or mode of living through interviews with people who know or have knowledge concerning the individual. This information may also be contained in an investigative consumer report obtained by employers as part of a preemployment investigation of applicants or otherwise.

The federal Fair Credit Reporting Act (FCRA), as discussed earlier, regulates the use of both credit reports and investigative consumer reports by employers. FCRA requires an employer to notify a job applicant in writing that an investigative consumer report has been ordered by the employer within three days from the time the report is requested. Significantly, FCRA prohibits employers from requesting or using an investigative consumer report to evaluate applicants or employees for positions for which they specifically applied. Consequently, such reports may be used principally for promotion decisions or perhaps for candidates contacted by search firms under consideration for positions they did not seek.

H. Considerations in Investigating Employees

What constitutes a proper and lawful investigation of employees varies with the reasonableness of the means employed in relation to its cause and purpose. Certain considerations can be highlighted.

The key to lawful investigations of employees is the giving of notice of such investigations. An employee with such notice is unlikely to demonstrate that he or she had a reasonable expectation of privacy in the observed or investigated activity. In any event, a legal opinion as to the lawfulness of the investigatory activity is advisable as a variety of federal, state, and judge-made laws may be applicable.

A diligent preemployment inquiry is increasingly essential for both legal and business reasons. Information generally available to the public, such as level of education, should be obtained or confirmed. References should be contacted. Information such as credit history and criminal record should be obtained or used advisedly. Arrest record information may be subject to challenge, and conviction records are most safely employed where the conviction is directly related to performance of the job sought.

Employers may retain private investigation firms or preemployment information service firms but should do so with care. Inquiry into the firm's licensing should be made and client references contacted. The assignment must be clearly defined and the methods to be used delineated. The employer may seek to negotiate an agreement that it be indemnified by the security firm for any liability the employer may be subjected to based on any aspect of the firm's investigation that proves to be unlawful.

The employer should periodically review the need for routine investigations such as preemployment investigations. Information should not be gathered when there is no need.

Surveillance activity should be limited to public places where no reasonable expectation of privacy may exist.

If monitoring performance or work site activities, either electronically or by computer, the employer should confirm, to the extent possible, the accuracy of any data obtained or relied upon. Often, a broader test sample more accurately portrays performance than a single snapshot sample.

The information obtained in an investigation should be kept confidential to the extent possible and appropriate. The more sensitive the information, the more essential it is that this practice be followed.

Employees may not be detained against their will during an investigation. An employee may sue for false imprisonment if he or she is detained without consent or authority of law.

Finally, criminal prosecutions based on information obtained in an investigation should be brought advisedly to avoid a claim of malicious prosecution. A dismissal of the charges coupled with a finding of an improper motive for bringing the action will generally support such a claim. It is safer for the employer to turn over all available information to the proper public authorities for a determination as to whether prosecution is warranted.

II. DISCLOSURE OF INFORMATION

Employers possess vast amounts of information about their employees related to such things as prior employment history, personal background, test scores, medical history, job references, disciplinary history, and performance evaluations. Employers have occasion, of course, to use and disclose the information they have gathered. Employees, in turn, have a great interest in ensuring that such information, particularly that which is disparaging in nature, not be imprudently disclosed.

The law of defamation provides employees with grounds for suing an employer that communicates false and disparaging information about the employee to a third party. Typically, in the employment setting, the disparaging information relates to the employee's ability to perform the job, trade, or profession. Disciplinary actions, performance evaluations, promotion and termination decisions, and job references are common settings in which the potential for the defamation of a current or former employee is present.

The elements of a defamation claim in the employment setting are reviewed in this section, and selected problem areas are discussed.

A. Elements of a Defamation Claim

The basic elements of a defamation claim are (1) a statement of fact concerning an individual, (2) that is false or substantially false, (3) that impugns the individual's character or abilities, and (4) that is published or communicated to a third party.

1. Statement Concerning an Individual

For a statement to be defamatory, it must be about an individual. Group defamation is unlikely to occur in the employment setting (for example, "the company's employees are incompetent") unless the disparaging information can reasonably be associated with certain individuals (for example, "the five members of the marketing department are incompetent").

The defamatory statement can be oral or by gesture or action (known as slander) or in writing (known as libel). For example, an employee told members of the personnel department and others that a co-worker criminally assaulted him, that the assaulting co-worker acted like a disturbed child and needed psychiatric help, and that he feared being "blown away" by the co-worker. These communications were found by a court to be defamatory subject to any defenses that might be raised. (*Misek-Falkoff v. Keller*) Defamatory statements in writing found, for example, in a letter of termination or a job reference may also constitute a basis for suit. (*Burger v. McGilley Memorial Chapels, Inc.*) Similarly, statements contained in press releases (*Nellis v. Miller*) and a memorandum from a hospital to the nursing agency that employed a nurse (*Murray v. Health East*) were found to support defamation claims.

The statement must be of fact or suggest that unstated facts support the statement. Generally, a mere statement of opinion does not constitute defamation. For example, a statement by a group of physicians that they "lacked confidence" in a colleague which caused him to be terminated by the hospital board was ruled merely an expression of opinion not subject to defamatory meaning. (*Gordon v. Lancaster Osteopathic Hosp. Ass'n*) Similarly, a doctor's statement to the press asking how a colleague could be right concerning his treatment "when the patient is dead" was also ruled to be protected opinion. (*Nanavati v. Burdette Tomlin Memorial Hosp.*) A New York court ruled in a labor dispute setting that the statement "#1 Scab Louise Steinhilber Sucks" was an expression of opinion not susceptible to proof of falsehood. (*Steinhilber v. Alphonse*) In contrast, an employee was permitted to sue his former employer based on a job reference stating that his attitude, dependability, and quantity of work were merely fair and the quality of his work was poor. The court concluded that these comments were mixed expressions of fact and opinion which the former employer implied were based on undisclosed facts. (*Nowik v. Mazda Motors of Am.*) Similarly, a supervisor's statement that he suspected that an employee sabotaged the company's computers was found to be defamatory despite the company's contention that the statement was merely an expression of opinion. (*Staples v. Bangor Hydro-Electric*)

It is often difficult to determine what constitutes statements of fact in the context of a defamation claim. One simple, unscientific method of distinguishing opinion from factual statements is to ask: Can the truth or falsity of the alleged defamatory statements be tested or demonstrated? If so, the statements are likely to be found to be factual; if not, the statements are likely to be considered pure opinion.

2. False Statement

To be defamatory, a statement must be false or substantially inaccurate. Truth is an absolute defense to a defamation claim. The owner of a contracting firm that employed nonunion employees at substandard wages was called "scab" in the midst of a labor dispute. The court concluded that this statement was not defamatory as "the statement, albeit unpleasant, was literally correct." (*Barss v. Tosches*) Similarly, an electronic message circulated among banks that a senior vice president could no longer act for the bank was ruled to be merely a statement of fact not subject to defamatory meaning. (*Bernhard v. UBAF Arab Am. Bank*) In contrast, the statement by a dentist to a patient that a former dental colleague was merely a hygienist not capable of performing complex procedures was defamatory. The dentist making the statement knew it to be false. (*Ingber v. Ross*)

3. Impugning Character or Abilities

One of an employee's most valuable assets is his or her good business reputation. Statements made impugning that reputation or suggesting incompetence, dishonesty, disloyalty, or criminal behavior are, if untrue, defamatory. The following statements were found by courts to impugn employees' business reputations and, as such, to be defamatory:

- The statement that the individual was terminated for stealing; (*Hennis v. O'Connor*)
- An accusation that an employee took papers from the employer's private files; (*Mercado v. Hoefler*)
- Claims that a salesman was not industrious, was fired because he sold merely on the basis of friendship, could not sell, and was hard to motivate; (*Stuempges v. Parke, Davis & Co.*)
- Statements by a union officer calling an employee "informer," "stooge," "stool pigeon," and "traitor to the union"; (*Soley v. Ampudia*)
- Three hundred employees were informed that a co-worker had driven away with company property in his truck without authority; (*Drennen v. Westinghouse Elec. Corp.*)

- The statement that a former employee was unethical; (*Prudential Ins. Co. of Am. v. Watts*)
- A refusal to comment on the reason for termination of an employee in an effort not to "embarrass" the former employee; (*Perry v. Cosgrove*) and
- The statement that a former employee was discharged for sound business reasons. (*Lent v. Huntoon*)

In contrast, courts have rejected defamation claims as not sufficiently impugning employees' business reputations based on statements that:

- A dietician quit at an inconvenient time and left a dirty kitchen; (*Meyer v. Allen*)
- An employee was retiring because of his bad health; (*Haggblom v. S.S. Silberblatt, Inc.*) and
- An employee was guilty of a single instance of poor performance. (*Shaw v. Consolidated Rail Corp.*)

Disparaging remarks about an employee's general character rather than the employee's business or professional reputation are also generally not defamatory. Mere name-calling generally does not provide a basis for a defamation claim. (*Wainman v. Bowler*) For example, one lawyer calling another lawyer a "regular nut," a "screwball," and "mishugenah" was found to be nothing but name-calling and not defamatory. (*Skolnick v. Nudelman*) It has also been ruled not defamatory to make snide remarks about a colleague's national origin even if they are meant to disparage the individual. In that case, co-workers made repeated references to a manager's Native American background by saying such things as, "(there are) all Indians here and no chiefs," and that if things did not change there would be only "one Indian left." These comments were found not to be defamatory because accurate reference to an individual's national origin is not derogatory. (*Gorwara v. AEL Indus.*)

Accusing an employee of sexual harassment, however, may be derogatory. In one case, a human resources officer accused her boss, a prison warden, of sexual harassment and he sued her for defamation. A jury rejected the human resources officer's claim that her statement was mere opinion and, therefore, constitutionally protected, and found for the plaintiff. (*Williams v. Garraghty*)

4. Publication

A defamatory statement must be published, that is, communicated to a third party, to violate the law. The communication must be understood as impugning the character or abilities of the defamed. For example, a defamatory remark made in Greek to one who does not speak Greek has not been published. (*Economopoulos v. A.G. Pollard Co.*) Publication has been found to occur where disparaging statements were communicated in the following ways:

- By dictating a letter; (*Arsenault v. Allegheny Airlines*)
- Through issuance of a news release; (*Nellis v. Miller*)
- By electronic mail; (*Misek-Falkoff v. Keller*)
- By teletype; (*Raffensberger v. Moran*)
- Orally in a meeting with staff; (*Norman v. General Motors Corp.*)
- In the barber's chair; (*Aronson v. Wiersma*)
- In a performance evaluation circulated to managers; (*Bals v. Verduzio*)
- In a disciplinary notice; (*Thompson v. Public Serv. Co.*) and
- In a letter of termination. (*Scherer v. Rockwell Int'l Corp.*)

The publication must be to a third party; the communication of a defamatory statement to the person defamed alone does not constitute publication of the defamation. Traditionally, intracorporate communications, that is, disparaging statements communicated among managers and employees of the same employer, were found by courts not to constitute publication for purposes of defamation law. The employer, in this setting, is viewed as the defamer, which cannot publish defamatory communication to itself. (*K-Mart Corp. v. Pendergrass*) Courts are increasingly willing, however, to recognize intracorporate publication. For example, Massachusetts has expressly rejected the notion that publication cannot occur within a corporation. In one Massachusetts case, a letter of termination accused an employee of aiding and abetting the misappropriation of funds by another employee. In that case, the letter was drafted by a manager, read by his secretary who dictated it to a second secretary who typed it, was given to her boss, who signed it, returned it to his secretary who then forwarded copies to the employee and various departments. The court found that the distribution within the company demonstrated that the letter had been published. (*Arsenault v. Allegheny Airlines*)

Each repetition or republication of a defamatory communication also constitutes a separate act of defamation. In the case of a document containing a defamatory communication, each new repetition of the defamatory statement constitutes a new basis for suit. However, under what is known as the "single publication" rule, multiple copies of the same document constitute merely a single publication subjecting the author or publisher to one claim of defamation. For example, an employer investigated claims of sexual harassment and produced various documents including a report and interview notes shown to several individuals and statements made to the alleged harasser after the investigation was completed. The employer concluded that harassment had occurred and transferred the alleged harasser who later sued. The court rejected his claim, based on the single publication doctrine, that each time the report or interview notes were read a new publication occurred. The court ruled, however, that the oral statements made at the disciplinary meeting based on the writings did constitute a separate publication. (*Stockley v. AT&T Info. Sys., Inc.*)

The mere potential for publication does not in fact satisfy the requirement of publication of a defamatory communication. For example, a defamatory statement contained in a personnel file not yet communicated and known only to the employee has not been published. (*Pressley v. Continental Can Co.*) Similarly, unintentional publication that is not negligently made will not be sufficient. For example, no publication occurred where an employee's wife eavesdropped on a telephone conversation between her husband and his employer (*Harbridge v. Greyhound Lines, Inc.*), or where a sealed letter addressed to an employee was opened by that employee's wife (*Scherer v. Rockwell Int'l Corp.*), or where a letter of termination was left on a file cabinet in the personnel office and was read by a co-worker. (*Cashio v. Holt*) Further, defamation that is procured or invited by the employee will not constitute publication. For example, a discharged employee asked his stepson and friend to pose as prospective employers to obtain job references from a former employee. The employer opined in response to these reference requests that the former employee was nearing retirement age and that his performance had recently deteriorated. The court concluded that the employer was not guilty of defamation because the alleged defamatory comments were "solicited" by the former employee and, consequently, he could not complain about any resulting damage to his reputation. (*Kelewae v. Jim Meagher Chevrolet, Inc.*)

Certainly the most notable recent development in the law of defamation as it relates to employment is the growing acceptance of what is known as the self-publication doctrine. In a traditional defamation case, the defamer communicates a disparaging remark to a third party about the defamed. What if the person communicating the disparaging communication is the person about whom the disparaging information relates? For example, what if a job applicant, rather than a former employer, informs a prospective employer that he or she was fired from his last job for theft? That information is true even though the job applicant denies that in fact such theft occurred. Until recently, most courts rejected the notion that a publication had occurred and denied any claim for defamation brought. For example, in a private meeting a supervisor accused a chief of a rail yard crew with violating company rules against intoxication and alcohol use on duty. The crew chief then told his crew of the allegation; he also later sued for defamation. The court rejected his claim, citing an 1838 decision that required the individual in this setting to "bear the consequences of his folly." (*Carson v. Southern Ry. Co.*)

An exception to this rule has increasingly been recognized where it is foreseeable that the disparaging information will be communicated by the employee to others such as prospective employers. The logic of this approach was offered by the Minnesota Supreme Court in a leading case:

> The concept of compelled self-publication does no more than hold the originator of the defamatory statement liable for damages caused by the statement where the originator knows, or should know, of circumstances whereby the defamed person has no reasonable means of avoiding publication of the statement or avoiding the resulting damages; in other words, in cases where the defamed person was compelled to publish the statement. In such circumstances, the damages are fairly viewed as the direct result of the originator's actions.

In that case, a number of employees were terminated for gross insubordination and, when asked on job interviews regarding their terminations, they explained the circumstances of their discharges. The employer, in contrast, disclosed only the employees' dates of employment and final job title. The employees sued for defamation in any event and won. The Minnesota Supreme Court, in reviewing the jury's decision, noted that the only alternative available to employees other than telling the truth was to lie. The court concluded, "Fabrication, however, is an unacceptable alternative." (*Lewis v. Equitable Life Assurance Soc'y*) Courts in the following states have adopted the self-publication rule: California (*McKinney v. Santa Clara*), New York (*Weldy v. Piedmont Airlines*), Colorado (*Churchey v. Adolph Coors Co.*), Georgia (*Colonial Stores, Inc. v. Barrett*), Missouri (*Neighbors v. Kirksville College of Osteopathic Medicine*), and Texas. (*Chasewood Constr. Co. v. Rico*)

While only a minority of jurisdictions have adopted the compelled self-publication doctrine, acceptance of the doctrine is clearly the trend.

B. Defenses to Defamation Claims

The fact that an employer has communicated disparaging information about an employee to a third party does not by itself establish an enforceable defamation claim. An employee must overcome additional hurdles in the form of employer defenses, the most prominent of which are (1) truth; (2) absolute privilege; (3) qualified privilege; and (4) consent.

1. Truth

A disparaging statement that is true cannot be defamatory. An honest belief in the truth of a statement that is not true is not enough; the statement must itself be true. (*Barss v. Tosches*) Defamation claims have been rejected where the press accurately reported the reasons for an employee's discharge (*Seabolt v. Westmoreland Coal Co.*), reports of rudeness to a customer were accurate (*Pratt v. Delta Air Lines*), and allegations that an employee threatened staff workers with acid, had a history of violence, and was making bombs in the laboratory were true. (*You v. Roe*) In contrast, claims that a termination was based on substantiated drug use were found not to defeat a defamation claim where it was alleged that the termination was also motivated by unrelated grounds. (*O'Brien v. Papa Gino's of Am.*)

2. Absolute Privilege

In limited circumstances, employers are entitled without limitation to defame their employees. The reasoning underlying such a rule is that, in these particular settings, uninhibited discussion is required by public policy to administer justice or permit the government to fully and properly carry out its functions. For example, an absolute privilege applies to statements made in the course of legislative, judicial, and quasi-judicial proceedings. Consequently, testimony offered at trial or in a pre-trial deposition is absolutely privileged. Information provided at the express request of a court or legislature is similarly protected (*Newman v. Legal Servs. Corp.*) as are reports required to be made to government agencies such as in cases of alleged child abuse. (*Lail v. Madisonville Child Care Project, Inc.*) Statements made in a judicial complaint not yet filed have been found, however, not to be absolutely privileged. (*Citizens State Bank v. Libertelli*)

Some courts, although not all, have ruled to be absolutely privileged statements made during unemployment insurance proceedings (*Magnan v. Anaconda Indus., Inc.*), grievance procedures pursuant to collective-bargaining agreements (*Green v. Hughes Aircraft Co.*), and to the police as part of a criminal complaint filed against an employee. (*Williams v. Taylor*) The absolute privilege has also been extended to fact-finding conferences held by the Equal Employment Opportunity Commission investigating claims of discrimination (*Ezekiel v. Jones Motor Co.*) and statements made to investigators in state human rights proceedings. (*Meyers v. Amerada Hess Corp.*)

3. Qualified Privilege

The defense most frequently invoked by employers is the qualified privilege defense. Unlike an absolute privilege, a qualified privilege may be lost or exceeded.

The qualified privilege defense recognizes and protects an employer's need to communicate information about its employees, including information critical of those employees, to others within its organization and sometimes to outsiders. Generally speaking, a qualified privilege extends to communications made in good faith between individuals or organizations with a shared interest in the matter discussed. The qualified privilege has been applied to communications such as statements made in the following settings:

- In office meetings related to the business; (*Burns v. Smith-Corona Marchant, Inc.*)
- In security reports; (*Zuniga v. Sears, Roebuck & Co.*)
- By a mental health worker that co-workers had sexual relations with a female patient who was a minor; (*Troxler v. Charter Mandala Ctr., Inc.*)
- Where the information concerned a sexual harassment investigation; (*Stockley v. AT&T Info. Sys., Inc.*)
- In the context of a performance evaluation; (*Price v. Conoco, Inc.*)
- As a part of a job reference; (*Haldeman v. Total Petroleum, Inc.*)
- To the employer's lawyers; (*Mathis v. Boeing Co.*) and
- Notification to the mother of a child allegedly physically abused at a child care center. (*Lail v. Madisonville Child Care Project, Inc.*)

The qualified privilege extends as well to third parties such as private investigators conducting background checks. (*DeSapio v. Kohlmeyer*)

The qualified privilege may be lost if the employer exceeds the scope of the privilege by, for example, disclosing the defamatory statements excessively to those without a need to know. (*Gibby v. Murphy*) The qualified privilege also may be lost based on the employer's negligence or failure to investigate adequately the defamatory statements. (*Banas v. Matthews Int'l Corp.*)

The most common challenge to the assertion of a qualified privilege is a claim of malice, that is, a showing of hostility, intent to injure, or lack of good faith. Malice in this context focuses on the motive of the speaker in making the defamatory statement. If malice is shown, the defamer forfeits his or her qualified privilege. Malice has been demonstrated, and a qualified privilege denied, where statements were made:

- Out of jealousy; (*Elbeshbeshy v. Franklin Inst.*)
- Out of spite; (*Swanson v. Speidel Corp.*)
- With full knowledge of their falsity; (*Ingber v. Ross*)
- Based on personal dislike; (*Nowik v. Mazda Motors of Am.*)
- With reckless indifference to the truth of those statements; (*Litman v. Massachusetts Mut. Life Ins. Co.*) and
- To injure a co-worker for rebuffing sexual advances. (*Bolling v. Baker*)

4. Consent

An employee who authorizes or consents to the publication of a defamatory statement may not bring a defamation action against his or her employer if the publication is within the bounds of the authorization or consent. For example, a policeman demanded the reasons for his termination during a meeting of the city board of aldermen. The mayor responded and the unflattering reasons were subsequently reported by the press. The policeman sued for defamation and the court ruled that the policeman had consented to the publication of the defamatory statement and dismissed the claim for defamation. (*Johnson v. Buckner*) In contrast, a request for an investigation into allegedly false reports about an employee did not constitute consent for further publication of the defamatory statements. (*Jerolamon v. Fairleigh Dickinson Univ.*) The consent here did not extend to the repetition of the defamatory statements but to a further investigation of them. The consent for publication was also exceeded in a case in which an employee consented for a psychologist to provide one type of report to the employer but instead the psychologist provided another type of report. (*McDermott v. Hughley*)

C. Damages

A variety of damages are awardable in defamation cases, including nominal, general, special, and punitive damages.

Nominal damages in this setting are the award of a minimal amount of money to one who has been defamed but has not suffered any compensable damages. The award is, in effect, symbolic, the sole purpose of which is vindication for the defamed. For example, damages to a former employee were reduced from $5,000 to $1 where the alleged loss of a bank loan caused by the former employer's defamation was found to be too speculative. (*Snodgrass v. Headco Indus.*)

General damages are peculiar to defamation actions and are awardable where injury to reputation occurs and damages are presumed, although not necessarily shown, to have occurred. General damages of $5,000 were awarded to a city councilman based on an erroneous report in a newspaper, which sold 35,000 copies, that he had come to city hall in a "drunken condition carrying a gun." (*Van Norman v. Peoria Journal-Star, Inc.*)

Special damages, unlike nominal and general damages, are never presumed and must be proved by specific evidence as to time, cause, and amount. Special damages include actual out-of-pocket expenses, such as medical expenses.

Punitive damages in the defamation context must be based upon a finding of actual malice, that is, publication of the defamatory statement with knowledge of its falsity or in reckless disregard of its truth or falsity. An employer will not be held liable for the punitive damages incurred by its agents or employees unless, in the words of one court, it has "authorized, participated in, consented to or ratified the conduct giving rise to such damages." (*Loughry v. Lincoln First Bank*) In that case, a bank employee alleged that his termination was the result of slanderous statements made by employees including a bank vice president. The statements insinuated that the employee was a cocaine user and had been guilty of larceny. He was fired because the bank "lost confidence" in him. The employee convinced a jury that the statements were in part in retaliation for his having embarrassed one of the defamers in front of his boss. The court rejected a punitive damages award of $105,000 against the bank because the bank or its management did not participate in or ratify the defamation. The court let stand other damages against the bank, however, and sustained punitive damage awards against the individual defamers.

D. Problematic Factual Settings

Defamation claims in the employment setting are most likely to arise in one of the following three settings: (1) employee screening and evaluations; (2) employee discipline and termination; and (3) job references. Each setting is reviewed below, along with practical advice on how to minimize the opportunity for such claims.

1. *Employee Screening and Performance Evaluations*

Employers screen employees for such things as criminal history, drug use or abuse, medical problems, and related matters. Presumably, the screening is conducted to deny or terminate employment if the results of the screening raise questions of the applicant's or employee's fitness for the position. Similarly, performance evaluations, if done correctly, will elicit honest assessments of an employee's job-related abilities and weaknesses.

Courts have generally ruled that employers have a qualified privilege when communicating to those with a need to know the results of screening tests or the substance of performance evaluations. For example, an employer with a serious employee drug problem implemented a random drug-testing policy under which anyone testing positive or refusing to be tested would be fired. At least nineteen employees were terminated over a two-day period under this policy. The terminations were reported in the press where one company official was quoted as saying, "If you know you are an illegal drug user and feel you are going to be caught, you have the option to leave the plant in a few moments and we will accept that as a voluntary quit." The nineteen employees sued for defamation. The court rejected the claim on privilege grounds, finding that the statement merely observed that an employee could take the test or quit and did not clearly state that anyone who refused the test was a drug addict. (*Baggs v. Eagle-Picher Indus.*)

Statements made in performance evaluations are also generally protected absent a showing of malice. (*Price v. Conoco, Inc.*) For example, supervisory comments submitted to supplement a performance evaluation included the observation that the employee lacked confidence in what she did, could not or did not want to be creative, did not understand or remember the content of correspondence, and had lost a $100,000 check. The court concluded that these and similar comments were directed at areas of the employee's performance that needed improvement and as such were privileged. The court reasoned that if this were not the case, "every time an employee was denied a raise on the basis of dissatisfaction with elements of their job performance, the employer could be subjected to a defamation suit." (*Frigon v. Morrison-Maierle, Inc.*)

2. Employee Disciplining and Terminations

Every disciplining or discharge for cause runs the risk of resulting in a defamation claim. While it may also be said that the disciplining or termination of a minority, woman, or older employee runs a similar risk of the filing of a discrimination claim, the situations nonetheless differ based on the different nature of the two types of actions. A termination for cause, the inability to satisfactorily perform the job, by definition satisfies one of the elements of a defamation claim. A necessary element of such a claim is admitted by the employer to be the basis for the personnel action where the challenged discipline or termination is for cause. In contrast, the employee's race, national origin, sex, or age are rarely offered as the reason for a disciplining or discharge and can never constitute cause for disciplining or termination. Put another way, an employee who is discharged for cause can point to that admitted fact as a basis for suing for defamation; in contrast, an employee suing on discrimination grounds has no comparable admission from the employer upon which to rely in establishing his or her claim but rather must establish this fact.

Indeed, defamation claims related to employee disciplining or discharge are the most common employee defamation claims. Tight control over the disclosure of the reasons for termination—for example, to whom such information is to be disclosed and to what degree—is crucial to limiting unintended defamation of employees.

One apparent option is not to disclose to any third party and, indeed, not even to the employee, the reasons for disciplinary action or discharge. That is generally not a viable option, however, for, among many other reasons, its damage to employee morale and relations. It is also antithetical to enforcement of any organization's rules and standards. Nonetheless, the deterrent effect of the threat of defamation action has instilled a healthy degree of caution in the manner in which many employers handle disciplinary and discharge situations.

An employer, of course, has legitimate reasons for disclosing to its employees the reasons for a co-worker's disciplining or discharge. Employers' principal legal defense to any defamation claim remains, of course, the qualified privilege defense. Courts have upheld the qualified privilege where the employer offered as its reason for the disclosure to co-workers of an employee's discipline or discharge for cause:

- Its legitimate business-related need to inform co-workers of the reason for the discharge; (*Garziano v. E.I. Du Pont de Nemours & Co.*)
- The need to exonerate the innocent where there are claims of wrongdoing; (*Ponticelli v. Mine Safety Appliance Co.*)
- Its proprietary interest where the employer had reason to believe that a cashier had stolen money; (*Schneider v. Pay 'N Save Corp.*)
- The company's interest in clarifying its policies and preventing future abuse of those policies; (*Deaile v. General Tel. Co.*)
- Its interest in maintaining morale and quieting rumors that may disrupt the business; (*Zinda v. Louisiana Pac. Corp.*) and
- Its obligation to investigate suspicions or potentially unlawful conduct of employees, in this case a claim of sexual harassment, and to subsequently disclose the results of the investigation. (*Scherer v. Rockwell Int'l Corp.*)

This privilege could be lost if the publication is excessive, false, based on facts not adequately investigated, or motivated by malice, among other reasons.

3. Job References

The singer Diana Ross was asked her opinion of certain former employees. She responded, in writing, that "I do not recommend these people." A court ruled that a jury could reasonably conclude that this statement suggested that it was based on unstated facts that were false and, consequently, was defamatory. (*Davis v. Ross*)

With decisions such as this, it is no surprise that many employers, if they respond to a job reference request at all, will limit their response to "name, rank, and serial number," that is, to information related to dates of employment, last position held, and last salary. Such an approach, if followed, will in almost all circumstances defeat a defamation claim based on such a job reference. (*Mathis v. Boeing Co.*) Neither employers nor employees gain, however, by these self-imposed limitations on the free disclosure of job performance information. In recognition of this fact, the California legislature in 1994 amended its civil code expressly to protect a "communication concerning the job performance of qualifications of an applicant for employment, based upon credible evidence, made without malice, by a current or former employer of the applicant to, and upon request of, the prospective employer." (Cal. Civ. Code §47(c))

As a general rule, the more fact-specific and verifiable a job reference is, the more likely it is that it will be found to be privileged. While pure statements of opinion are arguably protected by the constitution, any statement that reasonably implies a false assertion of fact can constitute defamation. (*Milkovich v. Lorain Journal Co.*) For example, a company official responded to a job reference request by stating, among other things, that the former employee "seemed detail oriented to the point of losing sight of the big picture," and that "[o]bviously he no longer worked for us and that might say enough." These statements were made even though the official had not supervised the former employee or read an evaluation. The official admitted his comments were not based on "real specific instances I can point to." The court determined that the statements were defamatory in that they were presented as expressions of fact. The court pointed out that the context was an interview intended to help the prospective employer determine the suitability of employment of an applicant. Under these circumstances, the company official giving the evaluation knew or should have known that his statements would be interpreted as factual evaluations of the former employee's qualifications. The court also concluded that the former employer had abused and thereby lost its qualified privilege to provide a job reference. The court reasoned that the evaluation was based on "rumor," "gossip," and "scuttlebutt" that was erroneously presented as fact. (*Sigal Constr. Corp. v. Stanbury*) In contrast, employers are privileged to offer negative job references where they are based on the evaluator's personal experience with the former employee (*Scholtes v. Signal Delivery Serv.*), on a careful, thorough investigation of the former employee's performance (*Rouly v. Enserch Corp.*), or on the former employee's own admission. (*Arsenault v. Allegheny Airlines*)

E. Guidelines for Limiting Defamation in the Workplace

The threat of defamation actions has no doubt had the therapeutic effect of making employers more cautious in disclosing negative information about their employees in any setting. Any good measure can, of course, be abused and an employer policy of not disclosing any information, like any overreaction, is on the broad scale counterproductive. A reasoned, responsible policy to the handling and disclosure of workplace information can be implemented and administered.

At the core of such a policy must be the following general principles:

- Only accurate, business-related information should be gathered and maintained under any circumstances;
- Information that cannot be verified or that lacks a substantial basis in fact should be ignored or discarded;
- Employee personnel and computer files should be periodically reviewed and purged of outdated or irrelevant information, particularly if it is disparaging in nature;

- Inquiries regarding or disclosing information related to an employee's personal life, practices, or tastes should be avoided unless they are clearly job-related;
- The disclosure of sensitive information must be limited to those with a demonstrable need to know;
- An employer should carefully investigate and determine if there is a substantial basis for any disparaging information about an employee before disclosing such information;
- All evaluations, disciplinary actions, and discharges should be handled or reviewed by the human resources department, if one exists, or a key manager or department, to provide consistency and quality control to the employer's information gathering and disclosure policies and practices;
- Consent and a release of claims should be obtained from an employee before any information about the employee is disclosed to third parties;
- Job references should only be provided in writing after consent has been obtained and should be limited to the questions asked; and
- The employer's information gathering and disclosure policy should be effectively communicated to all employees on a periodic basis and violations of that policy should be appropriately and consistently handled.

While even strict application and enforcement of these guidelines will not guarantee complete freedom from defamation claims, they will go a long way toward restricting the number of such claims filed. In this way, employers will be better able to defend themselves in the event of a defamation claim, and limit any damages that may be awarded by a court if defamation is found to have occurred.

6

EMPLOYEE TESTING

Employers in recent years have seen their discretion in terminating employees diminish, while witnessing an explosive growth in employment-related litigation and liability. Twenty years ago, a troublesome or dangerous employee was discharged without thought; today, many employers will pause before terminating the employee, or will not do it at all for fear of litigation. While employment in the United States is not for life, it is less at will than at any time since the nineteenth century.

One response to the diminution of at-will employment has been an increase in the care employers exercise when hiring employees. Mistakes in hiring can no longer be easily remedied by a pink slip. The drunk night watchman may still be drunk, but also may be legally disabled and entitled to reasonable accommodation for his disability. The thieving inventory clerk may still be a thief, but an employer is now less able to use a polygraph to substantiate its suspicions. Adding to the problem is the perception held by many employers, whether accurate or not, that problems affecting the workplace, such as drug and alcohol abuse and employee theft, are on the rise.

One manifestation of the greater care taken by employers in the hiring process and beyond is the more expansive use of testing as a screening device for undesirable traits and conditions in potential and current employees. Drug, alcohol, personality, and honesty tests are the most common of these screening devices. These and other employer screening devices, however, often push the limits of the law and come perilously close to unlawfully invading an applicant's or employee's privacy or to discriminating on the basis of disability or other unlawful grounds. On occasion, they have been found to do so. A review of the most common types of employee testing and the multitude of legal issues they implicate and rights they threaten follows.

I. DRUG AND ALCOHOL TESTING

The precise number of employees who use illegal drugs or abuse alcohol is unknown. What is evident is that the annual expense to employers due to employee accidents and injuries, absenteeism, reduced production, and lost inventory costs attributable to drug and alcohol abuse is in the billions of dollars.

Against this backdrop, it is not surprising that employers in increasing numbers have attempted to identify substance and alcohol abusers by testing both job applicants and employees. Drug tests merely indicate, however, whether an individual has used drugs in the recent past and not whether he or she was impaired either on the job, or at the time the test was given. In contrast, alcohol tests typically reveal alcohol consumption within the previous few hours but, in isolation, are not an adequate tool for determining an alcohol problem or possible impairment on the job. With both types of tests, the issue of accuracy and "false positive" results remains.

The strong public interest in limiting or eliminating drug or alcohol use that may impair an employee's performance is clear. It is also evident that the interest is of paramount importance in safety-sensitive positions. Applicants and employees have a strong interest as well in not having their privacy invaded or their off-the-job activities become the basis for an employment decision.

This section will address the limitations on employers in testing job applicants and employees for drug or alcohol use or abuse, and on their ability to terminate, discipline, or not hire an alcoholic or substance abuser.

A. Overview

1. *Types of Drug and Alcohol Testing*

Drug and alcohol testing can be administered both before and after employment commences. Preemployment examinations can screen out users of alcohol or drugs without regard for the applicant's on-the-job performance since, by definition, the applicant has not worked for the employer. Postemployment drug or alcohol tests may be administered:

- As part of a periodic medical examination;
- Based on a reasonable suspicion of impairment;
- Following an accident involving the employee; or
- Randomly.

The propriety of each kind of test depends on the type of work at issue, state privacy laws, and the conduct of the employee.

a. Drug Tests Tests for the detection of illegal substances have expanded significantly beyond the standard blood and urine tests to include the analysis of an individual's hair, the examination of eyes and pupils, and the testing of an individual's hand-eye coordination. Nonetheless, the most common drug tests remain those which screen an individual's urine for a range of illicit substances. Some of the more popular drug and alcohol screening tests include EMIT (enzyme-multiplied immunoassay technique), ELISA (enzyme-linked immunosorbent assay), RIA (radioimmunoassay), and the thin-layered chromatography (TLC technique). These tests are relatively inexpensive.

In the TLC technique, substances in an individual's urine are identified through observation of their movement and color. The TLC test results, however, may produce inaccuracies based on the intake of and reaction to certain foods. In comparison, RIA and EMIT examine the interaction between illicit substances and an individual's antibodies. As with TLC, these tests are not fool-proof since antibodies also react to legally prescribed drugs. For example, herbal teas, poppy seeds, and some over-the-counter medications, such as Contac, Sudafed, Advil, and Nuprin, may cause positive test results. While the incidents of false-positive results from these tests are relatively small, this provides little comfort to employees who lose their jobs because of the erroneous tests and to employers defending against subsequent litigation.

To minimize potential legal challenges and ensure the accuracy of test results, cautious employers follow up inexpensive screening tests that identify possible substance users with more sophisticated tests to confirm any positive results initially discovered. Indeed, such confirmatory testing is mandated by federal law in certain industries, such as transportation. Some of the more prevalent confirmatory drug tests available include gas-liquid chromatography, high-performance liquid chromatography, and gas chromatography/mass spectrometry (GC/MS). Courts have consistently upheld the accuracy of these confirmatory drug tests. (*Blankenship v. S. Carolina Elec. & Gas Co.*)

Drawbacks common to drug tests that sample urine include the inability to determine the precise timing of the drug use, the threat of contamination of the sample, and the possibility of false-positives based on the ingestion of certain foods and legal over-the-counter drugs. Consequently, the search for more certain and practical alternatives continues.

A newer and less widely accepted method of drug testing involves the radioimmunoassay analysis of elements embedded permanently in hair. The test is performed on at least one inch of hair cut from the crown and growing close to the scalp. Hair testing provides many advantages over urinalysis and blood testing because: (1) bodily functions and genital organs are not involved; (2) hair cannot be altered; (3) chain of custody problems, that is, the risk of contamination in the handling of the sample or of misidentification of samples, are minimized; and (4) rough estimates of usage can be made. One negative, however, is that hair testing is more expensive than urinalysis, and may not eliminate the need to confirm the results by GC/MS. (*Koch v. Harrah's Club*)

Another relatively new test seeks to determine possible impairment for any reason based on an employee's hand-eye coordination rather than substances in the blood or urine. Through the use of a computer-based video test, an employee's fitness for the job can be ascertained without resorting to invasive processes. This technique obviates many of the privacy invasion concerns raised by substance abuse testing, since it assesses only the employee's fitness for the job. This method has not yet been generally accepted and its utility remains in question.

b. Alcohol Tests Tests for the detection of alcohol consumption are comparable and often identical to those used for other substances. Through the use of screening and confirmatory tests (EMIT and GC/MS), the employer can confirm the presence of alcohol in an individual's blood or urine. Unlike drug ingestion— evidence of which remains in the urine, blood, or hair for extended periods of time—tests for alcohol use can measure only relatively recent consumption. Consequently, alcohol screening is effective in measuring impairment in the workplace but is vastly inaccurate in distinguishing an alcohol user from an alcohol abuser. As alcoholism is a disability, tests that focus on anything other than impairment while on the job risk challenge under federal, state, and local disability laws.

2. Mechanics of Testing

Drug tests in an overwhelming majority of cases involve the chemical testing of urine samples. The testing of blood samples, while more accurate, is a more difficult and expensive system to administer and, consequently, less practical for use in the employment setting. Alcohol testing as well is most often based on urine samples, although Breathalyzer tests are also employed.

The gathering of the test sample may be done on the employer's premises or at a designated laboratory, medical center, or physician's office. It is essential that the samples or specimens be clearly marked and that no contamination occur. Specimens that arrive at the testing site with evidence of tampering will be rejected.

The specimens are then analyzed by a clinical laboratory or testing service and the test results are provided to the employer. Some laboratories or testing services will provide coded results or otherwise ensure confidentiality. The key to any drug or alcohol testing, in addition to the accuracy of the results, is the integrity of the testing process and the chain of custody. If that chain is broken, the utility of the test results is significantly reduced, if not negated, as the employer will have difficulty demonstrating that the sample was a particular individual's or that it was not contaminated prior to the testing. Consequently, an employer will want assurances from the laboratory or testing service that it will document the chain of custody of each specimen to account for the integrity of the specimen by tracking its handling and storage from point of collection to final disposition. Laboratories and testing companies will generally agree as part of their service to provide litigation support (some will do it free of charge while others will charge a fee) to attest to the accuracy of test results and document the chain of custody.

Courts differ on the question of whether employers, laboratories, or testing services may be found liable for their negligence in the obtaining, handling, or testing of a specimen. The determining factor is whether, under the applicable state law, a duty of care is owed to the individual whose specimen is tested. For example, in an extreme example, an oilfield worker who was terminated after a laboratory erroneously reported a positive drug test result was awarded $4.1 million by a Kansas jury, including $3.4 million in punitive damages. (*Dick v. Koch Gathering Sys.*) In contrast, a federal appeals court ruled that under Texas law a laboratory could not be sued for negligence because it owed no duty to an employee who received a false positive drug-test result. (*Willis v. Roche Biomedical Laboratories, Inc.*)

At least one court has concluded that an employer would violate public policy if it failed to use drug-testing procedures that were "scientifically sound." The court reasoned that "an at will employee fired on the basis of a false positive, procured through second rate or negligent test procedures, would surely have a cause of action based on public policy for wrongful termination." The court further suggested that, while the employer owed a lesser duty to applicants than it did to employees, nonetheless, it was required to ensure that any drug tests used were reliable in design and application. In that case, the court found that the employer had used "the most advanced and accurate scientific procedures available" and dismissed the applicant's claims of negligence. (*Jevic v. Coca Cola Bottling Co.*) This latter view, however, has not been generally adopted. Most courts have rejected claims that employers owe employees or applicants a duty to conduct drug and alcohol testing in a fair, scientific, and non-negligent manner. (*DiTomaso v. Electronic Data Sys.*)

As the law develops in this area, employers, laboratories, and testing services can expect that courts will require greater care in the administration of drug and alcohol tests and in the analysis of test results where such test results play a role in an employment decision.

3. Confidentiality and Disclosure of Test Results

False accusations that an individual tested positive for drug or alcohol use are defamatory. (See Chapter 5 for a fuller discussion of defamation law.) For example, a railroad switchman was given a number of tests following an on-the-job injury that revealed, among other things, a trace of methadone, a drug commonly associated with the treatment of heroin addicts. A physician designated by the company reported this orally and in writing to the assistant manager of personnel who prepared a written report, in keeping with company procedure, relating the test results to seven company officials. The switchman was terminated as a result. A later test revealed the presence of a chemical compound in his system that resembled, but was not, methadone. The court ruled that there was enough evidence suggesting that the switchman was not a narcotics user to support a jury finding of defamation and an award of $200,000 in damages. (*Houston Belt & Terminal Ry Co. v. Wherry*)

Courts have similarly held that claims of drug use by employees reported by employers in press releases (*Record v. Whirlpool Corp.*) and to the police (*Norman v. General Motors Corp.*) stated claims of defamation that must be resolved at trial. In one instructive case, the court concluded that the employer did not defame its employees when it responded to press inquiries regarding drug testing on the job and the termination of employees who tested positive for drugs. The press learned of the drug testing from one of the employees and, although the employer confirmed the information, it did not provide names of the affected employees to the press. The court reviewed the published statements from the employer and concluded that, while the statements were defamatory, the employer was not liable for damages because the employer had a qualified privilege to disclose truthful information. (*Baggs v. Eagle-Picher Indus.*)

A defamation claim was also allowed to proceed to trial where an employee's supervisor told her in front of two other supervisors that "I know a person who is on drugs and you look like one." The court found that the supervisor knew in advance of the accusation that the employee was not "on drugs." (*Harris v. Hirsh*) In contrast, an employer lawfully informed the employees of an entire facility, and certain employees off the premises, that eight employees were discharged following an investigation into drug involvement. The court held that the employer had not acted with malice or had excessively circulated the information regarding the discharge. (*Harris v. Procter & Gamble Mfg. Co.*)

A clear lesson from these cases is that the results of drug and alcohol tests are extremely sensitive and must be kept confidential. Such information should be disclosed only to those within the company on a demonstrable need-to-know basis. Many employers keep test results in confidential, locked files separate from employees' personnel files as a means of limiting unauthorized or unintentional disclosure even though this is not required under the ADA as drug tests are not considered medical examinations. Further, such information should not be disclosed to anyone outside the company without the applicant's or employee's prior written consent.

B. Testing in the Public Sector

Workplace drug and alcohol testing of government employees and job applicants is subject to the protections afforded by the U.S. Constitution. Under the Fourth Amendment of the Constitution, individuals are guaranteed the right to be free from unreasonable governmental searches and seizures. Consequently, the government may not intrude upon an individual's sphere of privacy unless there is some reasonable ground for the intrusion. Since drug and alcohol tests have been interpreted to be "searches," testing of employees can occur only if the circumstances reveal testing is reasonable. What constitutes a reasonable search is dependent on the facts of each case and the type of testing involved.

1. Supreme Court Standards for Public-Sector Testing Programs

The Supreme Court has declared that the taking of urine, blood, and breath samples to conduct drug tests is within the Fourth Amendment's meaning of "search and seizure." (*Skinner v. Railway Labor Executives Ass'n*) Although "probable cause" is normally required before a search can ensue, the Supreme Court found that the Federal Railroad Administration's strong interest in regulating the conduct of certain employees to ensure the public safety "presents 'special needs' beyond normal law enforcement that may justify departures from the usual warrant and probable-cause requirements."

In reaching its decision, the Supreme Court employed a balancing test comparing the individual's privacy interests to the government's interest in testing for drug use or abuse. Since certain drugs and alcohol are quickly eliminated from an employee's bloodstream, the Supreme Court reasoned that requiring a warrant would "impede the achievement of the Government's objective." The Court stressed the high-risk nature of the employees' duties, noting that "even a momentary lapse of attention can have disastrous consequences." Consequently, it upheld testing after an accident or safety rule violation even absent individualized suspicion of drug or alcohol use.

In a second ruling decided the same day, the Supreme Court upheld the constitutionality of the U.S. Customs Service's drug-testing program. Unlike the railroad employees in *Skinner*, there was no indication that substance abuse was a problem among Customs Service employees. In balancing the interests at issue, the Court determined that Customs employees who are either involved in the interdiction of illegal drugs or required to carry firearms have a diminished expectation of privacy because they "reasonably should expect effective inquiry into their fitness and probity [for duty]." When weighed against the government's compelling interest in "safety and in the integrity of [the United States'] borders," the individual's diminished expectation of privacy was overcome. While recognizing that drug testing of employees with access to "truly sensitive information" was consti-tutionally permissible, the Court returned the case to the lower courts to determine whether the Customs Service defined the category too broadly by including such positions as electric equip-ment repairers, mail clerks, and messengers. (*National Treasury Employees Union v. Von Raab*)

These two leading Supreme Court decisions, unfortunately, leave several important issues unresolved, including which bal-ancing test factors are most important and whether any govern-ment interest would support a random, suspicionless testing pro-gram. These issues are likely to be addressed and resolved by the courts in the coming years.

2. Common Settings for Workplace Testing

Whether a particular type of testing policy will pass the Fourth Amendment prohibition against unreasonable searches and seizures depends on the basis for the test and the individual's reasonable expectation of privacy in that setting. The more intru-sive the testing and the more offensive to legitimate privacy in-terests, the greater the likelihood that the test will be found to be unreasonable.

Five legitimate settings have been identified to test for drugs and alcohol by government employers: applicant testing, regu-lar medical examination testing, reasonable suspicion testing, postaccident testing, and random testing. The application of the Fourth Amendment to each setting follows.

a. Applicant Testing Courts have held that a job applicant's privacy expectation is lower than that of a current employee on the assumption that job applicants have no legitimate expecta-tion of employment. For instance, the Federal Highway Administration's (FHA) drug testing of applicants has been up-held based on this diminished expectation and the FHA's com-pelling interest in the safety of the transportation industry. (*International Bhd. of Teamsters v. Department of Transp.*) In another decision, Justice Department testing of applicants for attorney positions was found proper based in part on the attorney's di-minished privacy expectations. In that case, the applicant (1) was aware of the testing requirement before applying; (2) did not have to apply for the position if opposed to submitting to the test; and (3) revealed extensive information, including past drug use, on his preemployment questionnaire. (*Willner v. Thornburgh*)

b. *Regular Medical Examination Testing* Public employers may require, as part of a periodic medical examination, that government employees submit to drug and alcohol tests. This testing is most likely to withstand scrutiny where it is designed to ensure that the employee can safely perform his or her job functions. Such testing has generally been construed as a minimal incursion into employees' privacy where medical examinations are a condition of continuing employment. (*International Bhd. of Teamsters v. Department of Transp.*)

c. *Reasonable Suspicion Testing* Public employers may require drug tests based on a reasonable suspicion that an employee is working while impaired by drugs or alcohol. The suspicion is generally based on the employee's erratic behavior or on a dramatic change in job performance and is particularly warranted where the individual has a history of substance abuse. Reasonable suspicion testing will withstand constitutional scrutiny if the employees to be tested are identified narrowly, the procedures for detecting impairment are reasonable, and government employees have been forewarned of the policy.

In balancing the government's legitimate reason for requiring the drug test against the individual's privacy interest, some courts have ruled that the government may not test employees whose jobs are not safety related based on off-duty drug use or alcohol impairment. (*National Treasury Employees Union v. Yeutter*)

Similarly, courts have struck down tests utilizing amorphous indicators of on-the-job drug use. Suspicion predicated on an application for a promotion or return to work following extended absence is an insufficient basis upon which to premise a test. (*Burka v. New York City Transit Auth.*) Although reasonable suspicion may be formed by reference to workplace rumors, the rumor must permit a reasonable inference that the employee used drugs. For example, a court ruled that the mayor of Pagedale, Missouri, violated the Fourth Amendment by requiring a police officer to undergo a drug test based solely on rumors and an anonymous tip that the officer was associating with a suspected drug dealer. (*Ford v. Dowd*)

d. Postaccident Testing The prevailing view is that postaccident testing is a form of "suspicionless" testing and, therefore, subject to a stricter scrutiny. Postaccident drug tests may be conducted primarily in two situations: where the employee's job classification involves high-risk duties; and where the accident is serious. The government must strike the proper balance between the two factors before requiring postaccident testing. For example, drug and alcohol testing of a bus driver who had a minor accident involving the striking of a pole while driving into a garage was upheld even where no injuries were caused and the damage was minimal. The court stated that the government's interest in protecting public safety outweighed the driver's privacy expectation particularly where its testing policy specifically provided that hitting a fixed object required an employee to undergo a drug test. (*Tanks v. Greater Cleveland Regional Transit Auth.*) In contrast, a postaccident testing program providing for testing of "all employees *involved* . . . in mishaps" was found to be constitutionally overbroad because it permitted testing of individuals who were not at fault. (*Plane v. United States*)

e. Random Testing The use of random drug tests is recognized as the strongest deterrent to employee drug use. Random testing also poses perhaps the greatest intrusion on an individual's rights and is the cause of most testing lawsuits. (*Government Employees v. Derwinski*) Random drug testing of government employees cannot be implemented absent a compelling governmental interest. Courts balance the countervailing interests of the government and employees and allow random testing only where:

- The employees at issue have a diminished expectation of privacy;
- The government's compelling interest in safety and national security outweighs the employees' diminished privacy interest; or

- It is necessary to maintain the integrity of the government's workforce.

Courts have upheld the right of employers to randomly test employees:

- Holding safety-sensitive positions such as pilots; (*Bluestein v. Skinner*)
- Working for railroads; (*Railway Labor Executives' Ass'n v. Skinner*)
- Involved in drug interdiction; (*Harmon v. Thornburgh*)
- Who must carry firearms as part of their job; (*National Fed'n of Fed. Employees v. Cheney*)
- Who work with chemical weapons; (*Thomson v. Marsh*)
- Who hold top secret national security clearances; (*Guiney v. Roache*) and
- Required to be physically fit. (*Doe v. City and County of Honolulu*)

For example, in *Bluestein v. Skinner*, the Federal Aviation Administration's regulations requiring random drug testing of various flight personnel, including employees in private commercial aviation, were challenged as unreasonable searches under the Fourth Amendment. The court rejected the challenge stating that the government's interest in ensuring aviation safety and deterring drug-related job impairment overcomes any invasion of employees' privacy interests.

3. Testing of Federal Employees

In September 1986, President Reagan issued Executive Order 12564, commonly referred to as the drug-free federal workplace policy. This Executive Order mandated that all federal executive agencies develop plans for achieving a drug-free workplace, including the implementation of drug-testing programs. In response, a vast majority of the approximately 135 federal agencies have approved plans for workplace drug testing of their employees. The U.S. Department of Health and Human Services has issued mandatory guidelines governing the implementation of federal employee drug and alcohol programs.

A common characteristic of the testing policies adopted is the requirement that employees in sensitive positions (where drug use would pose a danger to the public or national security) be tested along with (1) applicants for government employment; (2) government employees reasonably suspected of using drugs or alcohol; (3) employees involved in workplace accidents; and (4) employees in drug rehabilitation programs. Agencies are to conduct their drug programs pursuant to scientific and technical guidelines established by the Secretary of Health and Human Services. Any employee testing positive must be discharged unless the individual receives counseling or rehabilitation, and remains drug-free.

C. Testing in the Private Sector

Federal constitutional protections against unreasonable searches and seizures apply only to governmental intrusions into an individual's privacy. While private-sector employees and applicants for employment do not have so powerful a tool as the Constitution to combat workplace drug and alcohol testing (unless the private employer is found to be acting on behalf of the government), they are not without remedy. Indeed, lacking a single unifying basis for challenging such testing, employees and applicants have invoked a multitude of legal bases with varying success, including: state drug and alcohol testing laws; disability law; discrimination law; invasion of privacy claims under state constitutional, statutory, and judicial law; contract law; negligence law; defamation; public policy claims; and emotional distress claims. The result is an amalgam of restrictions creating varying boundaries for drug-testing programs depending on, among other things, the state in which the testing takes place and the industry involved.

Challenges to the propriety of testing in each of these realms require the balancing of the invasion of a person's privacy rights with an employer's "legitimate employment interest in seeking a drug-free work environment." Generally, the validity of private testing programs has been upheld if, under the facts presented, the testing was "appropriate . . . [and] the testing methods are reliable." (*Koch v. Harrah's Club*)

1. State Testing Laws

Those states that have enacted drug-testing laws (few have enacted alcohol-testing laws) have adopted widely divergent approaches.

The most common enactment mimics the Federal Drug-Free Workplace Act of 1988, which is discussed below, and requires state contractors and grantees to adopt and certify compliance with drug policies. Such policies must be communicated to employees and must prohibit drug use or abuse and designate appropriate sanctions for violations of the policy. California, Illinois, and South Carolina are examples of states with drug-free workplace laws. Other states, such as Connecticut, Maine, Montana, and Vermont, impose significant restrictions on workplace drug testing. Still others, such as Hawaii and Maryland, generally permit drug testing, but place limited procedural restrictions on the manner in which the testing is conducted or dictate the information to be provided to applicants or employees related to the testing.

Perhaps the state to take the most aggressive stand in favor of drug and alcohol testing in the workplace is Arizona. Under Arizona's law, preemployment, random, for-cause, periodic announced, postaccident, rehabilitation, and safety-sensitive job related drug testing is allowed as long as certain specified procedures are followed. Employers who take good-faith actions based on a positive drug or alcohol test and whose policies comply with the terms of the law are insulated from suit. In contrast, Rhode Island law prohibits employers from requiring an employee to submit to a drug test as a condition of continued employment unless the employer has reasonable grounds to believe that the employee's drug use is impairing work performance and the test is conducted in connection with a bona fide rehabilitation program.

Minnesota's law is an example of a state attempting to balance the privacy interests of employees and applicants with employers' interests in maintaining a workplace free from drugs and alcohol. The Minnesota law requires that drug and alcohol testing be performed pursuant to a written policy. A test may be required only of job applicants who have received a conditional offer of employment and such testing is required of all applicants for the position. Employers may require the testing of employees as part of a routine annual physical examination or randomly for employees in safety-sensitive positions. Drug and alcohol tests may also be required under the Minnesota law where the employer has a reasonable suspicion that the employee is under the influence of alcohol or drugs, has violated the employer's drug and alcohol policy while at work, has sustained a personal injury, or has caused a workplace accident.

The requirements of the Minnesota law, although limited to that state, nonetheless set forth useful guidelines for employers in other states with no such law or with less comprehensive or restrictive laws.

2. Disability

Of the federal statutes enacted by Congress, the laws that potentially have the most pronounced impact on drug testing in the private sector are the Americans With Disabilities Act (ADA) and the Vocational Rehabilitation Act of 1973 (Rehabilitation Act). Both statutes proscribe discrimination against the disabled, and depending upon the definition of "disabled," protected status may be accorded to drug addicts and alcoholics.

a. Americans With Disabilities Act The ADA makes it unlawful for employment determinations to be based solely on an individual's status as a present or former substance abuser or as an alcoholic. An employer may not deny employment opportunities to disabled individuals who are otherwise capable of performing the essential functions of the position.

An applicant or employee *"currently engaging* in the illegal use of drugs . . . " is not considered disabled for purposes of the ADA and is not protected by the law. (*Wormley v. Arkla*) Substance abusers are considered disabled if they are not current drug users. In contrast, alcoholic employees are afforded greater protection under the ADA. Employees whose alcohol intake does not affect on-the-job performance may not be discriminated against based solely on their status as alcoholics. An alcoholic employee, however, may not invoke his or her "disabled" status to excuse unsatisfactory job performance or poor attendance. The ADA provides expressly that an alcoholic may be judged against the "same qualification standards for employment or job performance and behavior [as] . . . other employees."

The ADA does not preclude employers from instituting testing practices to monitor illegal drug use. The ADA provides specifically that none of its provisions regarding the illegal use of drugs in the workplace or its identification of certain substance users as "disabled" should be construed to "encourage, prohibit, or authorize the conducting of drug testing for the illegal use of drugs by job applicants or employees or making employment decisions based on such test results."

b. Rehabilitation Act of 1973 The Rehabilitation Act, like the ADA, seeks to prevent an employer from discriminating against "qualified" handicapped individuals. Unlike the ADA, it applies only to those employers receiving federal contracts in excess of $2,500 and to participants in federally funded programs. For purposes of the Rehabilitation Act, a "handicapped individual" includes alcoholics and drug addicts.

Despite the Rehabilitation Act's inclusion of alcoholism and drug addiction as covered impairments, it specifically provides that a "handicapped" employee does not include an alcoholic or drug abuser whose current use prevents the individual from performing the duties mandated by the position, or poses a "direct threat" to property or another individual's safety. To attain "handicapped" status, employees must demonstrate that they are alcoholics or addicted to drugs; casual alcohol or drug use is insufficient. An employer will be required to reasonably accommodate a handicapped individual under the Rehabilitation Act and determine if performance problems are caused by the handicap. (*Teahan v. Metro-North Commuter R.R. Co.*) Courts differ as to whether an employer may distinguish an individual's disability from its consequences. For example, the court in the *Teahan* case ruled that the employer could not separate the employee's alco-

154 Primer on Individual Employee Rights, Second Edition

holism from his absenteeism. A second federal appeals court, however, upheld the discharge of a college football coach who alleged that his arrest for drunk driving, for which he was terminated, was attributable to his alcoholism. This court concluded that the Rehabilitation Act permitted the discharge for misconduct even if the misconduct could be traced to the employee's disability. The court reasoned that if this were not so, employers would be required to tolerate behavior from alcoholics that would not be tolerated from sober or nonalcoholic intoxicated employees. (*Maddox v. University of Tenn.*)

Under the Rehabilitation Act's regulations, preemployment drug tests are prohibited unless they are "job-related," compelled by "business necessity," and administered after a conditional employment offer has been extended. The Rehabilitation Act prohibits the administering of drug tests to current employees without reasonable suspicion of substance abuse.

3. Discrimination

Federal law, as well as many state and local laws, prohibits discrimination on the basis of race, age, sex, national origin, and related protected categories. Under these laws, a seemingly neutral employment policy is unlawful if it causes an adverse impact on one of the protected groups. Drug abusers, alcoholics, and users of drugs or alcohol generally are not protected groups. Still, a testing policy that causes an adverse impact on a protected group will be deemed unlawful unless the policy is shown to be job-related and consistent with business necessity. The breadth of the business necessity defense is uncertain, and the viability of a testing program will be determined only on a case-by-case basis.

4. Invasion of the Right to Privacy

Employees' privacy rights in the private sector, as discussed in Chapter 8, may derive from state constitutions, statutes, or case law. The extent of the protection against an invasion of privacy depends on applicable state law.

States such as Alaska, Arizona, California, Florida, Hawaii, Illinois, Louisiana, Massachusetts, Montana, South Carolina, and Washington have right-to-privacy provisions in their state constitutions. Some states, such as California and Montana, have applied these provisions to the private sector. For example, a California appellate court ruled that the state constitutional right to privacy applied to a private employer's drug-testing program. The court upheld a jury finding that the employer's random drug-testing policy violated the employee's right to privacy. (*Luck v. Southern Pac. Transp.*) A second California court ruled that a blanket requirement that all applicants undergo preemployment drug-screening examinations violated the privacy rights of those individuals in non–safety-sensitive positions. (*Loder v. The City of Glendale*) In contrast, the Alaska Supreme Court determined that the right to privacy in its state constitution does not extend to private parties and, consequently, did not provide grounds for challenging an employer's drug-screening program. (*Luedtke v. Nabors Alaska Drilling*)

A number of states, including Massachusetts, Rhode Island, and Wisconsin, have broad privacy statutes that could apply to drug and alcohol testing in the private sector.

Employees' right to privacy, as further discussed in Chapter 8, is also protected by case law in most states. Such privacy claims generally assert that the employer either improperly intruded upon the employee's "seclusion" or publicly disclosed private facts. For instance, a drug-testing program that required the observation of employees urinating was found to violate employee privacy. An employee who was terminated after two positive urinalysis tests under this program was awarded $125,000. (*Kelley v. Schlumberger Technology Corp.*)

In the preemployment testing area, courts have generally upheld an employer's right to (1) reject an applicant based on a positive drug test; (2) deny employment to an applicant refusing to submit to a preemployment drug test; and (3) condition an offer of employment on the passage of a drug test. For example, an applicant who interviewed for a district sales manager position was conditionally offered the position, subject to passage of a preemployment drug test. After taking the test, the applicant was notified that it indicated the presence of marijuana and his conditional offer was revoked. The applicant contested the propriety of the employer's actions on a variety of grounds including violation of his privacy rights. The court found that the preemployment drug test struck a balance between "the interest of the employer" in hiring drug-free employees, and "the legitimate privacy concerns of the prospective employee," and was therefore proper. The establishment of a testing program after commencement of employment also was found not to violate an employee's privacy rights. The court suggested two alternatives to at-will employees who receive notice that a drug-testing program was being imposed: accept the drug-testing program or quit. Merely continuing work after the drug program was announced was sufficient to constitute acceptance of the changed terms and conditions of employment. In short, the employee remained an at-will employee. (*Jennings v. Minco Technology Labs*)

Employers' use of random drug testing remains the most fertile ground for claims of privacy rights violations. Two cases illustrate the different approaches taken by courts in assessing the propriety of random drug testing. In one case, an employee refused to be tested under a random testing policy and was terminated. She sued, alleging that she was wrongfully terminated and that the random drug-testing program violated her privacy rights. The court rejected her claims, stating that based on the public policy in favor of eradicating drug use in the workplace and the absence of any contrary state legislation, the employer's random testing policy was "reasonable and [did] not violate the public policy of this state." (*Blankenship v. South Carolina Elec. & Gas Co.*)

In another case, a California court was more sympathetic to an employee's privacy rights claims. Following six years of at-will employment, a computer programmer in the engineering department was instructed to provide a urine sample and consent to substance testing. She refused to consent to the drug test, was fired, and sued on various grounds including violation of her privacy rights. In assessing the validity of the employer's random drug-testing scheme, the court determined that a private employer is bound by California's constitutional privacy rights provisions and can justify privacy rights encroachments only if the imposition is premised on a compelling employer interest. In this instance, given that the employee was a computer programmer, the court found that the employer's interest in railroad safety was not sufficient to warrant its intrusion into the programmer's privacy rights. (*Luck v. Southern Pac. Transp. Co.*)

5. Contract

Promises made by employers may be grounds for contract claims by employees challenging the implementation of drug and alcohol policies. These circumstances will be rare, however, as the employment-at-will doctrine, which is the law in all 50 states, allows for the termination of employees for any or no reason with certain limited, although ever-increasing, exceptions. Unless the employer has imposed on itself through words or actions a higher standard for termination, failure to abide by, or a violation of, a drug and alcohol policy will serve as a proper basis for termination. This is particularly so where a policy expressly required compliance and stated that discipline will result for failure to comply. For example, breach-of-contract claims were rejected when employees violated company policy which expressly provided that termination could result if the employee failed to:

- Take a drug or alcohol test; (*Greco v. Halliburton Co.*)
- Disclose the ingestion of any prescribed medicine and sign a consent form releasing this information to the employer; (*Mares v. Conagra Poultry Co.*) or
- Abide by company policy providing that drug use would result in termination. (*Horne v. J.W. Gibson Well Serv.*)

Courts have also rejected breach-of-contract claims where an offer of employment was revoked based on a positive drug test result (*Jevic v. Coca Cola Bottling Co.*) or the testing policy was implemented after employment commenced. (*Blankenship v. South Carolina Elec. & Gas Co.*)

Employees have successfully stated breach-of-contract claims where an employer allegedly failed to comply with the terms of its own testing policy (*Johnson v. Carpenter Technology Corp.*) or where the employer promised to terminate employees only for good cause and the issue was raised of whether termination for refusing to submit to drug testing constituted good cause. (*Luck v. Southern Pac. Transp. Co.*)

6. Public Policy

Terminations in violation of a clear mandate of public policy, that is, policy embodied in constitutional, statutory, or case law, are prohibited in a growing number of states. (See Chapter 7 for a discussion of the public policy exception.) Courts have generally found that drug- and alcohol-testing programs implemented by private employers do not violate public policy. Consequently, courts have rejected public policy claims based on:

- An employee's refusal to take a drug test; (*Blankenship v. South Carolina Elec. & Gas Co.*)
- The revocation of an offer of employment based on positive test results; (*Jevic v. Coca Cola Bottling Co.*) or
- The termination of employment based on a positive test result. (*Horne v. J.W. Gibson Well Serv.*)

A notable exception is the decision by the West Virginia Supreme Court limiting drug testing in private employment to circumstances in which the employer has a reasonable, good-faith, objective suspicion of employee drug use or where the employee's job responsibility involves public safety. The court in that case, balancing the employees' interest in individual privacy against the employer's right to ensure a safe and efficient workplace, rejected the employer's mandatory random testing program. (*Twigg v. Hercules Corp.*) New Jersey has adopted a similar balancing test that permits drug testing where the "employees' duties are so fraught with hazard that his or her attempts to perform them while in a state of drug impairment would pose a threat to co-workers, to the workplace, or to the public at large." (*Hennessey v. Coastal Eagle Point Oil Co.*) In contrast, courts in other states, including Texas (*Jennings v. Minco Technology Labs*) and South Carolina (*Blankenship v. South Carolina Elec. & Gas Co.*), have rejected public policy claims challenging random drug-testing programs on the ground that public policy does not prohibit and, indeed, may encourage such testing.

7. Infliction of Emotional Distress

Most states recognize claims for the intentional or negligent infliction of emotional distress for conduct so outrageous and extreme as to go beyond all possible bounds of decency. (See Chapters 7 and 9 for a full discussion of these emotional distress claims.)

Emotional distress claims related to drug and alcohol testing most often will be based on outrageous conduct related to the manner of testing, the manner in which the resulting discipline or termination was carried out, or the inappropriate disclosure of test results or alleged drug or alcohol use. For example, a court sustained a negligent infliction of emotional distress claim based on a drug-testing program that required employer representatives to observe employees urinating. (*Kelly v. Schlumberger Technology Corp.*) In contrast, the request that employees list medications used prior to testing was ruled not to constitute outrageous conduct. (*Mares v. Conagra Poultry Co.*)

The mere discharge from employment does not constitute outrageous conduct. For example, termination for refusing to sign a drug-testing consent form was found not to constitute outrageous conduct. (*Mares v. Conagra Poultry Co.*)

Terminations conducted in an outrageous manner, however, may support an emotional distress claim. For example, an employee who was chased and strangled by agents of the employer stated a claim for emotional distress. (*Bradbury v. Phillips Petroleum Co.*) In contrast, an employee's emotional distress claim was dismissed when she was suspended for refusing to take a random drug test, required to turn in her employee badge, and escorted from the building. (*Blankenship v. South Carolina Elec. & Gas Co.*)

An inappropriate or overbroad disclosure of test results or charges of drug or alcohol use or abuse could, in extreme circumstances, present a basis for an emotional distress claim. However, in one case, labelling employees illegal drug users when terminating them and failing to keep test results confidential were ruled to be insufficient to state an emotional distress claim. (*DiTomaso v. Electronic Data Sys.*)

D. Federal Regulation of Private-Sector Employers

Federal regulatory agencies are empowered to impose drug- and alcohol-testing requirements on private employers working in regulated industries whose work affects public safety, health, and welfare. Federal contractors and grantees are also required to promulgate drug policies and make a good-faith effort to maintain a drug-free workplace. A brief review of these federal mandates follows.

1. Federally Regulated Industries

Under the Omnibus Transportation Employee Testing Act of 1991, employers whose employees operate aircraft, public transportation, or commercial motor vehicles must test their employees for the use of alcohol or illegal drugs. The Department of Transportation and agencies within the Department such as the Federal Aviation Administration and the Federal Highway Administration must help ensure public safety by issuing rules and regulations requiring that airlines, railroads, commercial motor carriers, and operators of mass transportation conduct preemployment, reasonable suspicion, random, and postaccident drug and alcohol testing of employees performing safety-sensitive functions. These agencies may also require that affected employers conduct periodic testing of their employees in safety-sensitive positions. Further, this law requires that:

- Individual privacy in the collection of the sample be preserved to the fullest extent possible;
- Procedures be established ensuring the reliability and accuracy of the testing by laboratories;
- The confidentiality of the test results be preserved; and
- The selection of employees be in a nondiscriminatory manner.

The Department of Transportation has issued regulations (DOT Regulations) under the Omnibus Transportation Employee Testing Act designed to eliminate drug and alcohol use among a wide variety of transportation workers, including intrastate and interstate drivers of commercial, mass transit, and government vehicles. The DOT Regulations apply to approximately 7.4 million employees and preempt only those state drug-testing laws that would interfer with DOT compliance. Accordingly, if a state has drug-testing requirements more expansive than those of the DOT, the employer must be sure to comply with both state law and DOT Regulations.

Public and private employers who own or lease "commercial motor vehicles," or assign persons to operate such vehicles, are among those covered by the DOT Regulations. A "commercial motor vehicle" is a motor vehicle used in commerce to transport passengers or property (1) with a gross combination weight rating of 26,001 or more pounds inclusive of a towed unit with a gross vehicle weight rating of more than 10,000 pounds; (2) with a gross vehicle weight rating of 26,001 or more pounds; (3) designed to transport 16 or more passengers, including the driver; or (4) of any size used in the transportation of materials found to be hazardous for the purposes of the Hazardous Materials Transportation Act and required to be placarded under the Hazardous Materials Regulations. Among the employers not covered by the DOT Regulations are those employers who exclusively employ drivers not subject to commercial driver's license requirements, farmers, emergency response drivers, and firefighters exempted from commercial driver's license requirements; those employers subject to the Federal Transit Administration's alcohol and controlled substances testing requirements; and certain Department of Defense agencies that employ only active duty military personnel.

Any driver who operates a "commercial motor vehicle" and is subject to commercial driver's license requirements is required to submit to federally mandated drug and alcohol testing. Covered drivers may be full-time, regularly employed drivers; casual, intermittent, or occasional drivers; leased drivers; or independent contractors who are either directly employed by or under lease to an employer or who operate a commercial motor vehicle at the direction of or with the consent of an employer.

Covered employers must conduct preemployment, reasonable suspicion, random, postaccident, return-to-duty, and post-rehabilitation testing using DOT-specified procedures. Periodic testing is no longer required. A breath test is to be used in connection with alcohol screening; for controlled substances tests, a urine sample will be used. An employer must notify a driver, before administering a drug or alcohol test, that the test is required under the DOT Regulations. Testing for substances other than those specified by the DOT is strictly prohibited. The Regulations require "split sample" testing, that is, the splitting of a single urine sample into two, with the second vial being preserved in order to confirm, if required, the results of the first test.

Covered employers are also required to promulgate a policy on the misuse of drugs and alcohol and to distribute the policy prior to conducting any newly required test under the DOT Regulations. The policy must, in part, identify the categories of drivers subject to DOT testing requirements, provide notice of specific conduct prohibited by the Regulations, and specify the types of drug and alcohol testing to be conducted and the methods of testing. Employers must ensure that each covered driver signs a statement certifying receipt of the policy. The original of the signed statement must be maintained by the employer.

The DOT Regulations require that drivers who have engaged in drug or alcohol use in violation of the DOT standards be advised of resources available to resolve substance abuse problems. Thereafter, such drivers must be evaluated by a substance abuse professional. Employers should have on hand the names, addresses, and telephone numbers of substance abuse professionals and treatment programs. The DOT Regulations require covered employers to maintain records including, but not limited to, drug and alcohol test results, documented refusals by drivers to submit to required testing, and driver referrals to substance abuse professionals. In some instances, records must be maintained for at least five years.

Employers and drivers found to be in violation of the regulations may be subject to civil forfeiture penalties of up to $10,000.

2. Federal Contractors and Grantees

The Drug-Free Workplace Act of 1988 (DFWA), the text of which is included as Appendix D to this text, applies to any employer obtaining procurement contracts exceeding $25,000 from the federal government, and to anyone receiving federal grants.

Employers subject to its coverage must certify that they will establish and maintain drug-free workplaces. DFWA neither requires nor prohibits drug testing and does not create any protected status for applicants or employees who are substance abusers.

Specifically, the DFWA requires employers to implement antidrug programs that:

- Notify employees that illicit drugs and alcohol are banned from the workplace;
- Specify the disciplinary actions an employee will face for violating the policy, ranging from termination to completion of a rehabilitation program; and
- Institute programs informing employees about the drug-free policy and discussing treatment alternatives.

Payments forthcoming under a federal agency contract or grant are subject to suspension or termination if (1) a false certification claim is made, (2) the certification is violated through failure to effectuate DFWA's requirements, or (3) sufficient numbers of employees are convicted of criminal drug violations to indicate that a good-faith effort was not made to attain a drug-free workplace.

The Department of Defense (DOD) has issued specific regulations requiring that employers doing business with the DOD maintain a program for attaining a drug-free workforce. These regulations are intended to eliminate drug use both in and out of the workplace and support the use of random testing. Compliance with the DOD regulations is accomplished by the insertion of "affirmation clauses" within the contract of every contractor to the DOD, where the work (1) involves access to classified information or (2) is necessary to protect national security or the health and safety of those using or affected by the product or performance of the product. In addition, DOD regulations require that if the affirmation clause is violative of a collective-bargaining agreement, a good-faith effort must be made to renegotiate it when the agreement expires.

Among the obligations employers must agree to fulfill is a program for achieving a drug-free workforce. These programs should include:

- Employee assistance programs;
- Training of supervisors to assist and identify employee drug use;
- Identification of drug users, including the use of reasonable suspicion, postaccident, and random testing; and
- After-care testing of employees in "sensitive positions."

E. Testing of Union Employees

Employers with a unionized workforce cannot unilaterally implement or modify a drug- or alcohol-testing program. The employer has an obligation to bargain in good faith with the union over decisions to implement a testing program affecting current employees, including who to test, how the testing should be conducted, and the discipline to be accorded for a positive drug or alcohol test.

Organized labor's response to the implementation of testing has varied, from acquiescence to strong resistance. The variables influencing a particular union's position include the industry involved, the nature of work involved, whether public safety or health is implicated in the work, the strength of the union's bargaining position, and whether the testing is required by law. In one case, an employer posted a notice stating that drug and alcohol tests would be given whenever treatment was sought for injuries. Under the collective-bargaining agreement the employer was allowed to test only newly hired employees. The unilateral implementation of drug testing was found by the National Labor Relations Board (NLRB) to be a mandatory subject of bargaining because it was "plainly germane to the 'working environment'" and it was not "among those managerial decisions that lie at the core of entrepreneurial control." (*Johnson-Bateman Co.*)

Negotiations with unions are not required, however, when an employer implements a preemployment drug or alcohol testing program for applicants. The NLRB ruled that, unlike the testing of employees, the testing of applicants does not "vitally affect" the terms and conditions of employment. (*Star Tribune*)

As their members' exclusive bargaining representative, unions possess the power to enter into agreements regarding the drug and alcohol testing of their members. In one instance a union advanced a grievance on behalf of a member who alleged he was randomly tested in violation of his Fourth Amendment rights. The union entered into a settlement with the employer whereby the discharged employee—who had tested positive for marijuana—would be reinstated with partial back pay if he agreed to future drug testing. The employee refused to abide by the agreement's drug-testing provisions and sued both the union and his employer. The court held that the union could waive the employee's right against otherwise unreasonable random drug testing. Consequently, the employee was bound by the negotiated settlement. (*Bolden v. Southeastern Pennsylvania Transp. Auth.*) Such a waiver, however, must be "clear and unmistakeable." (*Johnson-Bateman Co.*)

The remedy for unlawful, unilateral implementation of a drug- or alcohol-testing policy generally is to rescind the policy and bargain with the union before implementing a new drug-testing program. In addition, an employee who was discharged or disciplined under the program may be reinstated with back pay or have his or her discipline rescinded. (*Storer Communications Inc.*)

F. Guidelines for Establishing Workplace Drug- and Alcohol-Testing Programs

There is no "best" way for an employer to draft and adopt a drug- and alcohol-testing policy. The unique characteristics of each employment environment will necessarily dictate the appropriateness of a given testing program. Initially, an employer must decide whether a testing program would serve an important purpose in that workplace with due concern for the privacy interests of applicants and employees. If the answer is yes, then the following factors should be considered when implementing a drug- or alcohol-testing program.

1. Drafting the Policy

The program should reflect the needs of the organization, focusing on the perceived problems, the program's goals, the company's available resources, and anticipated risks associated with implementing the testing policy.

2. Articulate Standards

A policy should clearly articulate (1) the prohibited substances and uses, (2) employees subject to the policy, (3) the type of testing to be used, (4) the settings under which testing will occur, and (5) the discipline for violating the policy or for testing positive.

3. Communication

The employer's drug- and alcohol-testing policy is best communicated to employees well in advance of its effective date, and should be included in employment applications and employee handbooks, rules, and notices. The policy's contents also should be communicated directly to employees at the time of orientation and periodically thereafter.

4. Supervisor Training

Supervisors should be trained to apply the policy properly. For example, supervisors should be trained to recognize the symptoms of alcohol and drug abuse and to properly document workplace disciplinary matters as they involve drug or alcohol use.

5. Procedural Guidelines

The program should adopt standardized procedures for administering the tests in a private and dignified manner and for monitoring the chain of custody of samples.

6. *Confidentiality*

Test results and claims of violation of the policy are best kept confidential. Information should be conveyed only on a need-to-know basis.

7. *Monitoring*

An employer should continually assess and monitor its program to ensure consistent application of its requirements and to ascertain whether modifications are needed.

II. HONESTY TESTING

Employers have a legitimate interest in determining the honesty of job applicants and employees. Employee theft is estimated to cost U.S. businesses more than $40 billion annually. Applicants and employees, however, have an equally substantial right not to have their privacy unduly infringed upon. Where the line is drawn between these two interests has long been in contention.

This section reviews the legal ramifications of the leading truth-verification devices such as polygraphs and what are known as paper and pencil honesty tests. In addition, employers should be aware that other truth-verification devices, such as voice stress analyzers, may be subject to the same legal limitations as polygraph tests and paper and pencil integrity tests. The federal government and most states regulate the use of lie detectors. Some states, such as New Jersey, address simply "lie detectors," or, in the cases of Maine and Michigan, "polygraph examinations." In contrast, New York regulates only "psychological stress evaluators" (which seek to detect deception as shown by changes in the subject's voice), and Wisconsin's law bars the psychological stress evaluator and other non-polygraph lie detectors.

A. Polygraphs

Polygraphs were the primary tool by which employers tested employee honesty until 1988 when Congress enacted the Employee Polygraph Protection Act (EPPA). The text of EPPA is re-produced as Appendix E to this text. Basically, the EPPA prohib-its most private employers (federal, state, and local governments are exempt) from requiring applicants or employees to submit to polygraph examinations. Three major exceptions exist.

First, employers who manufacture, distribute, or dispense controlled substances may administer polygraphs to job appli-cants who will have access to the substances and to employees where there has been a loss of the controlled substances.

Second, polygraphs may be administered to applicants for employment with private security firms providing services for industries whose businesses pose a public safety or security risk such as public transportation operations, water supply facilities, and facilities engaged in the production, transmission, or distri-bution of electric or nuclear power. Also included within this exception are private security firms hired to protect currency, negotiable instruments, precious commodities or instruments, or proprietary information.

Third, polygraphs may be administered as part of an ongo-ing investigation of a theft, embezzlement, or incident of sabo-tage that caused economic loss to the employer. The employer must have a reasonable suspicion that the employee was involved in the theft. Reasonable suspicion requires more than a general-ized suspicion about a group of employees. Rather, the employer must reasonably suspect a particular employee. Critically, the economic loss must be suffered by the employer rather than an employee. In one case, the court found that a hospital did not suffer a loss within the meaning of the EPPA because the theft of a doctor's money from his locker did not result in an economic loss to the hospital's business. *(Lyle v. Mercy Hosp. Anderson)*

Under the ongoing investigation exception, the employer must (1) give the employee written notice of the incident and the basis for testing the employee; (2) identify the loss; (3) demon-strate that the employee had access to the property; (4) provide the basis for the reasonable suspicion; (5) have the notice signed by a person authorized to bind the employer; and (6) retain the notice for three years. Failure to provide proper notice that meets all the statutory requirements will subject the employer to liabil-ity under the EPPA.

The EPPA places further procedural barriers before employers attempting to administer polygraphs, whether on a voluntary or involuntary basis, even in those limited settings in which polygraph examinations may be allowed. For example, before administering the test the employer must:

- Provide the employee with written notice that states, among other things, that the individual has a right to an attorney;
- Obtain a written statement from the employee acknowledging his or her rights under the EPPA;
- Provide the individual with an opportunity to review all questions to be asked during the test; and
- Refrain from conducting a test where a medical condition may cause abnormal reactions during the examination.

The examiner must be licensed by the state and may not administer more than five examinations per day. Polygraph examinations must last for 90 minutes or more and may be terminated at any time by the person being tested. The examiner may ask only questions presented to the individual before the test which may not be unduly intrusive.

The results of a polygraph may not be the sole reason for an employment decision. Before acting on those results, the employer must conduct a further interview with the individual, provide the employee with a copy of the questions and answers, and provide the employee with a written copy of the conclusions reached from the test. Rights under the EPPA may not be waived unless part of a written settlement of a pending matter. The Secretary of Labor is empowered to enforce the statute by seeking an injunction or civil damages of up to $10,000 for each violation.

State laws and union agreements that provide greater protection to employees or applicants are not preempted and, therefore, provide additional legal rights. States with their own polygraph laws applicable to private employers include Alaska, California, Connecticut, Delaware, Hawaii, Idaho, Illinois, Iowa, Maine, Maryland, Massachusetts, Michigan, Minnesota, Montana, Nebraska, Nevada, New Jersey, Oregon, Pennsylvania, Rhode Island, Tennessee, Utah, Vermont, Washington, West Virginia, and Wisconsin, as well as the District of Columbia.

Furthermore, the administration of polygraph examinations may subject employers to additional legal claims based upon privacy and related claims. For example, an employee who was discharged after being pressured into taking a polygraph test that invaded his privacy was awarded $358,000 for lost wages and benefits and $50,000 for defamation. The jury concluded that the employer had invaded the employee's privacy by inquiring about his off-the-job drug use and had defamed the employee by stating that he was terminated for using drugs. (*O'Brien v. Papa Gino's of Am.*) In another case, a federal court found that the state had intruded upon the privacy and associational interests of a police officer candidate, despite the fact that the inquiry was founded on a legitimate state interest, where the polygraph examiner conducted an unbounded, standardless inquiry into the candidate's sex life. (*Thorne v. City of El Segundo*)

Violations of polygraph laws may also provide the basis for a public policy claim (see Chapter 7 for a full discussion) entitling employees to punitive damages where the employer was found to have acted with an "evil motive or intent." In one case, $4 million in punitive damages was awarded to employees who were constructively discharged for refusing to submit to polygraph examinations. (*Moniodis v. Cook*) The jury found that the employer punished employees who refused to take polygraphs as part of an investigation into inventory shortages by changing their work hours and locations so as to make continued employment fruitless. Further, the employer was shown to have been aware of the statutory prohibition against requiring employees to submit to polygraph tests, but that it consciously elected to disregard the law.

B. Paper and Pencil Integrity Tests

The EPPA effectively eliminated polygraphs as a practical truth-verification device in most circumstances. As a result, a growing number of employers has sought alternative methods of assessing employee honesty. An increasingly popular approach is the use of what are called "paper and pencil" integrity or honesty tests. These tests, which require responses to a written questionnaire, are designed to identify individuals with a propensity for theft or counterproductive behavior. Employers then make employment decisions based on the results. The approaches used in these honesty tests vary. "Overt tests" ask directly about specific manifestations of dishonesty; personality-based tests seek to predict a range of work behaviors; "veiled purpose tests" purport to measure an individual's attitude toward dishonesty. An example of an overt test question would be, "Do you think it is stealing to take small items home from work?" A sample question from a personality-based test might be, "How prompt are you?" An example of a veiled purpose test question would be, "Are you a risk-taker?"

In 1991, the Office of Technology Assessment issued a report to Congress entitled *Truth and Honesty Testing*, in which it concluded that it is not possible, based on current research, to determine the validity of honesty tests in accurately predicting dishonesty. The report suggested four reasons why employers use honesty tests:

- To stem employee theft;
- To avoid "negligent-hiring" suits (See Chapter 9);
- To screen employees cost-effectively (it costs as little as $8 to administer each test); and
- To replace polygraphs that were effectively banned by the EPPA.

The report noted, however, that such tests raised serious questions of privacy and confidentiality. The report further questioned the appropriateness of predicting dishonesty where it is known that substantial numbers of test takers will be misclassified (studies reported that 73 to 97 percent of those identified as potentially dishonest did not steal from their employers).

Honesty tests are currently legal under federal law. A few states prohibit or limit the use of honesty and integrity examinations. Massachusetts prohibits employers from requesting job applicants to take written examinations that render a diagnostic interpretation of honesty. Rhode Island permits the use of honesty tests only to the extent that the results of such tests do not form the "primary basis" for employment decisions. While a

Minnesota statute prohibits the use of any "test purporting to test the honesty of any employee or prospective employee," the Minnesota Supreme Court has interpreted the statute to apply only to those tests that "measure psychological changes in the subject tested." (*Spannaus v. Century Camera*) A Wisconsin appellate court reached a similar conclusion under that state's polygraph law. (*Pluskota v. Roadrunner Freight Sys*)

Honesty tests would be subject to challenge if it was shown that they disproportionately impacted protected groups such as women or minorities. To date, no such claim has succeeded.

Honesty tests are also potentially vulnerable to legal challenge based on invasion of privacy grounds, particularly because the tests inquire about information and perceptions not clearly related to job performance. At least one court has ruled that intrusive questions posed to a job applicant in an employment questionnaire, if answered, would constitute an invasion of privacy. (*Cort v. Bristol Meyers Co.*)

Employers using honesty tests are less likely to invade an applicant's or employee's privacy and are better positioned to defend against legal challenges to such testing by complying with the following guidelines:

- Use only those tests that have been developed and validated for the positions that are being filled. Request and review a copy of the tester's validation study;
- Use such tests only for those positions in which honesty is clearly related to the job function;
- Eliminate test questions that are inherently offensive, and request support from the testing company for dubious questions;
- Monitor test results for potential adverse impact on protected groups;
- Administer tests in pleasant, nonthreatening, and private settings;
- Carefully select and train qualified staff to administer the tests;
- Do not rely on test results solely or even principally in making employment decisions;

- Ensure the confidentiality of test results and establish written guidelines on matters related to test security and data protection;
- Limit disclosure of test results to those with a demonstrable need to know, and do not disseminate test results to third parties without the consent of the test taker;
- Do not enter test results in personnel data bases or, in the alternative, ensure that data protection security measures limit access to test results;
- Periodically audit the procedures followed in administering such tests;
- Require applicants to sign an informed consent agreement and retain such forms;
- Determine the tester's willingness and ability to provide support in any litigation that may be brought based on the test, as well as his or her willingness to enter into a "hold harmless" agreement indemnifying the employer for any resulting liability;
- Obtain and comply with the Model Guidelines for Pre-Employment Integrity Testing Programs published by the Association of Personnel Test Publishers (1990); and
- Avoid characterizing those who fail to pass such tests as dishonest.

III. PERSONALITY OR PSYCHOLOGICAL TESTS

Honesty and integrity tests are, in the view of many, merely subsets of the broader personality or psychological tests available to employers. The latter seek to assess a wider range of personality traits and to predict a wider range of behaviors. Personality tests were developed principally for the mental pathology field to help identify mental disorders and to measure motivation. Their use in employee-selection matters is controversial, since personality tests tend to have low false-positive rates (test results designating a test taker as ill where in fact no illness is present) but a higher rate of false-negatives (indicating suitability where the individual is not suitable for a job or task). Among the most popular personality tests are the Sixteen Personality Factors Test, the Minnesota Multiphasic Personality Inventory, and the California Psychological Inventory.

Public employees in sensitive positions such as firefighters (*McKenna v. Fargo*) and school teachers (*Murray v. Pittsburgh Bd. of Educ.*) have traditionally been required to submit to personality or psychiatric examinations. Courts have reasoned that the public's compelling interest in employing emotionally stable individuals in sensitive positions outweighs the privacy interests of a government employee or applicant for a position. When the psychological exam goes beyond the normal bounds of such exams, however, the scales may tip in favor of the employee's interests. In one case, a police officer who was implicated, but never formally charged, in a child sex abuse case was instructed by a city manager to take a psychological test that included a penile plethysmograh test to measure his sexual arousal patterns. The court found that although the officer's privacy rights were not violated, the municipality may have violated the employee's constitutional rights. (*Harrington v. Almy*) When the case went to trial, a jury awarded the officer $960,000 in damages. (*Harrington v. Cole*)

Few cases have been reported in which a private employer's use of personality or psychological tests has been challenged. In one case, a journeyman carpenter hired to work in a nuclear power plant was required to take a psychological evaluation test so that he could enter vital areas of the plant unescorted. The test revealed that he had a "high likelihood" of being an alcoholic and he was terminated. The court ruled that a trial was required to determine whether, under Michigan's disability law, a particular propensity such as alcoholism affected the carpenter's ability to perform the requirements of the job. (*Adkerson v. MK-Ferguson Co.*) In the leading case, a California appeals court ruled that a psychological test that inquires into religious beliefs and sexual orientation violates the California Constitution's right of privacy and state antidiscrimination law. (*Soroka v. Dayton Hudson Corp.*) In that case, applicants for security officer positions were required to take a psychological test composed of 704 true–false questions including the following:

- "I feel sure there is only one true religion";
- "My soul sometimes leaves my body";
- "I believe in the second coming of Christ";
- "I believe that there is a Devil and a Hell in afterlife";
- "My sex life is satisfactory";
- "I am very strongly attracted to members of my own sex";
- "I have often wished I were a girl";
- "I have never indulged in any unusual sex practices"; and
- "I like to talk about sex."

The answers to the exam were sent to a consulting psychological firm that rated the test takers' responses based on five traits: emotional stability, interpersonal style, addiction potential, dependability and reliability, and socialization. The consulting firm then recommended whether to hire the applicant based on the ratings on these five traits, and the employer relied on those recommendations.

The court acknowledged that the employer had an interest in hiring emotionally stable security officers, but found that the employer had failed to demonstrate "that a person's religious beliefs or sexual orientation have any bearing on the emotional stability or on the ability to perform [a security officer's] job responsibilities." The court also concluded that the psychological examination violated state law prohibitions against discrimination on the basis of religious beliefs and political activities (the assertion of homosexual rights was viewed as a political right under California law). In a similar case, an employee alleged that the questions on a psychological test were a political litmus test designed to screen out progressive or Libertarian job candidates and was, therefore, a violation of California's prohibition of job discrimination based on political affiliations or participation. There was at least some basis for the claim since the court denied the employer's motion for summary judgment. (*Thompson v. Borg-Warner Protective Servs. Corp.*)

These decisions, while limited to California, will undoubtedly prompt further challenges to the use of personality or psychological tests. Such tests will be most vulnerable to challenge when (1) no compelling need for emotional stability for employment in the relevant position is shown, (2) the test ventures into such treacherous areas as political or religious beliefs or sexual interests or practices, and (3) the employer bases an employment decision wholly or in significant part on the test results.

IV. HIV TESTING AND RELATED ISSUES

Acquired Immune Deficiency Syndrome (AIDS) is caused by a virus (human immunodeficiency virus or "HIV") that attacks the body's immune system, leaving the body incapable of defending itself against certain opportunistic diseases, which, when left unchecked, are sometimes fatal. The virus is transmitted through blood as a result of blood transfusions, or shared needles used by intravenous drug users or through the exchange of body fluids in intimate sexual contact. Of those who are carriers of HIV, only about 25 percent actually develop AIDS. While medications may delay the illness's progress, no cure has yet been found for this deadly disease.

The Centers for Disease Control estimates that as many as 900,000 Americans are infected with HIV. In addition, more than 500,000 Americans have developed AIDS, and it is estimated that at least 300,000 Americans have died from AIDS-related diseases since the epidemic began in 1980.

It is now generally accepted that AIDS may not be transmitted through normal contact in the workplace. Consequently, fears related to transmission of the disease in the workplace may generally not be the basis for an employment decision.

Special concerns may apply in certain industries, such as the health care industry, where transmission of the disease is remotely possible in the normal course of a healthcare worker's duties. Under these circumstances, knowledge of exposure to the disease may be appropriate and may provide support for the testing of employees for exposure to HIV. In one case, a hospital lawfully dismissed a male licensed practical nurse who refused to disclose the results of an HIV test. The federal court reviewing the case concluded that a health care facility could require HIV testing of employees who could potentially transmit the virus to patients. In that case, the nurse was the homosexual roommate of an AIDS patient at the hospital, and the court found that the hospital had a substantial interest in providing a safe environment through infection control. (*Leckelt v. Board of Comm'rs of Hosp. Dist. No. 1*) Even assuming a worker in a sensitive position, such as a health care worker, was a carrier of HIV or had AIDS, a reasonable accommodation could be made in most circumstances and would be required under most applicable disability laws.

A. Testing for HIV

The tests currently in use do not test for the presence of the disease, but rather verify whether the individual is a carrier of HIV through detection of antibodies to the virus in the individual's system. The utility of such tests is lessened because an individual whose contact with the virus is recent may not have had enough time to develop antibodies and thus the exposure to the virus will not appear in the test results.

AIDS is a protected disability under the ADA and has been found to be protected under a number of state and local laws, including the laws of California, Iowa, Kentucky, Massachusetts, Michigan, Missouri, Nebraska, New Jersey, New York State and City, Pennsylvania, Rhode Island, Washington, and West Virginia. An HIV carrier who has not developed AIDS but is perceived as having the disease is also protected under these laws. Employees would not be protected under federal, state, and local disability laws where the absence of exposure to the virus may be a job requirement as may be the case in certain health care positions. For example, in one case, a court found that a doctor was not qualified to perform as an orthopedic surgeon because he was infected with HIV. (*Scoles v. Mercy Health Corp.*)

A number of states and municipalities, particularly those where the impact of the disease has been most dramatically felt, have adopted laws prohibiting employment discrimination or limiting employer testing for HIV. States with such laws include California, Florida, Kentucky, Massachusetts, Minnesota (state employees only), Nebraska, New Mexico, North Carolina, Pennsylvania (state employees only), Rhode Island, Texas, Washington, and Wisconsin. Municipalities with such laws include Berkeley, Los Angeles, Oakland, San Francisco, San Jose, West Hollywood, and Santa Clara County, California; Denver, Colorado (municipal workers only); Boston, Massachusetts; and Austin, Texas. Other jurisdictions, such as New York state, prohibit the administration of HIV tests without the informed consent of the subject of the test.

Preemployment HIV tests are unlawful under the ADA. Once an applicant is hired, the ADA permits employers to require medical examinations if the examination is given to all employees in a particular category, the results are kept confidential, and the results are not used to discriminate against disabled individuals. Medical examinations may also be administered to confirm an employee's continued ability to perform the essential functions of the position. Finally, medical examinations may be conducted as part of a voluntary employee health program.

B. Potential Legal Challenges

AIDS is a disease that breeds fear, ignorance, and prejudice. Due to the sensitive nature of the topic, many AIDS discrimination suits are settled privately. Thus, it is difficult to determine accurately the number of cases brought by applicants or employees who felt they were discriminated against on the basis of AIDS-related concerns.

Nonetheless, employers face potential legal challenges resulting from HIV testing. For example, disclosure of test results could be the basis for a defamation or invasion of privacy claim.

An employer may be liable for a defamation claim if it conveys information to a third party about an applicant or employee injurious to that person's reputation. For a defamation claim to succeed, the information disclosed must be false. Consequently, an employer who incorrectly informs co-workers that an employee tested positive for HIV may be liable to the employee for defamation.

In contrast, an invasion of privacy claim does not require that the information be false, but rather that it be private and that the disclosure inappropriately intrudes into the seclusion or private life of the individual. In one case, an employer was found to have violated an employee's right of privacy by forcing the employee to disclose that he had been diagnosed as having been exposed to HIV and by disclosing information regarding the employee's medical condition to other employees. (*Cronan v. New England Tel. & Tel. Co.*) As a result of the disclosure, co-workers called the afflicted employee at home and threatened him if he returned to work.

Employees have invoked the Employee Retirement Income Security Act of 1974 (ERISA) as well as the ADA to counter reductions by employers of company-provided medical coverage specifically for AIDS-related treatment. One employer's unilateral modification of health benefits to provide for a $25,000 cap on benefits for treatment of AIDS, compared with an original maximum of $1 million, was deemed not to be a breach of fiduciary duty in violation of ERISA. (*Owens v. Storehouse, Inc.*) In a similar case, a court upheld the reduction of benefits from $1 million to $5,000 and the discontinuance of chemical dependency benefits. (*McGann v. H & H Music*) The Equal Employment Opportunity Commission, however, in its Policy Guidance titled "EEOC Interim Guidance on Application of ADA to Health Insurance," has taken the position that such targeted reductions violate the ADA and has succeeded in settling a number of cases on that ground. (*EEOC v. Mason Tenders Dist. Council Welfare Fund*)

C. Employer Response

Employers often learn that an employee has AIDS or is an HIV carrier indirectly through the submission of medical forms by the employee, through rumors in the workplace, or from the employee directly, rather than through testing. Employers are well-advised to consider such an individual as being legally disabled and to treat that person as any other disabled applicant or employee. In particular, the employer may not consider the disability (in this case, either the disease AIDS or the presence of HIV in the body) in making employment decisions unless it is shown that the individual cannot perform the essential functions of the position as the result of the disability.

In addition, under most disability laws, an employer must reasonably accommodate an employee with a disability such as AIDS. The employer must be prepared to address the fears and concerns of co-workers should an applicant's or employee's AIDS become known, but not allow those fears or concerns to dictate or influence the employer's treatment of the disabled individual. The employer must also keep all information related to the employee's medical condition confidential, and such information should be disclosed only on a need-to-know basis. Finally, an employer's attempt to screen out individuals with HIV by refusing to hire or retain homosexuals or individuals whom the employer perceives to be homosexual would be subject to challenge under laws barring discrimination based upon sexual orientation.

V. GENETIC TESTING

For many years, employers have screened applicants for medical conditions that may interfere with performance of the job. Indeed, the preemployment physical has long been an accepted part of the hiring process.

No longer. The ADA precludes in most instances such preemployment testing, although medical examinations may be conducted after an offer of employment is made. An employer may withdraw an offer of employment based on the results of the examination if the criteria applied were job-related and consistent with business necessity and no reasonable accommodation could be made. In addition, medical examinations may be conducted under certain circumstances during employment to determine fitness for duty if the examinations are demonstrably job-related and consistent with business necessity.

Further, employers may monitor employee health, especially where the employees are exposed to toxic or hazardous substances, to assess compliance with safety and health laws and to meet the obligation to provide safe workplaces.

New technology allows employers to conduct testing to determine genetic predispositions or disorders. Genetic tests in the employment setting identify the presence or absence of traits that have been linked to occupational illnesses or diseases. Scientists have correlated certain genetic traits with workplace harms, for example, sickle-cell anemia may cause fainting at high altitudes. These correlations, however, have not been universally accepted. Further, the accuracy of genetic tests is in dispute. For these and other reasons, genetic testing is less popular with employers than may have previously been the case.

Nonetheless, employer incentives for the genetic screening of employees remains despite the great expense associated with such screening (the testing of one employee may cost as much as $2,000). In particular, by screening out employees who are genetically more susceptible to workplace harms, some employers argue that genetic testing will (1) permit employers to decrease their potential liability for future workplace injuries, (2) provide a safer workplace, (3) increase productivity by reducing absenteeism caused by illnesses associated with genetic susceptibilities to occupational hazards, and (4) better monitor employee exposure to harmful chemicals in the workplace.

Is it unlawful for an employer to make employment decisions based on the results of genetic tests? In most instances, yes. In few circumstances will an employer be able to show that testing the genetic makeup of an applicant or employee is job-related and required by business necessity. One possible exception is the chemical industry where genetic testing has historically been performed, although mostly for epidemiological purposes and monitoring the genetic effect of exposure to chemicals in the workplace, rather than for screening employees. Exceptional cases do exist. For example, an employer demonstrated job-relatedness and business necessity when it terminated an African-American man whose sickle-cell anemia caused a disabling back disease from a position entailing heavy manual labor. The court found the screening test not too "arbitrary, artificial, or unnecessary." (*Smith v. Olin Chem. Corp.*)

Genetic traits that determine eye color, skin pigment, or like characteristics, of course, are not likely to relate to the requirements of a job. Moreover, persons currently disabled as the result of a genetic disease are generally protected under federal and state disability laws. A person who has a genetic predisposition but is not currently affected may be protected under the disability laws as being "perceived" as having a disability.

Employers interested in performing genetic testing face further legal hurdles. Certain states, such as Florida, Iowa, North Carolina, Oregon, Rhode Island, and Wisconsin, expressly prohibit genetic testing by employers or discrimination based on certain genetic traits.

In addition, genetic diseases are often identified with discrete ethnic or racial groups, such as African-Americans and sickle-cell anemia, or Ashkenazi Jews and Tay-Sachs disease. Employers who deny job opportunities to individuals based on genetic diseases principally found in one racial or ethnic group may be subject to claims of discrimination.

Moreover, genetic information is particularly sensitive because it reveals an individual's innate sensitivities and susceptibilities. Inappropriate gathering or disclosure of such information may subject an employer to an invasion of privacy claim.

In sum, most employers who consider the genetic testing of employees generally reject such testing as simply being too intrusive, too costly, or too fraught with potential legal liability.

7

PUBLIC POLICY, WHISTLEBLOWING, AND CIVIC DUTIES

The discretion granted management under the employment-at-will doctrine has traditionally been trumpeted as giving the flexibility it needs to respond to a changing market and its business needs. Such flexibility comes at a high cost, however: the job security and due process interests of employees.

While termination at will remains the basic premise of U.S. employment law, its harsher applications are being challenged with increasing success. One such challenge with broad implications is the claim that an employment decision, typically a termination, violates a clear mandate of public policy.

Public policy, as used in this setting, refers to agreed-upon principles of law that transcend private concerns and serve to define our society's basic social, political, and civil rights. Courts in a majority of states now recognize that the at-will doctrine, while valid in most settings, must give way when a clear mandate of public policy would otherwise be offended. In these states, an employee may challenge his or her discharge under the public policy exception on the ground that it violates a clear mandate of a recognized public policy. The breadth of this exception and its application to any particular set of facts varies from state to state. Perhaps the most difficult problem in applying the public policy exception is in answering the question: What constitutes a clear mandate of public policy?

This chapter will explore the scope of the public policy exception by analyzing the varying definitions of public policy employed by the courts, the application of those definitions, the recognized sources of public policy, the nature of the damages recoverable, and the possible defenses to such claims.

Courts are not alone in limiting employer discretion based on the mandates of public policy or the performance of civic duties. For example, Congress and state legislatures have enacted whistleblower protection legislation and have reaffirmed the importance of certain civic duties such as voting, jury service, and military service by extending limited legal protection to employees performing such duties. These varied legislative protections are addressed in this chapter as well.

I. PUBLIC POLICY EXCEPTION
TO EMPLOYMENT AT WILL

The public policy exception is best viewed as an attempt by some courts to limit the abusive exercise of employers' discretion under the employment-at-will doctrine. Cases brought under this exception typically provide the most sympathetic facts for employees' claims. Employers, in contrast, are hard-pressed to defend actions that, though they are within the bounds of the at-will rule, still offend public policy. Just as the right of free speech may not encompass the right to shout "fire" in a crowded theater, so the right to terminate an employee at will may not include the right to do so in a manner or for a reason that violates a clear mandate of a recognized public policy. This protection generally has been extended as well to employees who are disciplined or suspended for a reason contrary to public policy. (*Garcia v. Rockwell Int'l Corp.*) This protection, however, has been found not to extend to employees covered by a union contract requiring "just cause" for discipline or dismissal for, by definition, these employees are not "employees-at-will." (*Hayes v. Zoological Soc'y of Cincinnati*)

The law has long struggled with the question of proper bounds of the concept of public policy in employment, as it has in other settings. In 1945, the Supreme Court, recognizing that the term "public policy" was vague, concluded that public policy was "to be ascertained by reference to the laws and legal precedents and not from general considerations of supposed public interests." (*Muschany v. United States*) The Illinois Supreme Court has noted, in the context of the public policy exception, that "the Achilles heel of the principle lies in the definition of public policy." (*Palmateer v. International Harvester Co.*)

A. Definition of Public Policy

A claim based on public policy must be rooted in established law and not on individual notions of the public good. Another requirement is a "clear mandate" of public policy, that is, an unambiguous statement of this policy. Further, this recognized policy must indeed be of public and not merely private concern.

1. Clear Mandate

The strongest and most direct statement of public policy is a constitutional, statutory, or regulatory provision or judicial decision specifically supporting the employee's claim. An employee, in referring to such authority in support of a public policy exception claim, is not suing under the cited authority, but rather is asking the court to view that authority as evidence of a public policy offended by the employer's actions.

An employee who can demonstrate that the employer's actions were contrary to a recognized and conspicuous basis for public policy will have satisfied the "clear mandate" requirement of the public policy exception. An issue arises, however, when the source and strength of the alleged public policy is less clear or is based on general notions of public policy without specific application to the facts at hand.

Employees are best positioned to invoke the public policy exception where they (1) perform an act required by law, (2) refuse to perform an act that the law prohibits, or (3) exercise a right that an employee is privileged by law to perform. (*Smith v. Calgon Carbon Corp.*)

a. *Act Required By Law* An employee who performs an act required by law and who is disciplined or discharged for doing so may claim the protection of the public policy exception. The following acts taken in furtherance of a legal duty to act have been found by courts to satisfy the clear mandate requirement:

- Complying with a request by the police that a movie theater projectionist empty the theater so that a burglary could be investigated; (*Girgenti v. Cali-Con, Inc.*) and
- Testifying under subpoena at an unemployment compensation hearing. (*Williams v. Hillhaven Corp.*)

In contrast, courts in some states have taken a narrower view of the scope of enforceable public policy and have ruled that no duty to act existed where:

- The employee exposed his supervisor's alleged violations of antitrust and tax laws where the court found no legal duty to "blow the whistle"; (*Adler v. American Standard Corp.*) and
- A flight engineer informed the Federal Aviation Authority of an airplane's excessive oil consumption. The state court reasoned that no state law right existed for employees terminated for seeking to enforce federal law. (*Rachford v. Evergreen Int'l Airlines*)

Courts differ on the difficult question of whether employees have a legal obligation to protect public health or safety where specific reporting requirements do not exist. An inspector at a nuclear power plant who reports a safety violation is merely performing his or her job; an employee in a position not related to safety who does the same thing is not so authorized. Similarly, a police officer acting to stop a crime is acting within his or her job description. Is there an obligation on an employee to become a citizen crime-fighter by policing an employer's practices?

The split between courts over the breadth of the public policy exception is apparent from the different conclusions reached by courts in Missouri and Illinois facing cases with nearly identical facts. In both cases, employees reported to K-Mart management the theft of services and merchandise by supervisory personnel. The Illinois court recognized this as an act in support of a clear mandate of public policy (*Belline v. K-Mart Corp.*); the Missouri court did not, because no statute, regulation, or constitutional provision was cited obligating the employee to enforce the law. (*Link v. K-Mart Corp.*)

The traditional view is that the law imposes no obligation on employees to take steps to enforce the law or to protect public health and safety. Consequently, courts applying the traditional view have found no clear mandate of law supporting such actions. For example, a warehouse supervisor who alleged that he was terminated for reporting what he believed to be the spill of a hazardous substance from a storage tank into an adjacent river was found not to have been terminated in violation of public policy. The court noted that under Pennsylvania law the supervisor had no responsibility for reporting spills or for disclosing management's cover-up. (*Smith v. Calgon Carbon Corp.*)

Courts in other states have taken a broader view of the scope of enforceable public policy and have upheld claims of "citizen crime-fighters." The Illinois Supreme Court is the leading proponent of this view. (*Palmateer v. International Harvester Co.*) These courts have emphasized that, while no law compels an individual to play such a role, public policy favors enforcement of the criminal code by citizens. The law furthers this end by shielding employees who volunteer information they reasonably believe indicates that crimes have been or are being committed or that serious threats to public health or safety are present. Once a clear mandate of public policy is discerned, in the view of these courts, the only issue is whether the employee's acts directly and significantly further that mandate. Consequently, employees who choose to enforce the law contrary to their employers' wishes and who are terminated as a result are gaining increasing legal protection for their actions.

Courts have sustained claims of a violation of a clear mandate of public policy even though the law did not compel an employee's act, as in the following representative cases where the employee was discharged for:

- Cooperating with a grand jury investigating the employer's anticompetitive business practices; (*Parnar v. Americana Hotels*)
- Assisting law enforcement officials in a "sting" operation to catch liquor store operators who sell liquor to minors; (*Kentucky Farmers Bank v. Nutter*)
- Supplying law enforcement authorities with information concerning the criminal acts of co-workers; (*Palmateer v. International Harvester Co.*) and
- Blowing the whistle on a bank's suspected laundering of Panamanian drug money. (*Potter v. Village Bank of New Jersey*)

Some courts have further determined that the employee need not be correct in his or her claim of illegal or unsafe activities. "[A]n employee's retaliatory discharge claim should not turn on the happenstance of whether the irregular conduct she reports is actually criminal. Public policy favors the exposure of apparently criminal activity. That the questionable conduct may later prove to be authorized and therefore legitimate is not dispositive." (*Belline v. K-Mart Corp.*) Moreover, the magnitude or insignificance of the alleged crime is not a determining factor for those courts taking a broad view of the public policy exception. Courts have sustained public policy claims even where the employee's complaints of illegal behavior involved "paltry sums" (*Belline v. K-Mart Corp.*) or possibly nothing more than theft of a $2 screwdriver. (*Palmateer v. International Harvester Co.*)

b. Refusal to Perform an Illegal Act Most courts recognizing the public policy exception have done so in settings in which employees are terminated for refusing to perform an illegal or arguably illegal act. Some courts, like the Texas Supreme Court, have limited the public policy exception to such circumstances. (*Sabine Pilot Serv., v. Hauck*)

Courts have held that employers violated public policy by terminating employees for refusing to do the following:

- Commit perjury before a state legislature; (*Petermann v. International Bhd. of Teamsters*)
- Violate a mine safety law; (*Shanholtz v. Monongahela Power Co.*)
- Violate state insurance laws; (*Harless v. First Nat'l Bank*)
- Engage in price-fixing; (*Tameny v. Atlantic Richfield Co.*)
- Practice medicine without a license; (*O'Sullivan v. Mallon*)
- Violate federal regulations limiting the number of hours a trucker can drive; (*Walt's Drive-A-Way Serv. v. Powell*)
- Submit false Medicaid information to the federal government; (*Webb v. HCA Health Servs.*)
- Participate in a supervisor's kickback scheme; (*Levito v. Hussman Food Serv.*)
- Provide misleading and erroneous design information to NASA; (*Lorenz v. Martin Marietta Corp.*)
- Conceal the illegal arrest and detention of a prisoner; (*Wagner v. City of Globe*)
- Expose one's buttocks; (*Wagenseller v. Scottsdale Memorial Hosp.*)
- Pump leaded gas into a car equipped to handle only unleaded gas in violation of the Clean Air Act; (*Phipps v. Clark Oil & Refining Corp.*)
- Take a lie detector test made unlawful by statute; (*Perks v. Firestone Tire & Rubber Co.*) and
- Serve alcohol to an intoxicated person. (*Woodson v. AMF Leisureland Ctrs.*)

A few jurisdictions have limited the public policy exception to those circumstances in which the employer affirmatively instructs the employee to violate the law, rather than where the employee passively refuses to perform an illegal act or performs an act required by law. For example, a stockbroker alleged that he was terminated because he discovered widespread insider trading and that his termination violated public policy in that he was required to disclose such information. The court found no violation under North Carolina law because the employer did not prohibit the employee from disclosing the alleged insider trading. (*Haburjak v. Prudential Bache Sec.*) This particularly narrow view, however, has not been widely accepted.

c. Exercise of Legal Right Jurisdictions that recognize the public policy exception have uniformly ruled that employers are not free to terminate employees for exercising a legal right.

The most common setting for such a finding is the termination of an employee for filing a workers' compensation claim. In the first significant case to recognize an exception on this basis, the Indiana Supreme Court reasoned that workers' compensation law establishes an employer's duty to compensate employees for work-related injuries and an employee's right to receive such compensation. An employer who terminates an employee for exercising a legal right such as filing a workers' compensation claim in effect relieves itself of the obligation imposed by law to compensate employees for their workplace injuries. This, in turn, serves to undermine an important public policy. The court concluded, "Retaliatory discharge for filing a workmen's compensation claim is a wrongful, unconscionable act and should be actionable in a court of law." (*Frampton v. Central Indiana Gas Co.*) Many courts have agreed, including courts in Arizona (*Douglas v. Wilson*), Arkansas (*Cross v. Coffman*), Illinois (*Kelsay v. Motorola, Inc.*), Iowa (*Springer v. Weeks & Leo Co.*), Kansas (*Murphy v. City of Topeka*), Kentucky (*Firestone Textile Co. v. Meadows*), Michigan (*Sventko v. Kroger Co.*), Nevada (*Hansen v. Harrah's*), New Jersey (*Lally v. Copygraphics*), North Dakota (*Krein v. Marian Manor Nursing Home*), Pennsylvania (*Bonham v. Dresser Indus.*), Tennessee (*Clanton v. Cain-Sloan Co.*), and West Virginia. (*Pritchett v. Affinity Mining Co.*) In contrast, a public policy exception claim was rejected where the discharge was not in retaliation for the filing of a workers' compensation claim but rather was in accordance with the employer's administrative policy of terminating all employees who miss more than 90 days of work. (*Fergerstrom v. Datapoint Corp.*)

Courts have applied the public policy exception to the exercise of the following legal rights:

- Jury duty service; (*Reuther v. Fowler & Williams, Inc.*)
- Membership in a union; (*Layne v. International Bhd. of Elec. Workers*)
- Contacting state department of labor regarding proper break-time; (*Weissman v. Crawford Rehabilitation Servs.*)

- Bringing a suit for payment of overtime wages; (*McClung v. Marion County Comm'n*) and
- Refusing to take a polygraph examination. (*Perks v. Firestone Tire & Rubber Co.*)

2. Public Versus Private Interest

Courts have, of course, recognized enforceable public policies where the policy is clearly expressed in a constitutional provision, statute, regulation, or judicial opinion, and the discharge offends that policy. Uncertainty arises, however, in settings in which the interest cited by the employee, while perhaps constituting a worthy cause or interest, may not be generally accepted or is one that furthers individual rather than societal interests.

For example, an executive sued under Maryland law alleging that he was terminated following a merger to avoid vesting of an equity interest in the company. The court dismissed the action because the executive could point to no public interest injured by his termination. (*Gould v. Maryland Sound Indus.*) In contrast, a salesman who alleged he was terminated to avoid payment of accrued commissions and vacation pay stated a claim under California law for a violation of public policy. (*Krisak v. Gourmet Coffees of America*) The different results in the two cases can be attributed to the fact that California law strongly mandates the prompt payment of wages and commissions while Maryland law leaves to the parties by way of contract the executive's equity interest in the company.

Courts have explored extensively the distinction between a "public" interest worthy of recognition and a "private" interest that would not support a public policy exception. Not all statutory rights establish "public" rights worthy of recognition under the public policy exception. For example, the Oregon Supreme Court has concluded that the statutory right of a stockholder to examine the company books does not constitute a sufficient public policy to support a public policy exception claim. In that case, the employee was allegedly terminated for exercising his statutory right as a stockholder to review his employer's books, which the court held to be a proprietary and not public right. (*Campbell v. Ford Indus.*)

The California Supreme Court has suggested a helpful test for distinguishing public from private interests, namely, whether the parties could expressly agree that no right or obligation exists. If so, then the interest is likely private. If not, then the right or obligation is likely rooted in law imposed on all and constitutes a public interest. (*Foley v. Interactive Data Corp.*) The following have been found to constitute public rather than private interests:

- Working conditions that present a threat to the health and safety of employees; (*Hentzel v. Singer Co.*)
- Incompetent medical care that resulted in patient deaths; (*Rosenfeld v. Thirteenth Street Corp.*)
- Violations of federal banking law that allegedly resulted in redlining; (*Hicks v. Clyde Federal Sav. & Loan Ass'n*)
- Repeated violations of a state food and drug act; (*Sheets v. Teddy's Frosted Foods*) and
- Preventing unauthorized access to important technical data related to military projects. (*Verduzco v. General Dynamics*)

In contrast, the following "private" interests were found to be insufficient to support a public policy exception claim:

- Arbitrating compensation dispute; (*Shearson Lehman Bros. v. Hedrich*)
- Writing and submitting to a newspaper a letter critical of the employer; (*Schultz v. Industrial Coils*)
- Submitting a letter critical of the employee's superior to the superior's boss; (*Sieverson v. Allied Stores Corp.*)
- Refusing to follow a superior's direction to give a patient an enema; (*Hinson v. Cameron*)
- Reporting to management that a supervisor was taking scrap wood home; (*Zaniecki v. P.A. Bergner & Co.*)
- Testifying at an internal grievance procedure; (*Miller v. SEVAMP, Inc.*)
- Objecting internally to the distribution of contaminated tooth polish; (*House v. Carter-Wallace, Inc.*)
- Engaging in an on-the-job romantic relationship that disrupted operations; (*Somers v. Westours, Inc.*)

- Consulting an attorney regarding a claim against the employer; (*Beam v. IPCO Corp.*)
- Attending law school at night; (*Scroghan v. Kraftco Corp.*) and
- Differing with management on how the company should run its business. (*Cain v. Kansas Corp. Comm'n*)

In one notable case, a branch manager reported to top management that his new supervisor was under investigation by the Federal Bureau of Investigation for embezzlement from his former employer, another bank. The branch manager felt that, inasmuch as his employer did business in the financial community, the company would have a legitimate interest in learning of the suspected criminal activity of a high executive. Instead, the branch manager was told not to discuss rumors and to forget what he heard. Two months later, he was terminated by his supervisor for performance reasons. The branch manager sued, alleging, among other things, a violation of public policy. The California Supreme Court rejected the claim, finding that no public interest had been implicated in his termination. The court inquired, in determining whether to find a public policy exception, whether the discharge "affects a duty which inures to the benefit of the public at large rather than to a particular employer or employee." If the laws at issue merely serve to regulate conduct between private individuals, the court reasoned, no fundamental public interest is implicated. The court concluded that the branch manager's disclosure of alleged criminal activity by his supervisor implicated only the private interest of his employer and, consequently, no exception to the employment-at-will doctrine based on public policy would be found. (*Foley v. Interactive Data Corp.*)

B. Sources of Public Policy

Public policy is not rooted in personal conviction but rather in accepted societal norms evidenced in a constitutional provision, statute, regulation, judicial decision, or, in limited circumstances, a professional code.

1. Constitutional Basis

Constitutions establish general principles by which a society is ordered. These principles tend to be broadly stated so that they may be adapted to the needs of succeeding generations. Statutes, in contrast, establish a body of law to be applied by courts to the facts of particular cases.

Employees relying on constitutional provisions to support public policy exception claims are not suing under that provision but rather are citing it as evidence of an accepted public policy. The argument for this position is clear—any principle appearing in a constitution is, by definition, part of the fundamental law of the land. The problem with such a position is that the vagueness of most constitutional terms allows for differing interpretations. Further, most "rights" appearing in the federal and state constitutions are principally limitations on the actions of government. For example, the "right" of free speech under the First Amendment is actually a bar against enactment by Congress of laws abridging that right. A private citizen is not prohibited by the Constitution from abridging the free speech rights of others. This being the case, do rights that appear in constitutions as limitations only on the actions of government constitute public policies enforceable against private employers? Courts are divided on this question.

Pennsylvania courts have consistently held that constitutional terms may not serve as enforceable public policies necessary for a public policy exception claim. For example, a Pennsylvania appeals court rejected a public policy claim based on the state constitution's prohibition against laws impairing the obligations of contracts, because the dispute was merely between private parties and did not involve the state. (*Booth v. McDonnell Douglas Truck Servs.*) In a second case, a court rejected an employee's claim that his forced resignation, after his employer learned that he had been indicted for theft, violated the constitutional presumption of innocence. (*Cisco v. United Parcel Serv.*) A similar claim based on the right of free speech has also been rejected. (*Yetter v. Ward Trucking Corp.*)

In contrast, a number of other courts have held, in the words of a federal appeals court, that constitutions are "a prime expression of public policy." In that case, an employee alleged that he was discharged for refusing to plant goods on a union shop steward to cause the steward to be fired. The court concluded that based on the protection afforded to union activity under the New Jersey Constitution the employee had stated a public policy claim. (*Radwan v. Beecham Labs.*)

The California Supreme Court found a fundamental public policy in the state constitution against sex discrimination and on that basis upheld an employee's right to bring a public policy claim against a private employer. The court rejected the argument that the relevant constitutional provision applied only to the state as employer as "largely irrelevant; the provision unquestionably reflects a fundamental *public policy* against discrimination in employment—public or private—on account of sex." (*Rojo v. Kliger*) Public policy exception claims have also been upheld based on constitutional, political, and associational freedoms, such as where an employee alleged he was fired for refusing to participate in his employer's lobbying efforts (*Chavez v. Manville Prods. Corp.*); and based on the constitutional prohibition against unlawful search and seizure and the right of privacy, such as where a rental agent refused to snoop through the apartments of tenants who owed money. (*Kessler v. Equity Mgmt.*)

Mere citation to a constitutional provision, of course, is not sufficient to sustain a public policy exception claim, even in those states recognizing a constitutional basis for such claims. For example, the constitutional right of freedom of association was held not to be applicable to a claim that termination resulted from an employee's association with a woman who was not his wife at the employer's convention. The court concluded that, while "freedom of association is an important social right, and one that ordinarily should not dictate employment decisions, . . . the right to 'associate with' a non-spouse *at an employer's convention* without fear of termination is hardly the kind of threat" to a recognized public policy to warrant protection. (*Staats v. Ohio Nat'l Life Ins.*) Similarly, a court rejected a public policy claim based on the constitutional right of free speech when it involved derogatory speech to an employer's customers and business contacts. (*Allen v. Safeway Stores*)

2. Statutory or Regulatory Basis

Employees most commonly cite statutes when alleging that their terminations offended a clear mandate of public policy. Unlike constitutional provisions, statutes are more likely to be narrowly focused and to represent a recent expression of legislative will. They also are more likely to apply to private and not merely public employers. Similarly, regulations issued by agencies with the mandate to enforce a particular law are also a commonly recognized source of public policy.

Workers' compensation laws have been most frequently invoked by employees seeking a remedy for an alleged wrongful discharge based on public policy. (*Springer v. Weeks & Leo Co.*) "The 'sure and certain relief' for an injured workman . . . would be largely illusory and do little for the workman's 'well-being' if the price were loss of his immediate livelihood." (*Krein v. Marian Manor Nursing Home*) The following are additional examples of legislation that has been successfully invoked in support of public policy exception claims:

- Federal antitrust laws; (*Haigh v. Matsushita Elec. Corp*)
- Perjury laws; (*Petermann v. International Bhd. of Teamsters*)
- State food and drug laws; (*Sheets v. Teddy's Frosted Foods*)
- State consumer protection laws; (*Harless v. First Nat'l Bank*)
- Labor laws; (*Glenn v. Clearman's Golden Cock Inn*)
- Jury duty laws; (*Nees v. Hocks*) and
- Environmental protection laws. (*Phipps v. Clark Oil & Ref. Corp.*)

Criminal statutes have generally, though not universally, been accepted as sources of public policy in this context. For example, a bank president alleged that he was terminated because he blew the whistle on the laundering of Panamanian drug money by his bank. The court, relying on federal law requiring the reporting of large cash transactions, found that the bank president was entitled to sue for wrongful discharge based on a violation of public policy. (*Potter v. Village Bank of New Jersey*) Courts have also sustained public policy claims based on a federal antifraud statute, such as when an engineer alleged he was terminated for objecting to inferior work performed by his employer on a NASA project (*Lorenz v. Martin Marietta Corp.*); and on laws against prostitution, such as when an employee alleged that her supervisor harassed her by requesting sex. (*Lucas v. Brown & Root, Inc.*)

The Arizona Supreme Court was confronted with the novel claim that a nurse was terminated for, among other reasons, refusing to "moon" an audience while on a rafting trip with hospital workers including her female boss. The court, professing "little expertise in the techniques of mooning," concluded that the termination offended public policy embodied in the criminal indecent exposure laws. The court found it irrelevant whether an actual violation of the criminal statute had occurred or whether the audience members were voyeurs who would not have been offended, but focused instead on whether important public policy interests embodied in the law were implicated by the mooning. "We are compelled to conclude that termination of employment for refusal to participate in public exposure of one's buttocks is a termination contrary to the policy of this state." (*Wagenseller v. Scottsdale Memorial Hosp.*)

Not all courts have found reference to a criminal statute sufficient to sustain a public policy claim. For example, a Florida appeals court refused to find a wrongful discharge based on state criminal law where a bartender was terminated for refusing to serve a drunk and belligerent patron. The court declined to "act where the legislature has chosen not to" by creating a civil remedy where the legislature has established solely criminal penalties. (*Ochab v. Morrison, Inc.*)

Regulations issued by agencies also may constitute enforceable public policies. (*Winkelman v. Beloit Memorial Hosp.*) For example, the North Carolina Supreme Court found a violation of public policy where an employer discharged a truck driver for refusing to drive more than ten hours per day and refusing to falsify travel logs in violation of Department of Transportation regulations. (*Coman v. Thomas Mfg. Co.*) Similarly, a hospital employee who was terminated for refusing to falsify Medicaid records in violation of federal Medicaid regulations was allowed to sue her employer on public policy grounds. (*Webb v. HCA Health Serv.*)

Mere invocation of a statute or regulation, of course, does not necessarily ensure the success of any employee's public policy violation claim. As noted by one court, "many ancient, anachronistic, and unenforced" statutes remain on the books. (*Peterson v. Browning*) The statute must also be directly applicable by its terms. A statute prohibiting the operation of an aircraft in a reckless manner was held not sufficient to sustain a public policy claim where an employee was discharged for reporting to management alleged safety violations by a pilot. (*Tritle v. Crown Airways*) A statute protecting public employee whistleblowers was held not sufficient to support a public policy claim of a corporate employee discharged for making critical remarks to customers about his employer's products. (*Wagner v. General Elec. Co.*) Further, some state courts have taken the position that they may not enforce public policy as evidenced in federal rather than their own state regulations. For example, three employees claimed they were wrongfully discharged in violation of Kentucky's public policy because the employer used the results of a polygraph exam as the basis for their terminations. The court rejected this claim stating that there was no constitutional or statutory provision in Kentucky limiting the use of polygraphs or their results in employment decisions. (*Stewart v. Pantry, Inc.*)

3. Common Law Grounds

The common law is the judge-made law first imported from Britain to the colonies that formed the basis for U.S. law. Imported with the common law was the tradition of empowering judges to make law and establish public policy. Courts' declarations of public policy, however, unless issued in the context of interpreting a constitutional term, may be overturned by legislative fiat. Further, courts' discretion to declare public policy is limited where the legislative or executive branches have "occupied" the field, that is, heavily legislated or regulated in the area. As the executive and legislative branches expand their reaches, the exclusive domain of the courts has decreased.

The public policy exception was created by the courts. Nonetheless, courts have relied predominantly on constitutional and legislative pronouncements of public policy to uphold such claims. This section concerns itself with those limited situations in which courts both announce and apply public policy without reference to a constitutional or legislative provision. In this regard, the Hawaii Supreme Court has cautioned that "courts should proceed cautiously if called upon to declare public policy" unless they can rely on some prior legislative or judicial expression on the subject. (*Parnar v. Americana Hotels*) Nonetheless, courts have generally recognized judicial decisions as authoritative sources of public policy. (*Thompto v. Coborn's Inc.*)

Law against fraud is one area governed in significant part by the courts. In one case, an employee of the subsidiary of a corporation cooperated in the internal investigation of the parent company and was fired, allegedly because of that cooperation. The employee's public policy exception claim was found to be valid based on the public policy against fraud. (*Schmidt v. Yardney Elec. Corp.*)

In a Kansas case, an employee in the corrections department was allegedly fired, at least in part, because her supervisor believed she was the source of a leak to the *Kansas City Times* that alleged favoritism in the department's hiring process. The court noted that no statute was violated by the employee's termination but that, nonetheless, a "very important source of public information concerning the operating of local and state governments" would be cut off if the termination were permitted on the alleged basis. The court concluded that the hiring of employees based on political connections rather than on qualifications was sufficiently harmful to the public interest to qualify it as the basis for a whistleblowing claim. (*Pilcher v. Board of County Comm'rs*) A court reached a similar decision where a worker at a Defense Department weapons plant complained to management about lax security and the use of inadequate materials in weapons assembly. The court concluded that a fundamental public interest had been invoked in preventing unauthorized persons from obtaining access to important technical data relating to military projects. (*Verduzco v. General Dynamics*)

In contrast, courts have declined to recognize enforceable public policies limiting the employment-at-will doctrine based on an employee's after-hours attendance in law school (*Scroghan v. Kraftco Corp.*), or fighting on the job, allegedly in self-defense. (*Smith v. American Greetings Corp.*)

4. *Professional Codes of Ethics*

Professional codes of ethics have been invoked as a basis of a public policy on which a professional employee can rely. That is not to say that the professions, which draft the codes governing their members, are empowered to establish public policy in the fashion of a legislature. Rather, the code may reflect or embody an enforceable public policy.

The leading decision in this area was issued by the New Jersey Supreme Court in *Pierce v. Ortho Pharmaceutical Corp.* Dr. Pierce, a director of medical research, refused to participate in the testing of an experimental drug that she thought would present a danger to test subjects. The employer disagreed and, in any event, further governmental approvals were required before testing on human subjects would begin. Dr. Pierce, citing the Hippocratic oath as the basis for her position, continued to refuse to participate in the project (though she acknowledged that such participation did not constitute malpractice). She alleged that she was forced to resign. The court acknowledged that "professionals owe a special duty to abide not only by federal and state law, but also by the recognized codes of ethics of their professions. That duty may oblige them to decline to perform acts required by their employers." Nonetheless, the court reasoned, an employee does not have the right to interfere with management's running of its business by refusing to perform a task based on the employee's personal morals. In that circumstance, no public policy would be implicated. The court rejected Dr. Pierce's claim because the Hippocratic oath, in the court's view, was framed too broadly to prohibit the research in that case. The court reasoned that to rule otherwise "would seriously impair the ability of drug manufacturers to develop new drugs according to their best judgment."

The California Supreme Court has similarly adopted a limited public policy claim in a case involving an in-house attorney based on a violation of "explicit and unequivocal ethical norms embodied in the Rules of Professional Responsibility." The court noted that the attorney may not, in raising the claim, disclose any client secrets causing a breach of the attorney–client privilege or the claim would have to be dismissed. (*General Dynamics Corp. v. Superior Court*)

In contrast, the Michigan Supreme Court has ruled, "The code of ethics of a private association does not establish public policy." (*Suchodolski v. Michigan Consol. Gas Co.*) In that case, the court held that an auditor who allegedly was terminated for disclosing practices such as poor fiscal management and sloppy internal accounting procedures, which violated the Code of Ethics of the Institute of Internal Auditors, was not terminated in violation of public policy.

As with other expressions of public policy, the extent to which professional codes may be relied on to support a public policy exception claim depends on the strength and specificity of the relevant code provision, its general applicability and acceptance, and the public rather than private interests that the code provision seeks to protect.

C. Defenses

State law governs defenses to public policy claims. In those states that do not recognize such an action, that in itself is the principal and definitive defense. In those states recognizing a public policy exception to the employment-at-will doctrine in only limited circumstances, an obvious defense is that the employee's claim does not fit within those limited bounds. Further, any public policy claim can be challenged if it is not based on a clear mandate of public policy as evidenced in a statute, constitution, regulation, or judicial decision.

Another defense exists where a public policy recognized by a court is preempted by a legislative body. The doctrine of preemption requires case law to give way to legislation where that legislation "occupies the field." A statute will preempt a court decision if a legislative body has established a pervasive scheme of regulation in the legal landscape in which the court is ruling. In this way, a potential conflict between the legislative and judicial branches may be avoided. For example, the federal law governing pension and welfare benefit plans—the Employee Retirement Income Security Act—has been found to "occupy the field" in this area, and state statutes and judge-made law, such as public policy claims, are generally preempted as a result. (*Ingersoll-Rand Co. v. McClendon*) In contrast, where the legislative enactment is limited and no intent to supersede all law in the area is expressed, courts may make law not contradictory to that enactment. For example, whistleblower laws are generally found not to preempt case law. (*Anderson v. Evergreen Internat'l Airlines*) In this way, judge-made law in the whistleblowing area supplements rather than supersedes legislation.

Public policy claims may be preempted by federal labor law or by a federal or state law addressing the same issue raised by the particular public policy claim. Federal labor law also preempts public policy claims based on rights created in a collective bargaining agreement or on rights requiring interpretation of terms of the agreement. A court will typically conclude in this setting that the just-cause provision in the relevant union contract will need to be interpreted and applied in reaching the merits of the public policy claim. As federal labor law governs such contracts, state law public policy claims will be found preempted in favor of federal law.

A public policy claim is not preempted, however, where "it poses no significant threat to the collective bargaining process and furthers a state interest in protecting the public transcending the employment relationship." (*Young v. Anthony's Fish Grottos*) For example, an employee's claim that he was terminated because he exercised his rights to privacy and free speech under state law by refusing to divulge the names of fellow drug-using employees was held not to be preempted by federal labor law because the state's statute provided the employee "with rights wholly separate from those afforded him under the Collective Bargaining Agreement and which could not be emasculated by such agreement." (*Paridis v. United Technologies*)

In addition, a union employee's public policy claim of retaliation for filing a workers' compensation claim was held by the Supreme Court not to be preempted by federal labor law because the claim was independent of the collective-bargaining agreement. (*Lingle v. Norge Div. of Magic Chef Co.*)

Public policy claims also may be preempted where a federal or state statute governs the issue raised by the claim. For example, the following statutes have been found to preempt public policy claims raising the same issues:

- State human rights law; (*Clay v. Advanced Computer Applications*) and
- Antiretaliation protection for whistleblowers under the federal Energy Reorganization Act. (*Chrisman v. Philips Indus.*)

D. Damages

Damages awardable in public policy cases may include an order of reinstatement, an injunction against continued or future violation of public policy, back pay, front pay, lost benefits, compensatory damages, punitive damages, attorneys' fees, and costs. A minority of states, including Arkansas, limit an employee's recovery to contract damages, that is, those damages that would put the employee in the same position as he or she would have been had public policy not been violated. (*Sterling Drug v. Oxford*) Consequently, future and punitive damages would not be awardable in such states.

Back pay is the most commonly awarded type of remedy in public policy cases. Back pay is the wages an employee would have earned but for the wrongful discharge through the time of the court's decision. Monies earned in the interim from other employment will generally be deducted from those sums.

Reinstatement to the employee's former or a comparable position may be awarded by the court. Among the factors for the court to consider are the feasibility of reinstatement and the employee's prospects for other employment. (*Stafford v. Electronic Data Sys.*) In lieu of reinstatement, a court may award front pay or future damages, that is, prospective damages such as pay for a period designated by the court following its decision.

Compensatory damages include a monetary award for pain and suffering, injury to reputation, expenses related to finding a new job, and other injuries caused by the employer's wrongful acts. For example, an employee who was terminated for filing a workers' compensation claim was awarded $150,000 in compensatory damages for, in the words of the court, "the humiliation of being falsely accused of lying on his employment application and having to see his wife clean houses to support them when he could not obtain other employment." (*Southwest Forest Indus. v. Sutton*) Attorneys' fees and expenses may be awarded to the employee who wins his or her public policy claim.

The following case demonstrates the range of damages awardable for public policy violations. A zoo keeper who witnessed a polar bear attack another keeper told inspectors for the Occupational Safety and Health Administration and the U.S. Department of Agriculture about the unsafe conditions at the zoo. The next day, she was demoted; after she refused the demotion, she was suspended. The zoo keeper obtained an injunction reinstating her to her former position. She later quit after being harassed following her reinstatement. She sued on public policy grounds and won. The court determined that reinstatment was inappropriate under these circumstances and awarded the zoo keeper front pay for one year in lieu of reinstatement, back pay of approximately $3,000, emotional distress damages of $10,000, costs, and attorneys' fees. (*Haynes v. Zoological Soc'y of Cincinnati*)

Punitive damages also may be awarded to punish an employer for outrageous conduct or for conduct that evidences an evil motive or reckless indifference to the rights of others and to deter such behavior in the future. Factors to be considered in assessing punitive damages include the character of the employer's act, the nature and extent of harm to the employee, and the financial status of the employer. Punitive damages were awarded to a barmaid who was discharged for refusing to serve alcoholic beverages to an intoxicated patron on the ground that the employer's actions evidenced a reckless disregard of the consequences to the public of its actions. (*Woodson v. AMF Leisureland Ctrs.*) In a notable case, one million dollars in punitive damages was found not to be excessive where an employer was found to have terminated an employee for filing a workers' compensation claim. (*Southwest Forest Indus. v. Sutton*)

II. WHISTLEBLOWING

The term "whistleblowing" is derived from the act of British constables—called "bobbies"—blowing their whistles after the commission of a crime to warn the public of any danger and to alert other law enforcement officers in the area. An employee whistleblower is one who discloses an employer's illegal or unsafe activities injurious to the public.

Whistleblower cases are a subset of public policy cases. Whistleblower statutes are attempts by legislative bodies to limit the harsher applications of the at-will doctrine to employees' actions in furtherance of public policy. Nonetheless, whistleblower cases, whether based on case law or legislative fiat, are distinct and constitute a significant enough body of law to warrant separate treatment here.

The whistleblower's case is a particularly difficult one for an employer to defend. If the claim is legitimate, the court is confronted with an employer seeking shelter behind the at-will doctrine to further its illegal or unsafe actions. As put by one justice of the Texas Supreme Court, "The judiciary should not ignore those unscrupulous employers who wield the powerful weapon of the pink slip to intimidate workers into silence in order to conceal and perpetuate activities in the workplace that endanger the public." (*Winters v. Houston Chronicle Publishing Co.*) It is no surprise then that whistleblower claims have spawned new rights for employees at the cost of management's full discretion under the at-will doctrine.

These new protections for employees have been both judicially and legislatively established. A review of developments in both domains follows.

A. Judicial Whistleblower Claims

Whistleblower claims make up a large number of challenges to the at-will doctrine on public policy grounds. To succeed, a whistleblower's actions must further a significant public policy and not merely the employee's own private interests or those of the employer. A reasonable belief in the truth of the claim has generally been found to be sufficient whether or not the claim ultimately turns out to have merit.

Whistleblowers have successfully challenged their terminations on public policy grounds where:

- A medical laboratory worker disclosed Medicaid fraud to her employer and law enforcement officials; (*Palmer v. Brown*)
- General Motors supervisors reported defects in brake installation; (*White v. General Motors Corp.*)
- An employee of an optical manufacturer threatened to report the company's failure to obey government regulations in the manufacture of eyeglass lenses; (*Boyle v. Vista Eyewear*)
- A barmaid refused to serve alcohol to an inebriated customer; (*Woodson v. AMF Leisureland Ctrs.*) and
- A record company employee alleged violations by company officials of federal antitrust law. (*Collier v. MCA, Inc.*)

In contrast, whistleblower claims have been rejected by courts taking a narrower view of the public policy exception where:

- A nursing home's removal of life-support systems conflicted with a nurse's religious beliefs; (*Farnam v. CRISTA Ministries*)
- An employee disclosed that his supervisor was receiving kickbacks; (*Adler v. American Standard Corp*) and
- An automobile mechanic was discharged for reporting to the state attorney general that the employer turned back the odometer mileage on a vehicle sold to the mechanic. (*Schriner v. Meginnis Ford Co.*)

One heavily disputed issue in whistleblower cases is whether internal reporting of the alleged illegal or unsafe activities of employers is an act in the *public* interest. Whistleblowers whose claims are made directly to public agencies are more likely to be found to be acting in the public interest. In one New Jersey case, a vice president of production and distribution alleged that his employer distributed a batch of toothpaste knowing it to be contaminated. The vice president expressed his opposition to the distribution of the product at a meeting of company executives and discussed the topic with his immediate supervisor. He made no effort to contact a government agency or otherwise oppose the distribution. He was terminated and alleged it was because of his stand on the distribution of the toothpaste. The court rejected his claim, finding that the vice president "did not take, or threaten to take, effective action to prevent distribution of the product, and in our view his alleged objections to distribution of the contaminated [toothpaste], expressed only to other executives of the corporation, do not provide grounds for maintenance of a wrongful discharge claim." (*House v. Carter-Wallace, Inc.*) Whistleblowers who go directly to a public agency without first attempting to address their claims internally, however, run the risk of claims of disloyalty or the exercise of poor judgment. Courts will often look more favorably on employees who first seek to resolve disputes internally, where the issue may typically be addressed most effectively and expeditiously, prior to "going public" with it unless to do so would be demonstrably fruitless.

B. Whistleblower Legislation

Whistleblower legislation is a patchwork of protection that varies depending on, among other things, the state law applicable to the claim, the industry in which the employee works, the nature of the work performed (for example, whether it is a safety-related position), and whether the employee works in the public or private sector. Legal protection is extended to all private-sector whistleblowers in a limited number of states, to a large number of government employees, to employees in environmental and public safety industries, and to government contractors under the federal False Claims Act of 1863, amended in 1986. A review of the law in these settings follows.

1. Private Sector

A number of states, including California, Connecticut, Hawaii, Maine, Maryland, Michigan, Minnesota, Nebraska, New Hampshire, New Jersey, New York, Oklahoma, Rhode Island, and Washington, have enacted whistleblower legislation protecting private-sector employees against retaliation for having blown the whistle on employers' illegal or unsafe actions.

The standards for protection vary. For example, the Maine law provides that an employer may not discriminate against an employee who in good faith (1) reports what the employee reasonably believes to be a violation of law or a practice that endangers the health or safety of the employee or others, (2) participates in a public proceeding, or (3) refuses to perform work that would expose the employee or others to serious injury or death. Under New York's law, an employer may not take retaliatory personnel action against an employee who discloses to a supervisor or public body an activity, policy, or practice of the employer that violates a law or regulation *and* creates a substantial and specific danger to public health or safety. Under both laws, the employee generally must raise the claim within the company first before "going public" with it.

Most whistleblower statutes require an employee to have a reasonable basis for a claim to be entitled to protection, though the claim need not ultimately be proven to be meritorious. In contrast, New York law requires that the employee blow the whistle on *actual* violations of law, rule, or regulation. (*Bordell v. General Elec. Co.*) Most whistleblower laws expressly provide that employees who knowingly make false charges are not entitled to protection.

Remedies under these laws generally include injunctive relief, reinstatement, back pay, restoration of lost benefits and seniority, and recovery for attorneys' fees and costs. Some state laws, such as New Jersey's, allow for punitive damages (*Abbamont v.*

Piscataway Bd. of Educ.), while the laws of other states, such as New York, do not. (*Bompane v. Enzolabs, Inc.*)

Common employer defenses to whistleblower claims include failure to comply with the procedural requirements of the statute, such as not filing a case in a timely manner (*Moore v. A.H. Riise Gift Shops*), and preemption by federal law in such heavily regulated areas as nuclear safety. (*Bordell v. General Elec. Co.*)

2. Public Sector

Whistleblower protection provided to government workers differs in one significant aspect from that offered to employees in the private sector. Waste, fraud, and mismanagement in a private corporation, while troublesome, does not rise to the level of a public concern. Private employers have the right to run their businesses, even inefficiently, without government intervention. The same is not the case with the government. Waste, fraud, and mismanagement in the government directly affects the public, if for no other reason than tax monies are wasted as a result. Consequently, whistleblowers disclosing waste, fraud, and mismanagement in the government are likely to be protected, while the same complaints in the private sector generally will not entitle the employee to legal protection.

Whistleblower protection is available to federal government employees and the employees of most state governments. Under the federal Civil Service Reform Act of 1978, a federal government agency or employer may not retaliate against an employee or applicant for disclosing what he or she believes to be a violation of law, rule, or regulation, or "gross mismanagement, a gross waste of funds, an abuse of authority, or a substantial and specific danger to public health or safety." The Office of the Special Counsel of the Merit Systems Protection Board is empowered to address complaints under this provision. Following investigation, the Special Counsel may recommend to the Merit Systems Protection Board that corrective action be taken, including ordering the reinstatement of the employee or the hiring of the applicant, and an award of full back pay and benefits, attorneys' fees, and costs. The Special Counsel also can recommend that disciplinary action be taken against offending supervisors or employees.

A majority of states, including Alaska, Arizona, California, Colorado, Connecticut, Delaware, Florida, Hawaii, Illinois, Indiana, Iowa, Kansas, Kentucky, Louisiana, Maine, Maryland, Michigan, Minnesota, Missouri, New Hampshire, New Jersey, New York, North Carolina, Oklahoma, Ohio, Oregon, Pennsylvania, Rhode Island, South Carolina, Tennessee, Texas, Utah, Washington, West Virginia, and Wisconsin, have enacted whistleblower statutes specifically protecting state government workers. In addition, government workers are protected under those state laws listed above that protect private-sector employees. Most of these state laws are modeled after the protection made available to federal employees. Often these provisions require exhaustion of all contractual and administrative remedies, such as internal appeal procedures, before filing of such a claim. (*McGregor v. Board of Comm'rs*)

The scope of protected employee activities varies from state to state. In some states, such as Alaska, California, Kentucky, and South Carolina, the statutory protection extends to employees who report violations of law, gross waste of public funds, abuse of authority, or acts that pose a substantial risk to public health or safety. Other states, including Delaware and Hawaii, only protect employees who report violations of law. Louisiana and Tennessee have the most limited statutory protection; Louisiana extends coverage only to those employees who report violations of environmental laws and Tennessee only to those who report the misuse of public education funds.

In a notable state employee whistleblower case, an architect for the state of Texas was terminated for reporting to agency officials in the Texas Department of Human Services and to a congressman that contractors were systematically being paid for work not performed. The jury awarded the architect $3.5 million in compensatory damages and $10 million in punitive damages. (*Green v. Texas Dep't of Human Servs.*) Texas is one of the few states that provides for compensatory and punitive damages under its whistleblower law.

3. Antiretaliation Provisions

A number of federal environmental, transportation, and health and safety statutes prohibit retaliation against employees who commence or participate in any proceeding under the Clean Air Act, the Federal Water Pollution Control Act, the Solid Waste Disposal Act, the Surface Mining Control and Reclamation Act, the Toxic Substances Act, the Safe Drinking Water Act, the Energy Reorganization Act, and the Occupational Safety & Health Act, among others.

The Supreme Court has determined that, at least in the case of the Energy Reorganization Act regulating the nuclear industry, the federal legislation does not preclude other legal challenges such as state whistleblower and emotional distress claims. (*English v. General Elec. Co.*) In *DeFord v. Secretary of Labor,* a manager of quality assurance at a Tennessee Valley Authority nuclear power plant participated in a government investigation of the plant at which time he expressed his concerns about quality assurance at the plant. He was subsequently transferred from a management position to a position where he performed mostly clerical functions, had no telephone, and shared a work table with a lower level engineer. The manager was found to have been discriminated against under the Energy Reorganization Act based on his participation in the government investigation. The court ordered that he be reinstated and that he was entitled to recover for the emotional injury he suffered as a result of the agency's action.

Courts have differed on the question of whether an employee must actually contact a government agency to warrant protection under an antiretaliation statute, or whether an internal complaint is sufficient to invoke the protection of these acts. Certain courts have taken a literal approach and concluded that participation in an actual legal or administrative proceeding with a government agency is required. (*Brown & Root, Inc. v. Donovan*) Others have rejected the notion that a formal proceeding must be involved and have instead extended protection to individuals whose internal complaints further the purposes of the legislation. For example, the termination of a quality assurance engineer at a nuclear power plant was ruled to be unlawful where the discharge was based on reports filed with management detailing quality assurance and safety problems. (*Kansas Gas & Elec. Co. v. Brock*)

4. False Claims Act

The stereotypical image of a whistleblower is of a conscience-ridden do-gooder who chooses the public good over private gain. This whistleblower is seen as an outcast, personally and professionally ostracized, and invariably fired. On occasion, a whistleblower has been reinstated or recovered damages from a court; more often, the whistleblower has nothing to show for his actions except unemployment, a damaged career, and an uncertain future.

A new breed of whistleblower has challenged that image in the 1990s. This whistleblower is a creature of Congress, brought to life by the revision of a Civil War–era statute known as the False Claims Act. This new form of whistleblowing may be not only morally cleansing (though good motives are not required) but enormously profitable as well.

The False Claims Act was enacted by Congress and signed into law by President Lincoln in 1863 to combat fraud against the government by Civil War contractors who mixed sawdust with the gunpowder provided to the armed forces. Under the Act, the Attorney General of the United States can recover damages and penalties from contractors who submit false or fraudulent claims for payment to the government or to another party, if the claims will ultimately result in a loss to the government. The Act also allows actions to be brought by private citizens who are entitled to share in the government's recovery. The Act was rarely used until 1986 when Congress reinvigorated the statute by, among other things, making it more profitable for a private citizen to initiate claims of contractor fraud.

To initiate a lawsuit, a private party must first notify the Justice Department, which then has 60 days to decide whether it wants to join the case. In the interim, the court does not make the suit public. The private party remains a litigant entitled to recover a portion of any damages ultimately awarded to the government, whether or not the Justice Department joins the case. Prior to the 1986 amendments, a private citizen could receive up to 25 percent of the proceeds of the action if the citizen proceeded with the action alone and up to 10 percent if the government took over the litigation. As revised, individuals must be awarded between 25 percent and 30 percent of the proceeds of those actions that the Justice Department does not join and between 15 percent and 25 percent in actions handled by the government.

The 1986 amendments also stiffened penalties against violators by raising them from $2,000 to $5,000 for each individual violation. Congress further broadened the category of those liable under the Act to include all contractors who submit false or fraudulent claims for payment "in reckless disregard or deliberate ignorance of the truth or falsity of the information and not merely those who intentionally do so."

Moreover, the False Claims Act and equivalent state enactments have made whistleblowing, at least in the government contractor area, an officially sanctioned act. The whistleblower in this setting is no longer the outsider acting on conscience but the fingers on the long arm of the law deputized to act on behalf of the government with the prospect of a substantial financial reward.

Since the 1986 amendments, the False Claims Act has, predictably, been increasingly invoked. Indeed, the number of False Claims Act suits swelled from 12 in 1987 to 220 in 1994.

In one case, an employee filed an internal complaint in which she alleged that her employer falsified ammunition test data. As a result of her complaint, two employees pled guilty to defrauding the government and the employer agreed to a $2.5 million settlement. After the settlement, the complaining employee's working conditions deteriorated and she resigned. More than five years later, she sued under the False Claims Act seeking her share of the settlement pot. The court found that she could proceed with her claim even though she had filed only an internal complaint and a lawsuit was never filed either by her or the government. (*Neal v. Honeywell, Inc.*)

In one of the largest awards in False Claims Act history, a whistleblower recovered $13.3 million and $2.6 million in legal costs against General Electric. (*United States ex rel. Taxpayers Against Fraud v. General Electric Co.*) In that case, General Electric had allegedly billed the U.S. for bribes it paid to an Israeli procurement official. General Electric and the government agreed to a settlement for $59.5 million in civil damages, $9.5 million in criminal fines, and $6,158,301 in restitution. They did not, however, resolve the issue of the whistleblower's share of the recovery and his legal fees. The Justice Department sought to limit the employee's recovery because, although he brought the fraud to the government's attention, he had remained silent for many months while the size of the fraud, and the size of his potential reward, grew. The whistleblower alleged, however, that he did not come forward because he feared that General Electric would punish him for his honesty and because he was afraid of the Israeli general who had accepted the bribes. The court found that his fears were reasonable but held, nevertheless, that since he failed to come forward sooner, he was not entitled to the 25% recovery provided in the False Claims Act but instead would be awarded 22.5% of the civil damages equaling 13,387,500.

III. INFLICTION OF EMOTIONAL DISTRESS

The notion that public policy mandates limitations on an employer's discretion also underlies lawsuits alleging employers' intentional infliction of emotional distress. The claim in this setting is that the employer's actions exceed all bounds of acceptable behavior in civilized society. A claim of emotional distress can be either a separate legal claim or a component of damages under other grounds for suit. In the latter case, compensation for the emotional distress caused by a legal wrong committed by an employer may be awarded as part of what is known as compensatory damages. For example, compensatory damages (damages for emotional distress or pain and suffering) are awardable under most discrimination, wrongful discharge, and negligence claims.

Courts have increasingly come to recognize infliction of emotional distress as a separate legal wrong and not merely as a type of damages available in another action. In those states recognizing an action for emotional distress, which may also be called an action for outrage or mental anguish, an employee must establish three basic elements to be entitled to damages: (1) extreme or outrageous actions; (2) intentional, reckless, or, in a limited number of states and circumstances, negligent conduct on the part of the employer or its agents; and (3) resulting severe emotional distress for the employee.

The offensive conduct must go beyond all bounds of decency and must be found to be utterly intolerable in a civilized society. Insults and indignities encountered in the normal course of employment are not compensable. Further, mere termination of employment does not constitute extreme or outrageous conduct although the basis for the termination or the manner in which it is conducted may be grounds for an emotional distress claim. For example, an employee alleged that he was terminated six days before Christmas because he refused to enforce an illegal privacy policy. The court permitted him to sue on his claim for emotional distress but ruled that he would have to show that the employer's offensive conduct went beyond "the mere fact of his termination." (*Thomason v. Mitsubishi Elec. Sales Am., Inc.*)

Courts have found extreme or outrageous conduct in the following circumstances:

- The conditioning of reemployment on a discharged employee's agreement to apologize to, work directly under, and attend church with a co-worker who had harassed the employee and his wife for eighteen months; (*Pratt v. Brown Mach. Co.*)
- A supervisor's remark implying adulterous and whorish conduct on the part of the employee's wife; (*Keehr v. Consolidated Freightways*)
- A supervisor's sexual assault of a female subordinate after he intentionally drugged her; (*Gilardi v. Schroeder*)
- Assigning an employee to go to a conference that had been cancelled for the purpose of setting her up to be fired for theft and dishonesty; (*McCool v. Hillhaven Corp.*)
- A supervisor coming to an employee's cubicle with two other employees who were larger than the employee, tell-

ing the employee that he was terminated, blocking his path when he wanted to go to the personnel department, preventing him from calling the personnel department, manhandling him, escorting him to and from the restroom, and then escorting him out of the company's building; (*Uebelacker v. Cincom Sys. Inc.*)

- A farm owner twice burglarizing his employee's residence, which was located on the farm, and sitting in front of the employee's residence in a car after notifying the employee that he was terminated, even though he knew of the employee's special need to live stress-free because of his children's delicate medical condition; (*Robbins v. Galbraith*)
- The discharge of a male employee for refusing to pull down his pants and expose himself to co-workers in an area that was in public view; (*Madani v. Kendall Ford, Inc.*)
- Racial harassment in the workplace; (*Agarwal v. Johnson*) and
- Sexual harassment in the workplace. (*Shrout v. Black Clawson Co.*)

Extreme or outrageous conduct is more likely to be found where supervisory authority is employed to inflict emotional distress or where the individuals causing the emotional distress have knowledge of the employee's particular susceptibility to such injury.

Mere uncooperative behavior or nastiness on the part of the employer is generally not sufficient to state a claim for emotional distress. For example, such claims have been denied in the following circumstances:

- The employer cursed at and embarrassed the employee; (*Byrnes v. Orkin Exterminating Co.*)
- The use of Polish jokes in the presence of a Polish employee; (*Pawelek v. Paramount Studios Corp.*)
- Termination for failure to report and pay for personal long-distance telephone calls; (*Lekich v. IBM Corp.*)
- The employee was escorted out of her employer's building by security guards after her supervisor and the company's president discussed her termination with her

in private and where other employees had been escorted out of the building; (*Wornick Co. v. Casas*)

- Two unconsented passionate kisses; (*Wolk v. Saks Fifth Avenue*)
- Age discrimination without repeated acts or a pattern of harassment; (*Brenimer v. Great W. Sugar Co.*)
- Compelling an employee to take two polygraph examinations as part of an investigation of a sizeable cash shortage; (*Buffolino v. Long Island Sav. Bank*) and
- Abuse by a supervisor that included yelling at the employee, criticizing his work, and authorizing another employee to switch offices with him in his absence. (*Merrick v. Northern Natural Gas Co.*)

To satisfy the obligation of intentional and reckless conduct, the employee must show that the individual causing the emotional distress sought to cause the emotional distress by his or her actions or otherwise had a reasonable certainty that it would result. Certain courts have recognized claims for negligent infliction of emotional distress where physical injury results. (See Chapter 9 for a more detailed discussion of this type of negligence claim.)

Finally, the emotional distress caused must be so severe that no reasonable person could be expected to endure it. Evidence supporting a claim of severe emotional distress includes the duration of the offensive behavior, its nature and intensity, and the circumstances under which it occurred. The employee will, of course, have to demonstrate that the employer's conduct actually caused severe emotional distress and may have to produce medical evidence of such an effect.

IV. CIVIC DUTIES

The obligations of citizenship include the performance of such civic duties as voting, jury duty, and military service. The law seeks to encourage such activities by requiring employers to facilitate and make accommodations for employees performing such civic functions.

A. Voting Time

Voting in elections for public office is, of course, a recognized civic duty. In furtherance of this public duty, a majority of states mandate that employers provide time off from work to vote in specified elections. These laws often vary with respect to the amount of time the employer must provide, whether the time off is compensable, and when the time off may be scheduled. Certain states require that the employee notify the employer that the worker intends to vote, and many allow the employer to exercise discretion in scheduling the time to be taken.

Although most state voting time laws apply to all employees who are eligible to vote, and to all elections—federal, state, general, primary, special, and local—exceptions do exist. In Massachusetts, for example, the law applies only to eligible employees in manufacturing, mechanical, and mercantile establishments, while Colorado's law applies only to municipal elections.

State laws vary greatly with respect to the amount of time that must be provided to vote, and the majority allow nonworking hours to be considered. New York, for example, provides that an employee who is registered to vote, but does not have four consecutive hours to vote, either between the opening of the polls and the beginning of the shift, or the end of the shift and the closing of the polls, must be given as much time off with pay as will, when added to nonworking time, enable the employee to vote, up to a maximum of two hours.

Several states do not provide a specific amount of time, but instead require a "sufficient" or "reasonable" amount of time to vote. California law, for example, provides that employees must be given as much time off work as will, when added to the time available outside working hours, enable them to vote, if they do not have sufficient time to vote outside of regular working hours.

Many states require that an employee must apply for time off to vote prior to election day. For example, Iowa requires that the application be in writing; West Virginia requires three days' notice; and Illinois and Kentucky mandate that the employee specify the particular hours of absence.

Under most state laws, employees must be paid for voting time. Exceptions include Wisconsin, which does not require that time off to vote be paid time, and Utah, which does not require pay if the employee is compensated on an hourly basis.

The Supreme Court has held voting time statutes to be lawful under the U.S. Constitution. (*Day-Brite Lighting v. Missouri*) Nonetheless, courts in certain states, including Illinois (*Heimgaertner v. Benjamin Elec. Mfg. Co.*) and Kentucky (*Illinois Cent. R.R. Co. v. Commonwealth*), have held that legislation requiring pay while voting violates due process and equal protection provisions of their state constitutions because employers as a group, rather than the general public, must carry the cost and burden of any such program. Certain states, such as Tennessee and Hawaii, allow wage deductions if the employee takes time off to vote but does not actually vote.

B. Jury Duty

Time off from work for jury duty service is provided under both federal and state laws.

The Jury Systems Improvement Act of 1978 (JSIA) provides protection for employees who report for federal jury service. Under the JSIA, an employer may not discharge, threaten to discharge, intimidate, or coerce employees solely because of their jury service. For example, an employer was held to have violated the JSIA by requiring that its employee make up time spent on jury duty by working evenings and Sundays and by threatening not to pay the difference between the employee's salary and jury pay. (*United States ex rel. Madonia v. Coral Springs Partnership*) Similarly, a court found that an employer violated the JSIA by providing an employee with an excuse letter that stated false reasons why he should not be put on a jury and by disciplining and treating the employee differently after his jury service. (*United States ex rel. Perkins v. Sara Lee Corp.*)

An employee on jury service is considered to be on furlough or leave of absence and must be treated accordingly. The JSIA also provides that the employee must be reinstated to his or her position without loss of seniority. The employee under the JSIA performing federal jury duty service also must be permitted to participate in insurance and other benefits in accordance with rules established by the employer relating to all leaves of absence. Thus, an employer violated the JSIA by refusing to pay its employee serving as an alternate juror during a protracted trial, when its previous established policy was to continue salary payments during jury service. The court found that such a deviation from previously established policy has a tendency to coerce and intimidate a juror in violation of the JSIA. (*United States v. Adamita*) The employee, however, must comply with the employer's reasonable notice requirements, if they exist, to benefit from the JSIA's provisions. In one case, the employee failed to notify his employers that he had to report for jury service and was terminated when he did not report for work. The court found that the employer had a reasonable notice requirement applicable to all absences and, therefore, the employee's discharge for not complying with the notice requirement did not violate the JSIA. (*In re Scott*)

An employee may sue to recover for violations of the JSIA. To establish a violation, the employee must demonstrate more than mere receipt of a notice of jury service or the fact of such service. For example, an immediate supervisor's isolated remark that the employee's manager was "not going to be happy about" his jury duty failed to establish that the employee had been fired for his jury service and not his poor attendance. (*Goodson v. Cigna Ins. Co.*) In contrast, a remark by an officer of the company in response to an employee's summons to serve as a grand juror, "You can't be here at work and do this, too," was sufficient to establish a violation of the JSIA, where no other valid reason for termination was offered. (*Johnson v. Appliance & T.V. Ctr.*) Similarly, a court found that an employer violated the JSIA when a manager responded, "Oh, great," when he was advised of the employee's jury service obligation, said that he was going to "get" the employee, and subsequently issued a disciplinary warning to the employee in connection with her jury service. The employee resigned as a result of the employer's conduct. (*Hill v. Winn-Dixie Stores, Inc.*) Although a jury found that the company violated the JSIA, the employee was not awarded back pay because she was not constructively discharged. A court may, however, excuse jury service of a key employee where the trial or grand jury proceeding may require more than 30 days of service and the employee's service would impose severe economic hardship on the employer.

An employer who violates the JSIA may be subject to a civil penalty of not more than $1,000 for each violation regarding each employee.

Many states have patterned their jury duty laws after the JSIA. Certain states, such as Georgia, extend legal protection beyond the jury service setting to cover work absences to attend any judicial proceeding, such as a subpoena or other court order or process. Similarly, Illinois protects those employees summoned to court by subpoena as witnesses to a crime. Other states have made it clear that their state statutory protection extends only to service on state court juries. Thus, in Florida, notwithstanding language in the jury duty statute referring to service "on any grand or petit jury in this state," the courts have held that those called for federal jury service are not protected by the state jury duty laws. (*Hill v. Winn-Dixie Stores, Inc.*)

Time off for jury service may or may not be paid, depending on the state. In Connecticut, for example, a full-time employee must be paid his or her regular wages for the first three full or partial days of jury service. Alabama provides for full-time employees to receive their usual compensation, less any money received for serving as a juror, for as many days as necessary to complete their jury service. Other states, such as New York, provide a minimum payment for daily wages, such as the first fifteen dollars for the first three days of jury service, if the employer has more than a certain number of employees (10 in New York). Arizona, on the other hand, provides for a leave of absence without pay.

Some states, such as Georgia, also forbid disciplining or otherwise penalizing employees for such time off and provide legal remedies to employees so penalized, including damages suffered by the employee, lost wages, reinstatement, and reasonable attorneys' fees. Punitive damages are available in some states. For example, in Nevada, punitive damages up to $50,000 may be collected, while in Idaho and Connecticut, violations may result in treble damages based on lost wages.

In addition to federal and state jury service statutes, the disciplining or discharge of an employee in retaliation for the employee's agreement to perform or actual performance of jury service has been found, as discussed earlier, to violate public policy. For example, in an Ohio case, an employee who served on jury duty and her mother who worked for the same company were terminated in retaliation for the daughter's serving on a jury. Both women were permitted to sue for wrongful discharge. (*Shaffer v. Frontrunner, Inc.*)

C. Reemployment Rights of Armed Services Veterans

Under federal law, employers are required to reemploy anyone who leaves a permanent job to enter active military duty. The resulting gap in employment is treated as a furlough or leave of absence. Employers do not have an obligation to pay wages unless the company has a policy or contractual provision that would apply to other employees on leaves of absence. Employers must, however, continue the employee's health coverage (if any) for up to 18 months if the employee pays the premium. If the employee's military service is for more than 31 days, the employee may be required to pay the full premium under the health plan plus a two percent surcharge. For service periods of less than 31 days, the employee may be charged only the full premium. If the employee has health insurance through a multi-employer plan, the plan may allocate the responsibility to pay for coverage. If the plan does not allocate responsibility, the employer assumes liability. Covered military service includes service in the Army, Navy, Marine Corps, Air Force, Coast Guard, the Reserve components of the military, the Army National Guard, the Air National Guard, the Public Health Service, and any other category of persons whom the President may designate in time of war or emergency.

Until December 12, 1990, an employee's right to reemployment following military service was principally embodied in the Vietnam Era Veterans' Readjustment Assistance Act of 1974, commonly known as the Veterans' Reemployment Rights Act (VRRA). Effective on December 12, however, the VRRA was replaced by the Uniform Services Employment and Reemployment Rights Act (USERRA). The relevant provisions of the USERRA are included as Appendix F to this text.

1. *Covered Employees*

USERRA applies to employees who are members, or who apply to be members, of any of the covered services and whose cumulative military service during employment with an employer lasts a total of five years or less. The five-year limitation does not apply, however, under certain circumstances. For example, if the employee is engaged in an initial period of obligated service that takes more than five years to complete, the employee may be entitled to reemployment under USERRA if certain other statutory conditions are met.

In addition to the membership or application requirement, the employee must have been honorably discharged and must apply for reemployment within the time frames set forth in the statute. If the employee's military service was less than 31 days, he or she must report to the employer for employment at the beginning of the first full regularly scheduled working period on the first calendar day following completion of service and the expiration of eight hours after a time for safe transportation back to his or her residence. If the period of service was for more than 31 days but less than 181 days, an application must be submitted to the employer no later than 14 days following the employee's completion of service. For service lasting more than 180 days, the employee must submit an application to the employer not later than 90 days after his or her completion of service. If the employee has been hospitalized as a result of his or her military service obligations, the time period for reporting may be extended for two years. This two-year hospitalization/convalescence extension can be further extended by the minimum time required to accommodate the circumstances beyond the employee's control that make reporting within the time limitations unreasonable or impossible.

Employers are obligated to reemploy only those employees who left a permanent job. A job is not permanent under USERRA if it is for a brief, nonrecurrent period and there is no reasonable expectation that the employment will continue indefinitely or for a "significant period."

The burden rests upon the employee to establish that he or she is a former employee returning from military service and that the application for reemployment is timely. In this regard, the employer may demand that the employee produce documentation to support the employee's claim that he or she is entitled to reemployment under USERRA.

2. Right to Reemployment

An employee returning from military service is entitled to reemployment. If the employee's military service lasted less than 91 days, he or she must be reemployed promptly in a position that the employee would have attained if continuously employed. The employer, however, is not required to place the returning employee in a position for which he or she is not qualified. If the employer claims that the returning employee is not qualified, it must be prepared to prove the employee's lack of qualifications and, moreover, must show that it made "reasonable efforts" to help the employee become qualified for the position. If the employee is not qualified, he or she must be reemployed in the position he or she previously held.

If the period of service was for more than 90 days, the employee is similarly entitled to a position in which he or she would have been employed but for the military service or a position of like seniority, status, and pay for which the employee is qualified. If the employee is not qualified for the position he or she would have held but for the military service or a similar position, the employee is entitled to be put in the position he or she held on the date of the commencement of service, or a like position. As the Supreme Court has stated in applying similar provisions under the VRRA, "the returning veteran 'does not step back on the seniority escalator at the point he stepped off. He steps back on at the precise point he would have occupied had he kept his position continuously during [his leave].'" (*Coffy v. Republic Steel Corp.*)

3. Disabled Veterans

An employee who sustained a service-connected disability and is not qualified to assume either the position he or she would have held but for the military service or the position held when he or she left (even after the employer attempts to accommodate the disability) is entitled to be promptly reemployed. The employer may meet this obligation by placing the employee in any other position of similar seniority, status, and pay for which the employee is qualified or for which the employee would become qualified with reasonable accommodations by the employer. Failing this, the employer must reemploy the returning employee in a position that is the nearest approximation to the former position, consistent with the circumstances of the employee's case.

4. Job Security

In addition to the broad reemployment rights the returning uniformed service member enjoys, he or she is also protected from the ravages of the employment-at-will rule for a brief period after returning to work. USERRA provides that if the employee's military service was for more than 180 days, the reemployed individual may not be discharged in the first year after returning to work except for cause. If the employee's service was for less than 180 days and more than 30 days, he or she may not be discharged during the first six months of reemployment except for cause.

5. Remedies

An employee denied rights or benefits conferred by the USERRA may initiate an action in federal court to recover "for any loss of wages or benefits" suffered because of the employer's unlawful action, and to obtain injunctive relief and liquidated damages in an amount equal to the employee's lost wages. In addition, the court may award the prevailing employee attorneys' fees, expert witness fees, and other litigation expenses.

8

LIFESTYLE AND PERSONAL PRIVACY ISSUES

The line between an employee's personal life and work life has, in recent years, become increasingly difficult to draw. Employees' activities, beliefs, interests, and lifestyles off the job can on occasion affect their ability to perform tasks required on the job. Increasingly, courts have been asked to delineate the extent to which management may condition the terms and benefits of employment on matters related to an applicant's or employee's lifestyle or personal preferences.

One commonly cited cause for employers' concerns regarding employees' lifestyles is a desire to contain rising health care costs. For example, smokers are often viewed as undesirable medical risks by cost-conscious employers. In response to rising health care costs, some employers now participate in "wellness" programs that seek to alter employees' lifestyles by encouraging exercise, improved diets, and other health-promoting activities.

Another significant concern cited by employers is workplace safety. Abuse of drugs and alcohol by employees can cause serious injury to co-workers and to the public, as well as to employers' operations and bottom lines. As a result, as discussed more fully in Chapter 6, testing for drugs has become commonplace. Current use of drugs or alcohol outside of the workplace (which may in turn affect performance on the job) can be grounds for discipline or discharge or for not being hired in the first place.

Counterbalancing these employer concerns are the strong social and constitutional notions of personal privacy arguing against employer intrusion into the personal lives and even bedrooms of employees.

The factual settings and court rulings raising lifestyle issues vary widely, and the legal rights of employees in this area are evolving with time. The legal, social, and political issues addressed in these cases are often as significant as the facts of the cases are colorful. The following lifestyle and personal privacy issues are addressed in this chapter: appearance and grooming; sexual harassment; relationships and related activities; sexual and reproductive freedom; and personal habits, conditions, and addictions. Introducing these topics will be a brief overview of privacy law as it applies to employees.

I. OVERVIEW OF EMPLOYEES' RIGHT TO PRIVACY

The law protecting an employee's right to privacy varies greatly depending on whether the employee works in the public or private sector. Constitutional protection of individual privacy rights, such as the prohibition against unreasonable searches and seizures, applies only to actions by the government and not to those of private employers. The Privacy Act of 1974, the most far-reaching federal law on the subject, applies solely to federal government employees. In contrast, employee privacy rights in the private sector, as is the case with so many individual employee rights, are dependent on a collection of diverse legal protections that vary from subject matter to subject matter and from state to state.

Some broad privacy protections for private-sector employees do exist. For example, Alaska and California recognize employees' right to privacy in their states' constitutions. A few other states, including Massachusetts, have enacted by statute broad employee privacy laws.

For the most part, however, employee privacy protection is derived from limited-purpose laws designed to protect one aspect of privacy. For example, a number of states limit the information that can be contained in or disclosed from personnel and medical files; similarly, the use of polygraphs in the workplace has been severely restricted by both federal and state law.

Perhaps the area of law that affords employees the broadest protection against the invasion of their privacy is the judge-made law known as the "privacy torts." The four privacy torts are (1) intrusion upon seclusion; (2) public disclosure of private facts; (3) publicity placing a person in a false light; and (4) appropriation of an employee's name or likeness without permission. Most states recognize each of these actions. Other states recognize only some. For example, New York recognizes by statute an action for appropriation but not the other privacy torts, while North Carolina does not recognize the false light action.

A review of the four privacy torts and their application to the employment setting follows.

A. Intrusion Upon Seclusion

An employer that intentionally intrudes, physically or otherwise, upon the solitude, seclusion, or private affairs of an employee may be liable for an invasion of privacy if the intrusion would be considered highly offensive to a reasonable person. The employer's legitimate needs to maintain an effective workforce will be weighed by a court against the degree and nature of the intrusion.

Courts have ruled that employers intruded upon the seclusion of their employees and violated their privacy rights where:

- A supervisor made offensive remarks, offers, demands, and threats including inquiries regarding the nature of the sex between the employee and her husband; (*Phillips v. Smalley Maintenance Servs.*)
- The principal officer of the company opened and read the private mail of another officer of the company; (*Vernars v. Young*)
- A manager broke open the employee's personal lock on a locker and went through the employee's personal belongings including her purse to investigate the theft of a watch; (*K-Mart Corp. v. Trotti*) and

- The employer improperly pressured the employee into taking a polygraph examination based on rumors of off-the-job drug use. (*O'Brien v. Papa Gino's*)

In contrast, intrusion upon seclusion claims have been rejected where:

- Co-workers asked a nurse why she left the hospital after her forced resignation; (*Avallone v. Wilmington Medical Ctr.*)
- The employer investigated claims by co-workers of a supervisor's inappropriate relationship with a subordinate by interviewing the company's full-time employees, reviewing written material voluntarily produced by the supervisor, and examining company records; (*Rogers v. IBM*)
- The company disclosed to a husband his wife's attendance record where, as a result, the husband committed suicide based on his correct conclusion that his wife was having an affair; (*Kobeck v. Nabisco, Inc.*)
- The supervisor sought but failed to induce an employee to enter into a "sexual liaison"; (*Ponton v. Scarfone*)
- A workplace drug test detected off-the-job drug use; (*DiTomaso v. Elec. Data Sys.*)
- The employer requested disclosure of medications being taken prior to the taking of a drug test; (*Mares v. Conagra Poultry Co.*) and
- The employer wrote to the physician of an employee on medical leave soliciting information regarding the employee's condition and ability to return to work. (*Saldana v. Kelsey-Hayes Co.*)

Failed attempts at an invasion of an employee's privacy are generally not a basis for suit. For example, no invasion of privacy occurred where the employee never stopped his car to permit an improper search (*Gretencord v. Ford Motor Co.*) or did not answer offensive and intrusive questions in a questionnaire. (*Cort v. Bristol-Myers Co.*) Further, no violation of privacy occurs where the employee is the source of the offensive disclosure. For example, a white female employee discussed with employees at work her affair with a black male co-worker. When highly offensive remarks regarding interracial relationships followed, she sued. The court rejected her invasion of privacy claim concluding that she waived her claim to privacy by making the affair a topic of office conversation. (*Moffett v. Gene B. Glick Co.*)

The dividing line between lawful surveillance and unlawful invasion of privacy is exemplified in a Maryland case in which a company hired a detective to observe a union activist. The detective discovered that the employee was having an affair, which was eventually disclosed to the employee's wife. The detective's investigation included observing the employee outside his home, outside his girlfriend's home, at various stores, and along public roads; placing a detection device on the employee's hotel room door; and monitoring the employee's actions from the bottom of the motel stairwell. The court determined that observing the employee in public places was lawful but ruled unlawful the placing of the detection device on the motel door and the monitoring of the employee's activities from the stairwell. (*Pemberton v. Bethlehem Steel Corp.*)

B. Public Disclosure of Private Facts

A second invasion of privacy action is based on unwarranted publicity given by an employer to the private facts of an employee's life. The matter publicized must be highly offensive to a reasonable person and of no legitimate concern to the public. A typical publicity case involves the disclosure to third parties of performance information or medical or psychological data regarding an employee.

A publicity action, while similar to a defamation claim (see Chapter 5 for a discussion of defamation law), nonetheless differs in significant ways. Most notably, truth is not a defense to a publicity action as it would be to a defamation action. For example, assume a supervisor announces to the assembled workforce that an employee has a venereal disease, and that this is true. The supervisor has both defamed the employee and invaded his or her privacy; however, the supervisor has a defense to the defamation claim, namely, the truth of the statement.

In contrast, truth will not serve as a defense to a publicity claim.

To succeed on an invasion of privacy claim, the publicity must be overly broad. Disclosure of private facts to an employee's union (*Davis v. Monsanto Co.*), to appropriate management personnel (*Beard v. Akzona, Inc.*), or to the employee's former wife (*Lodge v. Shell Oil Co.*) has been found not to constitute unlawful publicity. A court rejected a publicity claim based on the disclosure of the terms of a director of personnel's termination agreement to staff members. The court found that imparting this information to co-workers who wanted to know why the director of personnel was no longer employed was "appropriate." The court commented that even if those informed constituted the complete universe of interested persons, the disclosure by the employer did not constitute unlawful publicity but rather "a mere spreading of the word by interested persons in the same way rumors are spread." (*Wells v. Thomas*)

Publicity claims are often based on the inappropriate disclosure of employee medical information. For example, the disclosure of an employee's mastectomy to co-workers was ruled a sufficient basis for a publicity action. (*Miller v. Motorola, Inc.*) In another case, a physician retained by the company disclosed to management that an employee was "paranoid" and in need of psychiatric help. The court concluded that the employee did not authorize such disclosure and that he could sue the company for invasion of his privacy. (*Bratt v. IBM*) Similarly, an attorney was awarded almost $100,000 in damages after a senior partner in whom he had confided revealed to the attorney's co-workers that he was gay and was about to take an AIDS test. (*Borguez v. Ozer*) In contrast, the Mississippi Supreme Court rejected a publicity claim where a supervisor revealed to an employee's co-workers that the employee had had a hysterectomy. In that case, the employee, who worked as a decontamination laborer at a nuclear power plant, fainted on the job while working in a highly contaminated area. The fainting incident was apparently an aftereffect of the hysterectomy. Rumors spread throughout the plant, however, that the employee was the victim of radiation poisoning. A supervisor sought to squelch the rumors by disclosing the true cause of the fainting incident. The court ruled that while the fact of the hysterectomy was unquestionably private, the disclosure was privileged in that it was designed to calm the workers' fears of radiation poisoning and was not made out of ill will or spite. (*Young v. Jackson*) Similarly, a court rejected a publicity claim where a psychologist disclosed to management his diagnosis that an employee had a paranoid and obsessive personality that required reassignment to a less stressful position. The court reasoned that the employee had waived her right to privacy by authorizing release of any information obtained as part of the company's employee-assistance program and that publication had not occurred since the information was disclosed only to a few individuals. (*Childs v. Williams*)

The facts disclosed must be "private" for an invasion of privacy to occur. An employee's criminal record was found to be public information and, consequently, the disclosure of that public information was ruled not a violation of privacy. (*Baker v. Burlington Northern, Inc.*) The disclosure of private facts by the employee may serve as a waiver of an invasion of privacy claim. For example, a female employee who told others of her sexual encounters with her supervisor could not succeed on her invasion of privacy claim based on her supervisor's publication of this fact. (*Cummings v. Walsh Construction Co.*)

C. False Light

An employee's privacy may be invaded if the employer puts the employee in a "false light," that is, falsely attributes to the employee characteristics or beliefs not possessed, conduct not performed, or otherwise presents the person in a misleading and offensive manner. As with a public disclosure of private facts claim, a false light claim requires that the information be disclosed to the public broadly. Limited disclosure of the offensive information is not sufficient. (*Ledl v. Quik Pik Food Stores*)

An employee of an insurance company stated a false light claim where his employer accused him of leaking information from an investigation of fire loss claims to an arsonist and publicized this allegation. (*Todd v. South Carolina Farm Bureau Mut. Ins. Co.*) Similarly, an employee stated a cause of action for false light invasion of privacy where he alleged that the company provided to the employee's union, an arbitrator, and the State Attorney's Office, inaccurate and altered film of his activities after he sustained a work place injury, in order to portray inaccurately his physical condition. (*Allen v. Bethlehem Steel Corp.*) In contrast, the mere surveillance of employees based on union activity did not put the employees in a false light where the information gained and communicated was not misleading. (*International Union v. Garner*) Similarly, picket signs depicting the general manager of a plant as a "Little Hitler" operating a "Nazi concentration camp" were found to be mere expressions of opinions and not facts upon which a false light claim could be based. (*Yeager v. Local Union 20*)

D. Appropriation of Name or Likeness

An employer who appropriates for its own use or benefit an employee's name or likeness without consent may be found to have invaded the employee's privacy. Such cases, however, are rare as few employees have sufficient notoriety or reputations with sufficient market value to warrant the appropriation.

In one case, an employer continued to use the name of its former laboratory director after his job was terminated. The court concluded that the employer would be liable for the value of the benefit derived through use of the lab director's name if it was shown that the laboratory director did not license use of his name after his termination. (*Alonso v. Parfet*) Most appropriation cases involve the appropriation of likenesses or names for commercial value related to marketing or advertising. In a noncommercial setting, an employer was ruled to have unlawfully appropriated its employee's likeness for use during its safety education meetings. The employee had been seriously injured in an explosion that left a "gaping hole" the size of a fist in his upper thigh. Vivid pictures were taken at the hospital. The employer, without permission, used the pictures, including a particularly gruesome color photo, as a "shocker" in its safety training. The court concluded that the employer was guilty of appropriation and awarded the employee $250 (in 1968 dollars) plus the costs of the action. (*Lambert v. Dow Chem. Co.*)

An employee, of course, can consent expressly or by implication to the use of his or her likeness or name. For example, an employee who posed for a company photographer and whose photograph was used in such publications as *Time* and *Newsweek* was ruled to have waived the invasion of privacy claim he may have possessed. (*Johnson v. Boeing Airplane Co.*)

E. Defenses to Privacy Claims

The applicable defenses to privacy claims will depend on which privacy tort is asserted. For example, truth may be a defense to a false light claim where it generally would not be so for an intrusion into seclusion claim. Nonetheless, certain defenses generally applicable to privacy claims can be identified, namely, insufficient publicity; non-private matter; consent; waiver; failed attempt; and preemption.

An invasion of privacy claim generally requires that the private matter be publicized to a broad audience. Publicity limited to co-workers in the department in which the employee works or to those with a need to know within the organization will generally be acceptable, while a memorandum to all employees in a multinational corporation disclosing the same private information would not be.

The disclosure of information that is generally available to the public and, therefore, not private, will not serve as a basis for an invasion of privacy claim. Consequently, as noted earlier, the disclosure of an employee's criminal record did not constitute an invasion of privacy where, in contrast, the disclosure of a mastectomy did.

An employee may consent to the publicizing of private matters by posing for a company photographer, for instance, or by applying for a position that requires security clearance. The publicity, however, must be limited to the breadth of the consent. The filling out of a medical benefit form may serve as consent to the disclosure of information in the form to the human resources department, but would not serve as consent for circulation of the form to employees generally.

A waiver of an invasion of privacy claim is most likely to occur when the employee is a source, although not necessarily the only source, of the publicity related to private matters. While an employee's off-the-job romantic encounters are private matters, the employee's disclosure to co-workers of the details will serve as a waiver of an invasion of privacy claim even should others disclose the same, private information.

The law does not recognize "attempted" invasion of privacy as a basis for a claim. The contemplated illegal search that does not occur or the asking of invasive questions that are not answered will not, by itself, constitute a violation of law.

Finally, privacy claims may be preempted by federal law where those claims are based on rights established in a collective-bargaining agreement. (*In re Amoco Petroleum Additives Co.*)

II. APPEARANCE AND GROOMING

Employers may mandate that employees abide by reasonable dress, grooming, and appearance regulations. While a very limited number of jurisdictions, including the District of Columbia and the City of Santa Cruz, California, prohibit discrimination based on physical appearance, legal challenges to appearance and grooming standards typically allege discriminatory application of those standards—for example, by applying such standards to women exclusively or more strictly—rather than on privacy, constitutional, or related grounds.

Gender-neutral policies are the most likely to be found lawful. Employer grooming and appearance policies may require males and females to conform to different codes, however, without necessarily giving rise to liability for sex discrimination, provided that the restrictions are comparable and uniformly applied. (*Wislocki-Goin v. Mears*) For example, males-only necktie requirements have been held to be lawful. (*Fountain v. Safeway Stores*) In contrast, a "no-eyeglasses" policy applicable only to females has been ruled unlawful. (*Laffey v. Northwest Airlines*)

In *Craft v. Metromedia, Inc.*, the court ruled that a television station had not discriminated against an anchorwoman, Christine Craft, by removing her from her position, allegedly because, among other reasons, she was "too unattractive." The station had criticized Craft for her clothing and makeup, provided her with a copy of the book *Women's Dress for Success*, and assigned her a clothing consultant to help her select outfits for her on-air appearances. Male on-air personnel were similarly instructed by the station to "lose weight, to get better fitting clothes, to refrain from wearing sweaters under jackets, . . . to tie [a] necktie in a certain manner, . . . to try wearing contact lenses and to get a hair piece." The court concluded that the emphasis on the feminine stereotype of "softness" was "incidental to a true focus on consistency of appearance, proper coordination of colors and textures, the effects of studio lighting on clothing and makeup, and the greater degree of conservatism thought necessary in the Kansas City market" where the station aired.

Dress requirements demeaning to females or that reinforce stereotypical notions of female sexuality to induce business are unlawful. For example, requiring that a cocktail waitress wear "something low-cut and slinky" when she preferred wearing pantsuits was held to be unlawful discrimination. (*Priest v. Rotary*) Similarly, a policy that allows male retail clerks to wear business attire while requiring females to wear smocks is unlawful. (*O'Donnell v. Burlington Coat Factory*) In contrast, dress codes that appear at first glance to be discriminatory but that further a legitimate business purpose may be lawful. The Equal Employment Opportunity Commission ruled, for example, that a clothing store did not engage in sexual discrimination by requiring its female sales employees to wear swimsuits and a see-through or open robe while at work as part of the store's swimwear promotion. The Commission determined that employees would not have been subjected to unwelcome sexual conduct had they worn the required outfit and, therefore, the dress requirement did not violate federal law. (EEOC Dec. 85–9, May 7, 1985) Similarly, it is not unlawful to fire a female supervisor for refusing to dress like her male counterparts (*e.g.*, shirts with collars) rather than like female line workers (*e.g.*, tube tops) (*Andre v. Bendix Corp.*), or to fire a female attorney who refused to dress conservatively in keeping with the legal department's style. The attorney instead wore clothes that were, in the estimate of management, too "tight-fitting" and too "flashy." (*Bellissimo v. Westinghouse Elec. Corp.*) Further, a rule that allowed women to wear jewelry that was not "unusual or over-large" but prohibited male employees from doing so was found not to be discriminatory. (*Lockhart v. Louisiana-Pacific Corp.*)

Sex-based height and weight requirements have been upheld as nondiscriminatory where employers have regulated both males and females in a comparable fashion. Discriminatory application of such policies, however, or policies that reinforce sexual stereotypes will be subject to challenge. The airline industry has for many years strictly applied height and weight standards to flight attendants. Traditionally, flight attendants have been predominantly female. For example, American Airlines' flight attendants' policy manual stated that "a firm, trim silhouette, free of bulges, rolls, or paunches, is necessary for an alert, efficient image." Under American Airlines' old policy, a female flight attendant who was five-feet, five-inches tall could weigh no more than 129 pounds. Men were allowed to weigh significantly more based on the 1959 standard insurance chart used in the industry. American Airlines changed that policy in settlement of certain lawsuits by allowing female flight attendants to weigh 136 pounds at age 25 and up to 154 pounds at age 55. As part of the settlement, the airline agreed to reinstate with full back pay and benefits 15 flight attendants who were terminated and 150 who were suspended for having violated the old policy. (*Association of Professional Flight Attendants v. American Airlines*) Other airlines in recent years have followed suit and similarly relaxed their height and weight requirements for flight attendants.

Grooming policies that discriminate on the basis of race are unlawful. For example, "no-beard" policies that disproportionately affect African-American males with a hereditary skin condition that precludes frequent shaving are unlawful. (*Bradley v. Pizzaco of Nebraska*) Where a reasonable accommodation can be made, an employer may be obligated to make such accommodation. For example, the District of Columbia's argument that firefighters could not wear beards where beards would interfere with respiratory breathing devices was rejected because African-American firefighters with the disease affected by shaving could wear one-quarter inch beards without presenting a safety hazard. (*Kennedy v. Dixon*)

Stricter appearance regulations applied to police officers and other public servants generally have been upheld. For example, police regulations directed at the style and length of hair, sideburns, and mustaches, and that banned beards and goatees except for medical reasons, were upheld by the Supreme Court. (*Kelley v. Johnson*) Similarly, the challenge by two police officers disciplined for, among other reasons, wearing earring studs on and off duty was rejected. Moreover, the officers' attempts to hide the earrings while on duty by placing Band-Aids over them did not change the result. The court in that case emphasized that the community involved was small, the officers were generally known and recognized, and there was little difference in the public's perception of whether the officers were off duty or on duty. (*Rathert v. Peotone*)

Reasonable appearance regulations have also withstood employees' challenges based on freedom of religion. In *Goldman v. Weinberger*, the Supreme Court ruled that the First Amendment does not prohibit the U.S. Air Force from enforcing its uniform dress requirements, and thereby excluding the wearing of religious apparel. The Court thus held that an Orthodox Jew and ordained rabbi could be barred from wearing a yarmulke while on duty on an Air Force base.

III. SEXUAL HARASSMENT

Sexual harassment is a form of sex discrimination. It is also an egregious invasion of an employee's privacy and an increasingly visible legal issue. Perhaps no area of employment law raises more difficult issues of fact than those that arise in the area of sexual harassment.

The law in the area of sexual harassment divides into two categories: "quid pro quo" and "hostile environment" situations. A quid pro quo case is one in which a representative of management, rather than a co-worker, makes decisions regarding terms, conditions, or privileges of employment on the basis of submission to or rejection of sexual advances or demands for sexual favors; the employment decision is made without regard to whether the employee is otherwise entitled to it. In a hostile environment case, the employee is subjected to unwelcome sexual activities by a supervisor or co-worker that interfere with the terms, conditions, or privileges of employment. The sexual harassment in a hostile environment case must be so pervasive and offensive that it alters the conditions of employment and creates an intolerable working environment.

An employer will generally be found liable for the actions of its supervisors in a quid pro quo action and may be liable for the actions of its supervisors or employees in a hostile environment case if it had actual or constructive knowledge of the alleged harassment. Because sexual harassment must involve "unwelcome" sexual behavior, an employer defending a charge of sexual harassment may introduce evidence of the employee's provocative speech or dress to show that the challenged sexual activities were not offensive, but rather were welcomed. A sexual harassment claim may be brought as a claim for sex discrimination under Title VII of the Civil Rights Act of 1964 and also under state human rights laws, or as an assault or battery, a false imprisonment, an invasion of privacy, or an emotional distress claim.

A. Meritor Savings Bank v. Vinson

In the seminal sexual harassment case of *Meritor Savings Bank v. Vinson*, a female employee, a bank teller who became an assistant manager, alleged that her supervisor engaged in sexual harassment by compelling her to have sexual intercourse with him 40 to 50 times, fondling her in front of other employees, following her into the women's restroom, and forcibly raping her on several occasions. Although the employee testified that she feared losing her job, the terms and conditions of her employment were not expressly conditioned on her sexual relationship with her supervisor. She sued under Title VII specifically contending that the supervisor's activities created an unlawful hostile work environment. The Supreme Court held that the employee had alleged a viable sexual harassment claim, finding that federal law affords employees "the right to work in an environment free from discriminatory intimidation, ridicule and insult." To constitute a hostile environment, the harassment must be so severe or pervasive as to alter the conditions of employment and establish a hostile and abusive work environment. The focus, the Court indicated, is not whether any sexual conduct on the affected employee's part was voluntary, but rather whether the offensive actions were unwelcome.

The Supreme Court further clarified the requirements for establishing a claim of hostile work environment in *Harris v. Forklift Sys*. The Court ruled that the alleged harassing conduct must be severe and pervasive enough to create both an objectively and a subjectively hostile or abusive work environment. Thus, the work environment must be one that both a reasonable person would consider hostile and the victim actually perceives to be hostile. Factors to consider in determining whether the work environment is hostile or abusive are "the frequency of the discriminatory conduct; its severity; whether it is physically threatening or humiliating, or a mere offensive utterance; and whether it unreasonably interferes with an employee's work performance." The effect of the conduct on the employee's psychological well-being may also be considered, but proof of serious psychological harm is not required.

B. Unwelcome Conduct

The principal inquiries in any sexual harassment situation are whether the alleged harassment occurred and, if so, whether it was unwelcome. These determinations are made by reviewing the totality of the circumstances and must be based on a careful review of the facts.

Evidence of the welcomeness of a sexual advance includes the speech and dress of the target of the advances (*Meritor Savings Bank v. Vinson*), behavior encouraging attention of a sexual nature (*Weinsheimer v. Rockwell Int'l Corp.*), and acquiescence in offensive sexual conduct. (*Loftin-Boggs v. City of Meridian*) For example, a hostile environment claim was rejected where the complaining employee used vulgar language, inquired into the sex lives of married co-workers and whether they engaged in extramarital affairs, initiated sexual-oriented conversations, and shared her own sexual experiences with the alleged harassers. (*Gan v. Kepro Circuit Sys.*) In contrast, a federal appeals court ruled that the fact that a female employee posed nude for motorcycle magazines did not necessarily compel the conclusion that she solicited or found welcome a pattern of harassment that both preceded and followed the publication of the nude photographs. (*Burns v. McGregor Elec. Indus.*)

In another hostile environment case, the target of unwanted, lewd attention was awarded $300,000 in damages under Michigan's civil rights laws. In that case, the woman alleged that co-workers nicknamed her "Fluffy LeBush" after a pornography star, that a large poster of a naked woman in a pornographic pose hung on the assembly line, and that her male co-workers subjected her to "unwelcome touching" and requests for sexual favors. The jury and subsequently the appeals court on review found that although the employee participated in some of the horseplay, she nonetheless viewed the harassment as unwelcome and, consequently, found such actions to have constituted unlawful sexual harassment. (*Eide v. Kelsey-Hayes Co.*)

The best evidence of the unwelcomeness of a sexual advance in the workplace is a contemporaneous complaint or protest indicating that the particular conduct is offensive and will not be tolerated. That complaint can take a number of forms—written or oral, formal or informal. The stronger and more direct it is, however, the more effective it is likely to be and the more weight it will later be given by a court. In one case, a female employee alleged that for approximately fifteen years a manager harassed her by, among other things, asking if he could enter her hotel room on a business trip, to which she said no, by commenting that they should "go somewhere and make mad passionate love," and by making similar remarks on a regular basis. The court, in rejecting her claim, commented that it was "chagrined to learn that [the female employee] never communicated to [the manager] that his behavior was unwelcome or offensive. Harassment must be defined in context, and part of harassment is the repeated, unwanted nature of the conduct which is violative of the recipient's wishes." The court concluded that while the manager's behavior may have been presumptuous, it was not unlawful. (*Rose v. Figgie Int'l*)

A formal complaint or protest, while helpful in demonstrating the unwelcomeness of particular conduct, is not an essential element of a sexual harassment claim with due allowance made for the fear of repercussion of taking such action. For example, the president of a building and development firm hired a female architectural designer to supervise the company's custom homes division. Over a five-week period, the president harassed the designer by, among other things, commenting that she had a "good body" but if she worked out she would have a "great body"; commenting that she looked "good in tight jeans"; and grasping her hands and telling her in one instance that he liked women "with good looks and brains" and in a second instance that he put his women on a "pedestal." In each circumstance, the designer changed the subject or withdrew from his presence. In sustaining the designer's sexual harassment claim, the court concluded that where the employee did not affirmatively reject the advances but never invited them, "evidence that the employee consistently demonstrated her unalterable resistance to all sexual advances is enough to establish their unwelcomeness." The court commented that in evaluating the welcomeness of sexual overtures a court must consider "that the employee may reasonably perceive that her recourse to more emphatic means of communicating the unwelcomeness of the supervisor's sexual advances, as by registering a complaint, though normally advisable, may prompt the termination of her employment, especially when the sexual overtures are made by the owner of the firm." (*Chamberlin v. 101 Realty, Inc.*)

C. Quid Pro Quo Versus Hostile Environment Cases

A sexual harassment quid pro quo claim is established where the terms or conditions of employment are conditioned on the submission to or rejection of unwelcome sexual conduct. An act or a failure to act on the part of the harassed employee is what is being requested by the harassing supervisor or member of management.

This is not the case with hostile environment claims. The focus is less on the actions of the harassed employee (although they are relevant) than on the atmosphere established by supervisors or co-workers in which the harassed employee exists. To be unlawful, activities complained of must be sufficiently severe or pervasive so as to alter the conditions of the employee's work. In addition to the harassed employee's response to the offending conduct, relevant factors include the nature of the offensive conduct (*e.g.*, physical or verbal); its persistence; the threatening or nonthreatening quality of the conduct; the reasonableness or unreasonableness of the conduct; whether the harassers were supervisors or co-workers; the number of instances and people involved in the harassment; and the totality of the circumstances in which the alleged harassment occurred. While an abusive atmosphere by itself is not sufficient for a sexual harassment claim, a workplace setting in which abusive conduct is directed in particular against one sex is unlawful. (*Laughinghouse v. Risser*)

Sexual harassment against males has, under limited circumstances, also been recognized. In a leading case, two males were forced to have sex with their boss's secretary in a "modified ménage à trois" under a threat of job loss if they refused. The court found the company and manager guilty of both quid pro quo and hostile environment harassment, reasoning that the law protects both males and females from sexual harassment. The court upheld these claims despite a finding that the two men "contributed to the general tone of sexual innuendo" by ogling the secretary and making lewd proposals to female employees generally. The court reasoned that the men, despite their behavior, did not desire "intimate sexual contact" with the secretary. While both the company and the manager were held liable for sexual harassment, the claims against the secretary were dismissed because as a co-worker she could not be personally liable for unlawful discrimination as she could not provide or deny employment benefits to the complaining male employees. (*Showalter v. Allison Reed Group*)

An emerging area of sexual harassment law is the viability of claims involving members of the same sex. Some courts have rejected such claims outright on the ground that harassment by males against males or females against females cannot be because of the target's sex. (*Garcia v. Elf Atochem N. Am.*) Other courts find no basis for limiting the legal protection against sexual harassment to members of the opposite sex on the ground that the complaining party would not have been harassed "but for" his or her sex. (*Ecklund v. Fuisz Technology, Ltd.*) The division among the courts is so deep that resolution of the issue will likely await a ruling of the Supreme Court.

D. Unlawful Sexual Favoritism

As will be discussed later in this chapter, romance and sexual relationships in the office have increasingly been the cause of confusion, ill-feeling, and legal claims by both participants and nonparticipants in the romantic or sexual activity. One such common claim is sexual harassment raised by a subordinate who is coerced into the relationship by a manager. The legal impact of sexual harassment, however, is broader and may extend to affected third parties as well.

What if, rather than suffering the loss of tangible job benefits, the harassed employee actually gains unearned benefits? That employee nonetheless has a claim for sexual harassment although the harassed employee's damages may be somewhat limited. Perhaps equally significant, co-workers who were denied benefits gained by the favored employee may have a claim for what has been called unlawful sexual favoritism (EEOC Policy Guidance N-915-048, January 12, 1990) whether or not they were targets of the objectionable conduct. (*O'patka v. Menasha Corp.*) The rationale for this type of action is that sexual conduct is required to succeed in that workplace. In sum, legal claims resulting from sexual harassment may be available not only to the harassed employee but to co-workers as well, either because they lost out on tangible benefits or because of the offensiveness of the workplace atmosphere.

A female attorney employed by the Securities and Exchange Commission (SEC) successfully sued the Commission on sexual harassment grounds alleging unlawful sexual favoritism. The attorney alleged, and it was demonstrated, that romantic and sexual relationships among personnel in the office, including supervisors, abounded. The attorney's work relationship with her supervisors was admittedly poor. She attributed it to her complaints about excessive office romances; the SEC called her paranoid. The court acknowledged that she had some "adjustment" problems prior to her employment at the SEC, but concluded that her mental condition was caused or exacerbated by the environment in which she worked. The court concluded that romantic relationships and sexual conduct in the office were sufficiently pervasive to constitute a hostile work environment that injured the attorney's position in the workplace. (*Broderick v. Ruder*)

In *Priest v. Rotary*, a waitress was subjected to unwelcome sexual conduct by her employer, the restaurant owner. This conduct included putting his arms around her, placing his hands on her breasts and on her knee, kissing her, rubbing his body against hers, unzipping her uniform, and exposing himself to her. After the waitress complained to the owner about his behavior and asked him to stop on numerous occasions, he detrimentally affected her employment conditions by assigning her to work in a less desirable station, subjecting her to hostility and abuse, and eventually terminating her employment. In contrast, the owner gave preferential treatment to his consensual sexual partner and to other female employees who endured his sexual conduct. The court upheld the waitress's claim for sex discrimination based on the owner's preferential treatment of female employees who submitted to his sexual advances or tolerated his sexual conduct.

E. Employer Response to Harassment Claims

Employers who promptly investigate sexual harassment claims, particularly hostile environment cases, and take the proper remedial action (such as reprimand or discharge the employee engaging in harassment) may avoid liability. In *Swentek v. USAir,* a flight attendant brought a sexual harassment claim against the airline alleging, under Title VII, that a pilot exposed himself to her, put his hand up the skirt of her uniform, made numerous obscene comments to and about her, and made obscene telephone calls to her home. She alleged that these actions established a hostile work environment. Upon receiving the sexual harassment complaint, the airline performed an investigation and issued a written warning to the pilot pursuant to the airline's progressive discipline policy. Upon review, the court concluded that even though the pilot engaged in unwelcome sexual conduct, creating a sexually hostile working environment, the airline was not liable under the law because it took prompt and adequate remedial action upon learning of the problem.

When responding to claims of sexual harassment, the employer must consider the rights of the alleged harasser. Claims of sexual harassment are defamatory if proved to be false. Employers, however, are not obligated to clear the name of a supervisor falsely accused of harassment or sexual impropriety. (*Martin v. Baer*) Indeed, at least one employer has sued its manager for indemnification, that is, to recover a sum paid in settlement of a claim by a female former employee who claimed the manager had sexually harassed her. The manager admitted that on a business trip he entered the female employee's hotel room while drunk and naked and that in the office he said things to her such as "Susan, when you smoke, you look like a slut." The court found that the employer could pursue its claim against the manager for indemnification. (*Biggs v. Surrey Broadcasting Co.*)

The costs to an employer of a sexual harassment case can be substantial. Experience has shown that employers who take some or all of the following steps are best positioned to prevent, or at least minimize, such claims.

- Issue and strictly apply a specific policy prohibiting sexual harassment. Make sure that both supervisors and employees are familiar with the sexual harassment policy;
- Develop and implement a training program to inform supervisors what behavior constitutes sexual harassment and when and how to investigate claims;
- Develop an internal grievance procedure under which sexual harassment claims can be addressed and remedied without requiring the harassed employee to complain to the alleged harasser. Instruct all employees on what behavior is inappropriate and how to lodge a complaint;
- Do a visual survey of all work areas. If you see sexually explicit or discriminatory cartoons, centerfolds, pictures, or cartoons, remove them;
- Observe the language and behavior of supervisors and employees. If the language or behavior could be construed

as harassing or discriminatory toward men or women, ensure that your employees are counseled and told they could be fired if such language or behavior continues. Document this counseling;

- Ensure that "couples" do not work within the same chain of command; and
- Make sure that all sexual harassment claims are fully and promptly investigated and addressed.

IV. RELATIONSHIPS AND ACTIVITIES

Good relationships among employees in an office can bind colleagues by building a better working atmosphere and sense of collegiality, which in turn tends to promote greater efficiency and productivity (as well as profits for management).

Like any good thing, however, these general concepts have limits. Inevitably, there are lines that cannot be crossed. Family members working together may result in a cozy, comfortable workplace; it may also produce a destructive, circle-the-wagons response to management's decisions affecting individual family members. A work relationship among friends may build healthy competition and concern for each other's well-being; it may also carry with it unacceptable favoritism. An office romance may provide the office rumormongers with endless material and entertainment for their colleagues; it may also digress into on-site lovers' quarrels.

The law does not require a friendly or warm work setting. Indeed, social ostracism in the workplace is not unlawful. As stated by one judge, "There is no constitutional, statutory, or common law duty requiring an employee to be socially friendly with his or her co-employees. . . . Conversely, an employee does not have any 'right' to social friendship from his co-employees." (*Eserhut v. Heister*)

What follows is a review of the courts' attempts to balance the individual rights and interests of employees and the legitimate business interests of employers arising from familial and romantic relationships, both on and off the job.

A. Familial Relationships

The issue of family relationships in the workplace most typically arises in the context of nepotism rules that limit the employment opportunities of employees' relatives. The logic for nepotism rules is simple: Employees are likely to favor relatives, including their spouses, over other employees, and such favoritism serves to detract from a sense of fairness in the workplace.

Some companies encourage the employment of relatives. Arguments favoring such a policy include:

- Hiring of relatives is an effective recruiting tool;
- Relatives working together can create a warm, supportive family atmosphere in the workplace; and
- Employers lose their investment in an employee if a nepotism rule requires termination of a family member co-worker.

In contrast, the arguments supporting nepotism rules include assertions that the employment of relatives invites favoritism in the workplace with increased opportunities for:

- Breaches of security with family members working in tandem;
- Conflicts of interest;
- Bad feelings if a family member is disciplined, terminated, or not hired; and
- Family disputes or emergencies that will disrupt the workplace.

Nepotism rules have traditionally been found to be lawful in the face of constitutional (*Waters v. Geston County*) and common law (*Wright v. MetroHealth Medical Ctr.*) challenges. "No-spouse" rules, for example, limiting the ability of spouses to work in the same part of the company or even for the same company, have generally been held to be lawful where applied equitably to both men and women. In contrast, a rule that barred the employment of wives of employees but not husbands would be illegal (EEOC Dec. 70453, October 20, 1987) as would a rule that required the termination of the spouse who is not "head of the household." (*George v. Farmers Elec. Coop.*) A no-spouse rule, neutral on its face, that is applied discriminatorily to deny employment opportunities to women has been found unlawful. (*Yuhas v. Libby-Owens-Ford Co.*)

In contrast to valid "no-spouse" rules, "no-marriage" rules, that is, rules that bar the employment of individuals who are married, have been disfavored by courts. Such rules directly violate state "marital status" laws that prohibit discrimination in employment based on the fact that an individual is or is not married. Many states have enacted such laws. Nepotism rules have been challenged successfully in states such as California, Connecticut, and New York, which prohibit discrimination based on marital status.

No-marriage rules may also be unlawful on discrimination grounds. For example, in *Sprogis v. United Air Lines*, a stewardess challenged the airline's "no-marriage" rule for stewardesses as discriminatory based on sex. The court held that the airline's policy violated Title VII where the marital status rule was applicable only to stewardesses and had never been applied to any male employee in any position.

The decision of the Hawaii Supreme Court in *Ross v. Stouffer Hotel Co.* is instructive. In that case, two massage therapists, a man and a woman, lived together. Eleven days after one was hired to work in the same hotel as the other one already worked, they were married. The next year, the hotel was purchased and the new owner, applying a no-nepotism rule, offered each one the opportunity to transfer out of the department in which they both worked and, after they refused, terminated them both. The couple sued under Hawaii law barring discrimination on the basis of marital status and won. The court reasoned that the fact of their marriage was the cause of their terminations and noted, "Apparently continued cohabitation without going through a marriage ceremony would not have been a violation of the policy." The court discounted the hotel's argument that it was not the fact of their marriage but who they married that was the cause of their terminations. The court objected to what it called the Hobson's choice between either losing employment or seeking a divorce and cohabiting instead. Similarly, a state government nepotism rule that prevented the employment of a court clerk if that person had a relative on the police force was found to be unlawful as having a chilling effect on marriage. (*Hughes v. Lipscher*)

Favoritism based on family ties is not by itself unlawful. For example, Jack Thomas owned a general contracting business in which his son Steve was employed as a supervisor. Jeri Platner, a married employee, worked with Steve. Steve's wife, Savonda, worked part-time as a secretary. Savonda became extremely jealous of Platner, believing her husband and Platner were having an affair. One evening, Steve returned home late after having visited a co-worker in the hospital with a smudge on his collar that Savonda believed to be makeup. The next day, Savonda confronted Platner in the workplace, but she was later forced to apologize for the incident. Savonda later saw Platner wearing a bikini at an outing with co-workers present. Shortly after, Jack dismissed Platner, in the court's words, "to protect his son . . ., to quiet his daughter-in-law, and to preserve whatever he could of a conventional family unit environment for his grandchild." Platner sued, alleging sexual discrimination because she was fired due to this perceived office romance whereas Steve was not. The court rejected this claim, finding that the "ultimate basis for Platner's dismissal was not gender but simply favoritism for a close relative. However unseemly and regrettable nepotism may be as a basis for employment decisions in most contexts, it is clear that nepotism as such does not constitute discrimination." (*Platner v. Cash & Thomas Contractors, Inc.*)

The same analysis applies to the promotion of the white nephew of an interviewer over a black applicant. The court concluded, "A promotion decision motivated by favoritism toward relatives, however unfair, may be qualitatively different from a decision motivated by racial animus." (*Holder v. City of Raleigh*)

B. Romantic Relationships

Romance in the office is inevitable and has become more prevalent as a result of the greater percentage of working women and the longer hours worked by many Americans. One thing is for certain—it will not be eliminated by legal fiat.

Unlike sexual harassment, which is both unlawful and destructive to an employer's operations, romance in the office is neither necessarily unlawful nor harmful to an employer's business interests. It may become so, however, as a result of the positions held by the couple, their inappropriate behavior, or the detrimental effect of the relationship on normal business operations. At its worst, an office romance can interfere with normal work relationships, distort priorities, engender favoritism, and serve as an unhealthy office distraction. Moreover, where the romantic interest is unwelcome on one party's part, claims of sexual harassment may arise, and claims of unlawful sexual favoritism may be made by co-workers denied employment opportunities for which they were qualified. Distinguishing between consensual romantic relationships and unwelcome ones can be difficult. As one court of appeals judge noted, the difference between "invited, uninvited-but-welcome, offensive-but-tolerated, and flatly rejected" sexual advances may be difficult to determine (*Barnes v. Costle*)

On the other hand, office romances implicate basic individual associational and privacy rights and societal interests in marriage. Employers are not of a single mind as to whether to bar, limit, ignore, or encourage romance in the office. Surveys demonstrate that most employers have no established policies regarding personal relationships between their employees. Among the problems encountered when preparing such policies are defining the prohibited behavior, enforcing such rules, ensuring consistency in application, and limiting their application to on-the-job activities. Those few employers that have "no-fraternization," "no-dating," or similar rules have generally had those policies upheld in court when challenged. (*Crosier v. United Parcel Serv.*) Nepotism rules also come into play if the relationship results in marriage.

Whether or not a policy is implemented, legal challenges may result based on the employer's response to office romances. Grounds for such claims include sex discrimination, sexual harassment, marital status laws, wrongful discharge based on violations of public policy, the implied covenant of good faith and fair dealing, breach of contract, infliction of emotional distress, third-party interference with contract, and defamation.

Management is better able to sustain its legal position if its actions are the result of on-the-job rather than off-the-job activities. Courts tend to be more sympathetic to an employer's defense of its actions where the romance unduly affects the employer's operations as the result of on-the-job activities. On the other hand, an employer's attempt to dictate off-the-job employee activities that do not interfere with work performance are less likely to be sustained.

1. On-the-Job Romance

Courts have generally ruled that where a romance between a supervisor and subordinate is consensual, it is not unlawful (although it might be unprofessional) for the supervisor to favor the subordinate in employment matters. This determination might be different if the relationship were not consensual, in which case it would constitute sexual harassment, or if the sexual activity in the office were so pervasive as to raise issues of sexual favoritism.

A federal appeals court held that federal laws prohibiting sex discrimination were not violated when a male supervisor hired a female applicant with whom he was romantically involved rather than promoting qualified male employees. (*DeCintio v. Westchester County Medical Ctr.*) In so holding, the court distinguished between gender and sexual activity. The court concluded that the word "sex" as used by Congress in federal discrimination legislation "logically could only refer to membership in a class delineated by gender, rather than sexual activity regardless of gender."

Courts also generally have upheld enforcement of no romance and related policies as being legitimate exercises of management's prerogative to run its business operations in the way it sees fit. For example, courts have sustained the application of a "no-dating" policy (*Sears v. Ryder Truck Rental*), a "no-fraternization" rule (*Crosier v. United Parcel Serv.*), a "no romance with married associates" policy (*Federated Rural Elec. Ins. v. Kessler*), and a "no relatives on the same shift" policy (even though the two employees were only living together and were not married). (*Ward v. Frito-Lay, Inc.*)

In *Somers v. Westours, Inc.*, a female general manager and a male executive chef at a hotel became romantically involved. Their relationship severely disrupted the hotel's operations as they both came to work late, neglected their duties, played "grab ass" in the workplace, and were found drunk on the premises after work by a supervisor. On one occasion, the woman's separated husband threatened the male employee with a gun on the hotel's premises. The employer first counseled the two employees and then terminated them for ignoring the warning. Both employees sued and their claims of wrongful discharge, breach of contract, and violation of public policy were rejected.

It also is not unlawful merely to ask for romantic involvement and to be rebuffed, so long as no repercussions follow. A Florida appeals court ruled that it is not an invasion of privacy for a boss to seek to induce a subordinate's sexual favors through utterances rather than actions. (*Ponton v. Scarfone*) This result would have been different had the target of the solicitation suffered discriminatory treatment as a result or if the behavior was persistent or unseemly.

Bearing the boss's child may constitute proper grounds for termination of an employee, according to one federal court in Georgia. The court rejected a claim of sex discrimination (no claim of sexual harassment was raised), reasoning that the female subordinate "was not terminated because she was a woman, but because of her sexual relationship with [her boss] and the consequences thereof." (*Freeman v. Continental Technical Servs.*)

2. Off-the-Job Romance

Discipline or discharge for romantic or sexual activities off-the-job presents a more difficult issue and has resulted in varying responses by courts.

Convictions for sex crimes that detract from an employee's ability to perform the requirements of the job present perhaps the strongest case for discharge of employment based on off-the-job sexual activities. For example, a janitor at a veterans' hospital was held to be properly discharged following his conviction for sexually molesting his 11-year-old niece. The janitor, who was retarded, had argued that his discharge constituted disability discrimination. (*Watkins v. Turnage*) Similarly, a probationary police officer was terminated after it was learned that he had had sexual relations years before while an Explorer Scout with a 15-year-old girl, which constituted statutory rape. A federal appeals court denied the police officer's constitutional claims of privacy and associational rights, finding that the illegality of the police officer's acts "creates a substantial barrier to his successful assertion" of his claim. (*Fleisher v. City of Signal Hill*)

Discharges have similarly been upheld under the following circumstances:

- An employee refused to break off a relationship with a co-employee that admittedly took place on his own time and did not affect his performance; the court rejected the employee's wrongful discharge claim while still admitting that it may seem "harsh" that employers can terminate based on a "dislike of the employee's personal lifestyle"; (*Patton v. J.C. Penney Co.*)

- A female employee who willingly dated her supervisor, went to his parents' house, had sexual intercourse with him, and later accused the supervisor of rape, was found not to have a claim of sexual harassment against her employer; the court concluded that these off-the-job activities were not related to her employment; (*Capitol City Foods, Inc. v. Superior Court, Sacramento County*)

- An employee was terminated because of a prior sexual relationship he had with his current supervisor; (*Trumbauer v. Group Health Coop.*) and

- A female employee's termination was based on a prior sexual relationship with a male co-worker after the male co-worker's wife called management seeking her termination. The male employee's resignation was rejected and the female co-worker was terminated because she was the lesser skilled of the two employees. The court found no sex discrimination in this setting. (*C. Thorrez Indus. v. Michigan Dep't of Civil Rights*)

In contrast, discharges for off-the-job romances have been successfully challenged in other cases. For example, in *Rulon-Miller v. IBM.*, a successful manager for IBM in California was dating a former employee of IBM who now worked for a competitor. The jury found that the IBM manager had been terminated for her refusal to stop dating an employee of a competitor. IBM's strong privacy policy, which assures employment even though a manager may not approve of an employee's off-the-job behavior, was found by the jury to have been violated in this case and was used against IBM.

Similarly, the Kansas Supreme Court held that a married (but separated) male employee and an unmarried female co-worker who accompanied him on a business trip on her own time and at her own expense could challenge their terminations resulting from their trip. (*Morriss v. Coleman Co.*) The employees alleged that the employer had promised that their employment could be terminated only for just cause.

A police officer's constitutional right to freedom of association, which applies only to public and not private employees, was held violated where he was fired for dating the adopted daughter of a convicted felon and known organized crime figure. (*Wilson v. Taylor*) A married police officer successfully challenged his department's ability under the Constitution to terminate his employment because he cohabited with a married woman not his wife. The police department argued that such behavior was "unbecoming" of a police officer and cited an antiquated statute relating to illegal cohabitation between individuals not married to one another. (*Briggs v. North Muskegon Police Dep't*) In contrast, the discharge of a male police sergeant and a female police dispatcher for cohabitation in violation of department rules was found to be constitutional. (*Kukla v. Village of Antioch*)

In an extreme case, a woman who was drugged and raped by her boss while his wife slept next to them was held to have a claim for sexual discrimination, battery, and intentional infliction of emotional distress. When the boss's wife woke up to find an unconscious woman who worked for her husband in the bed next to her, she insisted that he fire her. The woman employee was awarded more than $160,000 in damages. (*Gilardi v. Schroeder*) In contrast, an employee who was discharged for refusing to allow his boss to date his wife did not state a sexual discrimination or harassment claim. The court relied on the absence of sexual advances or requests made by the employer to an employee, and on the fact that "no qualified potential employee was denied an employment opportunity because another employee submitted to sexual advances." (*Cairo v. OH Material Corp.*)

C. Off-the-Job Activities

An employee's off-the-job activities may, under certain circumstances, properly be taken into account by an employer in making employment decisions. To be permissible, it depends on, among other things, whether the employee is a public or private employee, the extent to which the off-the-job activities injure the employer's reputation or the employee's on-the-job performance, the nature of the activities and, if there is a lawsuit over the issue, the state in which the case is filed.

Public employees, who are guaranteed due process under federal and state constitutions, are less likely to suffer on-the-job repercussions for their off-the-job activities. For example, a municipal rule barring employment of police officers in the security field during their off-hours was held unconstitutional. (*Bowman v. Township of Pennsauken*) Similarly, a male California prison guard was reinstated to his job after being fired following an incident in which he was found in an elementary school parking lot in the evening wearing only female underwear, an unbuttoned shirt, and thongs. The California appellate court found an insufficient basis for concluding that the prison guard's job performance would be affected as a result of the incident, but rather found that the termination was caused in part by the animosity of the guard's co-workers to the employee's lifestyle. (*Yancey v. State Personnel Bd.*) In an extreme case, a court held that a Social Security Administration employee who murdered his girlfriend's paramour in a crime of passion was properly reinstated after serving his prison time despite the concerns of co-workers. The court concluded that his reinstatement would not adversely affect the efficiency of the agency. (*Horner v. Hardy*)

In contrast, a highway patrolman's off-the-job nudity was found to be grounds for dismissal. The patrolman in that case appeared nude in front of neighborhood women and children on several occasions despite receiving written warnings from his superiors to avoid such scenes. (*Anderson v. California State Personnel Bd.*) Similarly, a female law enforcement officer was forced to resign after her husband was found masturbating in the same room with a male colleague of hers. Her supervisor expressed concern about her ability to continue to work with her colleague. The court denied the female officer's various claims noting that homosexuality is not a fundamental right under the constitution. (*Dawson v. State Law Enforcement Div.*)

Private employers do not face the same constitutional restrictions on their activities as public employers and, consequently, have greater discretion in responding to employees' off-the-job activities. For example, a court found that an employee who had lost three fingers in a work-related accident was properly terminated when he called in sick so that he could shoot 18 holes of golf. The employer fired him on the spot when the employee tried in vain to justify the outing as being part of his doctor's recommended therapy. (*Georgia-Pacific Corp. v. Paperworkers Int'l Union*)

A number of states have enacted laws precluding employers from discriminating against applicants and employees for off-the-job lawful activities such as smoking, including Illinois, Minnesota, Nevada, New York, North Carolina, North Dakota and Wisconsin. Some states, such as New York, take a more expansive view and protect a wide range of off-duty activities including the employee's political activities and "legal recreational activities."

Job decisions based in part or in whole on social relationships off-the-job may be subject to challenge if unlawful discrimination underlies the decision. For example, an African-American maintenance supervisor was allowed to sue for race discrimination when a white hospital administrator selected a white employee with whom he had an after-hours social relationship for a promotion over the African-American supervisor. (*Roberts v. Gadsden Memorial Hosp.*) The court found that the qualifications of the employee who got the promotion "consisted of attending the same barbecues as [the hospital administrator] and becoming a 'drinking buddy' of the hospital administrator" and "that the promotion decision was nothing more than a typical 'good ol' boy' appointment." Similarly, the selection of a male "lifelong personal friend" over a better qualified female applicant for the position of assistant superintendent of police was found to support a claim of sex discrimination. (*Waldorf v. Board of Comm'rs*)

One court ruled that punishing employees for associating away from work with what the employer perceives to be "undesirables"—in this case, a union organizer—may violate public policy. The court reasoned that to allow an employer to punish an employee on such grounds would interfere with a private-sector employee's right of free association and speech. (*Ring v. River Walk Manor*) One California jury awarded more than $1 million to a network vice president who alleged that he was wrongfully terminated because he was not part of the network's "hard-drinking, hard-driving" crowd and instead went home to his wife rather than go drinking with his fellow executives. (*Boehm v. American Broadcasting Co.*)

In *Wagenseller v. Scottsdale Memorial Hosp.*, hospital personnel went on an eight-day camping and rafting trip. One woman, a nurse and paramedic coordinator, declined to participate in certain activities during the trip. In particular, she declined to "moon" the audience in a skit entitled "Moon River." The nurse alleged that her relationship with her supervisor deteriorated as a result, and eventually this led to her termination. The Arizona Supreme Court allowed the nurse to sue for wrongful discharge in violation of public policy, which in this instance meant the violation of the indecent exposure statute. The court wrote that "termination of employment for refusal to participate in public exposure of one's buttocks is a termination contrary to public policy. Even if, for instance, the employer might have ground to believe that all onlookers were voyeurs and would not be offended."

In sum, while off-the-job activities are generally not the province of the employer unless a tangible workplace impact is shown, employers maintain wide discretion in employment decisions unless discrimination or privacy laws or, in the case of public-sector employees, constitutional provisions are violated.

V. SEXUAL AND REPRODUCTIVE FREEDOM

Among the most controversial issues in U.S. law relate to a woman's right to have an abortion, the rights of pregnant women, and the legal rights of homosexuals.

As with any other privacy or employment law issue, an employer that bases its personnel actions on work performance rather than on an employee's medical condition—such as pregnancy—or on nonwork activities or lifestyle—such as having an abortion or one's sexual preference—is more likely to survive legal challenges based on any employment-related law.

A. Sexual Orientation

An employee's sexual orientation and off-the-job activities are unrelated to his or her on-the-job performance. Nonetheless, unless expressly prohibited, discrimination on the basis of sexual orientation is, at least on the surface, legal. Indeed, sexual orientation discrimination has become more widespread since the outbreak of the AIDS epidemic, a disease often associated with homosexuals.

Federal civil rights legislation does not protect against discrimination based on sexual orientation or sexual identity. For example, claims alleging discrimination based on the effeminate appearance of a male (*Smith v. Liberty Mut. Ins.*), homosexuality (*Sommers v. Budget Mktg.*), or transsexuality (*Ulane v. Eastern Airlines*) have been rejected. Claims of harassment based on sexual orientation also have been rejected under federal civil rights law. (*Dillon v. Frank*) Discrimination on the basis of sexual orientation is, however, expressly prohibited in nine states—California, Connecticut, Hawaii, Massachusetts, Minnesota, New Jersey, Rhode Island, Vermont, and Wisconsin—and in more than one hundred cities and counties, including Atlanta, New York, Philadelphia, San Francisco, Washington, D.C., and West Palm Beach. Homosexuality is not considered a disability under the Americans With Disabilities Act or related state disability laws and, consequently, homosexuals are provided with no protection under these laws based solely on their sexual orientation. However, discrimination based on a perception that a homosexual has or may develop AIDS, a protected disability, is unlawful.

Constitutional challenges to discrimination on the basis of sexual orientation have met with little success. For example, the Federal Bureau of Investigation was found not to have violated the Equal Protection Clause when it declined to hire a homosexual applicant for a special agent position. (*Padula v. Webster*) The Navy's policy of requiring the discharge of all homosexuals in its ranks was similarly found not to violate an individual's rights to privacy or equal protection. (*Dronenburg v. Zech*) Similarly, a sheriff's department did not violate the constitutional right of association of a female deputy for engaging in a homosexual relationship with another female officer. The deputy had contended that she was forced to quit after she was denied the opportunity to ride while off duty in the patrol car with her alleged lover. The court found the department's reason, to quell rumors in the community regarding the relationship, to be a legitimate, nondiscriminatory reason. (*Endsley v. Naes*) In addition, in *Shahar v. Bowers*, the court ruled that the Georgia Department of Law did not violate the plaintiff's constitutional rights to freedom of association, freedom of religion, equal protection under the law, or substantive due process when it withdrew its offer of employment from the plaintiff after learning that the plaintiff, a woman, was planning to marry another woman. The court reasoned that since Georgia law did not recognize same-sex marriages and prohibits consensual homosexual sodomy, hiring the plaintiff could adversely affect the Department's credibility with the public and conflict with the need to employ attorneys who act "with discretion, good judgment, and in a manner which does not conflict with the work of other Department attorneys."

Challenges to discrimination on the basis of sexual orientation have met with some limited success in wrongful discharge actions. In perhaps the most notable case, a former Shell Oil employee was awarded $5.3 million by a judge in California where he was discharged based on his off-the-job sexual activity. In that case, the employee, an executive at a bioscience facility, used his office computer to prepare invitations for a nude party at which group homosexual activity was planned. The invitation included a discussion of "safe sex." The court found the company's actions to be outrageous and concluded that the employee "was fired solely because he was a sexually active homosexual." The court discounted Shell Oil's contention that the employee's unauthorized use of his office computer warranted discharge and concluded that at best a reprimand was warranted. (*Collins v. Shell Oil Co.*)

A California court has determined that the right of privacy recognized in the state constitution prohibits the asking of questions related to sexual orientation on a psychological test unless the employer demonstrates a compelling need for the information. In that case, applicants for security guard positions were asked to respond to such statements as "I am very strongly attracted by members of my own sex" and "I have often wished that I was a girl." The employer's contention that the test was needed to screen out applicants who were emotionally unstable or unreliable or who had violent or addictive tendencies was rejected. (*Soroka v. Dayton Hudson Corp.*)

B. Pregnancy and Related Matters

1. Pregnancy

Federal law expressly prohibits discrimination based on "pregnancy, childbirth or related medical conditions." For example, a court awarded damages to both a pregnant waitress who was discharged for "looking tacky" as the result of her pregnancy and a co-worker who refused to discharge the pregnant employee as directed and was discharged herself as a result. The court rejected the restaurant's argument that its action was in the best interest of both mother and child. In addition to awarding back pay to the employees, the court awarded front pay (that is, compensation for a period of time after the court's decision) to the pregnant employee to compensate her for the fact that she was not earning the same in her subsequent employment as she had with the defendant restaurant. (*EEOC v. Red Baron Steak Houses*)

In another case, a female employee at a bank in Puerto Rico had been having an open and notorious affair with the bank's assistant comptroller who was married. She had a child out of wedlock in 1982 and the assistant comptroller secured employer-paid health coverage for the child. Both employees were fired in January 1987, when she returned from vacation pregnant. The bank, in response to her sex discrimination claim, alleged that she was fired for violating a bank rule requiring that employees conduct themselves with decency and morality. The court concluded that this was just a pretext, as evidenced by the fact that the bank had acquiesced in the relationship for at least five years and that the real reason for the bank's actions was her pregnancy. "Despite the bank's familiarity with the ongoing relationship, there was no evidence that any person in authority *ever* spoke to [the woman employee] about her love life, or suggested that she break off the liaison, until the day she was fired—shortly after her [pregnancy] had become apparent." (*Cumpiano v. Banco Santander Puerto Rico*)

In another case, two female employees of a property management company initially told their employer that they were not planning to have children in the near future; both, however, became pregnant within a few years of being hired. When each informed the employer of her pregnancy, they were each assured that their jobs would be available to them when they returned from maternity leave. Instead, one employee was terminated prior to her return to work, and the second returned to work to find her job responsibilities significantly reduced, and was terminated shortly thereafter. The jury awarded one woman $225,000 and the other $210,000 in compensatory damages, and awarded each $250,000 in punitive damages (*Rendine v. Pantzer*)

In contrast, a female employee informed the president of the corporation during her job interview that she was not planning to have any more children; she was, in fact, pregnant at the time and knew that she was pregnant. Two months later, after being hired, she informed the president of her pregnancy. The employer terminated her as an employee and entered into an independent contractor relationship with her instead. The president testified that he would have hired the woman had he known that she was pregnant, but that he felt betrayed and upset that she had lied to him. The Supreme Judicial Court of Massachusetts affirmed the jury's verdict in favor the employer. (*Lysak v. Seiler Corp.*)

Laws prohibiting discrimination on the basis of pregnancy also prohibit discrimination on the basis of pregnancy-related medical conditions. For example, in *Pacourek v. Inland Steel Co.* the court ruled that a medical condition preventing the employee from becoming pregnant naturally is a medical condition related to pregnancy and is thus covered by Title VII; the court also ruled that discrimination based on potential or intended pregnancy is unlawful. The right to have an abortion, as discussed further in the next section, also has been held to be encompassed by the concept of pregnancy-related medical conditions. (*Turic v. Holland Hospitality, Inc.*)

Furthermore, one court found in favor of a pregnant employee who used her employer's sick-leave policy to cover absences from work due to pregnancy-related illness and near-miscarriages and was terminated. The court stated, "[I]t is a violation of the [Pregnancy Discrimination Act] for an employer to deny a pregnant employee the benefits commonly afforded temporarily disabled workers in similar positions, or to discharge a pregnant employee for using those benefits." (*Byrd v. Lakeshore Hosp.*) On the other hand, an employee who was chronically late for work due to morning sickness during pregnancy failed to state a claim for discrimination. The court reasoned that the employer was required "to ignore an employee's pregnancy, but . . . not her absence from work, unless the employer overlooks the comparable absences of non-pregnant employees . . . in which event it would not be ignoring pregnancy at all." (*Troupe v. May Dep't Stores Co.*)

2. Abortion

Discrimination on the basis of having an abortion has been ruled unlawful. In *Doe v. First Nat'l Bank of Chicago*, Doe was instructed to complete five tasks before she went on vacation. She failed to do so because she took time off to have an abortion. Upon her return to work, she was terminated. The court held that an employee may not be discriminated against because she has had an abortion. Nonetheless, the court found that Doe had failed to complete assigned tasks and therefore was discharged for nondiscriminatory reasons. In addition, under the law of the District of Columbia, an employee who alleged that she was terminated because of her refusal to have an abortion stated successfully a claim for wrongful discharge. (*MacNabb v. MacCartee*)

Furthermore, in *Turic v. Holland Hospitality, Inc.*, the plaintiff, a hotel employee, was terminated because of an "uproar" that occurred in the workplace after she revealed that she was considering having an abortion. Many of the employee's co-workers, who had religious beliefs against abortion, were "very offended" by the discussions in the workplace regarding her possible abortion. While she chose to carry her pregnancy to term, the court ruled that discrimination on the basis of contemplation of having an abortion is unlawful. Finding that the employee had been discriminated against on that basis, the court awarded her back pay and compensatory and punitive damages.

3. *Reproductive Hazards and Fetal Protection Policies*

Certain chemicals used in the workplace pose dangers to employees exposed to them. Those with knowledge of the risk may be said to have assumed the occupational hazard. For example, an occupational hazard of being a running back for a professional football team is that you will be tackled and may be injured as a result. The running back chooses to assume that risk.

While the health and safety of a fetus is primarily the concern of the parents, the employer of a pregnant employee or an employee whose reproductive system has been damaged through workplace exposure to harmful chemicals runs the risk of liability for prenatal injuries under such legal principles as negligence and wrongful death. In response, a number of employers have developed and implemented reproductive-hazard or fetal protection policies designed to limit the chance of prenatal injuries. However benevolent, these policies tend to have a disproportionate impact on women.

The leading case in this area decided by the Supreme Court involved a fetal protection policy excluding women capable of bearing children from working in certain positions. The Court

ruled unequivocally that such an exclusionary policy constituted unlawful sex discrimination. (*Aerospace & Agric. Implement
Workers v. Johnson Controls Inc.*)

The Johnson Controls Corporation manufactures batteries.
Exposure to lead used in the process presents health risks to
employees and to fetuses. For years, the company simply warned
employees of the danger and urged fertile women expecting to
conceive children not to work in those areas. This policy changed
following indications that pregnant employees had critically high
lead levels (although no lost pregnancies were reported). Although there was evidence that lead also presented a health hazard to the reproductive systems of males, the company prohibited all women (and only women) from working in positions in
which they would be exposed to lead unless their inability to
bear children was medically documented. Among those who
challenged the policy was a woman who chose to be sterilized in
order to keep her position.

The Supreme Court held that the policy was discriminatory
on its face because it focused on the childbearing capacities of
women rather than the dangers to the fertility of members of
either sex. The Court noted that the obligation on the employer
was to concern itself with an employee's ability to perform a job
safely and efficiently and, "Decisions about the welfare of future
children must be left to the parents who conceive, bear, support,
and raise them rather than to employers who hire those parents."
The Court went on to say that the employer's "fear of prenatal
injury, no matter how sincere, does not begin to show that substantially all of its fertile women employees are incapable of doing their jobs." The Court acknowledged the potential for an
employer's liability for prenatal injuries suffered by the offspring
of its employees, but noted that the likelihood of liability would
be remote if the employer complied with applicable government
safety regulations, warned employees of known dangers, and did
not act negligently.

In short, reproductive hazard policies run the risk of being
found discriminatory unless they are based on accepted scientific evidence of the alleged risk; applied to both sexes equally
where the danger is present for both; narrowly drawn to limit
employment opportunities only to the extent necessary to neu-

tralize the hazard; and effectively communicated to employees exposed to the dangers.

Reproductive hazards can also raise important issues when it is the pregnant employee, rather than the employer, who is concerned with fetal protection. For example, an employer was held to have violated a state human rights law when a pregnant employee had a reasonable belief that spray paint fumes near her work area might be dangerous to her fetus, but the employer failed to make a reasonable effort to find a temporary position for her away from the danger or to place her in a safer position that was in fact available. (*Penn Mfg. v. Comm'n on Human Rights and Opportunities*) In contrast, in *Armstrong v. Flowers Hosp., Inc.,* the plaintiff, a nurse in her first trimester of pregnancy, was terminated because she refused to treat a patient who was HIV positive, believing that to do so would risk the health of her fetus. The court denied her claim of sex discrimination under Title VII, stating, "An employer is generally prohibited from deciding for a pregnant employee what course of action is best for her. This prohibition does not constitute a requirement that an employer make alternative work available."

Employee suits brought on behalf of their children alleging prenatal injury based on the employer's negligence may be precluded by state workers' compensation statutes which provide the exclusive remedies for workplace injuries. (*Bell v. Macy's California*) Remedies available to employees for prenatal injuries to their children under those circumstances would be those available under the applicable workers' compensation laws.

VI. PERSONAL HABITS, CONDITIONS, AND ADDICTIONS

Employees bring with them to the workplace—in addition to their job-related skills—personal habits, conditions, or addictions that may affect their performance on the job. An alcoholic may only drink off the job, but impaired performance on the job may be one manifestation of the disease. The Exxon Valdez oil spill disaster is a horrific example of the damage that can be caused by an alcoholic employee. The captain of the oil tanker was undergoing treatment for alcoholism under the company's employee assistance program at the time of the accident that resulted in billions of dollars of environmental and property damage and liability for the company. Can an employer base an employment decision not on an individual's present inability to perform the job—for example, where an employee arrives to work drunk—but rather on an individual's condition, such as alcoholism, or an individual's personal habit, such as smoking? Similarly, can an employer refuse to hire a smoker because smokers as a group are demonstrably more expensive to cover under its health plan?

Three trends have brought these issues into focus. First, society has become less tolerant of such habits as smoking and drinking, while simultaneously becoming more willing to recognize that such habits, where chronic, are disabling addictions. Indeed, in some states, the definition of protected disabilities has been broadened to include not merely drug addiction and alcoholism but such matters as obesity and stress-related conditions.

Second, as the cost of health coverage has increased dramatically, employers have become more cost-conscious. Consequently, many employers view with suspicion employees with habits, conditions, or addictions that may make them less productive employees and more expensive to cover with health insurance.

Third, employer intrusions in the lifestyle and off-the-job activities of employees or applicants have not gone unnoticed. Most notably, legislation designed principally to protect lawful activities away from the workplace in general, and off-the-job smoking in particular, have been enacted in a growing number of states.

A. Disability Law

Federal law and the law of 47 states (all except Alabama, Arkansas, and Mississippi) prohibit discrimination in private employment on the basis of disability. The Americans With Disabilities Act (ADA) applies to employers with 15 or more employees. The ADA does not preempt other federal or state laws that provide comparable or greater protection to the disabled. It is estimated that 43 million Americans—having more than 900 disabilities—are protected by these laws. Indeed, an employer is not only prohibited from discriminating but may have to accommodate reasonably persons with disabilities who are otherwise qualified for a position.

The application of disability laws to individuals with birth defects or diseases such as cancer is uncontroversial. A more difficult issue arises when the "disabilities" to be protected are emotional or mental rather than physical. The issue is complicated further by the question of the extent to which biology affects behavior. Is an individual obese because he or she lacks self-control at the dessert tray, or is it in the person's genes? Is an obese person disabled? Is someone who objects to cigarette smoke disabled or oversensitive? Is a supervisor who compulsively sexually harasses subordinates disabled or a deviant? These difficult issues increasingly will be addressed in the context of disability law.

Disability is generally defined under these laws as a physical or mental impairment that substantially limits one or more of the individual's major life activities, such as caring for oneself, walking, seeing, hearing, or speaking. A person who has a record or history of such an impairment or who is perceived as having such an impairment, whether or not he or she is actually so impaired, is generally protected under most disability laws. The scope of the definition of disability varies widely and, consequently, habits, conditions, or addictions that may be protected from discrimination in one state may not be so in another. For example, New York has declared obesity a protected disability (*State Div. of Human Rights v. Xerox Corp.*), while the Pennsylvania Supreme Court has rejected such a claim. (*Civil Serv. Comm'n of Pittsburgh v. Pennsylvania Human Relations Comm'n*) In one New York obesity case, a woman alleged that television personality David Susskind reneged on a job offer after she had resigned her prior employment. She alleged that she was told to come back for a job when she had lost some weight. The court ruled that this stated a claim for unlawful discrimination under New York law on the basis of obesity. Similarly, a New Jersey court held that an office manager who was terminated because management believed he was too heavy stated a claim for perceived disability based on obesity even if the office manager had not been shown to be actually disabled. (*Gimello v. Agency Rent-A-Car*)

The definition of disability has been further extended under some disability laws to include:

- Dyslexia; (*Fitzgerald v. Green Valley Area Educ. Agency*)
- A mastectomy involving substantial loss of muscle; (*Harrison v. Marsh*)
- Migraine headaches; (*Kimbro v. Atlantic Richfield Co.*)
- Manic depression; (*Gardner v. Morris*)
- Stiffening of the joints; (*Sisson v. Helms*)
- Hypersensitivity to tobacco smoke; (*Vickers v. Veterans Admin.*)
- AIDS; (*Severino v. Fire Control Dist.*)
- Alcoholism; (*Whitlock v. Donovan*) and
- Perceived mental impairment. (*Ashker v. IBM*)

Disability claims for the following conditions or diseases have been rejected:

- Venereal disease; (*Johnson v. Duckland Dairy Foods*)
- Hypersensitivity to criticism and low tolerance for stress; (*Pesterfield v. Tennessee Valley Auth.*)
- Addiction to marijuana; (*Rothweil v. Wetterau, Inc.*)
- Personality traits such as poor judgment and poor impulse control; (*Daley v. Koch*)
- Left-handedness; (*De La Torres v. Bolger*)
- Paranoid schizophrenia where the employee refused to take her medication; (*Franklin v. U.S. Postal Serv.*)
- Homosexuality; (*Blackwell v. U.S. Dep't of Treasury*) and
- Chronic lower back pain. (*Fuqua v. Unisys Corp.*)

Moreover, the ADA expressly excludes from coverage, among others, homosexuality, bisexuality, transvestism, exhibitionism, compulsive gambling, and kleptomania. Many state disability discrimination statutes, however, do not expressly contain similar exclusions. Nevertheless, some state courts have ruled that "sexual behavior disorders" are not covered by their state's disabilities laws. For example, in one case, a college professor claimed that his employer's decision to terminate him because he kissed one of his students violated the Maine Human Rights Act because he suffered from a "mental handicap of sexual addiction." The court found that although there is "no explicit exclusion of sexual behavior disorders from the definition of a disabled individual" in the Maine law, the professor's condition was not protected by the statute. (*Winston v. Maine Technical College Sys.*) In so holding, the court noted that the Maine law tracks federal antidiscrimination statutes, and federal law does not protect individuals from sexual behavior disorders.

B. Drug Use and Addiction

The application of disability laws to drug use and addiction raises difficult and controversial issues. Drug use has principally behavioral rather than biological roots, at least initially, and frequently involves illegal activity. Are drug users comparable to diabetics and tuberculosis victims? Moreover, society's interest in preserving employment opportunities for those addicted to drugs often runs counter to an employer's interest in maintaining a reliable and safe workforce.

Most disability laws, including the ADA, expressly exempt current use of drugs from protection and, consequently, an employer need not accommodate such drug use.

Former, rehabilitated, or rehabilitating drug users who are not current users are generally protected under disability laws.

C. Alcoholism

Alcoholism is a protected disability under the ADA, as well as under a number of state and local disability laws. Similarly, the Federal Rehabilitation Act of 1973 includes alcoholism as a disability unless current use of alcohol prevents the individual from performing the duties of the job or such current use constitutes a direct threat to the property or safety of others.

The protected status of the *condition* of alcoholism does not in any way limit an employer's ability to prohibit appearing for work under the influence of alcohol or drinking on the job. Further, alcoholics may be held to the same standards for job qualifications, performance, and behavior as all other employees or applicants. The difficult questions arise when the recovering or the borderline alcoholic uses alcohol in violation of company rules or abuses alcohol in a manner that affects work performance. Under such circumstances, the employer who has made a reasonable effort to accommodate the employee's alcoholism is generally entitled to take action for violation of company rules against alcohol use or alcohol-induced poor performance. The action must be based not on the individual's alcoholism but rather on the manifestation of that illness, even if the manifestation is the result of illness. Put another way, it is the drinking and not the fact that the individual is an alcoholic that must be the basis for the employer's actions. For example, the FBI did not discriminate against a special agent who was a recovering alcoholic by terminating the agent for his repeated drunkenness. (*Butler v. Thornburgh*)

An alcoholic must still be qualified for the position to be entitled to protection under most disability laws. A person who cannot perform the essential functions of the position because of a disability is not qualified. Disability laws generally protect individuals who are qualified for a position after reasonable accommodation in spite of, and not except for, their disability. (*Southeastern Community College v. Davis*)

D. Lawful Activities Laws

A number of states have enacted "lawful activities" laws, which prohibit employers from discriminating against employees for using lawful products or engaging in lawful activities off-premises on non-working time. States with lawful activities laws include Illinois, Minnesota, Nevada, New York, North Carolina, North Dakota, and Wisconsin. These laws do not prohibit distinctions made in insurance coverage based on an individual's lawful activities off-the-job.

The potential breadth and impact of these laws are broad. For example, a federal district court in New York, applying that state's law, allowed an employee to sue after she was allegedly demoted because she had a personal relationship and cohabited with a manager terminated by the president of the company. (*Pasch v. Katz Media Corp.*)

E. Smoking

Smoking in the workplace raises a number of troublesome personnel and legal questions. Emotions on the issue run high on all sides: Smokers object to limitations on their habit; nonsmokers insist on having a smoke-free workplace; and employers seek to limit their medical expenses by hiring or continuing to employ nonsmokers.

As a general rule, employers may limit or prohibit smoking in the workplace. Most states prohibit smoking in public places, which may include workplaces. Further, a number of state and local laws expressly prohibit smoking in the workplace except in specially designated areas or private offices. States that expressly prohibit smoking in the workplace include Alaska, Illinois, Iowa, Maine, Montana, Nebraska, New Hampshire, New Jersey, New York, Pennsylvania, Utah, Vermont, and Wisconsin. In one case under Illinois law, an employee who was allegedly forced to resign because she complained about smoking in the workplace was allowed to sue to recover the damages she may have suffered as the result of her employer's alleged retaliation. (*Pechan v. Dynapro, Inc.*)

Other states, such as Connecticut, Florida, and Rhode Island, require employers to accommodate the needs of nonsmokers who object to smoking in the workplace. The ADA expressly recognizes an employer's right to prohibit or restrict smoking in the workplace.

Sensitivity to smoke has been found to be a disability for which the employer must make reasonable accommodations in such states as California (*County of Fresno v. California Fair Hous. and Employment Comm'n*) and New Mexico (*Schober v. Mountain Bell Tel.*), and under the Federal Rehabilitation Act of 1973. (*Vickers v. Veterans Admin.*) Moreover, an employer's duty to provide a safe workplace has been interpreted by some courts as requiring employers to provide smoke-sensitive employees with a smoke-free environment. (*Shimp v. New Jersey Bell Tel.*)

Many employers have gone beyond merely limiting or prohibiting smoking in the workplace to refusing to hire smokers at all. These employers contend that by refusing to hire smokers they increase productivity while simultaneously decreasing their medical benefits costs.

Smokers' rights groups have succeeded in securing the enactment of legislation prohibiting employers from discriminating against employees and applicants based on their use of tobacco away from work as long as the individual complies with workplace smoking policies. States with such laws include Arizona, Connecticut, Indiana, Kentucky, Louisiana, Maine, Maryland, Minnesota, Mississippi, Nevada, New Hampshire, New Jersey, New Mexico, New York, Oklahoma, Oregon, Rhode Island, South Carolina, South Dakota, Virginia, West Virginia, and Wisconsin. For example, Nevada law prohibits an employer from discriminating against an applicant or employee who "engages in the lawful use in [Nevada] of any product outside the premises of the employer during his nonworking hours, if that use does not adversely affect his ability to perform his job or the safety of other employees."

9

NEGLIGENCE AND AN EMPLOYER'S DUTY OF CARE

The law imposes on all individuals a duty of care in the performance of certain acts. For example, the driver of a motor vehicle must operate it in a safe manner in accordance with accepted societal norms. The same standard of care is imposed on all people who operate motor vehicles, whether or not they are licensed to do so. Failure to satisfy this standard of care constitutes negligent behavior punishable under the law.

Negligence principles have long been applied to the employment setting. For example, employers have an obligation to provide a safe workplace to their employees, and a negligent failure to do so has long been held to be unlawful. In recent years, the scope and number of negligence claims submitted in employment-related matters have increased greatly. Basic principles of negligence law, however, have not changed. Rather, the duty of care imposed on employers by courts has expanded, rendering certain basic personnel functions potentially subject to challenge on negligence grounds.

Equally significant, negligence lawsuits against employers increasingly have been brought by third parties not involved in the employment relationship. For example, a third party who is assaulted by an employee may allege that the employer breached its duty of care by hiring or retaining the employee without detecting his or her potential violent propensities.

This chapter explores the expanding scope of negligence claims in the employment setting and potential employer defenses to such claims.

I. GENERAL NEGLIGENCE PRINCIPLES

The four basic elements of a negligence claim are (1) the existence of a duty or obligation to conform to a standard of conduct; (2) a failure to conform to the standard; (3) an injury or damage resulting from the conduct; and (4) a direct connection between the conduct and an injury. The standard of care for negligence in effect measures the degree of reasonable risk society is willing to place on a particular activity. A breach of that measure of acceptable risk constitutes negligence.

Returning to the motor vehicle example, drivers are obligated to operate their vehicles in a manner that does not present an unreasonable risk of injury to others. A driver whose vehicle strikes a pedestrian or another vehicle while the driver is operating it in an unsafe condition or manner—for example, by driving without headlights in the evening or by driving through a stop sign—would be guilty of negligence for causing or contributing to injury or damage. An intent to injure is not required for a finding of negligence. It is enough, in the case of the driver of the car, that the vehicle was driven in an unsafe manner or that the driver knew that the car itself was mechanically unsafe and that the injury or damage resulted. In contrast, a driver who purposefully runs over a pedestrian may be found guilty of intentional crimes such as assault, battery, or even manslaughter or homicide.

The standard of conduct is the same for all people no matter what their condition or individual characteristics. The same standard applies to the wise man as well as the fool, the athletically inclined as well as the awkward. Just as the distance for a 100-yard dash does not vary by competitor, the standard of care for negligence purposes applies uniformly to individuals and situations.

The traditional measure of this standard is a legal fiction known as the "reasonable man" standard. A failure to conform actions to what would be expected of a "reasonable man of ordinary prudence" in the same situation constitutes negligence.

A duty imposed by law, such as the duty to drive a car safely, is required for a negligence claim to exist. An obligation rooted in contract—an agreement between private parties—is not generally sufficient to serve as a basis for a negligence claim unless a separate and distinct duty is also imposed by law. Failure to satisfy the terms of a contract is simply a breach of contract and will not give rise to a negligence claim. For example, a truck driver who is required by his or her employer to arrive at work on time and to drive the truck safely and who fails to do either has breached the employment contract on both scores. The truck driver may also be found negligent in the unsafe manner in which the truck was driven. In contrast, there is no legal duty to arrive at work on time, only a contractual one.

II. NEGLIGENCE CLAIMS BY THIRD PARTIES OR CO-WORKERS

Employers under the traditional legal doctrine of "respondeat superior" are liable for injuries caused by employees in carrying out their responsibilities within the scope of their employment. For example, an employer employing a truck driver who had an accident during a delivery would be liable to the injured party under the theory of respondeat superior.

An employer may also be liable for injuries caused by the negligence of its employee *outside* the scope of the employee's job responsibilities. That same truck driver who picked up and assaulted a hitchhiker may subject his or her employer to liability on a number of negligence theories. The hitchhiker may sue, not as a result of actions taken by the employee in carrying out his or her responsibilities, but rather, as a result of the employer's negligence in hiring, supervising, training, or retaining the truck driver.

Such negligence claims are increasingly being filed against employers by customers, students, patients, and co-workers harmed by employees where the employer arguably had reason to know of the employee's dangerous propensities. Negligent hiring and the related claims of negligent training, supervision, and retention are the most notable of these actions.

A. Essential Elements of a Negligence Claim

The key elements of a negligence claim in the employment setting are the existence and breach of a legal duty, foreseeability, knowledge, proximate cause, and injury.

1. Existence and Breach of Legal Duty

To be found negligent, an employer will have to be shown to have breached a duty recognized by law such as a duty to drive a car safely. The legal expectations or duties imposed on employers have increased in recent years paralleling the expansion of employee rights. As an example, an employer's duty to provide a safe workplace at the beginning of the twentieth century and its duty at the century's end differ dramatically. Certainly, no turn-of-the-century employer would have found itself subject to suit for allowing smoking in the workplace.

While the legal obligations and expectations on employers have expanded rapidly, the precise scope and content of these newly recognized legal duties are far from certain or precise. Generally, a duty of care exists anytime there is a foreseeable risk of injury to others arising out of the failure to take the necessary steps to prevent such injury. The duty will be imposed where an employer knew or should have known that its workplace or employee was dangerous or had propensities that might cause injury to others or that its actions negligently performed or statements negligently made are likely to cause injury to a discernible party who had cause to and did rely on those actions or statements.

A court will decide if a legal duty exists by weighing the relationship of the parties, the nature of the risk, the public interest in the recognition of such a duty, and all the surrounding circumstances. (*Johnson v. Usdin Louis Co.*) "The greater the risk of harm, the higher the degree of care necessary to constitute ordinary care." (*Welsh Mfg. v. Pinkerton's, Inc.*)

2. Foreseeability

The foreseeability of the injury caused by the unfit employee is central to the determination of negligence. Entities with significant contact with the public, such as common carriers, hospitals and patient care facilities, churches and schools, realtors, and eating and drinking establishments, have a higher duty of care in selecting their employees. The foreseeability of injury to third parties caused by employees working in these settings is conspicuously greater.

In one case, a customer of a laundromat was severely beaten by an employee hired while on probation as part of the employer's agreement with a state-licensed juvenile resident treatment center. The juvenile employee was on probation for burglary and had been charged with molesting a child. The court determined that the customer could sue based on a claim of negligent hiring as the harm that actually occurred was foreseeable. The court concluded that the duty to select competent employees was not altered because the juvenile employee was hired in connection with a job program operated by a private rehabilitation center. The court further noted that the employer relied on the rehabilitation center to conduct the interviews, and that the employer did not ask the employee about his background. (*Nigg v. Patterson*) Similarly, the employer of a taxi driver who, when not given a tip, assaulted the rider with an iron bar and stole the rider's pants was held subject to suit for negligent hiring. (*Burch v. A&G Assocs.*)

The foreseeability of potential harm to third parties is, of course, greater where the employee's normal job duties entail sustained or close contact with the public. For example, the foreseeability of injury was found present in the following settings:

- Jobs with access to people's homes, such as exterminators (*Abbott v. Payne*), cable television installers (*D.R.R. v. English Enters., CATV*), apartment managers (*Ponticas v. KMS Invs.*), and real estate firms; (*Pruitt v. Pavelin*)

- Security guards; (*Welsh Mfg. Div. of Textron v. Pinkerton's, Inc.*)
- Common carriers, such as employers of taxi drivers (*Burch v. A&G Assocs.*), truck drivers (*Malorney v. B & L Motor Freight*), or ambulance services; (*Nazereth v. Herndon Ambulance Serv.*) and
- Employers who entrust employees with special responsibilities, especially dealing with children, such as church workers. (*J. v. Victory Tabernacle Baptist Church*)

There are, of course, situations where the particular injury to a third party was not a foreseeable risk created by hiring the employee. For example, an employer of a delivery driver who brought his dog with him on a delivery was not liable to a third party who drove over the dog and was attacked by the driver. (*Garcia v. Duffy*) In another case, a woman was raped in her home by a construction company employee who took drugs to combat depression while staying up late to finish a construction job bid. On his way home, he began to hallucinate and stopped near a house where a friend lived. He looked in the window, saw the woman, forced his way in, and raped her. The court found that the company had no duty of care toward the woman where it was not reasonably foreseeable, as in this case, that she would come into contact with the employee as a result of his employment. (*Chesterman v. Barmon*)

Similarly, a contractor successfully defended a negligent hiring claim based on its employee's rape of a dancer hired by the contractor's employees to dance at a Christmas party at the construction site. In that situation, the contractor could neither reasonably anticipate the dancer's presence on the premises nor the attack. (*Blenheim v. Dawsey & Hall, Ltd.*) Similarly, a laborer who was on parole for armed robbery visited his employer's premises after hours with a cocktail waitress and forcibly assaulted and beat the waitress with another employee's gun. The court, in rejecting a negligent hiring suit against the employer, reasoned that the waitress was not a customer, patron, or invitee of the employer and her injuries were not reasonably foreseeable. (*Baugher v. A. Hattersly & Sons*) A negligent retention claim was rejected where the court determined that the employer, a police department, could not foresee that two of its officers would commit a murder off-duty despite the officers' history of misconduct on the job. (*Watson v. City of Hialeah*)

Applicants or employees with criminal records present a particular problem for employers concerned with possible negligent hiring or retention claims based on subsequent criminal acts by such applicants or employees. The foreseeability of the subsequent crime is, of course, greater where a predisposition to commit such a crime has been shown. For this reason, employers have an interest in not hiring such applicants or retaining such employees. Society has a competing interest, however, in seeing that those convicted of a crime are integrated back into society, including obtaining gainful employment. Indeed, a number of states prohibit discrimination based on arrest and, to a lesser extent, criminal records. See discussion in Chapter 5.

The Florida Supreme Court, responding to the concern that "an employer who hires a person with a criminal record will be at substantial risk of liability for any intentional tort of that employee because of that past criminal record, irrespective of its connection to the conduct in issue," refused to hold an employer liable for negligent hiring or retention. In that case, the employee, who had been convicted of a drug offense in the military, stole a commuter airplane, took it for a joy ride, and crashed in the ocean shortly after takeoff, destroying the plane. The court concluded that the employer, which provided airport services, could not foresee that the employee "would take a joy ride in an easily identified commercial commuter plane that he had never flown before." (*Island City Flying Serv. v. General Elec. Credit*)

3. Knowledge

An employer will be liable for negligently hiring an employee not only where the employer knows that the employee is unfit for the job, but also where it is shown that, by using ordinary care, the employer *should* have known that the employee is unfit. For example, a supermarket was held subject to suit for failing to exercise ordinary care by not verifying references when hiring an employee to make home deliveries of groceries. The delivery person robbed and raped a customer in that case. (*Rosen-House v. Sloan's Supermarket*) In contrast, a restaurant was not liable for hiring a waitress who purposely poured a pot of hot coffee on a customer's back after the costumer threw a cup of coffee on her, because there was no evidence that she had violent or criminal tendencies. (*Odom v. Hubeny, Inc.*)

Employers will generally not be liable for failing to investigate an employee's past history if such a search would not reveal the particular unfitness or violent tendencies resulting in an injury. For example, the Baltimore Orioles were found not liable for the negligent hiring of two minor league players who assaulted a heckling fan after a game. The court determined that there was no evidence of violent tendencies in the players' backgrounds. (*Simmons v. Baltimore Orioles*) Of course, where such a search does reveal a prior history that demonstrates the employee's unfitness, a finding of negligence is likely.

4. Proximate Cause

For an employer to be held liable for negligent hiring, the type of conduct that renders an employee unfit for a job must also be the proximate cause of the injury. "The test of what was the proximate cause of an injury is whether, after the occurrence, the injury appears to be the reasonable and probable consequence of the act or omission of defendant, not whether a reasonable person could have foreseen the particular injury." (*Gaines v. Monsanto Co.*) An employer will not be liable if the type of conduct that resulted in the injury was unrelated to the type of conduct the employer should have discovered in investigating the employee's background and experience at the time of hire.

For example, in *Ponticas v. KMS Invs.*, the court found that an apartment complex owner's failure to investigate the criminal history of a resident manager was the proximate cause of a tenant's injuries following her rape by the manager. An investigation by the employer of a four-year period of unemployment would have disclosed that the resident manager had spent four years in prison for armed robbery and burglary. Instead, the employer negligently hired the manager and provided him with a pass key that gave him access to the tenant's apartment, which, in turn, facilitated the rape. Similarly, a church was held liable for negligently hiring an employee on probation from an aggravated sexual assault charge of a young girl for a position requiring that he be in contact with children. The employee repeatedly raped a 10-year-old girl soon after he was hired. (*J. v. Victory Tabernacle Baptist Church*)

In contrast, an employer was found not liable for hiring a truck driver with a suspended driver's license where the reason for the suspension—failure to pay a damage judgment—was not the proximate cause of an accident involving the truck driver in which a child was killed. (*Guillermo v. Brennan*) Similarly, a bank's hiring of a repossessor was not the proximate cause of an injury to a man who was struck by his own van when he tried to prevent its repossession. (*Texas Am. Bank v. Boggess*)

5. Injury

According to the Restatement of Torts, the term "injury" denotes that "there has been an invasion of a legally protected interest. . . ." (*Restatement (Second) of Torts*, § 7) The injury, if not privileged, may give rise to a cause of action. The most usual form of injury is the infliction of some degree of harm—a loss or detriment to a person. As the cases discussed in this section illustrate, injury is easily established in the negligent hiring context where the injury usually manifests itself as an assault and/or battery.

B. Negligent Hiring

Employers have a duty to use care in selecting their employees. An employer will be held liable for its employee's injurious conduct to a third party—a customer or co-worker—where the employee is unfit for the job or presents an unreasonable risk of injury to third parties and it is foreseeable that the employee would have contact with that class of person who was injured. The injury must be traceable to the employer's hiring of the unfit employee.

An important aspect of an employer's duty in selecting employees is the duty to investigate. Employers have an obligation to perform reasonable preemployment inquiries of any job applicant considered for employment or otherwise where the employer learns information or has reason to believe that it has breached, is breaching, or may breach a legal duty. This obligation is most conspicuous where the applicant will have or an employee already has extensive contact with the public or special access to non-public areas such as residences, or otherwise will occupy a position of trust. The obligation to make a background inquiry also will depend on the type of work to be done and whether opportunities will be present for potential harm to a third party or co-worker.

Where an employer has its own standard hiring practices or procedures, failure to follow them may support a claim of negligence against the employer. (*Haddock v. New York City*)

The failure to properly investigate an employee's background can, of course, have dire consequences. For example, the McDonald's Corporation was found negligent for failing to check the references of an employee who sexually abused a child in the restaurant's restroom. Such a search would have revealed a prior conviction for sexual assault. (*R.M. v. McDonald's Corp.*) An employer was negligent for not further investigating a truck driver's history after he denied having a criminal record during the job interview. The truck driver, who had a history of sexual assaults, raped a teenage hitchhiker. (*Malorney v. B & L Motor Freight*) In another case, an employer was held liable and ordered to pay $250,000 to a person injured by an unqualified driver. The employer was found to be grossly negligent in failing to request a list of traffic convictions, verify the employee's employment history, and confirm his driving skills or, in the alternative, train him on the equipment. (*North Houston Pole Line Corp. v. McAllister*)

While advisable, it may not always be simple or even feasible to conduct a thorough background search on job applicants. For example, criminal record information may not always be accessible and, under certain state laws, an employer is not permitted to inquire into a job applicant's criminal history unless the prehire convictions substantially relate to the job being filled. Indeed, some courts have reasoned that a rule requiring use of criminal history information would frustrate society's interest in rehabilitating and reintroducing into the mainstream people who are guilty of crimes. (*Ponticas v. KMS Invs.*) An employer may point to this legal limitation in defense of its failure to inquire into an applicant's criminal history. (*Guillermo v. Brennan*) Further, often on the advice of legal counsel, job references may not be obtainable from former employers. The Colorado Supreme Court has concluded that an employer has no duty to review an applicant's criminal records in the absence of evidence of an undue risk to the public or particular persons with whom the applicant will be in frequent contact. (*Connes v. Molalla Transp. Sys.*)

Despite these hurdles, a prudent employer seeking to fill a position with specific safety, health, and welfare concerns would be well advised to conduct a thorough investigation suitable to the setting. Preliminarily, the employer may seek to obtain written consent from the applicant expressly permitting the investigation. A diligent investigation would typically include a thorough interview and follow-up on any gaps in employment; a reasonable effort to obtain criminal history information; the contacting of job references; and the confirmation of representations made in the application, such as educational background. While such a diligent investigation may not always successfully predict the intentional or reckless misconduct by an employee who injures third parties, it may serve to minimize the employer's legal risk for negligence claims resulting from the hiring of the offending employee.

C. Negligent Training or Supervision

Negligent training or supervision claims are a subset of third-party negligence claims. The focus here is on the employer's failure to adequately train or supervise an employee in the basic responsibilities of the position, resulting in an injury to the public. A bus driver who drives the bus into a tree because he had never been shown the proper use of the gear shift, resulting in injuries to passengers, may subject the employer to negligent training claims. That same accident as a result of the bus driver, a known problem driver, being drunk instead raises the potential for a claim of negligent hiring, as discussed previously, or retention as discussed in the next section.

Negligent training or supervision claims are most likely to be raised in a setting in which the employer and its employees owe a special duty of care to the public due to the nature of the work, for example, where the relationship is based on trust, confidentiality, public safety, or health. An employer owes a greater duty of care in the training and supervision of an airline pilot than a foot messenger. In one case, a rookie police officer negligently applied his handcuffs to a suspect, causing permanent nerve damage and partially disabling the suspect. The New Hampshire Supreme Court, in upholding a negligence claim, noted that the police officer did not know the qualities of the handcuffs and emphasized that the officer had received no training. (*Cutter v. Town of Farmington*) Similarly, a blasting contractor assigned an employee to blast shale in a quarry. The blaster, who had no experience with shale, detonated blasts that devastated the quarry. The employer admitted that it had not trained the employee regarding the blasting of shale and had never inquired into the employee's experience in that regard. The contractor was held liable for the damage to the quarry. (*Watsontown Brick Co. v. Hercules Powder Co.*)

Employers increasingly are being found liable for negligently supervising employees who cause injuries to other employees or third parties while performing actions within the scope of their employment. Most states recognize negligent supervision claims; some, like Virginia, do not. (*Spencer v. General Elec. Co.*) States or courts that find employers and their employees to be in a "special relationship" requiring employers to protect against known hazards tend to recognize liability for negligent supervision; those that find that such a special relationship is not present in the employment relationship tend to reject such claims. In one case, an employer was found to be negligent for failing to supervise its employees at a company-sponsored Christmas party when an employee attending the party assaulted someone after the party had ended. (*Bradley v. Giess*) Similarly, an employee was found to have stated, under Tennessee law, a negligent supervision claim based on the alleged sexual assault of female employees by male co-workers. (*Hays v. Patton-Tully Transp. Co.*) In contrast, an Oregon court rejected a negligent supervision claim because, even assuming that a special relationship between the employer and its employees existed, the employee failed to allege that the employer knew or should have known of the manager's malfeasance. In that case, a store manager and certain employees taunted and harassed a security guard until he was removed from his position because they believed him to be homosexual. (*Whelan v. Albertson's, Inc.*)

D. Negligent Retention

An employer also may be liable for injuries to third parties for the improper retention of an unfit employee. As in the hiring situation, both the conduct and the type of injury must have been foreseeable. (*Dieter v. Baker Serv. Tools*)

An employer with knowledge or with reason to know of its employee's unfitness, who fails to take adequate steps in response, is vulnerable to a negligent retention claim.

An employer may learn of an employee's unfitness in a variety of ways, such as:

- Discovering an employee's criminal record after hiring the employee; (*Haddock v. New York City*)
- Receiving complaints or reports from third parties, such as tenants (*Corbally v. Sikras Realty*) or co-workers; (*Perkins v. Spivey*) or
- Witnessing an employee's conduct that suggests violent tendencies or unsuitability for the job. (*Foster v. Lodge*)

For example, a court ruled that an apartment complex owner could be sued for injuries resulting from the sexual abuse of two teenage tenants by a married couple employed by the owner as resident managers. The managers were generally known by tenants in the complex to be "swingers" and drug users. Liability in that case would depend on whether the owner had sufficient knowledge of the employees' dangerous propensities to support a negligent retention claim. (*Harvey Freeman & Sons v. Stanley*) Similarly, an employer that knew an employee had made sexual advances toward a co-worker and had a reputation of harassing female employees was ruled subject to suit on negligent retention grounds where the employee later killed the co-worker. (*Gaines v. Monsanto Co.*)

Once notified of an employee's dangerous or inappropriate propensities, an employer has an obligation to minimize dangers and prevent foreseeable injuries to third parties. (*Foster v. Lodge*) Appropriate responses may include further investigating the complaints or information obtained; warning or reprimanding the employee; training the employee; reassigning the employee; or discharging the employee. An employer also may be obligated to warn others about the employee's propensity for violent behavior. In one case, a railroad employer was held to be negligent for failing to warn a supervisor about an employee's violent tendencies, which were known to the employer, where the employee shot the supervisor after the supervisor reprimanded him. (*Smith v. National R.R. Passenger Corp.*)

Negligent retention claims have been established where:

- A supervisor who sexually harassed a subordinate was retained after the employer had actual notice of his "proclivity to engage in sexually offensive conduct"; (*Hogan v. Forsyth Country Club Co.*) and
- An employer retained a belligerent, ruthless, and violent man who sabotaged an oil drilling site. (*Plains Resources, Inc. v. Gable*)

In contrast, negligent retention claims were dismissed where:

- A radio station retained a reporter, knowing that he had been convicted of drunk driving; the reporter later killed a pedestrian while driving drunk off-duty; (*McQuade v. Arnett*)
- A sheriff retained a deputy whose wife told the sheriff that her husband had beaten her and threatened her life; the deputy later killed his wife while he was off-duty; (*Braswell v. Braswell*)
- A correctional department had received no complaints of harassment against a supervisor with an excellent work record prior to a claim of sexual harassment lodged against the supervisor; (*Kresko v. Rulli*) and
- A landlord retained a maintenance worker with criminal convictions for petty larceny and illegal dumping of trash (child abuse charges had been dropped) who later ab-

ducted, sexually assaulted, and murdered a tenant. (*Stubbs v. Panek*)

E. Employer as Social Host

Employers sometimes entertain employees. Employers also may request or require employees to host business contacts or clients in social settings. Problems may arise if alcohol is served at such functions. Employers may be held liable under the theory of vicarious liability for unlawful acts committed in the scope of employment. For example, an employer was held vicariously liable for compensatory and punitive damages where an employee drove home from a professional conference, at which he became intoxicated, and collided with another car, killing its passenger. The appeals court, sustaining the jury's verdict, noted that the company paid the employee's expenses and an officer of the company paid for the drinks. (*Carroll Air Sys. v. Greenbaum*)

Courts also are becoming increasingly receptive to claims of negligence based upon injuries resulting from the consumption of alcohol under these circumstances.

Traditionally, negligence claims failed in this setting because, among other reasons, the drinking of the alcohol rather than the furnishing of it was found to be the cause of the injury alleged. Exceptions were found where injuries resulted from the service of alcohol at company functions to minors (*Walker v. Key*) or to intoxicated employees. (*Dickinson v. Edwards*)

The scope of employer's potential liability, however, has expanded in recent years. For example, a company was held liable when an employee who became intoxicated at a Christmas party caused an accident while driving home. The court found that the employer could reasonably foresee at the time of the employee's departure that an accident could result from the employee's inebriated condition. (*Chastain v. Litton Sys.*) In contrast, an employer generally will not be held liable where it did not know that the employee was drunk or had a tendency to become intoxicated (*Baird v. Roach, Inc.*), or where the employer had no reason to know that the employee had consumed alcohol kept on the premises by the employer. (*Biel v. Alcott*)

Some courts have held that the employee's consumption of alcohol at a company function was sufficiently work-related to fall within the employee's scope of employment. (*Rodgers v. Kemper Constr. Co.*) In one case, a company was held liable where an employee had a few drinks with a customer of the employer on company premises after working hours. The court found that the employer benefitted from the employee's social contact with the customer such that the conduct was within the employee's scope of employment. The court also took into consideration the foreseeability and proximate cause of injury in determining whether the employee's intoxication occurred within the scope of employment. (*Childers v. Shasta Livestock Auction Yard*)

An employer that allows its employees to drink alcoholic beverages during business functions on or off the work site is increasingly likely to bear the burden of injuries proximately caused by the employees' intoxication. Thus employers are well advised to limit alcohol consumption at office or social functions and to make alternative transportation arrangements for inebriated employees.

III. NEGLIGENCE CLAIMS BY EMPLOYEES

Courts have become increasingly receptive to negligence claims brought by employees against their employers. Traditionally, negligence claims by employees focused on an employer's failure to provide a safe workplace. However, courts are increasingly imposing on employers a duty of care, for example, in the performance of the most significant aspects of personnel functions. The following provides a sampling of negligence claims available to employees, depending on state law and the facts of a particular case.

A. Safe Workplace

The law has long recognized an employer's duty to provide a safe workplace and to warn employees of physical dangers that would otherwise not be known. An employer is not the insurer against all injuries and is not required to provide the best or safest operations. Rather, an employer is obligated to exercise reasonable care in providing machinery, equipment, appliances, materials, and facilities. An employer's duty does not extend to the prevention of unlikely or unforeseeable occurrences, but rather is limited to dangers that may reasonably be anticipated. (*Murphy v. Owens-Corning Fiberglas Corp.*) Further, an employer is generally not obligated to warn against *obvious* dangers or to take precautions to avoid accidents caused by the negligence of its employees. (*Pomer v. Schoolman*)

The recognized practices of the industry in which the employer operates provide strong evidence of an acceptable standard of care. For example, where a fiberglass maker conducted testing and inspection in accordance with industry-wide practices, it was held not liable for providing an unsafe workplace contributing to an employee's pulmonary fibrosis. (*Murphy v. Owens-Corning Fiberglas Corp.*) In contrast, failure of an employer to abide by industry hygiene standards in the handling of asbestos was found to constitute negligence. (*Adkins v. GAF Corp.*) Similarly, a nurse's failure to abide by her employer hospital's own protocol by neglecting to use gloves while cleaning up an HIV-positive patient's blood was cited as a basis to defeat the claim of the nurse's estate against the doctor who operated on the patient. The nurse died of AIDS. Although the jury found that the doctor had been negligent, it concluded that the doctor's actions were not a "substantial factor" in causing the harm. (*James v. Nolan*)

In recent years, safe workplace claims have been successfully brought in the following settings:

- Where a convenience store clerk was murdered after her employer removed store security devices that may have prevented the crime; (*Havner v. E-Z Mart Stores*)
- Where an employer failed to provide a smoke-free workplace; (*McCarthy v. Department of Social & Health Servs.*) and
- Where employees were exposed to diseases not arising naturally from employment (*McCarthy v. Department of Social & Health Servs.*), such as carbon bisulfide poisoning

(*Pellerin v. Washington Veneer* Co.) or tuberculosis caused by gases and vapors. (*Depre v. Pacific Coast Forge Co.*)

In contrast, safe workplace claims have been rejected under the following sets of facts:

- Where an employee was sexually harassed; (*Perkins v. Spivey*)
- Where a restaurant's assistant manager seduced and impregnated a sixteen-year-old worker; (*Doe v. Western Restaurants Corp.*)
- Where an employee had idiosyncratic susceptibilities to fiberglass dust and heat due to his pulmonary fibrosis, which resulted in illness; (*Murphy v. Owens-Corning Fiberglas*) and
- Where one employee robbed his employer and killed a co-worker during the robbery. (*Vallejo v. Osco Drug, Inc.*)

Congress, in enacting the Occupational Safety and Health Act of 1970 (OSHA), in effect codified the common law obligation on employers to provide a safe workplace to their employees in its "general duty" clause. Numerous states have enacted related and complementary laws. Remedies under OSHA are not exclusive and claims brought under state law that supplement the federal law are not preempted. Indeed, the federal act expressly provides that it does not supersede or otherwise limit other federal and state laws and the common law. Actions enforcing the federal law are brought by the Department of Labor.

Generally, the standards for upholding an OSHA claim are less stringent than for a safe workplace claim. (*Morris v. Smith*) Whether the general duty clause encompasses workplace violence claims remains an unresolved question. In one case before a Department of Labor Administrative Law Judge (ALJ) (*Secretary of Labor v. Megawest Financial Inc.*), an employee was assaulted by a resident of a complex managed by the employer and OSHA issued a citation alleging a violation of the general duty clause. The Secretary of Labor presented evidence showing that the complex was one of the highest crime areas in Ft. Lauderdale, that the employees were subjected to verbal threats and abuse by residents, and that, on occasion, the employees were physically attacked during the performance of their duties. Further, a security guard had been hired but was later terminated because of costs even though the employees had requested security. The ALJ found that although hazards existed, the Secretary of Labor failed to establish that the employer was aware of the hazards. The ALJ further noted that when dealing with workplace violence, the introduction of a third-party human actor throws a "wild card" into the scenario for which the employer should not be held responsible under OSHA unless a high standard of proof is met showing that the employer had an ability to control the hazard.

Federal law further extends individual employee rights by providing under Section 11(c) of OSHA that employees who have a reasonable belief that a work assignment presents a serious risk of injury or death may not be discriminated against for refusing to perform that task. For example, a worker who was discharged for refusing to operate a paper cutting machine that he believed was unsafe was awarded his lost wages for the period he was out of work. (*Secretary of Labor v. H.M.S. Direct Mail Serv.*) In a leading case, the Supreme Court held that two employees were not required to work on an elevated mesh screen after a worker fell to his death two weeks earlier while performing a similar task on the same screen. The Court noted, however, that this was an extraordinary remedy and that the employees could be assigned to alternative work and could be entitled to lost wages only if they were suspended or discharged. (*Marshall v. Whirlpool Corp.*)

Employers also may be fined or imprisoned for their negligence in not providing a safe workplace. For example, a company was fined more than $1.5 million for 152 violations of OSHA's lead standards. (*Secretary of Labor v. Interstate Lead Co.*). In another case, a construction company and its president were convicted of criminal negligence based on the company's failure to adequately slope and shore a construction site trench, which resulted in the death of two workers. The president was fined $2000 and sentenced to 180 days in jail; the company was fined $10,000. (*Sabine Consol. v. Texas*) Similarly, two owners of a mercury reclamation facility were convicted, fined $10,000 each, and sentenced to serve weekends in jail for six months for falsifying business records and concealing their operations from the federal government. An employee was severely injured due to mercury poisoning while working at the facility. (*People v. Pymm*) While criminal actions against employers that fail to provide safe workplaces remain rare, the trend is clearly to bring such proceedings.

In sum, an employer that fails to provide a safe workplace for its employees may be subject not merely to the limited remedies under workers' compensation laws available to injured employees under that system, but negligence lawsuits with more substantial remedies and potential criminal penalties as well. As societal notions of what constitutes a "safe" workplace expand—for example, to include a smoke-free workplace—the potential rights of employees and liability of employers expands as well.

B. Negligent Misrepresentation

Effective and reasonable communication between employers and their employees and applicants for employment is at the heart of a successful employment relationship. Applicants, in considering the prospect of employment, and employers, in considering an applicant for employment, can be expected to rely on each other's representations in evaluating the potential benefits of establishing an employment relationship. Furthermore, the need for effective and honest communication does not dissipate in any way upon commencement of an employment relationship. To the contrary, the bonds and commitment between the parties to the established rather than merely prospective employment relationship are generally conceded to be greater.

The law governing the degree of care that employers and employees or applicants for employment must use in making representations to each other is, as with most topics in this book, evolving. The law of fraud is closely related to, though distinguishable from, the law of negligence. The law of fraud also applies in the employment context and, as it closely relates to the tort of negligent misrepresentation, is briefly discussed in this section.

The law of fraud (or deceit) and misrepresentation is rooted in the mores of the free marketplace. The traditional notion of *caveat emptor*, or the buyer beware, was as much a principle of business as it was of law. Parties to a commercial transaction were assumed to be vigilant against any deception by the other side. The law had little concern for any adversaries "whose acumen and sagacity are inferior to those of their adversaries" (REST. TORTS, Scope Notes, at 58 (1938)). The robust practices of the commercial marketplace did not permit such paternalism.

The commercial Darwinism of the nineteenth century met nicely the needs of a developing economic juggernaut. The limited scope of the law of deceit and misrepresentation, however, was ill-suited to address the needs of other categories of participants in the marketplace, such as homeowners, investors in financial marketplaces, consumers, and employees. These groups were far less equipped to participate fairly in the bustling and increasingly sophisticated commercial marketplace and were far more vulnerable to fraudulent and deceitful practices, due to a lack of both sophistication and access to relevant information. In response, the law adapted and expanded the protection available to participants in the marketplace generally and, in particular, to employees and applicants for employment. Most states now recognize that an employer is in a special relationship with an employee or potential employee requiring the exercise of reasonable care in making representations about the employment relationship. Not all states or courts agree. For example, an Oregon court determined that a university could not be held liable for its alleged misrepresentation to a professor in the hiring process. The court wrote, "Whatever duty an employer may owe to an employee in other contexts of the employment relationship, we know of no duty of an employer to act to further the economic interests of the employee in the negotiation of the employment contract." (*Conway v. Pacific Univ.*)

An employer who intentionally misstates a material term of the employment relationship has committed a fraud. Similarly, an employer who fails to exercise reasonable care in the communication of information material to the terms and conditions of employment—such as retirement, health, or other benefits—may be subject to a claim of negligent misrepresentation. (*Boucher v. Valus*) For example, an insurance company was held subject to suit for failing to live up to its promises to an agent regarding the number of policies he would be permitted to sell and the services he could provide to customers. (*Redies v. Nationwide Mut. Ins. Co.*) Similarly, an employer was found to have negligently misrepresented a material term of employment to 54 employees when it advised them that they could expect to work for at least three to five years based on orders it had already obtained—the employees were discharged after only one year. (*Barske v. Rockwell Int'l Corp.*)

To succeed on a negligent misrepresentation claim, an employee must demonstrate (1) a misrepresentation; (2) that the employer had the means of knowing or should have known the truth regarding the misrepresentation; (3) that the employee reasonably relied on the misrepresentation; and (4) that the employee was injured by relying on the employer's statements.

When an employer makes an incorrect or misleading statement or only partially discloses facts material to the employment relationship, it then has a duty to dispel any resulting mistaken impressions. For example, an employee was assured in his interview that the firm was a "profitable company," which, while true, was only the case for the prior two months. Failure to inform the employee that the company had not been profitable for the previous two years and three months was found sufficient to state a negligent misrepresentation claim. (*Harlan v. Intergy, Inc.*)

Similarly, a negligent misrepresentation claim was found to be cognizable where an employee was induced to relocate to Los Angeles based on the employer's representation that the company was financially secure and that the division in which the employee was to work was a "growth division" which the company had plans to expand; in fact, the company was planning a merger that would substantially increase the risk of elimination of the employee's position, had undergone its worst economic performance in its recent history, and was facing a bleak outlook. (*Lazar v. Superior Court*) The court also found that the employee stayed a claim under section 970 of the California Labor Code where the employer persuaded him to relocate by making false representations concerning the work. (Cal. Labor Code § 970) A proven violation of the Labor Code is a misdemeanor under California law.

Moreover, an innocent misrepresentation upon which an applicant relies may be held to be negligent if the employer had the means to determine the truth. (*D'Ulisse-Cupo v. Board of Directors*) Indeed, a misleading statement, even if accurate, may rise to the level of a misrepresentation under appropriate circumstances. For example, an employer responded to an employee's inquiry by indicating that the death benefit under the company's retirement plan "would not be as much" if one plan option was chosen over another. The employee relied on this representation and, when he died, his estate received $33,000 under the first option instead of $78,000, which would have been received under the second option. The court found the employer's statement to be a negligent misrepresentation reasoning that the employer, having undertaken to counsel the employee on the matter, was required to provide that advice clearly. (*Gediman v. Anheuser Busch, Inc.*)

Negligent misrepresentation claims often fail because of an employee's inability to demonstrate that the information communicated was false or misleading. For example, a court rejected a negligent misrepresentation claim based on comments during the job interview that "normally" an individual placed in the position sought "usually" stays for a number of years. The employee alleged that he relied on this representation and sued after he was terminated for poor performance in less than a year. The court concluded that no false information regarding the duration of employment had been provided. (*Roberts v. Conoco, Inc.*) Similarly, a claim that the employer negligently misrepresented that the employee would be terminated solely for good cause was rejected where the claim was based not on express statements but on "uncertain assurances" and a supervisor's course of conduct. (*Burdette v. Mepco/Electra, Inc.*)

Reliance on the employer's statement is essential to a negligent misrepresentation claim. Such a claim was rejected based on a failure to demonstrate reliance on claims of job security with the company. The employee had alleged that management assured him that the strength of the business would preclude layoffs and cutbacks. (*Hughlett v. Sperry Corp.*) A negligent misrepresentation claim based on reliance on oral representations made during the hiring process that are directly contradicted by the employment application and employee handbook was similarly rejected. (*Allen v. U.S. Fidelity & Guar.*)

The potential for negligent misrepresentation claims, coupled with the threat of breach-of-contract claims, are reasons for employers to exercise great care in the hiring process when making statements of fact, especially regarding the company's business prospects and the opportunities offered by the position. The dangers of overstatement are not merely dashed hopes and weakened morale, but also potential charges of negligence from employees who relied on the misrepresentations to their detriment.

C. Negligent Performance of Personnel Functions

Courts generally have declined to find that employers owe employees a duty of reasonable care in decision making and performing basic personnel functions. For example, the Montana Supreme Court rejected a negligence claim based on management's decision to reduce its workforce, finding that to do so would put a court or a jury in the "middle of general management decisions, in effect eviscerating the concept of employer latitude in decision-making." (*Heltborg v. Modern Mach.*) Similarly, courts have almost uniformly rejected claims of the negligent termination of at-will employees. For example, an employee committed suicide shortly after his termination. His widow brought suit alleging negligence, discrimination, and intentional infliction of emotional distress; she was awarded $700,000 by a jury on her negligence claim. A Texas appeals court overturned the jury verdict, finding that "there is no duty of care owed to an employee with respect to his discharge from employment or where the risk of harm from discharge is not reasonably foreseeable." (*Shell Oil Co. v. Humphrey*)

Employers have, on occasion, been held liable for failing to administer properly their own personnel procedures and policies where a duty of care is found to be present. Negligence principles have been applied to such personnel functions as the administration of tests, such as drug tests, polygraphs, or aptitude and skills tests; the maintenance of personnel records; and the evaluation of employees' performance. Such claims, to survive, must rise above mere claims for breach of contract. The extent of the duty of care to perform each of these personnel functions varies with the practice involved and the circumstances under which a particular claim arises.

1. Negligent Administration of Tests

Employers may test applicants and employees to determine aptitude, drug or alcohol use, or truthfulness. The results of these tests may be used to determine the employability of an applicant, the promotability of an employee, or, indeed, whether the employee may maintain his or her employment. The more significant the test, the more likely it is that an employer will be obligated to exercise due care in preparing, administering, and acting upon results of the examination. For example, an applicant for a government job took and was told that she passed a civil service exam and was awarded a position. Four months later, she was told that she actually had failed the exam and was fired. The Nebraska Supreme Court concluded that the now-terminated employee could sue for negligent grading of her exam because it was reasonably foreseeable that she would be injured when the accurate grade was discovered. (*Merrick v. Thomas*)

Claims based on the negligent administration of tests in the employment setting generally have been brought against professional testing companies and security firms that administer tests on behalf of an employer and who are often licensed to do so. The greater the employer's involvement in the process, however, the more likely it is that the employer will be subject to a duty of reasonable care. Of course, employers who administer such tests themselves remain directly liable to suit.

An employer was held liable for negligently implementing and administering a drug-testing program where, by requiring that employees be observed while providing a urine sample, it caused serious emotional distress to an employee. (*Kelley v. Schlumberger Technology Corp.*) In contrast, a court concluded that an employer need only ensure that the drug tests used be reliable in design and application. The employer in that case used the most advanced and accurate tests on the market and was held not to be obligated to administer a second test to confirm the positive results of the first test. (*Jevic v. Coca-Cola Bottling Co.*)

One court rejected a suit for negligence in the administration of a polygraph examination brought by an at-will employee, reasoning that since the employer was free to terminate the employee for no reason, "it was equally at liberty to discharge her for a reason based on incorrect information, even if that information was carelessly gathered." (*Johnson v. Delchamps, Inc.*) Similarly, a claim of negligent administration of a drug test based on an alleged violation of public policy was rejected where no specific violation of law was demonstrated. (*Weaver v. Coca-Cola Bottling Co.*)

A release of claims is often required before polygraphs, drug tests, and related examinations are administered. A knowing and voluntary waiver of a negligence claim is enforceable. (*Berube v. Fashion Ctr. Ltd.*) In contrast, one court refused to enforce such a waiver under Louisiana law on the ground of lack of consideration, that is, the employee failed to provide any benefit to the employer in exchange for the waiver of a legal right. (*Johnson v. Delchamps, Inc.*)

2. Negligent Performance Evaluation

There is generally no legal duty to conduct a performance evaluation in a proper manner. (*Pratt v. Delta Air Lines*) This duty may be imposed by contract but generally has not been found to exist as a separate and distinct duty imposed by law. (*Tollefson v. Roman Catholic Bishop*)

In a leading case, a former test driver for General Motors with a chronic absenteeism problem sued alleging that the company conducted his performance evaluation in a negligent manner by not informing him that he would be terminated for his absenteeism. The Michigan Supreme Court refused to recognize an action for negligent evaluation. The court found no duty imposed by law on employers to conduct evaluations in a certain manner, particularly where the employment is at will. The court reasoned that the law does not "impose on [the employer] a common-law obligation to evaluate or correctly evaluate [an employee] before exercising its right to discharge him at will. There is, thus, no right arising at common law as a matter of public policy, separate and distinct from any contractual right, to be evaluated or correctly evaluated before being discharged from employment."(*Ferrett v. General Motors Corp.*) Similarly, an employee's claim for negligent evaluation was rejected by a Pennsylvania federal district court. (*Mann v. J.E. Baker Co.*) In that case, the employee was discharged after receiving a favorable performance evaluation. She sued the employer alleging that if she had received an accurate evaluation, she would have had the opportunity to correct any performance deficiencies she may have had. The court dismissed her claim and held that she could not use a tort action to uphold rights arising from a contractual relationship.

A few courts have, however, suggested that an employer has a duty to use reasonable care in evaluating or reviewing the performance of its employees. The components of such a duty, as determined by these courts, include an obligation to perform the evaluation properly, to inform the employee of any performance deficiencies, to notify the employee that discharge was being considered, and to inform the employee that an improvement in performance is required. For example, one federal court concluded that an employer that had obligated itself to conduct performance reviews must exercise reasonable care in performing those reviews. In that case, the employer was found to be negligent in the performance evaluation prior to termination by not putting the employee on notice that his discharge was being considered if performance did not improve. (*Chamberlain v. Bissell, Inc.*)

3. Negligent Recordkeeping

A minority of courts have recognized an employer's duty to use reasonable care in maintaining or disclosing employment records. This duty includes not only the proper keeping of such records, but also care in disseminating the information contained in them. (*Quinones v. United States*)

In order to state a claim, an employee must demonstrate a failure by the employer to maintain records properly and a resulting injury. Such injuries include damage to the employee's reputation (*Quinones v. United States*); loss of future employment (*Bulkin v. Western Kraft E., Inc.*); and loss of promotions or salary increases that may be due. An employee must also demonstrate, as required with any negligence claim, a connection between the duty breached and the injury. In one dramatic case, an employer was found not liable for the alleged negligent disclosure of an employee's record of absenteeism to her husband. Based on this information, the employee's husband correctly concluded that his wife was seeing another man and committed suicide. The court found that the alleged negligent communication was not the proximate cause of the husband's death. (*Kobeck v. Nabisco, Inc.*)

IV. NEGLIGENT INFLICTION OF EMOTIONAL DISTRESS

Claims against employers for emotional distress may be based on either their intentional or negligent acts.

A claim for intentional infliction of emotional distress requires extreme or outrageous conduct that intentionally or recklessly causes serious emotional distress of a nature that no reasonable person could be expected to endure. An employee bringing such a claim must demonstrate that the extreme or outrageous behavior was the proximate cause of the injury. (Such claims are addressed in detail in Chapter 7.)

Courts in certain states have recognized claims for negligent rather than intentional infliction of emotional distress. An employee must show that the employer failed to satisfy the standard of care expected under those circumstances where emotional distress may have occurred. Outrageous conduct is not an element of this claim. (*Abston v. Levi Strauss & Co.*) The basic elements of a negligence claim—a duty, a breach of that duty, a foreseeable injury, and a showing that the injury was proximately caused by the breach—must be demonstrated to state a claim.

Certain states, such as Texas (*Williams v. Sealed Power Corp.*), have declined to recognize negligent infliction of emotional distress claims or, as in Ohio, have limited such claims to suits by bystanders to accidents who suffer severe emotional distress caused by having witnessed the accident. (*Flynn v. Fahlgren & Swink, Inc.*)

Negligent infliction of emotional distress claims in certain states have survived challenges in cases alleging:

- Racial harassment; (*Payne v. General Motors Corp.*)
- An agreement to withdraw discrimination charges based on a promise of benefits that were not provided; (*Miller v. Fairchild Indus.*)
- A nervous breakdown precipitated by a wrongful demotion; (*Sweeney v. Westvaco Co.*)
- Termination resulting from a refusal to fraudulently predetermine the winner of a raffle of donated hospital equipment; (*Beasly v. Affiliated Hosp. Prods.*) and
- A discharge based on age, which resulted in depression, embarrassment, distress, and shock. (*Abston v. Levi Strauss & Co.*)

Emotional distress claims brought against employers are particularly vulnerable to the defense that the sole remedy (while less lucrative) for such claims is under state workers' compensation laws as described more fully below. For example, negligent infliction of emotional distress claims in the following settings were held preempted by state workers' compensation laws:

- Coerced demotion; (*Dondero v. Lenox China*)
- Anti-Semitic harassment; (*Goldman v. Wilsey Foods*) and
- Age-based termination. (*Flynn v. New England Tel. Co.*)

Negligent infliction claims brought in court by union employees may also be preempted by federal labor law, also as described more fully below, which requires that all claims subject to a grievance procedure available under a union contract be resolved under those procedures. (*Jackson v. Southern Cal. Gas Co.*) In one case, a union employee challenged his discharge following a positive drug test under state tort law. The court found, however, that his claim was preempted by federal labor law since the collective-bargaining agreement gave the employer the right to test and discharge employees for the use of controlled substances. (*Clark v. Newport News Shipbuilding & Dry Dock Co.*)

V. DEFENSES TO NEGLIGENCE CLAIMS

A number of defenses are available to employers against negligence claims.

A. Workers' Compensation Laws

State workers' compensation laws provide the exclusive remedy for physical and emotional injuries arising out of or in the course and scope of employment. These laws are designed to provide employees with prompt payment for on-the-job injuries without regard for fault. Workers' compensation laws will generally preempt employee suits alleging on-the-job injuries whether based on intentional or negligent conduct.

For example, a garbage truck driver was stopped by his supervisor and reprimanded for allowing his daughter to accompany him and for being out of uniform in violation of department rules. An altercation ensued and the supervisor allegedly assaulted the driver, causing a concussion and a nervous disorder. The driver's suit alleging the negligent hiring and retention of the supervisor was found to be preempted by the state workers' compensation law because the injury arose out of and in the course of employment. (*Chinnery v. Virgin Islands*)

Negligence claims have also been found to be barred by the "exclusivity" provisions of workers' compensation laws where:

- An employee charged his employer with negligent hiring, training, and supervision based on his supervisor's alleged discrimination against him based on age; (*Bohm v. Trans World Airlines*)
- A federal employee alleged that the Tennessee Valley Authority failed to provide a smoke-free work environment; (*Carroll v. Tennessee Valley Auth.*)
- An airline reservation agent who was terminated for possession of marijuana aboard a flight alleged negligent infliction of emotional distress; (*Tachera v. United Airlines*)

- A store employee alleged negligent infliction of emotional distress based on her termination for failing to pass a polygraph examination; (*Johnson v. Delchamps, Inc.*)
- A security guard at a hospital was assaulted and raped by a psychiatric patient; (*Holland v. Norristown State Hosp.*)
- A store employee slipped and fell on ice outside of the store where she worked; (*Schwartz v. R. H. Macy & Co., Inc.*)
- A female employee raped by a co-worker alleged claims of negligent retention, supervision, and entrustment; (*Al-Dabbagh v. Greenpeace, Inc.*)
- A director of human resources alleged negligent infliction of emotional distress based on a claim that he was coerced into resigning; (*Dondero v. Lenox China*) and
- A female employee sued for negligent infliction of emotional distress based on claims of sexual harassment. (*Wangler v. Hawaiian Elec. Co.*)

Claims based on employees' actions that cause injury to others not in the course of employment are generally not barred by workers' compensation laws. For example, the negligent hiring claim of the family of an employee murdered by a co-worker was held not prohibited by the exclusivity of the workers' compensation law as the murder did not occur during the course of employment. (*Gaines v. Monsanto Co.*) State laws differ over the scope of claims covered by their workers' compensation laws. For example, under Ohio law, sexual harassment claims that seek remedies for psychological injuries are not cognizable under the state's workers' compensation law because only economic damages are covered. (*Crihfield v. Monsanto Co.*)

B. Preemption by Federal Labor Law

Employers whose workforces are partially or fully unionized enter into collective-bargaining agreements with the unions that set forth the terms of the relationship. In most instances, those agreements will establish a means for resolving disputes under the agreement, typically, through a grievance procedure ending in binding arbitration. Employee claims that are inextricably intertwined with the terms of the agreement are deemed preempted under federal labor law and must be resolved under the grievance procedures established by the parties. Examples of employer conduct that may be governed by collective-bargaining agreements include an employer's hiring and firing procedures, safety and health practices, disciplinary procedures and decisions, and discharges. The federal labor law preemption defense, of course, does not apply to the nonunion setting.

Examples of negligence claims that have been held to be preempted by federal labor law because they required interpretation of collective-bargaining agreements include alleged negligent administration of drug tests (*Hurst v. Consolidated Freightways*), negligent training (*Behrens v. John Hancock Mut. Life Ins. Co.*), negligent supervision (*Johnson v. Southwestern Bell Tel. Co.*), and negligent infliction of emotional distress. (*Jackson v. Southern Cal. Gas Co.*) Claims that do not require interpretation of a collective-bargaining agreement to resolve, such as a claim of racial discrimination (*Rasheed v. International Paper Co.*), are not preempted by federal labor law. (*Johnson v. AT&T Technologies*) Claims based on conduct that is viewed as particularly abusive— for example, claims resulting from an employer's act of pointing a shotgun at an employee—have been held to be an exception to the preemption rule and, consequently, are not preempted by federal labor law. (*Penrith v. Lockheed Corp.*) In one case, which is notable for its narrow view of federal labor law preemption, the court held that an employee's state law claims for assault and battery and intentional infliction of emotional distress were not preempted by federal labor law. (*Galvez v. Kuhn*) In that case, the employer had increased the speed of a conveyor belt, forcing the employee to keep up with the line and causing him to suffer a physical injury. The employer alleged that the employee's claims were nothing more than a safety and employment condition grievance masquerading as an assault and battery claim. The court found, however, that the employee's claims, camouflaged or not, should be taken at face value and were not subject to summary dismissal.

C. Contributory Negligence, Assumption of Risk, and Fellow Servant Defenses

The traditional defenses to negligence claims, historically known as the "unholy trinity"—contributory negligence, assumption of risk, and the "fellow servant" rule—successfully insulated employers from liability in most instances until the enactment of state workers' compensation laws early in this century. Contributory negligence is the theory that employees who fail to exercise reasonable care, and thereby contribute to their own workplace injury, cannot recover for that injury. Employees generally were held to have assumed the risk of dangers incident to their positions and, consequently, an employee's claim of an unsafe workplace could be rejected if a court found that the risk was inherent in the job or that the employee voluntarily assumed an additional risk. In addition, an employer was generally not held liable for injuries to its employees caused by the negligence of co-workers.

Workers' compensation statutes have provided a more efficient and certain remedy for workplace injuries, although with limited recoveries available, and have significantly narrowed or eliminated the traditional defenses available to employers for claims based on such injuries. These statutes generally hold employers liable for workplace injuries, regardless of fault, arising during the course of employment. Negligence on the part of an employee or co-worker is generally not a defense to a claim for workers' compensation. Consequently, the employers' contributory negligence, "fellow servant," and assumption of risk defenses, as such, have been severely limited or abolished as defenses to workplace injury claims under workers' compensation statutes. That is not to say that no defenses are available to employers under workers' compensation statutes. For example, most workers' compensation laws provide defenses to claims for willful misconduct on the part of the employee, violation of the law by an employee, self-inflicted injuries or injuries resulting from intoxication, or failure to abide by safety procedures.

Traditionally, under the contributory negligence doctrine, an employee who was even partially at fault could not recover for his or her injuries. A vast majority of states have replaced contributory negligence laws with comparative negligence laws, so that employers are liable to the degree of their fault. Consequently, the contributory negligence doctrine rarely is invoked to bar an employee's recovery for injuries.

An employer in most instances may no longer be able to avoid liability based on the claim that the employee assumed the risks of employment. Some states, such as Massachusetts, have by statute eliminated the defense. The assumption of risk defense may be invoked in the performance of certain specific professions or tasks. For example, athletes assume the risks associated with their sport, such as falling while fielding a baseball. (*Maddox v. New York City*) Even where the defense may still be viable under state law, the risk of injury in certain circumstances may be found to be so severe that no one would be presumed to have assumed it. In one case, such a defense failed where, over several years, an employee was raped repeatedly, threatened with death or bodily harm, and was subject to continued physical attacks by her supervisor. The employer's claim that she assumed the risk by remaining employed failed where there was a strong state policy against assuming the risk of an illegal act of another. (*Perkins v. Spivey*) An assumption of risk defense offered by a gas station operator also was rejected where the employer argued that a teenager who worked the overnight shift assumed the risk of being attacked. (*Exxon Corp. v. Tidwell*)

The fellow servant rule provides that no recourse is available to an employee injured by the negligence or fault of a fellow employee during the course of employment. The impact of the fellow servant rule has been severely diminished by the enactment of workers' compensation laws. Even in those limited circumstances where workers' compensation laws do not apply, courts have increasingly rejected the rule as being anachronistic and as serving no valid purpose. (*Buckley v. New York City*)

In sum, the defenses of contributory negligence, assumption of risk, and the fellow servant rule are of limited use to employers seeking to defend against a negligence claim.

D. Breach of Contract Not Sufficient

Contract claims and negligence claims are derived from different bases in the law. Contract law is based on the enforcement of private agreements; negligence law is based on the imposition of societal standards on the actions of all and does not require the assent of an individual for the standard to apply. You will not be held liable for breach of a contract that you never entered into, but you can be held liable for negligence for the manner in which you operate your motor vehicle, even though you never assented to the duty of care to be applied.

A negligence claim cannot be based solely on the existence of a breach of contract. (*Otis v. Zayre Corp.*) This is particularly so where the employee is an employee at will. (*Gossage v. Little Caesar Enters.*) Rather, an independent violation of the standard of care upon which a negligence claim may exist must be demonstrated. For example, a bus driver who is hired to drive his bus to a certain destination and fails to do so may be subject to a breach-of-contract claim. A claim of negligent performance of contract, based on the same set of facts, may not be maintained. If, however, it were shown that the bus did not arrive at its destination based on the driver's negligence, then a separate negligence claim seeking to enforce the societal standard of care for operating motor vehicles may be stated. Under this set of facts, the driver may be subject to a breach of contract claim by the employer and to negligence claims by those injured by the driver's conduct where the injuries were proximately caused by the driver's negligence.

E. Governmental Immunity

Public employers are generally immune from suit due to the sovereign immunity accorded governmental bodies. Under certain circumstances, however, public employers may be subject to suit for the actions of their employees. Two New York decisions are instructive. In the first, New York City hired a welfare recipient to work in a city park under a special welfare reform program. The employee responded to questions in the application that he had no arrest or conviction record. Four months after he began work, the City learned that he had a long criminal record, including charges of rape. The City did nothing and three months later the employee raped a nine-year-old girl. The girl's family sued for negligent retention of the employee and New York's highest court held that the city was not immune from suit. The court noted that the public interest in granting government employers broad discretion in exercising their judgment is outweighed where *discretionary* acts rather than *ministerial* or administrative tasks were at issue. The court concluded that since no judgment was exercised, as no review was made of the employee's criminal record after it was uncovered, no governmental immunity would apply. (*Haddock v. New York City*)

In contrast, the same court found the City of New York immune from suit where the City hired a police officer who had been convicted of disorderly conduct two years earlier. The City was sued for negligent hiring after the officer shot two brothers during an altercation while off-duty. The court pointed out that not every action of a government employee who exercises discretion is immune from suit but rather only the actual exercise of discretion. Nonetheless, the court concluded that, in the City's decision to hire the officer, "despite the known unfavorable information as to his character, [the claim] essentially arises from a misjudgment that was discretionary." (*Mon v. New York City*)

AFTERWORD

If this book were a novel written by Charles Dickens, its diverse strands and subplots would come together at the end in a frantic rush for closure and coherence. Of course, this is not a novel, I am not Charles Dickens, and, unfortunately, the topic of individual employee rights in the United States in the late twentieth century does not permit such comforting closure. Indeed, some would argue (with good cause) that the law of individual employee rights is most notable for its lack of coherence. As a consequence, often no simple or fully satisfying explanation exists for the differing approaches adopted or results achieved in the area of individual employee rights. While the temptation was strong at times in writing this book to attempt to impose order on the chaos of the law, I generally refrained from offering my thoughts unless the law had progressed sufficiently along to convey some basic and accepted guidance on the issue. This book is, after all, a primer and not an editorial, a book review, or a philosophical tract.

The text is now complete and I have been freed from merely reporting the state of the law. The question remains: why is it that the law of individual employee rights is so fractured? I offer the following thoughts on how we got to where we are in the increasingly important area of individual employee rights. Much of the answer is rooted in the structure of our legal system and, in particular, in the nature of the common law.

A vast majority of the rights characterized in this book as individual employee rights are rooted in the common law, that is, the judge-made law such as the law of contracts and torts imported from Great Britain by the colonists. Each state has adopted and adapted the common law to its own needs. The success of the common law in the United States is attributable, in significant part, to its ability to draw upon the ingenuity of individual judges and courts and on the experience of individual states in advancing the law of any particular jurisdiction. Each jurisdiction acts, in effect, as a laboratory in which new legal rights are tested. While generally not bound by the decisions of courts in other states, courts may review those decisions and are free to adopt the reasoning of those decisions that they find persuasive.

The state courts and legislatures, reflecting the different perspectives and needs of their citizens and constituencies, have taken very different approaches to the recognition and application of individual employee rights. As a general rule, the area of individual employee rights serves well as a litmus test for a particular state's views on the questions of the rights of labor unions and their members and on the proper balance between the needs of the business community and individual rights where the two conflict. For example, states that are known for being supportive of the labor movement and individual rights, such as California, Michigan, and New Jersey, generally have been receptive to individual employee rights claims. "Right-to-work" states, including many in the deep South, generally have been less receptive to such claims.

Moreover, as a consequence of history, Congress and the federal courts have intruded little in this area. The law of contracts and torts is simply viewed as the domain of the states not subject to federal regulation except in limited circumstances. As a result, federal law has done little to reduce the babble of the states.

Another key factor in the advancement of individual employee rights is the maturity of civil rights law as discussed in Chapter 1. The employment-at-will doctrine, the bedrock of pro-business employment law, today is viewed by many in our rights-oriented society as arbitrary and "un-American" in its inattention to individual rights. Further, those lawyers asserting their clients' rights under civil rights legislation have identified and exploited new opportunities to expand the limited bounds of individual employee rights. Their creative and persuasive application of the traditional notions of fairness and equity helped persuade state judges that the employment-at-will doctrine, strictly applied, had in certain settings outlived its usefulness.

This struggle is by no means over. As reflected in this book, the law in this area is being pulled and stretched regularly. New theories and expanded notions of existing legal rights are frequently proposed or invoked by attorneys for individual employees and by the courts in an effort to expand individual rights in the workplace. These efforts can be expected to continue and expand as we pass through the 1990s into the next century.

What developments can we expect to occur in the coming years? Just as important, what can we expect not to occur?

First, we are not likely to see a consensus reached among the states, at least not in the near future, on many of the issues addressed in this book. Supporting the preservation of the employment-at-will doctrine is the business community and the weight and inertia of tradition. Supporters of expanded individual rights in the workplace are, in fact, typically *individuals* and their counsel who often lack the resources to systematically challenge the well-established at-will doctrine. While change has come, it has come at a different pace and manner in each individual jurisdiction in keeping with the tradition of the common law.

Second, coherence is not likely to be imposed on employment law by Congress or the federal courts, which lack an incentive to intervene on a systematic basis into the domain of state law except in limited and extreme circumstances.

Third, state legislatures are likely to play an increasingly active role in defining the rights to be afforded individual employees. This has been the case, for example, in the whistleblowing area where a growing number of legislatures have recognized the rights of employees to disclose or object to unlawful or hazardous employer actions or practices. Similarly, the enactment of lawful activities laws in a majority of the states further demonstrates the active involvement of state legislatures in protecting the rights of employees.

Fourth, a more promising prospect is the privatization of employee dispute resolution. Simply put, litigation and administrative proceedings have proven to be burdensome and generally unsatisfactory means of resolving employment disputes for all parties to a dispute. Justice delayed is often justice denied, and resolution of employment disputes by means of litigation or agency proceedings is generally measured in years, not months. Moreover, the cost of such proceedings is often too great for either side to bear. Alternative means of dispute resolution such as arbitration, mediation, and peer review panels are, as a result, increasingly being employed. They may be voluntarily invoked as, for example, where the parties retain a retired judge to resolve their dispute or they may be mandated by the courts or agencies or under mandatory policies made a condition of employment by an increasing number of employers.

In short, the slow evolution of individual employee rights can be expected to continue in the coming years. With time, we can expect that the period of experimentation currently indulged in by the state courts and legislatures will be replaced by a period of consolidation. While there may not be uniformity across state lines, there will certainly be less diversity, thereby reducing the current babble of state law. In the interim, employers and employees are more likely to take it upon themselves to decide through negotiation, arbitration, or litigation, what the courts have struggled to do through decisional law, and state legislatures through legislation; that is, to determine the proper balance between the needs of the employer in a competitive marketplace and the rights to which an individual employee is entitled.

Appendix A

State Rulings Chart

This state-by-state chart is designed as a quick reference tool to show the availability of causes of action in three categories of employment at will cases: contract theory (employer policies, handbooks, and other representations), public policy, and the covenant of good faith and fair dealing. Whether the state has recognized a cause of action is noted under the proper header.

State	Employer Policies, Handbooks (Contracts)	Public Policy	Good-Faith Covenant
Alabama	Yes	Yes	Yes
Alaska	Yes	Yes	Yes
Arizona	Yes	Yes	No
Arkansas	Yes	Yes	Yes
California	Yes	Yes	Yes
Colorado	Yes	Yes	Yes
Connecticut	Yes	No	Yes
Delaware	No	Yes	NC
District of Columbia	Yes	Yes	NC
Florida	No	No	No
Georgia	Yes	No	NC
Hawaii	Yes	Yes	Yes
Idaho	Yes	Yes	No
Illinois	Yes	Yes	No
Indiana	No	Yes	Yes
Iowa	NR	Yes	No
Kansas	Yes	Yes	NC
Kentucky	NC	Yes	NC
Louisiana	NC	No	No
Maine	Yes	NC	No
Maryland	Yes	Yes	Yes
Massachusetts	NC	Yes	NC
Michigan	Yes	Yes	No
Minnesota	Yes	Yes	NC
Mississippi	NC	Yes	NC
Missouri	No	Yes	Yes
Montana	Yes	Yes	NC
Nebraska	NC	Yes	Yes
Nevada	NC	Yes	Yes
New Hampshire	Yes	Yes	No
New Jersey	Yes	Yes	NC
New Mexico	Yes	Yes	No
New York	Yes	No	NC
North Carolina	No	Yes	NC

State	Employer Policies, Handbooks (Contracts)	Public Policy	Good-Faith Covenant
North Dakota	NC	Yes	No
Ohio	Yes	Yes	NC
Oklahoma	Yes	Yes	No
Oregon	Yes	Yes	NC
Pennsylvania	NR	Yes	No
Puerto Rico	-	-	-
Rhode Island	NC	NC	NC
South Carolina	Yes	Yes	NC
South Dakota	Yes	Yes	No
Tennessee	No	Yes	NC
Texas	Yes	Yes	NC
Utah	Yes	Yes	NC
Vermont	Yes	Yes	NC
Virgin Islands	-	-	-
Virginia	NR	Yes	NR
Washington	Yes	Yes	No
West Virginia	Yes	Yes	NC
Wisconsin	Yes	Yes	No
Wyoming	Yes	Yes	Yes

NC—No cases or no clear expression.

NR—No definitive state ruling; there may be federal rulings in the subject area.

Notes: In some instances where Yes is noted, a court may merely have said that it would recognize a particular theory even though it may have found the elements necessary to prove the claim lacking in the case immediately before it. In addition, the accuracy of this chart will be affected by opinions not reported in Individual Employment Rights Cases (IER Cases) and Labor Relations Reference Manual (LRRM). It is intended as a point of departure and as an initial step only in any legal research undertaken by the user.

Source: BNA's *Individual Employment Rights Manual.*

Appendix B

Michigan's Access to Employee Records Law

Review Of Employees Records

Sec. 423.501. [Citation] — (1) This act shall be known and may be cited as the "Bullard-Plawecki employee right to know act."

(2) As used in this act:

(a) "Employee" means a person currently employed or formerly employed by an employer.

(b) "Employer" means an individual, corporation, partnership, labor organization, unincorporated association, the state, or an agency or a political subdivision of the state, or any other legal, business, or commercial entity which has 4 or more employees and includes an agent of the employer.

(c) "Personnel record" means a record kept by the employer that identifies the employee, to the extent that the record is used or has been used, or may affect or be used relative to that employee's qualifications for employment, promotion, transfer, additional compensation, or disciplinary action. A personnel record shall include a record in the possession of a person, corporation, partnership, or other association who has a contractual agreement with the employer to keep or supply a personnel record as provided in this subdivision. A personnel record shall not include:

(i) Employee references supplied to an employer if the identity of the person making the reference would be disclosed.

(ii) Materials relating to the employer's staff planning with respect to more than 1 employee, including salary increases, management bonus plans, promotions, and job assignments.

(iii) Medical reports and records made or obtained by the employer if the records or reports are available to the employee from the doctor or medical facility involved.

(iv) Information of a personal nature about a person other than the employee if disclosure of the information would constitute a clearly unwarranted invasion of the other person's privacy.

(v) Information that is kept separately from other records and that relates to an investigation by the employer pursuant to [Sec. 423.509].

(vi) Records limited to grievance investigations which are kept separately and are not used for the purposes provided in this subdivision.

(vii) Records maintained by an educational institution which are directly related to a student and are considered to be education records under section 513(a) of title 5 of the family educational rights and privacy act of 1974, 20 U.S.C. 1232g.

(viii) Records kept by an executive, administrative, or professional employee that are kept in the sole possession of the maker of the record, and are not accessible or shared with other persons. However, a record concerning an occurrence or fact about an employee kept pursuant to this subparagraph may be entered into a personnel record if entered not more than 6 months after the date of the occurrence or the date the fact becomes known.

Sec. 423.502. [Scope; limitations] — Personnel record information which was not included in the personnel record but should have been as required by this act shall not be used by an employer in a judicial or quasi-judicial proceeding. However, personnel record information which, in the opinion of the judge in a judicial proceeding or in the opinion of the hearing officer in a quasi-judicial proceeding, was not intentionally excluded in the personnel record, may be used by the employer in the judicial or quasi-judicial proceeding, if the employee agrees or if the employee has been given a reasonable time to review the information. Material which should have been included in the personnel record shall be used at the request of the employee.

Sec. 423.503. [Employee's right to review records] — An employer, upon written request which describes the personnel record, shall provide the employee with an opportunity to periodically review at reasonable intervals, generally not more than 2 times in a calendar year or as otherwise provided by law or a collective bargaining agreement, the employee's personnel record if the employer has a personnel record for that employee. The review shall take place at a location reasonably near the employee's place of employment and during normal office hours. If a review during normal office hours would require an employee to take time off from work with that employer, then the employer shall provide some other reasonable time for the review. The employer may allow the review to take place at another time or location that would be more convenient to the employee.

Sec. 423.504. [Copy of records; fee] — After the review provided in [Sec. 423.503], an employee may obtain a copy of the information or part of the information contained in the employee's personnel record. An employer may charge a fee for providing a copy of information contained in the personnel record. The fee shall be limited to the actual incremental cost of duplicating the information. If an employee demonstrates that he or she is unable to review his or her personnel record at the employing unit, then the employer, upon that employee's written request,

shall mail a copy of the requested record to the employee.

Sec. 423.505. [Removal or correction] — If there is a disagreement with information contained in a personnel record, removal or correction of that information may be mutually agreed upon by the employer and the employee. If an agreement is not reached, the employee may submit a written statement explaining the employee's position. The statement shall not exceed 5 sheets of 8½ inch by 11-inch paper and shall be included when the information is divulged to a third party and as long as the original information is a part of the file. If either the employer or employee knowingly places in the personnel record information which is false, then the employer or employee, whichever is appropriate, shall have remedy through legal action to have that information expunged.

Sec. 423.506. [Exclusivity] — (1) An employer or former employer shall not divulge a disciplinary report, letter of reprimand, or other disciplinary action to a third party, to a party who is not a part of the employer's organization, or to a party who is not a part of a labor organization representing the employee, without written notice as provided in this section.

(2) The written notice to the employee shall be by first-class mail to the employee's last known address, and shall be mailed on or before the day the information is divulged from the personnel record.

(3) This section shall not apply if any of the following occur:

(a) The employee has specifically waived written notice as part of a written, signed employment application with another employer.

(b) The disclosure is ordered in a legal action or arbitration to a party in that legal action or arbitration.

(c) Information is requested by a government agency as a result of a claim or complaint by an employee.

Sec. 423.507. [Prior review] — An employer shall review a personnel record before releasing information to a third party and, except when the release is ordered in a legal action or arbitration to a party in that legal action or arbitration, delete disciplinary reports, letters of reprimand, or other records of disciplinary action which are more than 4 years old.

Sec. 423.508. [Prohibition] — (1) An employer shall not gather or keep a record of an employee's associations, political activities, publications, or communications of nonemployment activities, except if the information is submitted in writing by or authorized to be kept or gathered, in writing, by the employee to the employer. This prohibition on records shall not apply to the activities that occur on the employer's premises or during the employee's working hours with that employer that interfere with the performance of the employee's duties or duties of other employees.

(2) A record which is kept by the employer as permitted under this section shall be part of the personnel record.

Sec. 423.509. [Separate records] — (1) If an employer has reasonable cause to believe that an employee is engaged in criminal activity which may result in loss or damage to the employer's property or disruption of the employer's business operation, and the employer is engaged in an investigation, then the employer may keep a separate file of information relating to the investigation. Upon completion of the investigation or after 2 years, whichever comes first, the employee shall be notified that an investigation was or is being conducted of the suspected criminal activity described in this section. Upon completion of the investigation, if disciplinary action is not taken, the investigative file and all copies of the material in it shall be destroyed.

(2) If the employer is a criminal justice agency which is involved in the investigation of an alleged criminal activity or the violation of an agency rule by the employee, the employer shall maintain a separate confidential file of information relating to the investigation. Upon completion of the investigation, if disciplinary action is not taken, the employee shall be notified that an investigation was conducted. If the investigation reveals that the allegations are unfounded, unsubstantiated, or disciplinary action is not taken, the separate file shall contain a notation of the final disposition of the investigation and information in the file shall not be used in any future consideration for promotion, transfer, additional compensation, or disciplinary action.

Sec. 423.510. [Construction] — This act shall not be construed to diminish a right of access to records as provided in Act No. 442 of the Public Acts of 1976, being sections 15.231 to 15.246 of the Michigan Compiled Laws, or as otherwise provided by law.

Sec. 423.511. [Penalty] — If an employer violates this act, an employee may commence an action in the circuit court to compel compliance with this act. The circuit court for the county in which the complainant resides, the circuit court for the county in which the complainant is employed, or the circuit court for the county in which the personnel record is maintained shall have jurisdiction to issue the order. Failure to comply with an order of the court may be punished as contempt. In addition, the court shall award an employee prevailing in an action pursuant to this act the following damages:

(a) For a violation of this act, actual damages plus costs.

(b) For a wilful and knowing violation of this act, $200.00 plus costs, reasonable attorney's fees, and actual damages. (Secs. 423.501 to 423.511, as enacted by P.A. 397, L. 1978)

Source: BNA's *Individual Employment Rights Manual.*

Appendix C

Worker Adjustment And Retraining Notification Act

Following is the text of The Worker Adjustment and Retraining Notification Act, which, with some exceptions, requires employers to provide 60 days' advance notice of plant closings and layoffs. The law (PL 100-379, 102 Stat 890, 29 USC §§2101-2109) automatically became law on Aug. 4, 1988, without the president's signature, and took effect, except where noted, on Feb. 4, 1989.

29 U.S.C. s 2101
TITLE 29—LABOR
CHAPTER 23—WORKER ADJUSTMENT AND RETRAINING NOTIFICATION

Sec. 2101. Definitions; exclusions from definition of loss of employment

(a) *Definitions.* As used in this chapter—

(1) the term "employer" means any business enterprise that employs—

(A) 100 or more employees, excluding part-time employees; or

(B) 100 or more employees who in the aggregate work at least 4,000 hours per week (exclusive of hours of overtime);

(2) the term "plant closing" means the permanent or temporary shutdown of a single site of employment, or one or more facilities or operating units within a single site of employment, if the shutdown results in an employment loss at the single site of employment during any 30-day period for 50 or more employees excluding any part-time employees;

(3) the term "mass layoff" means a reduction in force which—

(A) is not the result of a plant closing; and

(B) results in an employment loss at the single site of employment during any 30-day period for—

(i)(I) at least 33 percent of the employees (excluding any part-time employees); and

(II) at least 50 employees (excluding any part-time employees); or

(ii) at least 500 employees (excluding any part-time employees);

(4) the term "representative" means an exclusive representative of employees within the meaning of section 159(a) or 158(f) of this title or section 152 of Title 45;

(5) the term "affected employees" means employees who may reasonably be expected to experience an employment loss as a consequence of a proposed plant closing or mass layoff by their employer;

(6) subject to subsection (b) of this section, the term "employment loss" means (A) an employment termination, other than a discharge for cause, voluntary departure, or retirement, (B) a layoff exceeding 6 months, or (C) a reduction in hours of work of more than 50 percent during each month of any 6-month period;

(7) the term "unit of local government" means any general purpose political subdivision of a State which has the power to levy taxes and spend funds, as well as general corporate and police powers; and

321

(8) the term "part-time employee" means an employee who is employed for an average of fewer than 20 hours per week or who has been employed for fewer than 6 of the 12 months preceding the date on which notice is required.

(b) *Exclusions from definition of employment loss.* (1) In the case of a sale of part or all of an employer's business, the seller shall be responsible for providing notice for any plant closing or mass layoff in accordance with section 2102 of this title, up to and including the effective date of the sale. After the effective date of the sale of part or all of an employer's business, the purchaser shall be responsible for providing notice for any plant closing or mass layoff in accordance with section 2102 of this title. Notwithstanding any other provision of this chapter, any person who is an employee of the seller (other than a part-time employee) as of the effective date of the sale shall be considered an employee of the purchaser immediately after the effective date of the sale.

(2) Notwithstanding subsection (a)(6) of this section, an employee may not be considered to have experienced an employment loss if the closing or layoff is the result of the relocation or consolidation of part or all of the employer's business and, prior to the closing or layoff—

(A) the employer offers to transfer the employee to a different site of employment within a reasonable commuting distance with no more than a 6-month break in employment; or

(B) the employer offers to transfer the employee to any other site of employment regardless of distance with no more than a 6-month break in employment, and the employee accepts within 30 days of the offer or of the closing or layoff, whichever is later.

Sec. 2102. Notice required before plant closings and mass layoffs

(a) *Notice to employees, state dislocated worker units, and local governments.* An employer shall not order a plant closing or mass layoff until the end of a 60-day period after the employer serves written notice of such an order—

(1) to each representative of the affected employees as of the time of the notice or, if there is no such representative at that time, to each affected employee; and

(2) to the State dislocated worker unit (designated or created under title III of the Job Training Partnership Act [29 U.S.C.A. s 1651 et seq.]) and the chief elected official of the unit of local government within which such closing or layoff is to occur.

If there is more than one such unit, the unit of local government which the employer shall notify is the unit of local government to which the employer pays the highest taxes for the year preceding the year for which the determination is made.

(b) *Reduction of notification period.* (1) An employer may order the shutdown of a single site of employment before the conclusion of the 60-day period if as of the time that notice would have been required the employer was actively seeking capital or business which, if obtained, would have enabled the employer to avoid or postpone the shutdown and the employer reasonably and in good faith believed that giving the notice required would have precluded the employer from obtaining the needed capital or business.

(2)(A) An employer may order a plant closing or mass layoff before the conclusion of the 60-day period if the closing or mass layoff is caused by business circumstances that were not reasonably foreseeable as of the time that notice would have been required.

(B) No notice under this chapter shall be required if the plant closing or mass layoff is due to any form of natural disaster, such as a flood, earthquake, or the drought currently ravaging the farmlands of the United States.

(3) An employer relying on this subsection shall give as much notice as is practicable and at that time shall give a brief statement of the basis for reducing the notification period.

(c) *Extension of layoff period.* A layoff of more than 6 months which, at its outset, was announced to be a layoff of 6 months or less, shall be treated as an employment loss under this chapter unless—

(1) the extension beyond 6 months is caused by business circumstances (including unforeseeable changes in price or cost) not reasonably foreseeable at the time of the initial layoff; and

(2) notice is given at the time it becomes reasonably foreseeable that the extension beyond 6 months will be required.

(d) *Determinations with respect to employment loss.* For purposes of this section, in determining whether a plant closing or mass layoff has occurred or will occur, employment losses for 2 or more groups at a single site of employment, each of which is less than the minimum number of employees specified in section 2101(a)(2) or (3) of this title but which in the aggregate exceed that minimum number, and which occur within any 90-day period shall be considered to be a plant closing or mass layoff unless the employer demonstrates that the employment losses are the result of separate and distinct actions and causes and are not an attempt by the employer to evade the requirements of this chapter.

Sec. 2103. Exemptions.

This chapter shall not apply to a plant closing or mass layoff if—

(1) the closing is of a temporary facility or the closing or layoff is the result of the completion of a particular project or undertaking, and the affected employees were hired with the understanding that their employment was limited to the duration of the facility or the project or undertaking; or

(2) the closing or layoff constitutes a strike or constitutes a lockout not intended to evade the requirements of this chapter. Nothing in this chapter shall require an employer to serve written notice pursuant to section 2102 (a) of this title when permanently replacing a person who is deemed to be an economic striker under the National Labor Relations Act: [29 U.S.C.A. s 151 et seq.]: Provided, That nothing in this chapter shall be deemed to validate or invalidate any judicial or administrative ruling relating to the hiring of permanent replacements for economic strikers under the National Labor Relations Act.

Sec. 2104. Administration and enforcement of requirements.

(a) *Civil actions against employers.*

(1) Any employer who orders a plant closing or mass layoff in violation of section 2102 of this title shall be liable to each aggrieved employee who suffers an employment loss as a result of such closing or layoff for—

(A) back pay for each day of violation at a rate of compensation not less than the higher of—

(i) the average regular rate received by such employee during the last 3 years of the employee's employment; or

(ii) the final regular rate received by such employee; and

(B) benefits under an employee benefit plan described in section 1002 (3) of this title, including the cost of medical expenses incurred during the employment loss which would have been covered under an employee benefit plan if the employment loss had not occurred.

Such liability shall be calculated for the period of the violation, up to a maximum of 60 days, but in no event for more than one-half the number of days the employee was employed by the employer.

(2) The amount for which an employer is liable under paragraph (1) shall be reduced by—

(A) any wages paid by the employer to the employee for the period of the violation;

(B) any voluntary and unconditional payment by the employer to the employee that is not required by any legal obligation; and

(C) any payment by the employer to a third party or trustee (such as premiums for health benefits or payments to a defined contribution pension plan) on behalf of and attributable to the employee for the period of the violation.

In addition, any liability incurred under paragraph (1) with respect to a defined benefit pension plan may be reduced by crediting the employee with service for all purposes under such a plan for the period of the violation.

(3) Any employer who violates the provisions of section 2102 of this title with respect to a unit of local government shall be subject to a civil penalty of not more than $500 for each day of such violation, except that such penalty shall not apply if the employer pays to each aggrieved employee the amount for which the employer is liable to that employee within 3 weeks from the date the employer orders the shutdown or layoff.

(4) If an employer which has violated this chapter proves to the satisfac-

tion of the court that the act or omission that violated this chapter was in good faith and that the employer had reasonable grounds for believing that the act or omission was not a violation of this chapter the court may, in its discretion, reduce the amount of the liability or penalty provided for in this section.

(5) A person seeking to enforce such liability, including a representative of employees or a unit of local government aggrieved under paragraph (1) or (3), may sue either for such person or for other persons similarly situated, or both, in any district court of the United States for any district in which the violation is alleged to have occurred, or in which the employer transacts business.

(6) In any such suit, the court, in its discretion, may allow the prevailing party a reasonable attorney's fee as part of the costs.

(7) For purposes of this subsection, the term, "aggrieved employee" means an employee who has worked for the employer ordering the plant closing or mass layoff and who, as a result of the failure by the employer to comply with section 2102 of this title did not receive timely notice either directly or through his or her representative as required by section 2102 of this title.

(b) *Exclusivity of remedies.*

The remedies provided for in this section shall be the exclusive remedies for any violation of this chapter. Under this chapter, a Federal court shall not have authority to enjoin a plant closing or mass layoff.

Sec. 2105. Procedures in addition to other rights of employees.

The rights and remedies provided to employees by this chapter are in addition to, and not in lieu of, any other contractual or statutory rights and remedies of the employees, and are not intended to alter or affect such rights and remedies, except that the period of notification required by this chapter shall run concurrently with any period of notification required by contract or by any other statute.

Sec. 2106. Procedures encouraged where not required.

It is the sense of Congress that an employer who is not required to comply with the notice requirements of section 2102 of this title should, to the extent possible, provide notice to its employees about a proposal to close a plant or permanently reduce its workforce.

Sec. 2107. Authority to prescribe regulations.

(a) The Secretary of Labor shall prescribe such regulations as may be necessary to carry out this chapter. Such regulations shall, at a minimum, include interpretative regulations describing the methods by which employers may provide for appropriate service of notice as required by this chapter.

(b) The mailing of notice to an employee's last known address or inclusion of notice in the employee's paycheck will be considered acceptable methods for fulfillment of the employer's obligation to give notice to each affected employee under this chapter.

Sec. 2108. Effect on other laws.

The giving of notice pursuant to this chapter, if done in good faith compliance with this chapter, shall not constitute a violation of the National Labor Relations Act [29 U.S.C.A. s 151 et seq.] or the Railway Labor Act.

Sec. 2109. Report on employment and international competitiveness.

Two years after Aug. 4, 1988, the Comptroller General shall submit to the Committee on Small Business of both the House and Senate, the Committee on Labor and Human Resources, and the Committee on Education and Labor a report containing a detailed and objective analysis of the effect of this chapter on employers (especially small-and medium-sized businesses), the economy (international competitiveness), and employees (in terms of levels and conditions of employment). The Comptroller General shall assess both costs and benefits, including the effect on productivity, competitiveness, unemployment rates and compensation, and worker retraining and readjustment. (Effective February 4, 1989, expect that the authority of the Secretary of Labor under Sec. 2107 took effect August 4, 1988.)

Source: BNA's *Individual Employment Rights Manual.*

Appendix D

Fair Credit Reporting Act

Text of Title VI of the Consumer Credit Protection Act, relating to credit reporting agencies, known as the Fair Credit Reporting Act, Pub. L. 90-321 (codified as 15 USC 1681-1681t), October 26, 1970; as added by Pub. L. 91-508, April 25, 1971. The text below appears as last added to by Pub. L. 102-537, October 27, 1992, effective January 1, 1993.

Sec. 1681. Congressional findings and statement of purpose

(a) *Accuracy and fairness of credit reporting*

The Congress makes the following findings:

(1) The banking system is dependent upon fair and accurate credit reporting. Inaccurate credit reports directly impair the efficiency of the banking system, and unfair credit reporting methods undermine the public confidence which is essential to the continued functioning of the banking system.

(2) An elaborate mechanism has been developed for investigating and evaluating the credit worthiness, credit standing, credit capacity, character, and general reputation of consumers.

(3) Consumer reporting agencies have assumed a vital role in assembling and evaluating consumer credit and other information on consumers.

(4) There is a need to insure that consumer reporting agencies exercise their grave responsibilities with fairness, impartiality, and a respect for the consumer's right to privacy.

(b) *Reasonable procedures*

It is the purpose of this subchapter to require that consumer reporting agencies adopt reasonable procedures for meeting the needs of commerce for consumer credit, personnel, insurance, and other information in a manner which is fair and equitable to the consumer, with regard to the confidentiality, accuracy, relevancy, and proper utilization of such information in accordance with the requirements of this subchapter.

Sec. 1681a. Definitions; rules of construction

(a) Definitions and rules of construction set forth in this section are applicable for the purposes of this subchapter.

(b) The term "person" means any individual, partnership, corporation, trust, estate, cooperative, association, government or governmental subdivision or agency, or other entity.

(c) The term "consumer" means an individual.

(d) The term "consumer report" means any written, oral, or other communication of any information by a consumer reporting agency bearing on a consumer's credit worthiness, credit standing, credit capacity, character, general reputation, personal characteristics, or mode of living which is used or expected to be used or collected in whole or in part for the purpose of serving as a factor in establishing the consumer's eligibility for (1) credit or insurance to be used primarily for personal, family, or household purposes, or (2) employment purposes, or (3) other purposes authorized under section 1681b of this title. The term does not include (A) any report containing information solely as to transactions or experiences between the consumer and the person making the report; (B) any authorization or approval of a specific extension of credit directly or indirectly by the issuer of a credit card or similar device; or (C) any report in which a person who has been requested by a third party to make a specific extension of credit directly or indirectly to a consumer conveys his decision with respect to such request, if the third party advises the consumer of the name and address of the person to whom the request was made and such person makes the disclosures to the consumer required under section 1681m of this title.

(e) The term "investigative consumer report" means a consumer report or portion thereof in which information on a consumer's character, general reputation, personal characteristics, or mode of living is obtained through personal interviews with neighbors, friends, or associates of the consumer reported on or with others with whom he is acquainted or who may have knowledge concerning any such items of information. However, such information shall not include specific factual information on a consumer's credit record obtained directly from a creditor of the consumer or from a consumer reporting agency when such information was obtained directly from a creditor of the consumer or from the consumer.

(f) The term "consumer reporting agency" means any person which, for monetary fees, dues, or on a cooperative nonprofit basis, regularly engages in whole or in part in the practice of assembling or evaluating consumer credit information or other information on consumers for the purpose of furnishing consumer reports to third parties, and which uses any means or facility of interstate commerce for the purpose of preparing or furnishing consumer reports.

(g) The term "file," when used in connection with information on any consumer, means all of the information on that consumer recorded and retained by a consumer reporting agency regardless of how the information is stored.

(h) The term "employment purposes" when used in connection with a consumer report means a report used for the purpose of evaluating a consumer for employment, promotion, reassignment or retention as an employee.

(i) The term "medical information" means information or records obtained, with the consent of the individual to whom it relates, from licensed physicians or medical practitioners, hospitals, clinics, or other medical or medically related facilities.

(j) *Definitions Relating to Child Support Obligations*

(1) Overdue support—The term "overdue support" has the meaning given to such term in section 666(e) of title 42.

(2) State or local child support enforcement agency—The term "State or local child support enforcement agency" means a State or local agency which administers a State or local program for establishing and enforcing child support obligations.

[Subsection (j) added by Pub.L. 102-537, eff. Jan. 1, 1993]

Sec. 1681b. Permissible purposes of consumer reports

A consumer reporting agency may furnish a consumer report under the following circumstances and no other:

(1) In response to the order of a court having jurisdiction to issue such an order, or a subpoena issued in connection with proceedings before a Federal grand jury.

(2) In accordance with the written instructions of the consumer to whom it relates.

(3) To a person which it has reason to believe—

(A) intends to use the information in connection with a credit transaction involving the consumer on whom the information is to be furnished and involving the extension of credit to, or review or collection of an account of, the consumer; or

(B) intends to use the information for employment purposes; or

(C) intends to use the information in connection with the underwriting of insurance involving the consumer; or

(D) intends to use the information in connection with a determination of the consumer's eligibility for a license or other benefit granted by a governmental instrumentality required by law to consider an applicant's financial responsibility or status; or

(E) otherwise has a legitimate business need for the information in connection with a business transaction involving the consumer.

[As amended by Pub.L. 101-73, Aug. 9, 1989)

Sec. 1681c. Reporting of obsolete information prohibited

(a) *Prohibited items*

Except as authorized under subsection (b) of this section, no consumer reporting agency may make any consumer report containing any of the following items of information:

(1) cases under title 11 or under the Bankruptcy Act that, from the date of entry of the order for relief or the date of adjudication, as the case may be, antedate the report by more than 10 years.

(2) Suits and judgments which, from date of entry, antedate the report by more than seven years or until the governing statute of limitations has expired, whichever is the longer period.

(3) Paid tax liens which, from date of payment, antedate the report by more than seven years.

(4) Accounts placed for collection or charged to profit and loss which antedate the report by more than seven years.

(5) Records of arrest, indictment, or conviction of crime which, from date of disposition, release, or parole, antedate the report by more than seven years.

(6) Any other adverse item of information which antedates the report by more than seven years.

(b) *Exempted cases*

The provisions of subsection (a) of this section are not applicable in the case of any consumer credit report to be used in connection with—

(1) a credit transaction involving, or which may reasonably be expected to involve, a principal amount of $50,000 or more;

(2) the underwriting of life insurance involving, or which may reasonably be expected to involve, a face amount of $50,000 or more; or

(3) the employment of any individual at an annual salary which equals, or which may reasonably be expected to equal $20,000, or more.

[As amended by Pub.L. 95-598, Nov. 6, 1978]

Sec. 1681d. Disclosure of investigative consumer reports

(a) *Disclosure of fact of preparation*

A person may not procure or cause to be prepared an investigative consumer report on any consumer unless—

(1) it is clearly and accurately disclosed to the consumer that an investigative consumer report including information as to his character, general reputation, personal characteristics, and mode of living, whichever are applicable, may be made, and such disclosure (A) is made in a writing mailed, or otherwise delivered, to the consumer, not later than three days after the date on which the report was first requested, and (B) includes a statement informing the consumer of his right to request the additional disclosures provided for under subsection (b) of this section; or

(2) the report is to be used for employment purposes for which the consumer has not specifically applied.

(b) *Disclosure on request of nature and scope of investigation*

Any person who procures or causes to be prepared an investigative consumer report on any consumer shall, upon written request made by the consumer within a reasonable period of time after the receipt by him of the disclosure required by subsection (a)(1) of this section, shall make a complete and accurate disclosure of the nature and scope of the investigation requested. This disclosure shall be made in a writing mailed, or otherwise delivered, to the consumer not later than five days after the date on which the request for such disclosure was received from the consumer or such report was first requested, whichever is the later.

(c) Limitation on liability upon showing of reasonable procedures for compliance with provisions—No person may be held liable for any violation of subsection (a) or (b) of this section if he shows by a preponderance of the evidence that at the time of the violation he maintained reasonable procedures to assure compliance with subsection (a) or (b) of this section.

Sec. 1681e. Compliance procedures

(a) *Identity and purposes of credit users*

Every consumer reporting agency shall maintain reasonable procedures designed to avoid violations of section 1681c of this title and to limit the furnishing of consumer reports to the purposes listed under section 1681b of this title. These procedures shall require that prospective users of the information identify themselves, certify the purposes for which the information is sought, and certify that the information will be used for no other purpose. Every consumer reporting agency shall make a reasonable effort to verify the identity of a new prospective user and the uses certified by such prospective user prior to furnishing such user a consumer report. No consumer reporting agency may furnish a consumer report to any person if it has reasonable grounds for believing that the consumer report will not be used for a purpose listed in section 1681b of this title.

(b) *Accuracy of report*

Whenever a consumer reporting agency prepares a consumer report it shall follow reasonable procedures to assure maximum possible accuracy of the information concerning the individual about whom the report relates.

Sec. 1681f. Disclosures to governmental agencies

Notwithstanding the provisions of section 1681b of this title, a consumer reporting agency may furnish identifying information respecting any consumer, limited to his name, address, former addresses, places of employment, or former places of employment, to a governmental agency.

Sec. 1681g. Disclosures to consumers

(a) Information on file; sources; report recipients

Every consumer reporting agency shall, upon request and proper identification of any consumer, clearly and accurately disclose to the consumer:

(1) The nature and substance of all information (except medical information) in its files on the consumer at the time of the request.

(2) The sources of the information; except that the sources of information acquired solely for use in preparing an investigative consumer report and actually used for no other purpose need not be disclosed: Provided, That in the event an action is brought under this subchapter, such sources shall be available to the plaintiff under appropriate discovery procedures in the court in which the action is brought.

(3) The recipients of any consumer report on the consumer which it has furnished—

(A) for employment purposes within the two-year period preceding the request, and

(B) for any other purpose within the six-month period preceding the request.

(b) *Exempt information*

The requirements of subsection (a) of this section respecting the disclosure of sources of information and the recipients of consumer reports do not apply to information received or consumer reports furnished prior to the effective date of this subchapter except to the extent that the matter involved is contained in the files of the consumer reporting agency on that date.

Sec. 1681h. Conditions of disclosure to consumers

(a) *Times and notice*

A consumer reporting agency shall make the disclosures required under section 1681g of this title during normal business hours and on reasonable notice.

(b) *Identification of consumer*

The disclosures required under section 1681g of this title shall be made to the consumer—

(1) in person if he appears in person and furnishes proper

identification; or

(2) by telephone if he has made a written request, with proper identification, for telephone disclosure and the toll charge, if any, for the telephone call is prepaid by or charged directly to the consumer.

(c) *Trained personnel*

Any consumer reporting agency shall provide trained personnel to explain to the consumer any information furnished to him pursuant to section 1681g of this title.

(d) *Persons accompanying consumer*

The consumer shall be permitted to be accompanied by one other person of his choosing, who shall furnish reasonable identification. A consumer reporting agency may require the consumer to furnish a written statement granting permission to the consumer reporting agency to discuss the consumer's file in such person's presence.

(e) *Limitation of liability*

Except as provided in sections 1681n and 1681o of this title, no consumer may bring any action or proceeding in the nature of defamation, invasion of privacy, or negligence with respect to the reporting of information against any consumer reporting agency, any user of information, or any person who furnishes information to a consumer reporting agency, based on information disclosed pursuant to section 1681g, 1681h, or 1681m of this title, except as to false information fur-

nished with malice or willful intent to injure such consumer.

Sec. 1681i. Procedure in case of disputed accuracy

(a) *Dispute; reinvestigation*

If the completeness or accuracy of any item of information contained in his file is disputed by a consumer, and such dispute is directly conveyed to the consumer reporting agency by the consumer, the consumer reporting agency shall within a reasonable period of time reinvestigate and record the current status of that information unless it has reasonable grounds to believe that the dispute by the consumer is frivolous or irrelevant. If after such reinvestigation such information is found to be inaccurate or can no longer be verified, the consumer reporting agency shall promptly delete such information. The presence of contradictory information in the consumer's file does not in and of itself constitute reasonable grounds for believing the dispute is frivolous or irrelevant.

(b) *Statement of dispute*

If the reinvestigation does not resolve the dispute, the consumer may file a brief statement setting forth the nature of the dispute. The consumer reporting agency may limit such statements to not more than one hundred words if it provides the consumer with assistance in writing a clear summary of the dispute.

(c) *Notification of consumer dispute in subsequent consumer reports*

Whenever a statement of a dispute is filed, unless there is reasonable grounds to believe that it is frivolous or irrelevant, the consumer reporting agency shall, in any subsequent consumer report containing the information in question, clearly note that it is disputed by the consumer and provide either the consumer's statement or a clear and accurate codification or summary thereof.

(d) *Notification of deletion of disputed information*

Following any deletion of information which is found to be inaccurate or whose accuracy can no longer be verified or any notation as to disputed information, the

332 Primer on Individual Employee Rights, Second Edition

consumer reporting agency shall, at the request of the consumer, furnish notification that the item has been deleted or the statement, codification or summary pursuant to subsection (b) or (c) of this section to any person specifically designated by the consumer who has within two years prior thereto received a consumer report for employment purposes, or within six months prior thereto received a consumer report for any other purpose, which contained the deleted or disputed information. The consumer reporting agency shall clearly and conspicuously disclose to the consumer his rights to make such a request. Such disclosure shall be made at or prior to the time the information is deleted or the consumer's statement regarding the disputed information is received.

Sec. 1681j. Charges for disclosures

A consumer reporting agency shall make all disclosures pursuant to section 1681g of this title and furnish all consumer reports pursuant to section 1681i(d) of this title without charge to the consumer if, within thirty days after receipt by such consumer of a notification pursuant to section 1681m of this title or notification from a debt collection agency affiliated with such consumer reporting agency stating that the consumer's credit rating may be or has been adversely affected, the consumer makes a request under section 1681g or 1681i(d) of this title. Otherwise, the consumer reporting agency may impose a reasonable charge on the consumer for making disclosure to such consumer pursuant to section 1681g of this title, the charge for which shall be indicated to the consumer prior to making disclosure; and for furnishing notifications, statements, summaries, or codifications to person designated by the consumer pursuant to section 1681i(d) of this title, the charge for which shall be indicated to the consumer prior to furnishing such information and shall not exceed the charge that the consumer reporting agency would impose on each designated recipient for a consumer

report except that no charge may be made for notifying such persons of the deletion of information which is found to be inaccurate or which can no longer be verified.

Sec. 1681k. Public record information for employment purposes

A consumer reporting agency which furnishes a consumer report for employment purposes and which for that purpose compiles and reports items of information on consumers which are matters of public record and are likely to have an adverse effect upon a consumer's ability to obtain employment shall—

(1) at the time such public record information is reported to the user of such consumer report, notify the consumer of the fact that public record information is being reported by the consumer reporting agency, together with the name and address of the person to whom such information is being reported; or

(2) maintain strict procedures designed to insure that whenever public record information which is likely to have an adverse effect on a consumer's ability to obtain employment is reported it is complete and up to date. For purposes of this paragraph, items of public record relating to arrests, indictments, convictions, suits, tax liens, and outstanding judgments shall be considered up to date if the current public record status of the item at the time of the report is reported.

Sec. 1681l. Restrictions on investigative consumer reports

Whenever a consumer reporting agency prepares an investigative consumer report, no adverse information in the consumer report (other than information which is a matter of public record) may be included in a subsequent consumer report unless such adverse information has been verified in the process of making such subsequent consumer report, or the adverse information was received within the three-month period preceding the date the subsequent report is furnished.

Sec. 1681m. Requirements on users of consumer reports

(a) *Adverse action based on reports of consumer reporting agencies*

Whenever credit or insurance for personal, family, or household purposes, or employment involving a consumer is denied or the charge for such credit or insurance is increased either wholly or partly because of information contained in a consumer report from a consumer reporting agency, the user of the consumer report shall so advise the consumer against whom such adverse action has been taken and supply the name and address of the consumer reporting agency making the report.

(b) *Adverse action based on reports of persons other than consumer reporting agencies*

Whenever credit for personal, family, or household purposes involving a consumer is denied or the charge for such credit is increased either wholly or partly because of information obtained from a person other than a consumer reporting agency bearing upon the consumer's credit worthiness, credit standing, credit capacity, character, general reputation, personal characteristics, or mode of living, the user of such information shall, within a reasonable period of time, upon the consumer's written request for the reasons for such adverse action received within sixty days after learning of such adverse action, disclose the nature of the information to the consumer. The user of such information shall clearly and accurately disclose to the consumer his right to make such written request at the time such adverse action is communicated to the consumer.

(c) *Reasonable procedures to assure compliance*

No person shall be held liable for any violation of this section if he shows by a preponderance of the evidence that at the time of the alleged violation he maintained reasonable procedures to assure compliance with the provisions of subsections (a) and (b) of this section.

Sec. 1681n. Civil liability for willful noncompliance

Any consumer reporting agency or user of information which willfully fails to comply with any requirement imposed under this subchapter with respect to any consumer is liable to that consumer in an amount equal to the sum of—

(1) any actual damages sustained by the consumer as a result of the failure;

(2) such amount of punitive damages as the court may allow; and

(3) in the case of any successful action to enforce any liability under this section, the costs of the action together with reasonable attorney's fees as determined by the court.

Sec. 1681o. Civil liability for negligent noncompliance

Any consumer reporting agency or user of information which is negligent in failing to comply with any requirement imposed under this subchapter with respect to any consumer is liable to that consumer in an amount equal to the sum of—

(1) any actual damages sustained by the consumer as a result of the failure;

(2) in the case of any successful action to enforce any liability under this section, the costs of the action together with reasonable attorney's fees as determined by the court.

Sec. 1681p. Jurisdiction of courts; limitation of actions

An action to enforce any liability created under this subchapter may be brought in any appropriate United States district court without regard to the amount in controversy, or in any other court of competent jurisdiction, within two years from the date on which the liability arises, except that where a defendant has materially and willfully misrepresented any information required under this subchapter to be disclosed to an individual and the information so misrepresented is material to the establishment of the defendant's liability to that individual under this subchapter, the action may be brought at any time within two years after discovery by the individual of the misrepresentation.

Sec. 1681q. Obtaining information under false pretenses

Any person who knowingly and willfully obtains information on a consumer from a consumer reporting agency under false pretenses shall be fined not more than $5,000 or imprisoned not more than one year, or both.

Sec. 1681r. Unauthorized disclosures by officers or employees

Any officer or employee of a consumer reporting agency who knowingly and willfully provides information concerning an individual from the agency's files to a person not authorized to receive that information shall be fined not more than $5,000 or imprisoned not more than one year, or both.

Sec. 1681s. Administrative enforcement

(a) *Federal Trade Commission; powers*

Compliance with the requirements imposed under this subchapter shall be enforced under the Federal Trade Commission Act by the Federal Trade Commission with respect to consumer reporting agencies and all other persons subject thereto, except to the extent that enforcement of the requirements imposed under this subchapter is specifically committed to some other government agency under subsection (b) hereof. For the purpose of the exercise by the Federal Trade Commission of its functions and powers under the Federal Trade Commission Act, a violation of any requirement or prohibition imposed under this subchapter shall constitute an unfair or deceptive act or practice in commerce in violation of section 5(a) of the Federal Trade Commission Act and shall be subject to enforcement by the Federal Trade Commission under section 5(b) thereof with respect to any consumer reporting agency or person subject to enforcement by the Federal Trade Commission pursuant to this subsection, irrespective of whether that person is engaged in commerce or meets any other jurisdictional tests in the Federal Trade Commission Act. The Federal Trade Commission shall have such procedural, investigative, and enforcement powers, including the power to issue procedural rules in enforcing compliance with the requirements imposed under this subchapter and to require the filing of reports, the production of documents, and the appearance of witnesses as though the applicable terms and conditions of the Federal Trade Commission Act were part of this subchapter. Any person violating any of the provisions of this subchapter shall be subject to the penalties and entitled to the privileges and immunities provided in the Federal Trade Commission Act as though the applicable terms and provisions thereof were part of this subchapter.

(b) *Other administrative bodies*

Compliance with the requirements imposed under this subchapter with respect to consumer reporting agencies and persons who use consumer reports from such agencies shall be enforced under—

(1) section 1818 of title 12, in the case of—

(A) national banks, and Federal branches and Federal agencies of foreign banks, by the Office of the Comptroller of the Currency;

(B) member banks of the Federal Reserve System (other than national banks), branches and agencies of foreign banks (other than Federal branches, Federal agencies, and insured State branches of foreign banks), commercial lending companies owned or controlled by foreign banks, and organizations operating under section 25 or 25(a) of the Federal Reserve Act, by the Board of Governors of the Federal Reserve System; and

(C) banks insured by the Federal Deposit Insurance Corporation (other than members of the Federal Reserve System) and insured State branches of foreign banks, by the Board of Directors of the Federal Deposit Insurance Corporation;

(2) section 1818 of title 12, by the Director of the Office of Thrift Supervision,

in the case of a savings association the deposits of which are insured by the Federal Deposit Insurance Corporation;

(3) the Federal Credit Union Act, by the Administrator of the National Credit Union Administration with respect to any Federal credit union;

(4) subtitle IV of title 49, by the Interstate Commerce Commission with respect to any common carrier subject to such subtitle;

(5) the Federal Aviation Act of 1958, by the Secretary of Transportation with respect to any air carrier or foreign air carrier subject to that Act; and

(6) the Packers and Stockyards Act, 1921 (except as provided in section 406 of that Act), by the Secretary of Agriculture with respect to any activities subject to that Act.

The terms used in paragraph (1) that are not defined in this subchapter or otherwise defined in section 1813(s) of title 12) shall have the meaning given to them in section 3101(b) of title 12.

(c) *Enforcement under other authority*

For the purpose of the exercise by any agency referred to in subsection (b) of this section of its powers under any Act referred to in that subsection, a violation of any requirement imposed under this subchapter shall be deemed to be a violation of a requirement imposed under that Act. In addition to its powers under any provision of law specifically referred to in subsection (b) of this section, each of the agencies referred to in that subsection may exercise, for the purpose of enforcing compliance with any requirement imposed under this subchapter any other authority conferred on it by law.

[As amended by Pub.L. 98-443, Oct. 4, 1984; Pub.L. 101-73, Aug. 9, 1989; Pub.L. 102-242, Dec. 19, 1991; Pub.L. 102-550, Oct. 28, 1992]

Sec. 1681s-1. Information on overdue child support obligations

Notwithstanding any other provision of this subchapter, a consumer reporting agency shall include in any consumer report furnished by the agency in accordance with section 1681b of this title, any information on the failure of the consumer to pay overdue support which—

(1) is provided—

(A) to the consumer reporting agency by a State or local child support enforcement agency; or

(B) to the consumer reporting agency and verified by any local, State, or Federal Government agency; and

(2) antedates the report by 7 years or less.

Sec. 1681t. Relation to State laws

This subchapter does not annul, alter, affect, or exempt any person subject to the provisions of this subchapter from complying with the laws of any State with respect to the collection, distribution, or use of any information on consumers, except to the extent that those laws are inconsistent with any provision of this subchapter, and then only to the extent of the inconsistency.

[*Editor's note:* Formerly known as section 622 of Pub.L. 90-321, this section was renumbered as section 623 by Pub.L. 102-537, Oct. 27, 1992, eff. Jan. 1, 1993]

Appendix E

Omnibus Transportation Employee Testing Act of 1991

Following is text of the Omnibus Transportation Employee Testing Act of 1991, which was approved by the House and Senate as part of the Department of Transportation and Related Agencies Appropriations Act, 1992 (H.R. 2942). The measure, which President Bush signed into law (P.L. 102-143) on October 28, 1991, provides for drug and alcohol testing of persons who operate aircraft, trains, and commercial motor vehicles.

SECTION 1. Short Title. This title may be cited as the "Omnibus Transportation Employee Testing Act of 1991".

SECTION 2. Findings. The Congress finds that—(1) alcohol abuse and illegal drug use pose significant dangers to the safety and welfare of the Nation;

(2) millions of the Nation's citizens utilize transportation by aircraft, railroads, trucks, and buses, and depend on the operators of aircraft, trains, trucks, and buses to perform in a safe and responsible manner;

(3) the greatest efforts must be expended to eliminate the abuse of alcohol and use of illegal drugs, whether on duty or off duty, by those individuals who are involved in the operation of aircraft, trains, trucks, and buses;

(4) the use of alcohol and illegal drugs has been demonstrated to affect significantly the performance of individuals, and has been proven to have been a critical factor in transportation accidents;

(5) the testing of uniformed personnel of the Armed Forces has shown that the most effective deterrent to abuse of alcohol and use of illegal drugs is increased testing, including random testing;

(6) adequate safeguards can be implemented to ensure that testing for abuse of alcohol or use of illegal drugs is performed in a manner which protects an individual's right of privacy, ensures that no individual is harassed by being treated differently from other individuals, and ensures that no individual's reputation or career development is unduly threatened or harmed; and

(7) rehabilitation is a critical component of any testing program for abuse of alcohol or use of illegal drugs, and should be made available to individuals, as appropriate.

SECTION 3. Testing to enhance aviation safety. (a) Title VI of the Federal Aviation Act of 1958 (49 App. U.S.C. 1421 et seq.) is amended by adding at the end thereof the following:

Sec. 614. Alcohol and controlled substances testing.

(a) *Testing Program.—* (1) *Program for employees of carriers.*—The Administrator shall, in the interest of aviation safety, prescribe regulations within twelve months after the date of enactment of this section. Such regulations shall establish a program which requires air carriers and foreign air carriers to conduct preemployment, reasonable suspicion, random, and post-accident testing of airmen, crew-

337

members, airport security screening contract personnel, and other air carrier employees responsible for safety-sensitive functions (as determined by the Administrator) for use, in violation of law or Federal regulation, of alcohol or a controlled substance. The Administrator may also prescribe regulations, as the Administrator considers appropriate in the interest of safety, for the conduct of periodic recurring testing of such employees for such use in violation of law or Federal regulation.

(2) *Program for FAA employees.*— The Administrator shall establish a program applicable to employees of the Federal Aviation Administration whose duties include responsibility for safety-sensitive functions. Such program shall provide for preemployment, reasonable suspicion, random, and post-accident testing for use, in violation of law or Federal regulation, of alcohol or a controlled substance. The Administrator may also prescribe regulations, as the Administrator considers appropriate in the interest of safety, for the conduct of periodic recurring testing of such employees for such use in violation of law or Federal regulation.

(3) *Suspension; revocation; disqualification; dismissal.*—In prescribing regulations under the programs required by this subsection, the Administrator shall require, as the Administrator considers appropriate, the suspension or revocation of any certificate issued to such an individual, or the disqualification or dismissal of any such individual, in accordance with the provisions of this section, in any instance where a test conducted and confirmed under this section indicates that such individual has used, in violation of law or Federal regulation, alcohol or a controlled substance.

(b) *Prohibition on Service.*—(1) *Prohibited act.*—It is unlawful for a person to use, in violation of law or Federal regulation, alcohol or a controlled substance after the date of enactment of this section and serve as an airman, crewmember, airport security screening contract personnel, air carrier employee responsible for safety-sensitive functions (as determined by the Administrator), or employee of the Federal Aviation Administration with responsibility for safety-sensitive functions.

(2) *Effect of rehabilitation.*—No individual who is determined to have used, in violation of law or Federal regulation, alcohol or a controlled substance after the date of enactment of this section shall serve as an airman, crewmember, airport security screening contract personnel, air carrier employee responsible for safety-sensitive functions (as determined by the Administrator), or employee of the Federal Aviation Administration with responsibility for safety-sensitive functions unless such individual has completed a program of rehabilitation described in subsection (c) of this section.

(3) *Performance of prior duties prohibited.*—Any such individual determined by the Administrator to have used, in violation of law or Federal regulation, alcohol or a controlled substance after the date of enactment of this section who—

(A) engaged in such use while on duty;

(B) prior to such use had undertaken or completed a rehabilitation program described in subsection (c);

(C) following such determination refuses to undertake such a rehabilitation program; or

(D) following such determination fails to complete such a rehabilitation program, shall not be permitted to perform the duties relating to air transportation which such individual performed prior to the date of such determination.

(c) *Program for Rehabilitation.*—(1) *Program for employees of carriers.*— The Administrator shall prescribe regulations setting forth requirements for rehabilitation programs which at a minimum provide for the identification and opportunity for treatment of employees referred to in subsection (a)(1) in need of assistance in resolving problems with the use, in violation of law or Federal regulation, of alcohol or controlled substances. Each air carrier and foreign air carrier is encouraged to make such a program available to all of its employees in addition to those employees referred to in subsection (a)(1). The Administrator shall determine the circumstances under which such employees shall be required to participate in such a program. Nothing in this subsection shall preclude any air carrier or foreign air carrier from establishing a program under this subsection in cooperation with any other air carrier or foreign air carrier.

(2) *Program for FAA employees.*— The Administrator shall establish and maintain a rehabilitation program which at a minimum provides for the identification and opportunity for treatment of those employees of the Federal Aviation Administration whose duties include responsibility for safety-sensitive functions who are in need of assistance in resolving problems with the use of alcohol or controlled substances.

(d) *Procedures for Testing.*—In establishing the program required under section (a), the Administrator shall develop requirements which shall—

(1) promote, to the maximum extent practicable, individual privacy in the collection of specimen samples;

(2) with respect to laboratories and testing procedures for controlled substances, incorporate the Department of Health and Human Services scientific and technical guidelines dated April 11, 1988, and any subsequent amendments thereto, including mandatory guidelines which—

(A) establish comprehensive standards for all aspects of laboratory controlled substances testing and laboratory procedures to be applied in carrying out this section, including standards which require the use of the best available technology for ensuring the full reliability and accuracy of controlled substances tests and strict procedures governing the chain of custody of specimen samples collected for controlled substances testing;

(B) establish the minimum list of controlled substances for which individuals may be tested; and

(C) establish appropriate standards and procedures for periodic review of laboratories and criteria for certification and revocation of certification of laboratories to perform controlled substances testing in carrying out this section;

(3) require that all laboratories involved in the controlled substances testing of any individual under this section shall have the capability and facility, at such laboratory, of performing screening and confirmation tests;

(4) provide that all tests which indicate the use, in violation of law or Federal regulation, of alcohol or a controlled substance by any individual shall be confirmed by a scientifically recognized method of testing capable of providing quantitative data regarding alcohol or a controlled substance;

(5) provide that each specimen sample be subdivided, secured, and labelled in the presence of the tested individual and that a portion thereof be retained in a secure manner to prevent the possibility of tampering, so that in the event the individual's confirmation test results are positive the individual has an opportunity to have the retained portion assayed by a confirmation test done independently at a second certified laboratory if the individual requests the independent test within 3 days after being advised of the results of the confirmation test;

(6) ensure appropriate safeguards for testing to detect and quantify alcohol in breath and body fluid samples, including urine and blood, through the development of regulations as may be necessary and in consultation with the Department of Health and Human Services;

(7) provide for the confidentiality of test results and medical information (other than information relating to alcohol or a controlled substance) of employees, except that the provisions of this paragraph shall not preclude the use of test results for the orderly imposition of appropriate sanctions under this section; and

(8) ensure that employees are selected for tests by nondiscriminatory and impartial methods, so that no employee is harassed by being treated differently from other employees in similar circumstances.

(e) *Effect on Other Laws and Regulations.*—(1) *State and local law and regulations.*—No State or local government shall adopt or have in effect any law, rule, regulation, ordinance, standard, or order that is inconsistent with the regulations promulgated under this section, except that the regulations promulgated under this section shall not be construed to preempt provisions of State criminal law which

impose sanctions for reckless conduct leading to actual loss of life, injury, or damage to property, whether the provisions apply specifically to employees of an air carrier or foreign air carrier, or to the general public.

(2) *Other regulations issued by administrator.*—Nothing in this section shall be construed to restrict the discretion of the Administrator to continue in force, amend, or further supplement any regulations issued before the date of enactment of this section that govern the use of alcohol and controlled substances by airmen, crewmembers, airport security screening contract personnel, air carrier employees responsible for safety-sensitive functions (as determined by the Administrator), or employees of the Federal Aviation Administration with responsibility for safety-sensitive functions.

(3) *International obligations.*—In prescribing regulations under this section, the Administrator shall only establish requirements applicable to foreign air carriers that are consistent with the international obligations of the United States, and the Administrator shall take into consideration any applicable laws and regulations of foreign countries. The Secretary of State and the Secretary of Transportation, jointly, shall call on the member countries of the International Civil Aviation Organization to strengthen and enforce existing standards to prohibit the use, in violation of law or Federal regulation, of alcohol or a controlled substance by crew members in international civil aviation.

(f) *Definition.*—For the purposes of this section, the term 'controlled substance' means any substance under section 102(6) of the Controlled Substances Act (21 U.S.C. 802(6)) specified by the Administrator.

(b) That portion of the table of contents of the Federal Aviation Act of 1958 relating to title VI is amended by adding at the end thereof the following:

Sec. 614. Alcohol and controlled substances testing.

(a) Testing program.
(b) Prohibition on service.
(c) Program for rehabilitation.
(d) Procedures.
(e) Effect on other laws and regulations.
(f) Definition.

SECTION 4. Testing to enhance railroad safety.

Section 202 of the Federal Railroad Safety Act of 1970 (45 U.S.C. 431) is amended by adding at the end thereof the following:

(r)(1) In the interest of safety, the Secretary shall, within twelve months after the date of enactment of this subsection, issue rules, regulations, standards, and orders relating to alcohol and drug use in railroad operations. Such regulations shall establish a program which—

(A) requires railroads to conduct preemployment, reasonable suspicion, random, and post-accident testing of all railroad employees responsible for safety-sensitive functions (as determined by the Secretary) for use, in violation of law or Federal regulation, of alcohol or a controlled substance;

(B) requires, as the Secretary considers appropriate, disqualification for an established period of time or dismissal of any employee determined to have used or to have been impaired by alcohol while on duty; and

(C) requires, as the Secretary considers appropriate, disqualification for an established period of time or dismissal of any employee determined to have used a controlled substance, whether on duty or not on duty, except as permitted for medical purposes by law and any rules, regulations, standards, or orders issued under this title.

The Secretary may also issue rules, regulations, standards, and orders, as the Secretary considers appropriate in the interest of safety, requiring railroads to conduct periodic recurring testing of railroad employees responsible for such safety sensitive functions, for use of alcohol or a controlled substance in violation of law or Federal regulation. Nothing in this subsection shall be construed to restrict the discretion of the Secretary to continue in force, amend, or further supplement any rules, regulations, standards, and orders governing the use of alcohol and controlled substances in railroad operations issued before the date of enactment of this subsection.

(2) In carrying out the provisions of this subsection, the Secretary shall develop requirements which shall—

(A) promote, to the maximum extent practicable, individual privacy in the collection of specimen samples;

(B) with respect to laboratories and testing procedures for controlled substances, incorporate the Department of Health and Human Services scientific and technical guidelines dated April 11, 1988, and any subsequent amendments thereto, including mandatory guidelines which—

(i) establish comprehensive standards for all aspects of laboratory controlled substances testing and laboratory procedures to be applied in carrying out this subsection, including standards which require the use of the best available technology for ensuring the full reliability and accuracy of controlled substances tests and strict procedures governing the chain of custody of specimen samples collected for controlled substances testing;

(ii) establish the minimum list of controlled substances for which individuals may be tested; and

(iii) establish appropriate standards and procedures for periodic review of laboratories and criteria for certification and revocation of certification of laboratories to perform controlled substances testing in carrying out this subsection;

(C) require that all laboratories involved in the controlled substances testing of any employee under this subsection shall have the capability and facility, at such laboratory, of performing screening and confirmation tests;

(D) provide that all tests which indicate the use, in violation of law or Federal regulation, of alcohol or a controlled substance by any employee shall be confirmed by a scientifically recognized method of testing capable of providing quantitative data regarding alcohol or a controlled substance;

(E) provide that each specimen sample be subdivided, secured, and labelled in the presence of the tested individual and that a portion thereof be retained in a secure manner to prevent the possibility of tampering, so that in the event the individual's confirmation test results are positive the individual has an opportunity to have the retained portion assayed by a confirmation test done independently at a second certified laboratory if the individual requests the independent test within three days after being advised of the results of the confirmation test;

(F) ensure appropriate safeguards for testing to detect and quantify alcohol in breath and body fluid samples, including urine and blood, through the development of regulations as may be necessary and in consultation with the Department of Health and Human Services;

(G) provide for the confidentiality of test results and medical information (other than information relating to alcohol or a controlled substance) of employees, except that the provisions of this subparagraph shall not preclude the use of test results for the orderly imposition of appropriate sanctions under this subsection; and

(H) ensure that employees are selected for tests by nondiscriminatory and impartial methods, so that no employee is harassed by being treated differently from other employees in similar circumstances.

(3) The Secretary shall issue rules, regulations, standards, or orders setting forth requirements for rehabilitation programs which at a minimum provide for the identification and opportunity for treatment of railroad employees responsible for safety-sensitive functions (as determined by the Secretary) in need of assistance in resolving problems with the use, in violation of law or Federal regulation, of alcohol or a controlled substance. Each railroad is encouraged to make such a program available to all of its employees in addition to those employees responsible for safety sensitive functions. The Secretary shall determine the circumstances under which such employees shall be required to participate in such program. Nothing in this paragraph shall preclude a railroad from establishing a program under this paragraph in cooperation with any other railroad.

(4) In carrying out the provisions of this subsection, the Secretary shall only establish requirements that are consistent with the international obligations of the United States, and the Secretary shall take into consideration any applicable laws and regulations of foreign countries.

(5) For the purposes of this subsection, the term 'controlled substance'

means any substance under section 102(6) of the Controlled Substances Act (21 U.S.C. 802(6)) specified by the Secretary.

SECTION 5. Testing to enhance motor carrier safety. (a)(1) The Commercial Motor Vehicle Safety Act of 1986 (49 App. U.S.C. 2701 et seq.) is amended by adding at the end the following new section:

Sec. 12020. Alcohol and controlled substances testing.

(a) *Regulations.*—The Secretary shall, in the interest of commercial motor vehicle safety, issue regulations within twelve months after the date of enactment of this section. Such regulations shall establish a program which requires motor carriers to conduct preemployment, reasonable suspicion, random, and post-accident testing of the operators of commercial motor vehicles for use, in violation of law or Federal regulation, of alcohol or a controlled substance. The Secretary may also issue regulations, as the Secretary considers appropriate in the interest of safety, for the conduct of periodic recurring testing of such operators for such use in violation of law or Federal regulation.

(b) *Testing.*—(1) *Post-accident testing.*—In issuing such regulations, the Secretary shall require that post-accident testing of the operator of a commercial motor vehicle be conducted in the case of any accident involving a commercial motor vehicle in which occurs loss of human life, or, as determined by the Secretary, other serious accidents involving bodily injury or significant property damage.

(2) *Testing as part of medical examination.*—Nothing in subsection (a) of this section shall preclude the Secretary from providing in such regulations that such testing be conducted as part of the medical examination required by subpart E of part 391 of title 49, Code of Federal Regulations, with respect to those operators of commercial motor vehicles to whom such part is applicable.

(c) *Program for Rehabilitation.*—The Secretary shall issue regulations setting forth requirements for rehabilitation programs which provide for the identification and opportunity for treatment of operators of commercial motor vehicles who are determined to have used, in violation of law or Federal regulation, alcohol or a controlled substance. The Secretary shall determine the circumstances under which such operators shall be required to participate in such program. Nothing in this subsection shall preclude a motor carrier from establishing a program under this subsection in cooperation with any other motor carrier.

(d) *Procedures for Testing.*—In establishing the program required under subsection (a) of this section, the Secretary shall develop requirements which shall—

(1) promote, to the maximum extent practicable, individual privacy in the collection of specimen samples;

(2) with respect to laboratories and testing procedures for controlled substances, incorporate the Department of Health and Human Services scientific and technical guidelines dated April 11, 1988, and any subsequent amendments thereto, including mandatory guidelines which—

(A) establish comprehensive standards for all aspects of laboratory controlled substances testing and laboratory procedures to be applied in carrying out this section, including standards which require the use of the best available technology for ensuring the full reliability and accuracy of controlled substances tests and strict procedures governing the chain of custody of specimen samples collected for controlled substances testing;

(B) establish the minimum list of controlled substances for which individuals may be tested; and

(C) establish appropriate standards and procedures for periodic review of laboratories and criteria for certification and revocation of certification of laboratories to perform controlled substances testing in carrying out this section;

(3) require that all laboratories involved in the testing of any individual under this section shall have the capability and facility, at such laboratory, of performing screening and confirmation tests;

(4) provide that all tests which indicate the use, in violation of law or Federal regulation, of alcohol or a controlled substance by any individual shall be confirmed by a scientifically recognized method of testing capable of providing quantitative data regarding alcohol or a controlled substance;

(5) provide that each specimen sample be subdivided, secured, and labelled in the presence of the tested individual and that a portion thereof be retained in a secure manner to prevent the possibility of tampering, so that in the event the individual's confirmation test results are positive the individual has an opportunity to have the retained portion assayed by a confirmation test done independently at a second certified laboratory if the individual requests the independent test within three days after being advised of the results of the confirmation test;

(6) ensure appropriate safeguards for testing to detect and quantify alcohol in breath and body fluid samples, including urine and blood, through the development of regulations as may be necessary and in consultation with the Department of Health and Human Services;

(7) provide for the confidentiality of test results and medical information (other than information relating to alcohol or a controlled substance) of employees, except that the provisions of this paragraph shall not preclude the use of test results for the orderly imposition of appropriate sanctions under this section; and

(8) ensure that employees are selected for tests by nondiscriminatory and impartial methods, so that no employee is harassed by being treated differently from other employees in similar circumstances.

(e) *Effect on Other Laws and Regulations.* —(1) *State and local law and regulations.* —No State or local government shall adopt or have in effect any law, rule, regulation, ordinance, standard, or order that is inconsistent with the regulations issued under this section, except that the regulations issued under this section shall not be construed to preempt provisions of State criminal law which impose sanctions for reckless conduct leading to actual loss of life, injury, or damage to property, whether the provisions apply specifically to commercial motor vehicle employees, or to the general public.

(2) *Other regulations issued by secretary.* —Nothing in this section shall be construed to restrict the discretion of the Secretary to continue in force, amend, or further supplement any regulations governing the use of alcohol or controlled substances by commercial motor vehicle employees issued before the date of enactment of this section.

(3) *International obligations.* —In issuing regulations under this section, the Secretary shall only establish requirements that are consistent with the international obligations of the United States, and the Secretary shall

take into consideration any applicable laws and regulations of foreign countries.

(f) *Application of Penalties.*—(1) *Effect on other penalties.*—Nothing in this section shall be construed to supersede any penalty applicable to the operator of a commercial motor vehicle under this title or any other provision of law.

(2) *Determination of sanctions.*— The Secretary shall determine appropriate sanctions for commercial motor vehicle operators who are determined, as a result of tests conducted and confirmed under this section, to have used, in violation of law or Federal regulation, alcohol or a controlled substance but are not under the influence of alcohol or a controlled substance, as provided in this title.

(g) *Definition.*—For the purposes of this section, the term 'controlled substance' means any substance under section 102(6) of the Controlled Substances Act (21 U.S.C. 802(6)) specified by the Secretary.

(2) The table of contents of the Commercial Motor Vehicle Safety Act of 1986 (Public Law 99-570; 100 Stat. 5223) is amended by adding at the end thereof the following:

Sec. 12020. Alcohol and controlled substances testing.

(b)(1) The Secretary of Transportation shall design within nine months after the date of enactment of this Act, and implement within fifteen months after the date of enactment of this Act, a pilot test program for the purpose of testing the operators of commercial motor vehicles on a random basis to determine whether an operator has used, in violation of law or Federal regulation, alcohol or a controlled substance. The pilot test program shall be administered as part of the Motor Carrier Safety Assistance Program.

(2) The Secretary shall solicit the participation of States which are interested in participating in such program and shall select four States to participate in the program.

(3) The Secretary shall ensure that the States selected pursuant to this subsection are representative of varying geographical and population characteristics of the Nation and that the selection takes into consideration the historical geographical incidence of commercial motor vehicle accidents involving loss of human life.

(4) The pilot program authorized by this subsection shall continue for a period of one year. The Secretary shall consider alternative methodologies for implementing a system of random testing of operators of commercial motor vehicles.

(5) Not later than thirty months after the date of enactment of this Act, the Secretary shall prepare and submit to the Congress a comprehensive report setting forth the results of the pilot program conducted under this subsection. Such report shall include any recommendations of the Secretary concerning the desirability and implementation of a system for the random testing of operators of commercial motor vehicles.

(6) For purposes of carrying out this subsection, there shall be available to the Secretary $5,000,000 from funds made available to carry out section 404 of the Surface Transportation Assistance Act of 1982 (49 App. U.S.C. 2304) for fiscal year 1992.

(7) For purposes of this subsection, the term "commercial motor vehicle" shall have the meaning given to such term in section 12019(6) of the Commercial Motor Vehicle Safety Act of 1986 (49 App. U.S.C. 2716(6)).

SECTION 6. Testing to enhance mass transportation safety.—(a) As used in this section, the term—

(1) "controlled substance" means any substance under section 102(6) of the Controlled Substances Act (21 U.S.C. 802(6)) whose use the Secretary has determined has a risk to transportation safety;

(2) "person" includes any corporation, partnership, joint venture, association, or other entity organized or existing under the laws of the United States, or any State, territory, district, or possession thereof, or of any foreign country;

(3) "Secretary" means the Secretary of Transportation; and

(4) "mass transportation" means all forms of mass transportation except those forms that the Secretary determines are covered adequately, for purposes of employee drug and alcohol testing, by either the Federal Railroad Safety Act of 1970 (45 U.S.C. 431 et seq.) or the Commercial Motor Vehicle Safety Act of 1986 (49 App. U.S.C. 2701 et seq.).

(b)(1) The Secretary shall, in the interest of mass transportation safety, issue regulations within twelve months after the date of enactment of this Act. Such regulations shall establish a program which requires mass transportation operations which are recipients of Federal financial assistance under section 3, 9, or 18 of the Urban Mass Transportation Act of 1964 (49 App. U.S.C. 1602, 1607a, or 1614) or section 103(e)(4) of title 23, United States Code, to conduct preemployment, reasonable suspicion, random, and post-accident testing of mass transportation employees responsible for safety-sensitive functions (as determined by the Secretary) for use, in violation of law or Federal regulation, of alcohol or a controlled substance. The Secretary may also issue regula-

tions, as the Secretary considers appropriate in the interest of safety, for the conduct of periodic recurring testing of such employees for such use in violation of law or Federal regulation.

(2) In issuing such regulations, the Secretary shall require that post-accident testing of such a mass transportation employee be conducted in the case of any accident involving mass transportation in which occurs loss of human life, or, as determined by the Secretary, other serious accidents involving bodily injury or significant property damage.

(c) The Secretary shall issue regulations setting forth requirements for rehabilitation programs which provide for the identification and opportunity for treatment of mass transportation employees referred to in subsection (b)(1) who are determined to have used, in violation of law or Federal regulation, alcohol or a controlled substance. The Secretary shall determine the circumstances under which such employees shall be required to participate in such program. Nothing in this subsection shall preclude a mass transportation operation from establishing a program under this section in cooperation with any other such operation.

(d) In establishing the program required under subsection (b), the Secretary shall develop requirements which shall—

(1) promote, to the maximum extent practicable, individual privacy in the collection of specimen samples;

(2) with respect to laboratories and testing procedures for controlled substances, incorporate the Department of Health and Human Service scientific and technical guidelines dated April 11, 1988, and any subsequent amendments thereto, including mandatory guidelines which—

(A) establish comprehensive standards for all aspects of laboratory controlled substances testing and laboratory procedures to be applied in carrying out this section, including standards which require the use of the best available technology for ensuring the full reliability and accuracy of controlled substances tests and strict procedures governing the chain of custody of specimen samples collected for controlled substances testing;

(B) establish the minimum list of controlled substances for which individuals may be tested; and

(C) establish appropriate standards and procedures for periodic review of laboratories and criteria for certification and revocation of certification of laboratories to perform controlled substances testing in carrying out this section;

(3) require that all laboratories involved in the testing of any individual under this section shall have the capability and facility, at such laboratory, of performing screening and confirmation tests;

(4) provide that all tests which indicate the use, in violation of law or Federal regulation, of alcohol or a controlled substance by any individual shall be confirmed by a scientifically recognized method of testing capable of providing quantitative data regarding alcohol or a controlled substance;

(5) provide that each specimen sample be subdivided, secured, and labelled in the presence of the tested individual and that a portion thereof be retained in a secure manner to prevent the possibility of tampering, so that in the event the individual's confirmation test results are positive the individual has an opportunity to have the retained portion assayed by a confirmation test done independently at a second certified laboratory if the individual requests the independent test within three days after being advised of the results of the confirmation test;

(6) ensure appropriate safeguards for testing to detect and quantify alcohol in breath and body fluid samples, including urine and blood, through the development of regulations as may be necessary and in consultation with the Department of Health and Human Services;

(7) provide for the confidentiality of test results and medical information (other than information relating to alcohol or a controlled substance) of employees, except that the provisions of this paragraph shall not preclude the use of test results for the orderly imposition of appropriate sanctions under this section; and

(8) ensure that employees are selected for tests by nondiscriminatory and impartial methods, so that no employee is harassed by being treated differently from other employees in similar circumstances.

(e)(1) No State or local government shall adopt or have in effect any law, rule, regulation, ordinance, standard, or order that is inconsistent with the regulations issued under this section, except that the regulations issued under this section shall not be construed to preempt provisions of State criminal law which impose sanctions for reckless conduct leading to actual loss of life, injury, or damage to property, whether the provisions apply specifically to mass transportation employees, or to the general public.

(2) Nothing in this section shall be construed to restrict the discretion of the Secretary to continue in force, amend, or further supplement any regulations governing the use of alcohol or controlled substances by mass transportation employees issued before the date of enactment of this Act.

(3) In issuing regulations under this section, the Secretary shall only establish requirements that are consistent with the international obligations of the United States, and the Secretary shall take into consideration any applicable laws and regulations of foreign countries.

(f)(1) As the Secretary considers appropriate, the Secretary shall require—

(A) disqualification for an established period of time or dismissal of any employee referred to in subsection (b)(1) who is determined to have used or to have been impaired by alcohol while on duty; and

(B) disqualification for an established period of time or dismissal of any such employee determined to have used a controlled substance, whether on duty or not on duty, except as

permitted for medical purposes by law or any regulations.

(2) Nothing in this section shall be construed to supersede any penalty applicable to a mass transportation employee under any other provision of law.

(g) A person shall not be eligible for Federal financial assistance under section 3, 9, or 18 of the Urban Mass Transportation Act of 1964 (49 App. U.S.C. 1602, 1607a, or 1614) or section 103(e)(4) of title 23, United States Code, if such person—

(1) is required, under regulations prescribed by the Secretary under this section, to establish a program of alcohol and controlled substances testing; and

(2) fails to establish such a program in accordance with such regulations.

Source: BNA's *Individual Employment Rights Manual.*

Appendix F

Employee Polygraph Protection Act Of 1988

Following is the text of the Employ-
ee Polygraph Protection Act of 1988.
The measure was signed into law by
President Reagan on June 27, 1988,
(PL 100-847, 102 Stat 646), and is codi-
fied as 29 U.S.C.A. 2001, et seq. Regula-
tions for implementation of the act
appear at IERM 595:1251.

The law bars most tests for pre-em-
ployment screening, but allows tests to
be administered to employees who are
reasonably suspected of workplace
theft or other incidents causing the
employer economic loss.

The law provides an exemption for
drug companies and federal, state, or
local governments, and does not apply
to testing administered for national-
defense or security reasons. It allows
pre-employment testing of security
guards and employees who will have
direct access to controlled substances.

Sec. 2001. Definitions.

As used in this chapter:

(1) *Commerce.*—The term "commerce" has the meaning provided by
section 203(b) of this title.

(2) *Employer.*—The term "employer" includes any person acting directly
or indirectly in the interest of an employer in relation to an employee or
prospective employee.

(3) *Lie detector.*—The term "lie detector" includes a polygraph, deceptio-
graph, voice stress analyzer, psychological stress evaluator, or any other
similar device (whether mechanical or
electrical) that is used, or the results
of which are used, for the purpose of

rendering a diagnostic opinion regarding the honesty or dishonesty of an
individual.

(4) *Polygraph.*—The term "polygraph" means an instrument that—

(4)(A) records continuously, visual-
ly, permanently, and simultaneously
changes in cardiovascular, respiratory,
and electrodermal patterns as minimum instrumentation standards; and

(4)(B) is used, or the results of which
are used, for the purpose of rendering
a diagnostic opinion regarding the
honesty or dishonesty of an individual.

(5) *Secretary.*—The term "Secretary" means the Secretary of Labor.

Sec. 2002. Prohibitions on lie de-tector use.

Except as provided in sections 2006
and 2007 of this title, it shall be unlawful for any employer engaged in or
affecting commerce or in the production of goods for commerce—

(1) directly or indirectly, to require,
request, suggest, or cause any employee or prospective employee to take or
submit to any lie detector test;

(2) to use, accept, refer to, or inquire
concerning the results of any lie detector test of any employee or prospective
employee;

(3) to discharge, discipline, discriminate against in any manner, or deny
employment or promotion to, or
threaten to take any such action
against—

(3)(A) any employee or prospective
employee who refuses, declines, or fails
to take or submit to any lie detector
test, or

(3)(B) any employee or prospective employee on the basis of the results of any lie detector test; or

(4) to discharge, discipline, discriminate against in any manner, or deny employment or promotion to, or threaten to take any such action against, any employee or prospective employee because—

(4)(A) such employee or prospective employee has filed any complaint or instituted or caused to be instituted any proceeding under or related to this chapter,

(4)(B) such employee or prospective employee has testified or is about to testify in any such proceeding, or

(4)(C) of the exercise by such employee or prospective employee, on behalf of such employee or another person, of any right afforded by this chapter.

Sec. 2003. Notice of protection.

The Secretary shall prepare, have printed, and distribute a notice setting forth excerpts from, or summaries of, the pertinent provisions of this chapter. Each employer shall post and maintain such notice in conspicuous places on its premises where notices to employees and applicants to employment are customarily posted.

Sec. 2004. Authority of the Secretary.

(a) In general

The Secretary shall—

(a)(1) issue such rules and regulations as may be necessary or appropriate to carry out this chapter;

(a)(2) cooperate with regional, State, local, and other agencies, and cooperate with and furnish technical assistance to employers, labor organizations, and employment agencies to aid in effectuating the purposes of this chapter; and

(a)(3) make investigations and inspections and require the keeping of records necessary or appropriate for the administration of this chapter.

(b) Subpoena authority

For the purpose of any hearing or investigation under this chapter, the Secretary shall have the authority contained in sections 49 and 50 of Title 15.

Sec. 2005. Enforcement provisions.

(a) *Civil penalties*

(a)(1) *In general.* Subject to paragraph (2), any employer who violates any provision of this chapter may be assessed a civil penalty of not more than $10,000.

(a)(2) *Determination of amount.* In determining the amount of any penalty under paragraph (1), the Secretary shall take into account the previous record of the person in terms of compliance with this chapter and the gravity of the violation.

(a)(3) *Collection.* Any civil penalty assessed under this subsection shall be collected in the same manner as is required by subsections (b) through (e) of section 1853 of this title with respect to civil penalties assessed under subsection (a) of such section.

(b) *Injunctive actions by the Secretary.* The Secretary may bring an action under this section to restrain violations of this chapter. The Solicitor of Labor may appear for and represent the Secretary in any litigation brought under this chapter. In any action brought under this section, the district courts of the United States shall have jurisdiction, for cause shown, to issue temporary or permanent restraining orders and injunctions to require compliance with this chapter, including such legal or equitable relief incident thereto as may be appropriate, including, but not limited to, employment, reinstatement, promotion, and the payment of lost wages and benefits.

(c) *Private civil actions*

(c)(1) *Liability.* An employer who violates this chapter shall be liable to the employee or prospective employee affected by such violation. Such employer shall be liable for such legal or equitable relief as may be appropriate, including, but not limited to, employment, reinstatement, promotion, and the payment of lost wages and benefits.

(c)(2) *Court.* An action to recover the liability prescribed in paragraph (1) may be maintained against the employer in any Federal or State court of competent jurisdiction by an employee or prospective employee for or on behalf of such employee, prospective employee, and other employees or prospective employees similarly situated. No such action may be commenced more than 3 years after the date of the alleged violation.

(c)(3) *Costs.* The court, in its discretion, may allow the prevailing party (other than the United States) reasonable costs, including attorney's fees.

(d) *Waiver of rights prohibited.* The rights and procedures provided by this chapter may not be waived by contract or otherwise, unless such waiver is part of a written settlement agreed to and signed by the parties to the pending action or complaint under this chapter.

Sec. 2006. Exemptions.

(a) *No application to Governmental employers.* This chapter shall not apply with respect to the United States Government, any State or local government, or any political subdivision of a State or local government.

(b) *National defense and security exemption*

(b)(1) *National defense.* Nothing in this chapter shall be construed to pro-hibit the administration, by the Federal Government, in the performance of any counterintelligence function, of any lie detector test to—

(b)(1)(A) Any expert or consultant under contract to the Department of Defense or any employee of any contractor of such Department; or

(b)(1)(B) any expert or consultant under contract with the Department of Energy in connection with the atomic energy defense activities of such Department or any employee of any contractor of such Department in connection with such activities.

(b)(2) *Security.* Nothing in this chapter shall be construed to prohibit the administration, by the Federal Government, in the performance of any intelligence or counterintelligence function, of any lie detector test to--

(b)(2)(A)(i) any individual employed by, assigned to, or detailed to, the National Security Agency, the Defense Intelligence Agency, or the Central Intelligence Agency,

(b)(2)(A)(ii) any expert or consultant under contract to any such agency,

(b)(2)(A)(iii) any employee of a contractor to any such agency,

(b)(2)(A)(iv) any individual applying for a position in any such agency, or

(b)(2)(A)(v) any individual assigned to a space where sensitive cryptologic information is produced, processed, or stored for any such agency; or

(b)(2)(B) any expert, or consultant (or employee of such expert or consultant) under contract with any Federal Government department, agency, or program whose duties involve access to information that has been classified at the level of top secret or designated as being within a special access program under section 4.2(a) of Executive Order 12356 (or a successor Executive Order).

(c) *FBI contractors exemption.* Nothing in this chapter shall be construed to prohibit the administration, by the Federal Government, in the performance of any counterintelligence function, of any lie detector test to an employee of a contractor of the Federal Bureau of Investigation of the Department of Justice who is engaged in the performance of any work under the contract with such Bureau.

(d) *Limited exemption for ongoing investigations.* Subject to sections 2007 and 2009 of this title, this chapter shall not prohibit an employer from requesting an employee to submit to a polygraph test if—

(d)(1) the test is administered in connection with an ongoing investigation involving economic loss or injury to the employer's business, such as theft, embezzlement, misappropriation, or an act of unlawful industrial espionage or sabotage;

(d)(2) the employee had access to the property that is the subject of the investigation;

(d)(3) the employer has a reasonable suspicion that the employee was involved in the incident or activity under investigation; and

(d)(4) The employer executes a statement, provided to the examinee before the test, that—

(d)(4)(A) sets forth with particularity the specific incident or activity being investigated and the basis for testing particular employees.

(d)(4)(B) is signed by a person (other than a polygraph examiner) authorized to legally bind the employer.

(d)(4)(C) is retained by the employer for at least 3 years, and

(d)(4)(D) contains at a minimum—

(d)(4)(D)(i) an identification of the specific economic loss or injury to the business of the employer,

(d)(4)(D)(ii) a statement indicating that the employee had access to the property that is the subject of the investigation, and

(d)(4)(D)(iii) a statement describing the basis of the employer's reasonable suspicion that the employee was involved in the incident or activity under investigation.

(e) *Exemption for security services*

(e)(1) *In general.* Subject to paragraph (2) and sections 2007 and 2009 of this title, this chapter shall not prohibit the use of polygraph tests on prospective employees by any private employer whose primary business purpose consists of providing armored car personnel, personnel engaged in the design, installation, and maintenance of security alarm systems, or other uniformed or plainclothes security personnel and whose function includes protection of--

(e)(1)(A) facilities, materials, or operations having a significant impact on the health or safety of any State or political subdivision thereof, or the national security of the United States, as determined under rules and regulations issued by the Secretary within 90 days after June 27, 1988, including—

(e)(1)(A)(i) facilities engaged in the production, transmission, or distribution of electric or nuclear power,

(e)(1)(A)(ii) public water supply facilities,

(e)(1)(A)(iii) shipments or storage of radioactive or other toxic waste materials, and

(e)(1)(A)(iv) public transportation, or

(e)(1)(B) currency, negotiable securities, precious commodities or instruments, or proprietary information.

(e)(2) *Access.* The exemption provided under this subsection shall not apply if the test is administered to a prospective employee who would not be employed to protect facilities, materials, operations, or assets referred to in paragraph (1).

(f) *Exemption for drug security, drug theft, or drug diversion investigations*

(f)(1) *In general.* Subject to paragraph (2) and sections 2007 and 2009 of this title, this chapter shall not prohibit the use of a polygraph test by any employer authorized to manufacture, distribute, or dispense a controlled substance listed in schedule I, II, III, or IV of section 812 of Title 21.

(f)(2) *Access.* The exemption provided under this subsection shall apply—

(f)(2)(A) if the test is administered to a prospective employee who would have direct access to the manufacture, storage, distribution, or sale of any such controlled substance; or

(f)(2)(B) in the case of a test administered to a current employee, if—

(f)(2)(B)(i) the test is administered in connection with an ongoing investigation of criminal or other misconduct involving, or potentially involving, loss or injury to the manufacture, distribution, or dispensing of any such controlled substance by such employer, and

(f)(2)(B)(ii) the employee had access to the person or property that is the subject of the investigation.

Sec. 2007. Restrictions on use of exemptions.

(a) *Test as basis for adverse employment action*

(a)(1) *Under ongoing investigations exemption.* Except as provided in paragraph (2), the exemption under subsection (d) of section 2006 of this title shall not apply if an employee is discharged, disciplined, denied employment or promotion, or otherwise discriminated against in any manner on the basis of the analysis of a polygraph test chart or the refusal to take a polygraph test, without additional supporting evidence. The evidence required by such subsection may serve as additional supporting evidence.

(a)(2) *Under other exemptions.* In the case of an exemption described in subsection (e) or (f) of such section, the exemption shall not apply if the results of an analysis of a polygraph test chart are used, or the refusal to take a polygraph test is used, as the sole basis upon which an adverse employment action described in paragraph (1) is taken against an employee or prospective employee.

(b) *Rights of examinee.* The exemptions provided under subsections (d), (e), and (f) of section 2006 of this title shall not apply unless the requirements described in the following paragraphs are met:

(b)(1) *All phases.* Throughout all phases of the test—

(b)(1)(A) the examinee shall be permitted to terminate the test at any time;

(b)(1)(B) the examinee is not asked questions in a manner designed to degrade, or needlessly intrude on, such examinee;

(b)(1)(C) the examinee is not asked any question concerning—

(b)(1)(C)(i) religious beliefs or affiliations,

(b)(1)(C)(ii) beliefs or opinions regarding racial matters,

(b)(1)(C)(iii) political beliefs or affiliations,

(b)(1)(C)(iv) any matter relating to sexual behavior; and

(b)(1)(C)(v) beliefs, affiliations, opinions, or lawful activities regarding unions or labor organizations; and

(b)(1)(D) the examiner does not conduct the test if there is sufficient written evidence by a physician that the examinee is suffering from a medical or psychological condition or undergoing treatment that might cause abnormal responses during the actual testing phase.

(b)(2) *Pretest phase.* During the pretest phase, the prospective examinee—

(b)(2)(A) is provided with reasonable written notice of the date, time, and location of the test, and of such examinee's right to obtain and consult with legal counsel or an employee representative before each phase of the test;

(b)(2)(B) is informed in writing of the nature and characteristics of the tests and of the instruments involved;

(b)(2)(C) is informed, in writing—

(b)(2)(C)(i) whether the testing area contains a two-way mirror, a camera, or any other device through which the test can be observed,

(b)(2)(C)(ii) whether any other device, including any device for recording or monitoring the test, will be used, or

(b)(2)(C)(iii) that the employer or the examinee may (with mutual knowledge) make a recording of the test;

(b)(2)(D) is read and signs a written notice informing such examinee--

(b)(2)(D)(i) that the examinee cannot be required to take the test as a condition of employment,

(b)(2)(D)(ii) that any statement made during the test may constitute additional supporting evidence for the purposes of an adverse employment action described in subsection (a) of this section,

(b)(2)(D)(iii) of the limitations imposed under this section,

(b)(2)(D)(iv) of the legal rights and remedies available to the examinee in the polygraph test is not conducted in accordance with this chapter, and

(b)(2)(D)(v) of the legal rights and remedies of the employer under this chapter (including the rights of the employer under section 2008(c)(2) of this title); and

(b)(2)(E) is provided an opportunity to review all questions to be asked during the test and is informed of the right to terminate the test at any time.

(b)(3) *Actual testing phase.* During the actual testing phase, the examiner does not ask such examinee any question relevant during the test that was not presented in writing for review to such examinee before the test.

(b)(4) *Post-test phase.* Before any adverse employment action, the employer shall—

(b)(4)(A) further interview the examinee on the basis of the results of the test; and

(b)(4)(B) provide the examinee with—

(b)(4)(B)(i) a written copy of any opinion or conclusion rendered as a result of the test, and

(b)(4)(B)(ii) a copy of the questions asked during the test along with the corresponding charted responses.

(b)(5) *Maximum number and minimum duration of tests.* The examiner shall not conduct and complete more than five polygraph tests on a calendar day on which the test is given, and shall not conduct any such test for less than a 90-minute duration.

(c) *Qualifications and requirements of examiners.* The exemptions provided under subsections (d), (e), and (f) of section 2006 of this title shall not apply unless the individual who conducts the polygraph test satisfies the requirements under the following paragraphs:

(c)(1) *Qualifications.* The examiner—

(c)(1)(A) has a valid and current license granted by licensing and regulatory authorities in the State in which the test is to be conducted, if so required by the State; and

(c)(1)(B) maintains a minimum of a $50,000 bond or an equivalent amount of professional liability coverage.

(c)(2) *Requirements.* The examiner—

(c)(2)(A) renders any opinion or conclusion regarding the test--

(c)(2)(A)(i) in writing and solely on the basis of an analysis of polygraph test charts,

(c)(2)(A)(ii) that does not contain information other than admissions, information, case facts, and interpretation of the charts relevant to the purpose and stated objectives of the test, and

(c)(2)(A)(iii) that does not include any recommendation concerning the employment of the examinee; and

(c)(2)(B) maintains all opinions, reports, charts, written questions, lists, and other records relating to the test for a minimum period of 3 years after administration of the test.

Sec. 2008. Disclosure of information.

(a) *In general.* A person, other than the examinee, may not disclose information obtained during a polygraph test, except as provided in this section.

(b) *Permitted disclosure.* A polygraph examiner may disclose information acquired from a polygraph test only to—

(b)(1) the examinee or any other person specifically designated in writing by the examinee;

(b)(2) the employer that requested the test; or

(b)(3) any court, governmental agency, arbitrator, or mediator, in accordance with due process of law, pursuant to an order from a court of competent jurisdiction.

(c) *Disclosure by employer.* An employer (other than an employer described in subsection (a), (b), or (c) of section 2006 of this title) for whom a polygraph test is conducted may disclose information from the test only to—

(c)(1) a person in accordance with subsection (b) of this section or

(c)(2) a governmental agency, but only insofar as the disclosed information is an admission of criminal conduct.

Sec. 2009. Effect on other laws and agreements.

Except as provided in subsections (a), (b), and (c) of section 2006 of this title, this chapter shall not preempt any provision of any State or local law or of any negotiated collective bargaining agreement that prohibits lie detector tests or is more restrictive with respect to lie detector tests than any provision of this chapter. (29 U.S.C. §2001-2009, effective six months after June 27, 1988)

Source: BNA's *Individual Employment Rights Manual.*

Appendix G

New Jersey's Conscientious Employee Law
(Whistleblower Law)

Whistleblower Protection

Sec. 34:19-1. Short title—This act shall be known and may be cited as the "Conscientious Employee Protection Act."

Sec. 34:19-2. Definitions—As used in this act:

a. "Employer" means any individual, partnership, association, corporation or any person or group of persons acting directly or indirectly on behalf of or in the interest of an employer with the employer's consent and shall include all branches of State Government, or the several counties and municipalities thereof, or any other political subdivision of the State, or a school district, or any special district, or any authority, commission, or board or any other agency or instrumentality thereof.

[Ed. note: A school board may be held liable under the theory of respondeat superior for violations of the act by a school principal and superintendent who recommended the termination of an industrial arts teacher after he complained about the school metal shop's inadequate ventilation, where the principal and superintendent acted within the scope of their employment, and a statutory requirement that an employee act with the employer's "consent" does not mean that employee conduct must be sanctioned as "official policy." *Abbamont v. Piscataway Bd. Of Education,* 10 IER Cases 242 (NJ SupCt 1994).

The definition of employer as an individual acting "on behalf of or in the interest of an employer with the employer's consent" does not exclude acts of corporate officers to defraud an employer, since such activity may hurt the public as well. Coverage depends on whether the public, not the employer or corporate stockholders, are injured by acts reported by a whistleblower. *Littman v. Firestone Tire & Rubber Co.,* 709 F.Supp 461, 4 IER Cases 1023 (DC SNY 1989).]

b. "Employee" means any individual who performs services for and under the control and direction of an employer for wages or other remuneration.

c. "Public body" means: (1) the United States Congress, and State legislature, or any popularly-elected local governmental body, or any member or employee thereof;

(2) any federal, State, or local judiciary, or any member or employee thereof, or any grand or petit jury;

(3) any federal, State, or local regulatory, administrative, or public agency or authority, or instrumentality thereof;

(4) any federal, State, or local law enforcement agency, prosecutorial office, or police or peace officer;

(5) any federal, State or local department of an executive branch of government; or

(6) any division, board, bureau, office, committee, or commission of any

of the public bodies described in the above paragraphs of this subsection.

d. "Supervisor" means any individual with an employer's organization who has the authority to direct and control the work performance of the affected employee, who has authority to take corrective action regarding the violation of the law, rule or regulation of which the employee complains, or who has been designated by the employer on the notice required under section 7 of this act.

e. "Retaliatory action" means the discharge, suspension or demotion of an employee, or other adverse employment action taken against an employee in the terms and conditions of employment.

Sec. 34:19-3. Employer retaliatory action; protected employee actions—An employer shall not take any retaliatory action against an employee because the employee does any of the following:

a. Discloses, or threatens to disclose to a supervisor or to a public body an activity, policy or practice of the employer or another employer, with whom there is a business relationship, that the employee reasonably believes is in violation of a law, or a rule or regulation promulgated pursuant to law;

[Ed. note: A school board, through its superintendent and principal, violated the act when the two, acting within the scope of their employment, recommended the termination of an industrial arts teacher for complaining about the school metal shop's inadequate ventilation. The teacher had been warned that he would not receive tenure after raising his complaints, which were based on a reasonable belief that the ventilation deficiencies violated regulatory standards and contradicted a clear mandate of public policy as set forth in the "New Jersey Industrial Arts Education Safety Guide." *Abbamont v. Piscataway Bd. Of Education*, supra.

The act does not cover an employee's discharge for his repeated objections to his supervisor about the promotion to a sales-manager position of an individual who lacked the real-estate license required by N.J. law for those who deal directly with customers,

where he never attempted to complain to any public body, and the whistleblowing must be to a supervisor who is someone other than the alleged wrongdoer. While the employee discussed the licensing situation with his supervisor's brother, who also was a company official, there is no evidence that he was terminated for circumventing his supervisor and bringing his concerns to superiors or any regulatory authority, and the statute does not apply to his discussion of the issue with a company official who was not in the relevant chain of command. *Boyinis v. Marriott Ownership Resorts, Inc.*, 855 F.Supp. 862, 9 IER Cases 1024 (DC NVa 1994).

An employee who was discharged after asking that his employer investigate alleged internal fraud failed to state a claim under the act, which does not apply to activity that injures only a corporation and its shareholders and not the public at large. In addition, the employee failed to prove his claim, where he had been notified of his proposed discharge two weeks before he discussed the fraud with his employer. *Littman v. Firestone Tire & Rubber Co.*, 715 F.Supp. 90, 4 IER Cases 1023 (DC SNY 1989).

No wrongful discharge claim was stated by an employee who had voiced her disapproval of certain business practices that she believed violated federal law and company policy, where the employee admitted that she was not discharged for questioning the alleged illegal actions and that she had been encouraged to report questionable practices. *Moore v. Merrill Lynch, Pierce, Fenner & Smith Inc.*, 7 IER Cases 1849 (DC NJ 1991).]

b. Provides information to, or testifies before, any public body conducting an investigation, hearing, or inquiry into any violation of law, or a rule or regulation promulgated pursuant to law by the employer or another employer, with whom there is a business relationship,; or

c. Objects to, or refuses to participate in any activity, policy or practice which the employee reasonably believes:

(1) is in violation of a law, or a rule or regulation promulgated pursuant to law;

(2) is fraudulent or criminal; or

(3) is incompatible with a clear mandate of public policy concerning the public health, safety or welfare or protection of the environment.

[Ed. note: A nursing-home physician discharge merely for objecting to a staffing level that he believed to be a violation of public policy would violate the act, but his discharge for refusing to treat three times the number of patients regularly assigned to him due to the temporary absence of other physicians would not violate the act under the circumstances. The evidence suggests that the employer agreed with the physician's complaints, was attempting to remedy the understaffing problem, and discharged the physician because he refused to render service to the patients temporarily assigned to him. No law or regulation established the physician-staffing levels that would be violated, the physician's job description required that he accept the duties of vacationing co-workers, and he had a professional obligation to render medical treatment to the best of his ability in difficult circumstances. *Fineman v. New Jersey Dept. of Human Services,* 9 IER Cases 895 (NJ SuperCt AppDiv 1994).

A veterinary doctor who was discharged allegedly for objecting to his employer's funding of research on a drug because he believed it posed a potential human health hazard fails to state a claim, where the employer's decision to research the drug aggressively did not violate a clear mandate of public policy. *Young v. Schering Corp.,* 645 A.2d 1238, 9 IER Cases 1651 (NJ SuperCt AppDiv 1994).

A hospital's blood-bank supervisor, who was discharged after he destroyed blood samples to show his objection to, or refusal to participate in, the hospital's allegedly defective blood-identification practices, fails to state a claim. The supervisor admitted that the hospital's system of storing pre-admission blood samples worked well until understaffing and clerical problems caused him to re-evaluate the procedure, he never expressed his concern to hospital officials nor apprised accrediting agencies of the problems, and a means of protest less drastic than the destruction of blood samples was readily available. The state statute does not require an employee to use the least intrusive method to object to an employer's practices, but it also does not provide blanket immunity to an employee for assaultive or destructive behavior, however well intended. *Haworth v. Deborah Heart and Lung Center,* 638 A.2d 1354, 9 IER Cases 1085 (NJ SuperCt AppDiv 1994).]

Sec. 34:19-4. Disclosure to public body; requirement of notice and opportunity to correct—The protection against retaliatory action provided by this act pertaining to disclosure to a public body shall not apply to an employee who makes a disclosure to a public body unless the employee has brought the activity, policy or practice in violation of a law, or a rule or regulation promulgated pursuant to law to the attention of a supervisor of the employee by written notice and has afforded the employer a reasonable opportunity to correct the activity, policy or practice. Disclosure shall not be required where the employee is reasonably certain that the activity, policy or practice is known to one or more supervisors of the employer or where the employee reasonably fears physical harm as a result of the disclosure provided, however, that the situation is emergency in nature.

Sec. 34:19-5. Violations; civil action—Upon a violation of any of the provisions of this act, an aggrieved employee or former employee may, within one year, institute a civil action in a court of competent jurisdiction. Upon the application of any party, a jury trial shall be directed to try the validity of any claim under this act specified in the suit. All remedies available in common law tort actions shall be available to prevailing plaintiffs. These remedies are in addition to any legal or equitable relief provided by this act or any other statute. The court may also order:

a. An injunction to restrain continued violation of this act;

b. The reinstatement of the employee to the same position held before the retaliatory action, or to an equivalent position;

c. The reinstatement of full fringe benefits and seniority rights;

d. The compensation for lost wages, benefits, and other remuneration;

e. The payment by the employer of reasonable costs, and attorney's fees;

f. Punitive damages; or

g. An assessment of a civil fine of not more than $1,000.00 for the first violation of the Act and not more than $5,000.00 for each subsequent violation, which shall be paid to the State Treasurer for deposit in the General Fund.

[Ed. note: Punitive damages are available against a school board under the act, where statutory language permitting the recovery of all remedies available at common law implies recovery of punitive damages. The policy implications of awarding punitive damages against public entities are addressed by the heightened standard of awarding them only if conduct is particularly egregious and involves willful indifference or the actual participation of managers or supervisors. Allowing punitive damages against a public entity does not implicitly repeal the prohibition against such damages in the New Jersey Tort Claims Act, where the whistleblower statute is remedial, while the tort-claims statute disavows any remedial purpose and operates to compensate tort victims without imposing excessive financial burdens on taxpayers. Whether punitive damages should be awarded is a question for the jury. *Abbamont v. Piscataway Bd. Of Education*, supra.

An award of attorneys' fees is strictly in the court's discretion, in view of the act's discretionary language, its lack of fee-shifting provisions correlating reasonable attorneys' fees to "prevailing party" status such as those in civil-rights statutes, and the intention reflected in the act to afford employees a range of remedies. *Moody v. Township of Marlboro,* 855 F.Supp. 685, 9 IER Cases 1041 (DC NJ 1994).

An employee who was suspended because he opposed a policy that he contended was illegal is entitled to an award of reasonable attorneys' fees, where the jury awarded him one week's pay, there is no indication that he had any questionable subjective motivation in bringing the action or that the action was frivolous, and the act's policy of deterring retaliation properly extends to his unjustified suspension. An award of $25,000 in fees, rather than the $175,000 he requested, is reasonable, where he prevailed on his claim under the act but his federal constitutional claims were dismissed. The degree of relief obtained by a plaintiff in relation to the scope of the litigation as a whole is an essential factor in determining a reasonable fee award under the act. *Moody v. Township of Marlboro,* supra.

An in-house attorney who alleged that he was constructively discharged after questioning the legality of a proposal to transmit to him certain trade secrets contained in documents under seal of the court may maintain an action for money damages and attorneys' fees under the Act without impinging on the New Jersey Supreme Court's authority to regulate the practice of law. *Parker v. M&T Chemicals,* 566 A.2d 215, 4 IER Cases 1766 (NJ SuperCt AppDiv 1989).

The act does not preclude an employee from pursuing alternate claims for compensation for work previously done, since whistleblowers do not waive their right to compensation independent of the statute. *Flaherty v. The Enclave,* 605 A.2d 301, 7 IER Cases 921 (NJ SuperCt LawDiv 1992).

A veterinary doctor's amended complaint alleging that he was discharged for warning his employer that test results revealing adverse effects of a drug should be reported to government agencies is barred by the one-year statute of limitations. The amended complaint does not relate back to the date of the original complaint—which alleges discharge for objecting to the employer's funding of research on another veterinary drug—since it was filed 20 months after the original complaint was dismissed and pleads entirely new facts. *Young v. Schering Corp.,* supra.

The act's one-year statute of limitations began to run:

• when an employee was discharged, rather than when she complained about the alleged illegal activity. *Moore v. Merrill Lynch, Pierce, Fenner & Smith Inc.,* supra.

• when an employer rejected an employee's attempt to withdraw his allegedly coerced resignation, rather than on the date his employer reassigned him following his alleged refusal to violate the law. *Dondero v. Lenox China,* 5 IER Cases 819 (DC NJ 1990).

A state rule under which evidence of a settlement is inadmissible to prove liability does not bar admission of the parties' workers' compensation settlement in an action under the act by an industrial arts teacher who alleged that he was terminated for complaining about inadequate ventilation in the school metal shop. The settlement was offered to prove that the teacher had a reasonable belief that safety standards were violated because of illnesses he suffered as a result of working in the unventilated shop, and not to prove workers' compensation liability. *Abbamont v. Piscataway Bd. Of Education,* supra.]

Sec. 34:19–6. Award of attorney's fees and costs to employer; action without basis in law or fact—A court, upon notice of motion in accordance with the Rules Governing the Courts of the State of New Jersey, may also order that reasonable attorneys' fees and court costs be awarded to an employer if the court determines that an action brought by an employee under this act was without basis in law or in fact. However, an employee shall not be assessed attorneys' fees under this section if, after exercising reasonable and diligent efforts after filing a suit, the employee files a voluntary dismissal concerning the employer, within a reasonable time after determining that the employer would not be found to be liable for damages.

Sec. 34:19–7. Informing employees of protections and obligations under act; name of person designated to receive notices—An employer shall conspicuously display notices of its employees' protections and obligations under this act, and use other appropriate means to keep its employees so informed. Each notice posted pursuant to this section shall include the name of the person or persons the employer has designated to receive written notifications pursuant to section 4 of this act.

Sec. 34:19–8. Effect of act on rights, privileges, or remedies of employees under other laws, regulations, or agreements—Nothing in this act shall be deemed to diminish the rights, privileges, or remedies of any employee under any other federal or State law or regulation or under any collective bargaining agreement or employment contract; except that the institution of an action in accordance with this act shall be deemed a waiver of the rights and remedies available under any other contract, collective bargaining agreement, State law, rule or regulation or under the common law. (Secs. 34:19–1 to 34:19–8, as enacted by Ch. 105, L. 1986, and as last amended by Ch. 12, L. 1990)

[Ed. note: Common-law wrongful-discharge claims for whistleblowing are pre-empted by the statute, but claims for breach of contract and breach of the covenant of good faith and fair dealing are not pre-empted. *Flaherty v. The Enclave*, supra.

Claims for wrongful discharge, malicious interference with advantageous business relationships, harassment, and intentional infliction of emotional distress are waived in view of an employee's suit under the statute, since they relate directly to his discharge claim. However, his claim for severance pay was not waived, since it is essentially a contractual cause of action stemming from his employer's personnel policies. Nor did the employee waive his common-law claims of defamation, slander, and malicious interference with his prospective employment opportunities based on statements made by his supervisor. Proof of these claims does not depend on a showing of retaliation, as does his statutory claim.

The act does not cover actions that might affect an employment relationship between the employee and a third party. *Young v. Schering Corp.*, supra.

Arbitration—An insurance-company subsidiary president who alleges that he was discharged for refusing to submit fraudulent financial data to the state department of insurance must arbitrate his claim, where his employment agreement contains an arbitration clause sufficiently broad to encompass statutory claims, federal law favors the enforcement of arbitration clauses, and provisions in the act suggesting judicial resolution of claims are pre-empted by federal law. Arbitration does not deprive the president of substantive rights afforded by the statute, since all remedies available from a court may be awarded by an arbitrator, and differences in discovery do not preclude arbitration of statutory claims.

The president's claims against the parent company and its chief financial officer are subject to the arbitration clause, even though the officer was a non-party to the contract and the parent had assigned the contract to its subsidiary, where claims are dependent upon an agency relationship with the subsidiary, the parent and officer come within the statutory definition of "employer," and the parent, as a signatory to the contract, remains obligated under it despite the assignation.

The claim is subject to the Federal Arbitration Act, even though the subsidiary was a New Jersey corporation selling automobile insurance only in New Jersey, since the subsidiary of necessity engaged in activities involving interstate commerce whenever its policyholders had accidents outside New Jersey. *Bleumer v. Parkway Insurance Co.*, 10 IER Cases 31 (NJ SuperCt LawDiv 1994).]

Source: BNA's *Individual Employment Rights Manual.*

Appendix H

Uniformed Services Employment and Reemployment Rights Act of 1994

Selected sections of the Uniform Services Employment and Reemployment Rights Act that was signed into law October 13, 1994 (P.L. 103-353), which replaces the Veterans' Reemployment Rights Act, are reprinted below. The law prohibits employers from discriminating against individuals because of past, present, or future membership in a uniformed service and provides employees certain reemployment rights. Covered individuals with service-connected disabilities who are not qualified for the positions they would have attained but for the military service, or for the positions they left, even after "reasonable efforts" by the employer to accommodate their disabilities, must be reemployed in other positions with similar seniority, status, and pay. Codified at 38 USC §4301 et seq., the law repeals former §4307 pertaining to disabled veterans reemployment rights. The new disability provisions (§4313(a)(3)) are retroactive to August 1, 1990, while the new anti-discrimination provisions are effective October 13, 1994.

UNIFORMED SERVICES RIGHTS ACT

Table of Contents

SUBCHAPTER I—GENERAL

Sec. 4301. Purposes; Sense of Congress

(a) The purposes of this chapter are —

(1) to encourage noncareer service in the uniformed services by eliminating or minimizing the disadvantages to civilian careers and employment which can result from such service;

(2) to minimize the disruption to the lives of persons performing service in the uniformed services as well as to their employers, their fellow employees, and their communities, by providing for the prompt reemployment of such persons upon their completion of such service under honorable conditions; and

(3) to prohibit discrimination against persons because of their service in the uniformed services.

(b) It is the sense of Congress that the Federal Government should be a model employer in carrying out the provisions of this chapter.

Sec. 4302. Relation to Other Law and Plans or Agreements

(a) Nothing in this chapter shall supersede, nullify or diminish any Federal or State law (including any local law or ordinance), contract, agreement, policy, plan, practice, or other matter that establishes a right or benefit that is more beneficial to, or is in addition to, a right or benefit provided for such person in this chapter.

(b) This chapter supersedes any State law (including any local law or ordinance), contract, agreement, policy, plan, practice, or other matter that reduces, limits, or eliminates in any manner any right or benefit provided by this chapter, including the establishment of additional prerequisites to the exercise of any such right or the receipt of any such benefit.

Sec. 4303. Definitions

For the purposes of this chapter —

(1) The term "Attorney General" means the Attorney General of the United States or any person designated by the Attorney General to carry out a responsibility of the Attorney General under this chapter.

(2) The term "benefit," "benefit of employment," or "rights and benefits" means any advantage, profit, privilege, gain, status, account, or interest (other than wages or salary for work performed) that accrues by reason of an employment contract or agreement or an employer policy, plan, or practice and includes rights and benefits under a pension plan, a health plan, an employee stock ownership plan, insurance coverage and awards, bonuses, severance pay, supplemental unemployment benefits, vacations, and the opportunity to select work hours or location of employment.

(3) The term "employee" means any person employed by an employer.

(4)(A) Except as provided in subparagraphs (B) and (C), the term "employer" means any person, institution, organization, or other entity that pays salary or wages for work performed or that has control over employment opportunities, including —

(i) a person, institution, organization, or other entity to whom the employer has delegated the performance of employment-related responsibilities;

(ii) the Federal Government;

(iii) a State;

(iv) any successor in interest to a person, institution, organization, or other entity referred to in this subparagraph; and

(v) a person, institution, organization, or other entity that has denied initial employment in violation of section 4311.

(B) In the case of a National Guard technician employed under section 709 of title 32, the term "employer" means the adjutant general of the State in which the technician is employed.

(C) Except as an actual employer of employees, an employee pension benefit plan described in section 3(2) of the Employee Retirement Income Security Act of 1974 (29 U.S.C. 1002(2)) shall be deemed to be an employer only with respect to the obligation to provide benefits described in section 4318.

(5) The term "Federal executive agency" includes the United States Postal Service, the Postal Rate Commission, any nonappropriated fund instrumentality of the United States, any Executive agency (as that term is defined in section 105 of title 5) other than an agency referred to in section 2302(a)(2)(C)(ii) of title 5, and any military department (as that term is defined in section 102 of title 5) with respect to the civilian employees of that department.

(6) The term "Federal Government" includes any Federal executive agency, the legislative branch of the United States, and the judicial branch of the United States.

(7) The term "health plan" means an insurance policy or contract, medical or hospital service agreement, membership or subscription contract, or other arrangement under which health services for individuals are provided or the expenses of such services are paid.

(8) The term "notice" means (with respect to subchapter II) any written or verbal notification of an obligation or intention to perform service in the uniformed services provided to an employer by the employee who will perform such

service or by the uniformed service in which such service is to be performed.

(9) The term "qualified," with respect to an employment position, means having the ability to perform the essential tasks of the position.

(10) The term "reasonable efforts," in the case of actions required of an employer under this chapter, means actions, including training provided by an employer, that do not place an undue hardship on the employer.

(11) Notwithstanding section 101, the term "Secretary" means the Secretary of Labor or any person designated by such Secretary to carry out an activity under this chapter.

(12) The term "seniority" means longevity in employment together with any benefits of employment which accrue with, or are determined by, longevity in employment.

(13) The term "service in the uniformed services" means the performance of duty on a voluntary or involuntary basis in a uniformed service under competent authority and includes active duty, active duty for training, initial active duty for training, inactive duty training, full-time National Guard duty, and a period for which a person is absent from a position of employment for the purpose of an examination to determine the fitness of the person to perform any such duty.

(14) The term "State" means each of the several States of the United States, the District of Columbia, the Commonwealth of Puerto Rico, Guam, the Virgin Islands, and other territories of the United States (including the agencies and political subdivisions thereof).

(15) The term "undue hardship," in the case of actions taken by an employer, means actions requiring significant difficulty or expense, when considered in light of —

(A) the nature and cost of the action needed under this chapter;

(B) the overall financial resources of the facility or facilities involved in the provision of the action; the number of persons employed at such facility; the effect on expenses and resources, or the impact otherwise of such action upon the operation of the facility;

(C) the overall financial resources of the employer; the overall size of the business of an employer with respect to the number of its employees; the number, type, and location of its facilities; and

(D) the type of operation or operations of the employer, including the composition, structure, and functions of the work force of such employer; the geographic separateness, administrative, or fiscal relationship of the facility or facilities in question to the employer.

(16) The term "uniformed services" means the Armed Forces, the Army National Guard and the Air National Guard when engaged in active duty for training, inactive duty training, or full-time National Guard duty, the commissioned corps of the Public Health Service, and any other category of persons designated by the President in time of war or emergency.

Sec. 4304. Character of Service

A persons entitlement to the benefits of this chapter by reason of the service of such person in one of the uniformed services terminates upon the occurrence of any of the following events:

(1) A separation of such person from such uniformed service with a dishonorable or bad conduct discharge.

(2) A separation of such person from such uniformed service under other than honorable conditions, as characterized pursuant to regulations prescribed by the Secretary concerned.

(3) A dismissal of such person permitted under section 1161(a) of title 10.

(4) A dropping of such person from the rolls pursuant to section 1161(b) of title 10.

SUBCHAPTER II—EMPLOYMENT AND REEMPLOYMENT RIGHTS AND LIMITATIONS; PROHIBITIONS

Sec. 4311. Discrimination Against Persons Who Serve in the Uniformed Services and Acts of Reprisal Prohibited

(a) A person who is a member of, applies to be a member of, performs, has performed, applies to perform, or has an obligation to perform service in a uniformed service shall not be denied initial employment, reemployment, retention in employment, promotion, or any benefit of employment by an employer on the basis of that membership, application for membership, performance of service, application for service, or obligation.

(b) An employer shall be considered to have denied a person initial employment, reemployment, retention in employment, promotion, or a benefit of employment in violation of this section if the persons membership, application for membership, service, application for service, or obligation for service in the uniformed services is a motivating factor in the employers action, unless the employer can prove that the action would have been taken in the absence of such membership, application for membership, performance of service, application for service, or obligation.

(c)(1) An employer may not discriminate in employment against or take any adverse employment action against any person because such person has taken an action to enforce a protection afforded any person under this chapter, has testified or otherwise made a statement in or in connection with any proceeding under this chapter, has assisted or otherwise participated in an investigation under this chapter, or has exercised a right provided for in this chapter.

(2) The prohibition in paragraph (1) shall apply with respect to a person regardless of whether that person has performed service in the uniformed services and shall apply to any position of employment, including a position that is described in section 4312(d)(1)(C).

* * *

Sec. 4313. Reemployment Positions

(a) Subject to subsection (b) (in the case of any employee) and sections 4314 and 4315 (in the case of an employee of the Federal Government), a person entitled to reemployment under section 4312, upon completion of a period of service in the uniformed services, shall be promptly reemployed in a position of employment in accordance with the following order of priority:

(1) Except as provided in paragraphs (3) and (4), in the case of a person whose period of service in the uniformed services was for less than 91 days —

(A) in the position of employment in which the person would have been employed if the continuous employment of such person with the employer had not been interrupted by such service, the duties of which the person is qualified to perform; or

(B) in the position of employment in which the person was employed on the date of the commencement of the service in the uniformed services, only if the person is not qualified to perform the duties of the position referred to in subparagraph (A) after reasonable efforts by the employer to qualify the person.

(2) Except as provided in paragraphs (3) and (4), in the case of a person whose period of service in the uniformed services was for more than 90 days —

(A) in the position of employment in which the person would have been employed if the continuous employment of such person with the employer had not been interrupted by such service, or a position of like seniority, status and pay, the duties of which the person is qualified to perform; or

(B) in the position of employment in which the person was employed on the date of the commencement of the service in the uniformed services, or a position of like seniority, status and pay, the duties of which the person is qualified to perform, only if the person is not qualified to perform the duties of a position referred to in subparagraph (A) after reasonable efforts by the employer to qualify the person.

(3) In the case of a person who has a disability incurred in, or aggravated during, such service, and who (after reasonable efforts by the employer to accommodate the disability) is not qualified due to such disability to be employed in the position of employment in which the person would have been employed if the continuous employment of such person with the employer had not been interrupted by such service—

(A) in any other position which is equivalent in seniority, status, and pay, the duties of which the person is qualified to perform or would become qualified to perform with reasonable efforts by the employer; or

(B) if not employed under subparagraph (A), in a position which is the nearest approximation to a position referred to in subparagraph (A) in terms of seniority, status, and pay consistent with circumstances of such persons case.

(4) In the case of a person who (A) is not qualified to be employed in (i) the position of employment in which the person would have been employed if the continuous employment of such person with the employer had not been interrupted by such service, or (ii) in the position of employment in which such person was employed on the date of the commencement of the service in the uniform services for any reason (other than disability incurred in, or aggravated during, service in the uniformed services), and (B) cannot become qualified with reasonable efforts by the employer, in any other position of lesser status and pay which such person is qualified to perform, with full seniority.

(b)(1) If two or more persons are entitled to reemployment under section 4312 in the same position of employment and more than one of them has reported for such reemployment, the person who left the position first shall have the prior right to reemployment in that position.

(2) Any person entitled to reemployment under section 4312 who is not reemployed in a position of employment by reason of paragraph (1) shall be entitled to be reemployed as follows:

(A) Except as provided in subparagraph (B), in any other position of employment referred to in subsection (a)(1) or (a)(2), as the case may be (in the order of priority set out in the applicable subsection), that provides a similar status and pay to a position of employment referred to in paragraph (1) of this subsection, consistent with the circumstances of such person's case, with full seniority.

(B) In the case of a person who has a disability incurred in, or aggravated during, a period of service in the uniformed services that requires reasonable efforts by the employer for the person to be able to perform the duties of the position of employment, in any other position referred to in subsection (a)(3) (in the order of priority set out in that subsection) that provides a similar status and pay to a position referred to in paragraph (1) of this subsection, consistent with circumstances of such person's case, with full seniority.

* * *

SUBCHAPTER III—PROCEDURES FOR ASSISTANCE, ENFORCEMENT, AND INVESTIGATION

Sec. 4321. Assistance in Obtaining Reemployment or Other Employment Rights or Benefits

The Secretary (through the Veterans Employment and Training Service) shall provide assistance to any person with respect to the employment and reemployment rights and benefits to which such person is entitled under this chapter. In providing such assistance, the Secretary may request the assistance of existing Federal and State agencies engaged in similar or related activities and utilize the assistance of volunteers.

Sec. 4322. Enforcement of Employment or Reemployment Rights

(a) A person who claims that —

(1) such person is entitled under this chapter to employment or reemployment rights or benefits with respect to employment by an employer; and

(2)(A) such employer has failed or refused, or is about to fail or refuse, to comply with the provisions of this chapter; or

(B) in the case that the employer is a Federal executive agency, such employer or the Office of Personnel Management has failed or refused, or is about to fail or refuse, to comply with the provisions of this chapter, may file a complaint with the Secretary in accordance with subsection (b), and the Secretary shall investigate such complaint.

(b) Such complaint shall be in writing, be in such form as the Secretary may prescribe, include the name and address of the employer against whom the complaint is filed, and contain a summary of the allegations that form the basis for the complaint.

(c) The Secretary shall, upon request, provide technical. assistance to a potential claimant with respect to a complaint under this subsection, and when appropriate, to such claimant's employer.

(d) The Secretary shall investigate each complaint submitted pursuant to subsection (a). If the Secretary determines as a result of the investigation that the action alleged in such complaint occurred, the Secretary shall resolve the complaint by making reasonable efforts to ensure that the person or entity named in the complaint complies with the provisions of this chapter.

(e) If the efforts of the Secretary with respect to a complaint under subsection (d) are unsuccessful, the Secretary shall notify the person who submitted the complaint of —

(1) the results of the Secretary's investigation; and

(2) the complainant's entitlement to proceed under the enforcement of rights provisions provided under section 4323 (in the case of a person submitting a complaint against a State or private employer) or section 4324 (in the case of a person submitting a complaint against a Federal executive agency).

(f) This subchapter does not apply to any action relating to benefits to be provided under the Thrift Savings Plan under title 5.

Sec. 4323. Enforcement of Rights With Respect to a State or Private Employer

(a)(1) A person who receives from the Secretary a notification pursuant to section 4322(e) of an unsuccessful effort to resolve a complaint relating to a State (as an employer) or a private employer may request that the Secretary refer the complaint to the Attorney General. If the Attorney General is reasonably satisfied that the person on whose behalf the complaint is referred is entitled to the rights or benefits sought, the Attorney General may appear on behalf of, and act as attorney for, the person on whose behalf the complaint is submitted and commence an action for appropriate relief for such person in an appropriate United States district court.

(2) A person may commence an action for relief with respect to a complaint if that person —

(A) has chosen not to apply to the Secretary for assistance regarding the complaint under section 4322(c);

(B) has chosen not to request that the Secretary refer the complaint to the Attorney General under paragraph (1); or

(C) has been refused representation by the Attorney General with respect to the complaint under such paragraph.

(b) In the case of an action against a State as an employer, the appropriate district court is the court for any district in which the State exercises any authority or carries out any function. In the case of a private employer the appropriate district court is the district court for any district in which the private employer of the person maintains a place of business.

(c)(1)(A) The district courts of the United States shall have jurisdiction, upon the filing of a complaint, motion, petition, or other appropriate pleading by or on behalf of the person claiming a right or benefit under this chapter —

(i) to require the employer to comply with the provisions of this chapter;

(ii) to require the employer to compensate the person for any loss of wages or benefits suffered by reason of such employer's failure to comply with the provisions of this chapter; and

(iii) to require the employer to pay the person an amount equal to the amount referred to in clause (ii) as liquidated damages, if the court determines that the employer's failure to comply with the provisions of this chapter was willful.

(B) Any compensation under clauses (ii) and (iii) of subparagraph (A) shall be in addition to, and shall not diminish, any of the other rights and benefits provided for in this chapter.

(2)(A) No fees or court costs shall be charged or taxed against any person claiming rights under this chapter.

(B) In any action or proceeding to enforce a provision of this chapter by a person under subsection (a))2) who obtained private counsel for such action or proceeding, the court may award any such person who prevails in such action or proceeding reasonable attorney fees, expert witness fees, and other litigation expenses.

(3) The court may use its full equity powers, including temporary or permanent injunctions, temporary restraining orders, and contempt orders, to vindicate fully the rights or benefits of persons under this chapter.

(4) An action under this chapter may be initiated only by a person claiming rights or benefits under this chapter, not by an employer, prospective employer, or other entity with obligations under this chapter.

(5) In any such action, only an employer or a potential employer, as the case may be, shall be a necessary party respondent.

(6) No State statute of limitations shall apply to any proceeding under this chapter.

(7) A State shall be subject to the same remedies, including prejudgment interest, as may be imposed upon any private employer under this section.

* * *

Sec. 4326. Conduct of Investigation; Subpoenas

(a) In carrying out any investigation under this chapter, the Secretary's duly authorized representatives shall, at all reasonable times, have reasonable access to, for purposes of examination, and the right to copy and receive, any documents of any person or employer that the Secretary considers relevant to the investigation.

(b) In carrying out any investigation under this chapter, the Secretary may require by subpoena the attendance and testimony of witnesses and the production of documents relating to any matter under investigation. In case of disobedience of the subpoena or contumacy and on request of the Secretary, the Attorney General may apply to any district court of the United States in whose jurisdiction such disobedience or contumacy occurs for an order enforcing the subpoena.

(c) Upon application, the district courts of the United States shall have jurisdiction to issue writs commanding any person or employer to comply with the subpoena of the Secretary or to comply with any order of the Secretary made pursuant to a lawful investigation under this chapter and the district courts shall have jurisdiction to punish failure to obey a subpoena or other lawful order of the Secretary as a contempt of court.

(d) Subsections (b) and (c) shall not apply to the legislative branch or the judicial branch of the United States.

Source: BNA's *Fair Employment Practices Manual.*

Appendix I

New York: Smokers' Rights Law

Following is the text of a New York law prohibiting job bias for participation in political activities, recreational activities and legal use of consumable products during non-working hours and off of the employer's premises. The law is codified in the New York Statutes, Labor Law, Vol. 20, Section 201-d, the law, effective January 1, 1993, reads as amended by Ch. 778, L. 1992.

EMPLOYEE'S PROTECTION FROM DISCRIMINATION FOR ENGAGEMENT IN LEGAL ACTIVITIES

Sec. 201-d. Discrimination Against the Engagement in Certain Activities

1. Definitions. As used, in this section:

a. "Political activities" shall mean (i) running for public office, (ii) campaigning for a candidate for public office, or (iii) participating in fund-raising activities for the benefit of a candidate, political party or political advocacy group;

b. "Recreational activities" shall mean any lawful. leisure-time activitiy, for which the employee receives no compensation and which is generally engaged in for recreational purposes, including but not limited to sports, games, hobbies, exercise, reading and the viewing of television, movies and similar material;

c. "Work hours" shall mean, for purposes of this section, all time, including paid and unpaid breaks and meal periods, that the employee is suffered, permitted or expected to be engaged in work, and all time the employee is actually engaged in work. This definition shall not be referred to in determining hours worked for which an employee is entitled to compensation under any law including article nineteen of this chapter.

2. Unless otherwise privided by law, it shall be unlawful for any employer or employment agency to refuse to hire, employ or license, or to discharge from employment or otherwise discriminate against an individual in compensation, promotion or terms, conditions or privileges of employment because of:

a. an individual's political activities outstide of working hours, off of the employer's premises and without use of the employer's equipment or other property, if such activities are legal, provided however, that this paragraph shall not apply to persons whose employment is defined in paragraph six of subdivision (a) of section seventy-nine-h of the civil rights law, and provided further that this paragraph shall not apply to persons who would otherwise be prohibited from engaging in political activity pursuant to chapter 15 of title 5 and subchapter III of chapter 73 of title 5 of the USCA;

b. an individual's legal use of consumable products prior to the beginning or after the conclusion of the employee's work hours and off the employer's premises and without use of the employer's equipment or other property;

c. an individual's legal recreational activities outside work hours, off of the employer's premises and without use of the employer's equipment or other property; or

d. an individual's membership in a union or any exercise of rights granted under Title 29, USCA, Chapter 7 or under article fourteen of the civil service law.

3. The provisions of subdivision two of this section shall not be deemed to protect activity which:

a. creates a material conflict of interest related to the employer's trade secrets, proprietary information or other proprietary or business interest;

b. with respect to employees of a state agency as defined in sections seventy-three and seventy-four of the public officers law respectively, is in knowing violation of subdivision two, three, four, five, seven, eight or twelve of section seventy-three or of section seventy-four of the public officers law, or of any executive order policy, directive, or other rule which has been issued by the attorney general regulating outside employment or activities that could conflict with employees' performance of their offical duties;

c. with respect to employees of any employer as defined in section twenty-seven-a of this chapter, is in knowing violation of a provision of a collective bargaining agreement concerning ethics, conflicts of interest, potential conflicts of interest, or the proper discharge of official duties;

d. with respect to employees of any employer as defined in section twenty-seven-a of this chapter who are not subject to section seventy three or seventy-four of the public officers law, is in knowing violation of article eighteen of the general municipal law or any local law, administrative code provision, charter provision or rule or directive of the mayor or any agency head of a city having a population of one million or more, where such law, code provision, charter provision, rule or directive concerns ethics, conflicts of interst, potential conflicts of interest, or the proper discharge of official duties and otherwise covers such employees; and

e. with respect to employee other than those of any employer as defined in section twenty-seven-a of this chapter, violates a collective bargaining agreement or a certified or licensed professional's contractual obligation to devote his or her entire compensated working hours to a single employer, provided however that the provisions of this paragraph shall apply only to professionals whose compensation is at least fifty thousand dollars for the year nineteen hundred ninety-two and in subsequent years is an equivalent amount adjusted by the same percentage as the annual increase or decrease in the consumer price index.

4. Notwithstanding the provisions of subdivision three of this section, an employer shall not be in violation of this section where the employer takes action based on the belief either that; (i) the employer's actions were required by statute, regulation, ordinance or other governmental mandate, (ii) the employer's actions were permissible pursuant to an established substance abuse or alcohol program or workplace policy, professional contract or collective bargaining agreement, or (iii) the individual's actions were deemed by an employer or previous employer to be illegal or to constitute habitually poor performance, incompetency or misconduct.

5. Nothing in thi section shall apply to persons who, on an individual basis, have a professional service contract with an employer and the unique nature of the services provided is such that the employer shall be permitted, as part of such professional service contract, to limit the off-duty activities which may be engaged in by such individual.

6. Nothing in this section shall prohibit an organization or employer from offering, imposing or having in effect a health, disability or life insurance policy that makes distinctions between employees for the type of coverage or the price of coverage based upon the employees' recreational activities or use of consumable products, provided that differential premium rates charged employees reflect a differential cost to the employer and that employers provide employees with a statement delineating the differential rates used by the carriers providing insurance for the employer, and provided further that such distinctions in type or price of coverage shall not be utilized to expand, limit or curtail the rights or liabilities of any party with regard to a civil cause of action.

7. a. Where a violation of this section is alleged to have occurred, the attorney general may apply in the name of the people of the state of New York for an order enjoining or restraining the com-

mission or continuance of the alleged unlawful acts. In any such proceeding, the court may impose a civil penalty in the amount of three hundred dollars for the first violation and five hundred dollars for each subsequent violation.

b. In addition to any other penalties or actions otherwise applicable pursuant to this chapter, where a violation of this section is alleged to have occurred an aggrieved individual may commence an action for equitable relief and damges.

Source: BNA's *Fair Employment Practices Manual.*

TABLE OF CASES

A

C

G

H

M

N

Purgess v. Sharrock, 33 F.3d 134 (2d Cir. 1994),   20, 22

Pytlik v. Professional Resources, Ltd., 887 F.2d 1371, 4 IER Cases 1523 (10th Cir. 1989),   65

Q

Quinones v. United States, 492 F.2d 1269, 1 IER Cases 42 (3d Cir. 1974),   301, 302

R

R. M. v. McDonald's Corp., No. 89-CV-17012 (D. Colo. 1991),   284

R. R. Donnelly & Sons Co. v. Fagan, 767 F. Supp. 1259, 6 IER Cases 985 (S.D.N.Y. 1991),   77

Rachford v. Evergreen Int'l Airlines, Inc., 596 F. Supp. 384, 1 IER Cases 559, 117 LRRM 3195 (N.D. Ill. 1984),   186

Radwan v. Beecham Labs., 850 F.2d 147 (3d Cir. 1988), aff'd, 932 F.2d 960 (3d Cir. 1991),   195

Raffensberger v. Moran, 336 Pa. Super. 97 (1984),   122

Railway Labor Executives' Ass'n. v. Skinner, 934 F.2d 1096, 6 IER Cases 833 (9th Cir. 1991),   149

Rasheed v. International Paper Co., 826 F. Supp. 1377 (S.D. Ala. 1993),   306

Rathert v. Village of Peotone, 903 F.2d 510, 5 IER Cases 918 (7th Cir. 1990), cert. denied, 111 S. Ct. 297, 5 IER Cases 1376 (1990),   239

Record v. Whirlpool Corp., 6 IER Cases 221 (E.D. Ky.), aff'd, 951 F.2d 350 (6th Cir. 1991),   143

Redies v. Nationwide Mut. Ins. Co., 711 F. Supp. 570, 4 IER Cases 1644 (D. Colo. 1989),   296

Rehmann, Robson & Co. v. McMahan, 187 Mich. App. 36 (1991), appeal denied 438 Mich. 857 (1991),   73

Reid v. Sears, Roebuck & Co., 790 F.2d 453, 1 IER Cases 451 (6th Cir. 1986),   24, 25, 37

Reisner v. Recco Temporary Serv., Inc., 136 A.D.2d 686 (N.Y. App. 2d Dep't 1988),   19

Rendine v. Pantzer, 141 N.J. 292 (1995),   263

Renny v. Port Huron Hosp., 427 Mich. 415, 1 IER Cases 1560 (1986),   64

Reprosystem, B.V. v. SCM Corp., 727 F.2d 257 (2d Cir.), cert. denied, 469 U.S. 828 (1984),   18

Reuther v. Fowler & Williams, Inc., 255 Pa. Super. 28, 115 LRRM 4690 (Pa. 1978),   190

Richardson v. Hotel Corp. of Am., 332 F. Supp. 519, 3 FEP Cases 1031 (E.D. La. 1971),   aff'd, 468 F.2d 951, 5 FEP Cases 323 (5th Cir. 1972),   103

Ring v. River Walk Manor, Inc., 596 F. Supp. 393 (D. Md. 1984),   259

Ritchie v. Michigan Consol. Gas Co., 163 Mich. App. 358, 3 IER Cases 242 (1987),   31

Robbins v. Finlay, 645 P.2d 623 (Utah 1982),   32

Robbins v. Galbraith, 9 IER Cases 1776 (E.D. Pa. 1994),   216

Roberts v. Conoco, Inc., 717 F. Supp. 724, 4 IER Cases 1235 (D. Colo. 1989),   297

Roberts v. Gadsden Memorial Hosp., 835 F.2d 793, 45 FEP Cases 1246 (11th Cir. 1988),   258

Robertson v. Atlantic Richfield Petroleum Prods. Co., 371 Pa. Super. 49, 2 IER Cases 1433 (1987),   48

Rodgers v. Kemper Constr. Co., 50 Cal. App. 3d 608 (1975),   290

Rodie v. Max Factor & Co., 256 Cal. Rptr. 1, 4 IER Cases 215 (Cal. App. 1989),   14

Rogers v. IBM, 500 F. Supp. 867, 115 LRRM 4608 (W.D. Pa. 1980),   230

Rojo v. Kliger, 52 Cal. 3d 65, 6 IER Cases 530, 54 FEP Cases 1446 (1990),   195

Rose v. Elmhurst College, 62 Ill. App. 3d 824 (1978),   47

Rose v. Figgie Int'l, 56 FEP Cases 41 (W.D. Mich. 1990), aff'd, 919 F.2d 739 (6th Cir. 1990),   243

Rosenfeld v. Thirteenth Street Corp., 4 IER Cases 770 (Okla. 1989), opinion withdrawn, (Apr. 19, 1993),   192

Rosen-House v. Sloan's Supermarket, Inc., N.Y.L.J. p.18 (Sept. 27, 1988), aff'd, 148 A.D.2d 1020 (N.Y. App. 1st Dep't 1989),   282

Ross v. Stouffer Hotel Co., 816 P.2d 302 (Haw. 1991),   250

Rothweil v. Wetterau, Inc., 820 S.W.2d 557, 57 FEP Cases 356, 6 IER Cases 1510 (Mo. App. 1991),   270

V

Vallejo v. Osco Drug, Inc. 743 S.W.2d 423 (Mo. App. 1988), 292

Van Norman v. Peoria Journal-Star, Inc., 31 Ill. App. 2d 314 (1961), 129

Velo-Bind v. Scheck 485 F. Supp. 102 (S.D.N.Y. 1979), 73

Verduzco v. General Dynamics, 742 F. Supp. 559, 5 IER Cases 1113 (S.D. Cal. 1990), 192, 199

Vernars v. Young, 539 F.2d 966 (3d Cir. 1976), 229

Vickers v. Veterans Admin., 549 F. Supp. 85, 29 FEP Cases 1197 (W.D. Wash. 1982), 270, 273

Vollrath v. Georgia-Pacific Corp., 899 F.2d 533, 5 IER Cases 34 (6th Cir.), *cert. denied*, 498 U.S. 940 (1990), 52

Voorhees v. Guyan Mach. Co., 191 W. Va. 450, 9 IER Cases 1465 (1994), 21

W

Wagenseller v. Scottsdale Memorial Hosp., 147 Ariz. 370, 1 IER Cases 526, 119 LRRM 3166 (1985), 57, 189, 197, 259

Wagner v. General Elec. Co., 760 F. Supp. 1146, 6 IER Cases 684 (E.D. Pa. 1991), 198

Wagner v. Globe, 150 Ariz. 82, 1 IER Cases 501 (1986), 189

Wainman v. Bowler, 176 Mont. 91 (1978), 121

Waldorf v. Board of Comm'rs., 857 F.2d 1047, 48 FEP Cases 209 (5th Cir. 1988), 259

Walker v. Goodson Farms, Inc., 90 N. C. App. 478 (1988), 61

Walker v. Key, 101 N.M. 631 (App. 1984), 289

Walker v. South Cent. Bell Tel. Co., 904 F.2d 275, 5 IER Cases 1373, 53 FEP Cases 433 (5th Cir. 1990), 103

Walt's Drive-A-Way Serv., Inc. v. Powell, 638 N.E.2d 857, 10 IER Cases 789 (Ind. App. 1994), 189

Wanamaker v. Columbian Rope Co., 740 F. Supp. 127, 60 FEP Cases 764 (N.D.N.Y. 1990), 27

Wangler v. Hawaiian Elec. Co., 742 F. Supp. 1465, 5 IER Cases 1063 (D. Haw. 1990), 305

Ward v. Frito-Lay, Inc., 95 Wis. 2d 372, 115 LRRM 4320 (App. 1980), 253

Waters v. Gaston County, 57 F.3d 422, 68 FEP Cases 414, 11 IER Cases 403 (4th Cir. 1995), 249

Watkins v. L. M. Berry & Co., 704 F.2d 577 (11th Cir. 1983), 114

Watkins v. Turnage, 883 F.2d 70 (4th Cir. 1989), 255

Watson v. City of Hialeah, 552 So. 2d 1146 (Fla. App. 1989), 281

Watsontown Brick Co. v. Hercules Powder Co., 265 F. Supp 268 (M.D. Pa. 1967), *aff'd*, 387 F.2d 99 (3d Cir. 1967), 286

Watts v. Union Pac. R.R., 796 F.2d 1240, 122 LRRM 3036 (10th Cir. 1986), 258

Weaver v. Coca-Cola Bottling Co., 805 F. Supp. 10, 7 IER Cases 1267 (W.D. Va. 1992), 300

Webb v. HCA Health Serv., Inc., 300 Ark. 613, 4 IER Cases 1869 (1989), 189, 198

Weiner v. McGraw-Hill, Inc., 57 N.Y.2d 458, 118 LRRM 2689 (1982), 9

Weinsheimer v. Rockwell Int'l Corp., 754 F. Supp. 1559, 34 FEP Cases 828 (M.D. Fla. 1990), *aff'd*, 949 F.2d 1162, 57 FEP Cases 1224 (11th Cir. 1991), 241

Weinzirl v. Wells Group, Inc., 234 Kan. 1016 (1984), 41

Weissman v. Crawford Rehabilitation, Inc., 10 IER Cases 900 (Colo. App. 1995), *cert. granted*, (March 18, 1996), 190

Weldy v. Piedmont Airlines, 4 IER Cases 1846 (W.D.N.Y. 1989), 125

Wells v. Thomas, 569 F. Supp. 426 (E.D. Pa. 1983), 21, 232

Welsh Mfg. v. Pinkerton's, Inc., 474 A.2d 436 (R.I. 1984), 279, 280

Whelan v. Albertson's, Inc., 129 Or. App. 501 (1994), 287

Whitco Indus. Inc. v. Kopani, 514 N.E.2d 840, 2 IER Cases 1684 (Ind. App. 1987), 28

White v. General Motors Corp., Inc., 908 F.2d 669, 6 IER Cases 231 (10th Cir. 1990), *cert. denied*, 498 U.S. 1069 (1991), 206

Whitlock v. Donovan, 598 F. Supp. 126, 36 FEP Cases 425 (D.D.C. 1984), *aff'd without op.*, 790 F.2d 964, 45 FEP Cases 520 (1986), 270

Wilde v. Houlton Regional Hosp., 537 A.2d 1137, 2 IER Cases 1883 (Me. 1988), 61

Y

Z

INDEX

A

Abortion 260, 264–65
Absolute privilege
  See Privilege, Absolute
Acceptance of contracts
  See Contracts, Acceptance
Acquired Immune Deficiency Syndrome
  See AIDS
"After-acquired" evidence 100–01
Age discrimination 101, 131, 154, 217, 303, 304
AIDS and AIDS testing 109, 176–80, 232, 260, 261, 291
Air Force, United States 222, 239
Alabama 221, 268
Alaska 23, 56, 82, 88, 155, 169, 210, 228, 273
Alcohol and alcoholism 61, 124, 137, 152–54, 174, 189, 206, 227, 267-68, 270, 271-72, 289–90
Alcohol testing
  See Drug testing
Americans With Disabilities Act of 1990 83, 106-07, 144, 152, 179, 180, 260, 268, 271, 273
Antipiracy agreements
  See Non-solicitation clauses or agreements
Appearance and grooming 236–39
Application, Job
  See Job application

Appropriation of likeness tort
  See Privacy
Arbitration agreements 42, 64, 306
Arizona 56, 88, 102, 151, 155, 190, 197, 210, 221, 259, 274
Arkansas 71, 83, 85, 190, 203, 268
Army, United States 222
Arrests and convictions
  See Criminal history or records
Ashkenazi Jews 182
Assault or battery 240, 256, 276, 280, 283, 292, 304, 306
Assignment of inventions
  See Invention assignment agreements
Assignment of patents
  See Patent assignment agreements
Assumption of risk 307–08
Atlanta, Georgia 260
Attorney General 212
Attorneys' fees 82, 105, 114, 203-04, 208-09, 221, 225
Austin, Texas 178

B

Background checks 98, 99
Back pay
  See Damages
Bankruptcy 19
Benefits, lost
  See Damages
Berkeley, California 177–78

Punitive damages
  See Damages, Punitive

Q

Qualified privilege
  See Privilege, Qualified or conditional
Quantum meruit
  See Quasi-contract
Quasi–contract   15, 18-19

R

Race discrimination and
  harassment   65, 131, 154, 216, 238,
  251, 258, 303, 306
Radioimmunoassay (RIA)   139, 140
Railway Labor Act of 1926   3
Reagan, Ronald   149
Reduction-in-force
  See Layoffs
Reference letters   82
References, Job
  See Job references
Rehabilitation Act of 1973   107, 152,
  153-54, 271, 273
Reinstatement   16, 30, 32, 100, 203, 204,
  208, 221
Release of claims
  See Waivers
Religion, freedom of   239, 261
Relocation   11, 13, 14, 17-18, 41, 56,
  94-95
Reorganization   60, 94–95
Reproductive hazards   265–67
Republication
  See Publication
Reserves, military   203–207
Respondeat superior   277
Restrictive covenants   22, 66–79
Resume fraud   98, 100, 102
Resume verification   99–101
Retaliation   20, 188, 190, 202, 203, 209,
  211–12, 222, 273
Retirement   27, 31, 38, 39, 51, 124, 295
Rhode Island   82, 83, 151, 155, 169, 171,
  177, 182, 208, 210, 260, 273, 274
Right to know legislation   81, 85–88
Romantic relationship
  Off-the-job   236, 253, 254–57, 261
  On-the-job   192, 245–46, 248, 252,
  253–54

S

Safe Drinking Water Act   211
Safe workplace   109, 180, 273, 275, 278,
  290–94, 307
Salary and wages
  See Compensation
San Francisco, California   178, 260
San Jose, California   178
Santa Clara County, California   178
Santa Cruz, California   236
Searches and seizures   98, 99, 107–111,
  144–45, 150, 195, 230, 231, 236
Secretary of Labor   104, 169, 293
Securities and Exchange
  Commission   245–46
Security guards and firms   110, 112, 117,
  262, 280, 287, 293, 305
Self-publication rule
  See Publication
Severance pay   13, 31, 40, 65
Sex discrimination   65, 131, 154, 236-39,
  246, 252, 254, 256, 259, 266, 267
Sexual favoritism   245–46, 252
Sexual harassment and assault   48, 64,
  101, 121, 123, 127, 132, 215, 216, 239-
  48, 252, 254, 255, 256, 286, 287, 288,
  289, 292, 305
  Hostile environment   239, 240–44,
  246, 247
  Quid pro quo   239–40, 243–45
  Unwelcome conduct   240, 241–43
Sexual orientation or preference   174,
  175, 180, 232, 258, 260-62, 287
Shop right rule   78
Sick time and leave   31, 264
Sickle cell anemia   181–82
Single publication rule
  See Publication
Sixteen Personality Factors Test
  See Personality tests
Slander   118, 129
Smoke-free workplace   42, 54, 273, 291,
  294, 304
Smokers and smoking   227, 258, 268,
  269, 273–74, 278
Social Security Administration   257
Solicitation of Clients or Employees
  See Non-solicitation clauses or
  agreements
Solid Waste Disposal Act   211
South Carolina   88, 151, 155, 158, 210,
  274